Information Systems Auditing and Assurance

James A. Hall
Lehigh University

Team Director: Richard Lindgren
Acquisitions Editor: Rochelle J. Kronzek
Developmental Editor: Diane M. Van Bakel
Marketing Manager: Danial H. Silverburg
Production Editor: Kara ZumBahlen
Media Production Editor: Lora Craver
Manufacturing Coordinators: Doug Wilke And Michelle D. Allen
Cover Design: Jennifer Martin-Lambert
Cover Image: © 1999, PhotoDisc, Inc.
Production House: Cover to Cover Publishing, Inc.
Compositor: Janet Sprowls, Cover to Cover Publishing, Inc.
Printer: West Group

Printed in the United States of America.
 5 6 7 8 9 10

International Thomson Publishing Europe
Berkshire House
168-173 High Holborn
London, WC1V7AA, United Kingdom

Nelson ITP, Australia
102 Dodds Street
South Melbourne
Victoria 3205 Australia

Nelson Canada
1120 Birchmount Road
Scarborough, Ontario
Canada M1K 5G4

International Thomson Publishing Southern Africa
Building 18, Constantia Square
138 Sixteenth Road, P.O. Box 2459
Halfway House, 1685 South Africa

International Thomson Editores
Seneca, 53
Colonia Polanco
11560 Mexico D.F. Mexico

International Thomson Publishing Asia
60 Alberta Street #15-01
Albert Complex
Singapore 189969

International Thomson Publishing Japan
Hirakawa-cho Kyowa Building, 3F
2-2-1 Hirakawa-cho, Chiyoda-ku
Tokyo 102, Japan

You can request permission to use material from this text through the following phone and fax numbers:
telephone: 1-800-730-2214   fax: 1-800-730-2215

Or you can visit our Web site at **http://www.thomsonrights.com**

Library of Congress Cataloging-in-Publication Data

Hall, James A., 19--
    Information systems auditing and assurance / James A. Hall. -- 1st
 ed.
     p.   cm.
    ISBN 0-324-00318-8 (soft cover : alk. paper)
     1. Electronic data processing--Auditing.   I. Title.
 QA76.9.A93H35 2000
 658'.0558--dc21   99-28300

This book is printed on acid-free paper.

BRIEF TABLE OF CONTENTS

TABLE OF CONTENTS

1

AUDITING, ASSURANCE, AND INTERNAL CONTROL   1

2

COMPUTER OPERATIONS   32

3

DATA MANAGEMENT SYSTEMS   76

4

SYSTEMS DEVELOPMENT AND MAINTENANCE ACTIVITIES   117

5

ELECTRONIC COMMERCE SYSTEMS   166

8

AUDITING THE REVENUE CYCLE   290

9

AUDITING THE EXPENDITURE CYCLE   344

10

FRAUD AND FRAUD DETECTION   392

PREFACE

This book is not an encyclopedic treatment of computer assurance issues. Instead, I have tried to keep it short and to the point, while providing a faithful representation of the field. I have sought to address central concerns and have attempted to present them in plain language. I have focused on the professional needs of the typical accounting major who has a limited background in systems. An overview of the relevant technology and systems issues is provided for each major topic. For some students, this material may be a useful review of the topics that are typically covered in a formal systems course. For students who have not had such a course, the overview is sufficiently detailed to bring them up to speed on the issues.

DISTINGUISHING FEATURES OF THE TEXT

RISK ASSESSMENT APPROACH

The first chapter presents a risk assessment model that identifies key areas of potential computer risk. These include operations, data management, systems development, systems maintenance, electronic commerce, and computer applications. This model provides a framework for the remainder of the text. The issues most relevant to the auditor's assurance responsibilities in each of these risk areas are developed in subsequent chapters. For clarity and comparability, the chapters are structured along similar lines. They begin with a discussion of the operational features and/or technologies employed in the area. Then the nature of the risks and the controls that can be implemented to mitigate risks are explained. Finally, specific audit objectives are defined, and suggested audit procedures to achieve those objectives are presented.

CAREFULLY FOCUSED BODY OF MATERIAL

The text focuses on the most important topics pertaining to the auditor's computer assurance responsibilities. In Chapter 1, an important distinction is drawn between the auditor's traditional attestation function and the emerging field of assurance services. The evolution of the accounting profession is expected to follow the assurance services model. The material outlined in this chapter relates to tasks normally conducted by auditors while providing computer assurance. The text examines what constitutes an assurance audit, who performs audits, and how audits are structured. Internal control concerns that underlie SAS 78 are reviewed, and the risk assessment model is discussed, which forms the basis for the rest of the book.

Chapter 2 examines the assurance issues related to computer operations. The chapter opens with a review of the advantages and potential risks associated with both centralized and distributed information technology (IT) structures. Next, auditor concerns pertinent to the computer center are examined and the key elements of a disaster recovery plan are discussed. The risks, controls, and audit issues pertaining to multi-user operating systems employed by networks and mainframes are then examined. The chapter concludes with a review of audit concerns unique to the personal computer (PC) environment.

Chapter 3 deals with assurance issues pertaining to data management systems. This material is approached from the perspective of two commonly used models: the *flat-file* model and the *database* model. Private ownership of data, which characterizes the flat-file model, is the root cause of several problems that inhibit entity-wide data integration. On the other hand, data sharing and centralized control of data are the heart of the database philosophy. The philosophies and technologies underlying both approaches create special audit issues, which are examined at length in the chapter.

The key activities that constitute the systems development life cycle (SDLC) are explored in Chapter 4. The risks, controls, and audit issues related to systems planning, systems analysis, conceptual design, system selection, detailed design, systems implementation, and system maintenance are discussed.

Chapter 5 deals with the ever-evolving topic of electronic commerce (EC). Electronic commerce encompasses diverse business activities including electronic trading of goods and services, on-line delivery of digital products, electronic funds transfer (EFT), electronic trading of stocks, and direct consumer marketing. Electronic commerce, however, is not a new phenomenon. For years, companies have engaged in electronic data interchange (EDI) over private networks. Today, driven by the Internet revolution, EC is dramatically expanding and undergoing radical changes. The modern auditor needs to be familiar with the technologies, risks, controls, and audit issues associated with EC. Hardware failures, software errors, and unauthorized access from remote locations can expose an organization's accounting system to unique threats.

The use of Computer Assisted Audit Tools and Techniques (CAATTs) for performing tests of application controls is the topic of Chapter 6. The chapter begins with an extensive description of application controls organized into three classes: input controls, process controls, and output controls. Both the *black box* and *white box* approaches to testing application controls are examined. The latter approach requires a detailed understanding of the application's logic. Five CAATT approaches used for testing application logic are examined. These are the *test data method, base case system evaluation, tracing, integrated test facility*, and *parallel simulation*.

Chapter 7 examines the use of CAATTs for data extraction and analysis. Auditors make extensive use of these tools in gathering accounting data for testing application controls and in performing substantive tests. In an IT environment, the records needed to perform such tests are stored in computer files and databases. Understanding how data are organized and accessed is central to using data extraction tools. For this reason, a thorough review of common flat-file and database structures are provided. Data extraction software falls into two general categories: *embedded audit modules* (EAM) and *general audit software* (GAS). The chapter describes the features, advantages, and disadvantages of both. The chapter closes with a review of the key features of ACL, the leading GAS product on the market.

Auditing procedures associated with the revenue and expenditure cycles are examined in Chapters 8 and 9, respectively. Each chapter begins with a review of alternative technologies employed in legacy systems and modern computer systems. This is followed by the audit objectives, controls, and tests of controls that an auditor would normally perform to gather the evidence needed to limit the scope, timing, and extent of substantive tests. Finally, substantive tests related to audit objectives are explained and illustrated using ACL software.

Finally, Chapter 10 examines the two closely related topics of ethics and fraud. It begins with a survey of ethical issues that highlight the organization's conflicting responsibilities to its employees, shareholders, customers, and the general public. Management, employees, and auditors need to recognize the implications of new information technologies for such traditional issues as working conditions, the right to privacy, and the potential for fraud.

No major aspect of the independent auditor's role has caused more concern for the public accounting profession than the auditor's responsibility for detecting fraud during an audit. Although the term *fraud* is very familiar in today's financial press, it is not always clear what constitutes fraud. The nature and meaning of fraud are examined, employee fraud and management fraud are differentiated, fraud-motivating forces are explained, and common fraud techniques are reviewed. The chapter outlines the key features of SAS 82, *Consideration of Fraud in a Financial Statement Audit*, and presents the results of a fraud research project conducted by the Association of Fraud Examiners. It concludes with a review of ACL tests that auditors can perform to help them detect fraud.

PEDAGOGICAL AIDS PROVIDED

The following features of the text are designed to assist the learning process:

- Each chapter is preceded by a clearly stated set of learning objectives.
- Each chapter is followed by an extensive set of review questions, discussion questions, multiple-choice questions, and problems of varying degrees of difficulty.
- Key terms are highlighted in the text and listed at the end of the chapters.

HANDS-ON EXPOSURE TO ACL SOFTWARE

ACL software is used throughout the world by public accounting firms and internal audit departments for data extraction and analysis. A fully functional version of ACL and associated data files are available with the text to provide students with hands-on audit experience.

SUPPLEMENTS

SOLUTIONS MANUAL

A solutions manual containing answers to all of the end-of-chapter questions and problems is available.

ACL COMPACT DISC

ACL for Windows software, data files, and an instruction manual are contained on the CD that accompanies the text. Adobe® Acrobat software needs to be installed on the user's computer to retrieve and print the instruction manual.

WEB SITE

Visit our Web site at **http://isauditing.swcollege.com**

ACKNOWLEDGEMENTS

I wish to extend my sincere appreciation to ACL for allowing their software to be bundled with this text. I would also like to thank the project team at South-Western College Publishing—Rick Lindgren, Team Director; Rochelle Kronzek, Acquisitions Editor; Dan Silverburg, Marketing Manager; Lora Craver, Media Production Editor; and Doug Wilke, Manufacturing Coordinator—for their support and guidance in developing this book. In particular, I owe a debt of gratitude to my Developmental Editor, Diane Van Bakel, and my Production Editor, Kara ZumBahlen, for their tireless dedication to this project.

DEDICATION

To my mother and my father's memory.

ABOUT THE AUTHOR

James A. Hall is Associate Professor of Accounting and Information Systems at Lehigh University, Bethlehem, PA. After his discharge from the U.S. Army, he entered the University of Tulsa in 1970 and received a BSBA in 1974 and an MBA in 1976. He earned his Ph.D from Oklahoma State University in 1979. Hall has worked in industry in the fields of systems analysis and computer auditing and has served as consultant in these areas to numerous organizations.

Professor Hall has published articles in the *Journal of Accounting, Auditing & Finance, Management Accounting, Journal of Computer Information Systems, The Journal of Accounting Education, The Review of Accounting Information Systems,* and other professional journals. He is the author of *Accounting Information Systems,* 2nd Edition, published by South-Western College Publishing.

chapter **1**

AUDITING, ASSURANCE, AND INTERNAL CONTROL

Recent developments in **information technology (IT)** have had a tremendous impact on the field of **auditing**. IT has inspired the reengineering of traditional business processes to promote more efficient operations and to improve communications within the entity and between the entity and its customers and suppliers. These advances, however, have introduced new risks that require unique internal controls. They have engendered the need for new techniques for evaluating controls and for assuring the security and accuracy of corporate data and the information systems that produce it.

This chapter presents an overview of computer auditing. We begin with a general discussion of alternative audit approaches. We then review the internal control concerns that underlie SAS 78. Finally we examine a framework for risk assessment that identifies seven areas of computer risk. The remainder of the text is based upon this framework.

LEARNING OBJECTIVES

After studying this chapter, you should:

- Know the difference between attest services and assurance services and be able to explain the relationship between these two types of auditing.
- Understand the structure of an audit and have a firm grasp of the conceptual elements of the audit process.
- Understand internal control objectives promulgated by SAS 78.
- Understand how the unique features of the computer environment must be taken into account to achieve the control objectives specified in SAS 78.
- Be familiar with the key areas of risk in the IT environment.

ATTEST SERVICES VERSUS ASSURANCE SERVICES

An important starting point for this body of material is to draw a distinction between the auditor's traditional attestation function and the emerging field of **assurance services**. The attest service is defined as:

an engagement in which a practitioner is engaged to issue, or does issue, a written communication that expresses a conclusion about the reliability of a written assertion that is the responsibility of another party. (SSAE No. 1, AT Sec. 100.01)

The following requirements apply to attestation services:

• Attestation services require written assertions and a practitioner's written report.
• Attestation services require the formal establishment of measurement criteria or their description in the presentation.
• The levels of service in attestation engagements are limited to examination, review, and application of agreed-upon procedures.

Assurance services constitute a broader concept that encompasses, but is not limited to, attestation. The relationship between these services is illustrated in Figure 1–1.

Assurance services are professional services that are designed to improve the quality of information, both financial and nonfinancial, used by decision-makers. The domain of assurance services is intentionally unbounded so that it does not inhibit the growth of future services that are currently unforeseen. For example, assurance services may be contracted to provide information about the quality or marketability of a product. Alternatively, a client may need information about the efficiency of a production process or the effectiveness of their network security system. Assurance services are intended to help people make better decisions by improving information. This information may come as a by-product of the attest function, or it may ensue from an independently motivated review.

The evolution of the accounting profession is expected to follow the assurance services model. All of the "Big Five" professional services firms have now renamed their traditional audit functions "Assurance Services." The organizational unit responsible for conducting IT audits is named either *IT Risk Management*, *Information Systems Risk Management*, or *Operational Systems Risk Management (OSRM)* and typically is a division of assurance services.

The material outlined in this chapter relates to tasks normally conducted by OSRM professionals while performing an IT audit. In the pages that follow we examine what constitutes an audit, who performs audits, and how audits are structured. Keep in mind, however, that in many cases the purpose of the audit task, rather than the task itself, defines the service being rendered. Therefore, the issues and procedures described in this text apply to the broader context of assurance services, which include,

FIGURE 1–1

Relationship Between Assurance Services and Attest Services

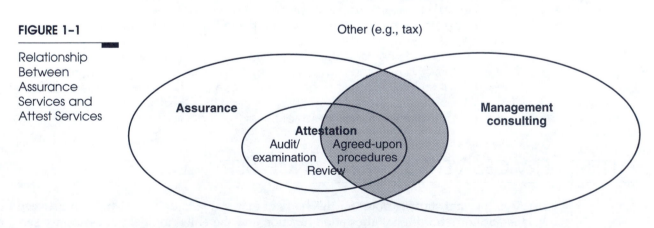

SOURCE: Based on the AICPA *Special Committee Report on Assurance Services.*

but are not limited to, attest services. They also relate directly to the internal audit function.

WHAT IS A FINANCIAL AUDIT?

A financial audit is an independent attestation performed by an expert—the auditor— who expresses an opinion regarding the presentation of financial statements. The auditor's role is similar in concept to a judge who collects and evaluates evidence and renders an opinion. A key concept in this process is *independence*. The judge must remain independent in his or her deliberations. The judge cannot be an advocate of either party in the trial, but must apply the law impartially based on the evidence presented. Likewise, the independent auditor collects and evaluates evidence and renders an opinion based on the evidence. Throughout the audit process, the auditor must maintain his or her independence from the client organization. Public confidence in the reliability of the company's internally produced financial statements rests directly on their being evaluated by an independent expert auditor.

The public expression of the auditor's opinion is the culmination of a systematic audit process that involves three conceptual phases: (1) familiarization with the organization's business, (2) evaluating and testing internal controls, and (3) assessing the reliability of financial data. Later in this section, we examine the specific elements of the audit process.

AUDITING STANDARDS

The product of the attestation function is a formal written report that expresses an opinion about the reliability of the assertions contained in the financial statements. The auditor's report expresses an opinion as to whether the financial statements are in conformity with *generally accepted accounting principles*. External users of financial statements are presumed to rely on the auditor's opinion about the reliability of financial statements in making decisions. To do so, users must be able to place their trust in the auditor's competence, professionalism, integrity, and independence. Auditors are guided in their professional responsibility by the ten *generally accepted auditing standards (GAAS)* presented in Figure 1–2.

Auditing standards are divided into three classes: general qualification standards, field work standards, and reporting standards. GAAS establishes a framework for prescribing auditor performance, but it is not sufficiently detailed to provide meaningful guidance in specific circumstances. To provide specific guidance, the American Institute of Certified Public Accountants (AICPA) issues *Statements on Auditing Standards (SASs)* as authoritative interpretations of GAAS. SASs are often referred to as *auditing standards*, or *GAAS*, although they are not the ten generally accepted auditing standards.

STATEMENTS ON AUDITING STANDARDS

The first SAS (SAS 1) was issued by the AICPA in 1972. Since then, many SASs have been issued to provide auditors with guidance on a spectrum of topics, including methods of investigating new clients, procedures for collecting information from attorneys regarding contingent liability claims against clients, and techniques for obtaining background information on the client's industry.

Statements on Auditing Standards are regarded as authoritative pronouncements because every member of the profession must follow their recommendations or be able

FIGURE 1–2

Generally
Accepted
Auditing
Standards

GENERALLY ACCEPTED AUDITING STANDARDS		
General Standards	**Standards of Field Work**	**Reporting Standards**
1. The auditor must have adequate technical training and proficiency.	1. Audit work must be adequately planned.	1. The auditor must state in the report whether financial statements were prepared in accordance with generally accepted accounting principles.
2. The auditor must have independence of mental attitude.	2. The auditor must gain a sufficient understanding of the internal control structure.	2. The report must identify those circumstances in which generally accepted accounting principles were not applied.
3. The auditor must exercise due professional care in the performance of the audit and the preparation of the report.	3. The auditor must obtain sufficient, competent evidence.	3. The report must identify any items that do not have adequate informative disclosures.
		4. The report shall contain an expression of the auditor's opinion on the financial statements as a whole.

to show why a SAS does not apply in a given situation. The burden of justifying departures from SAS falls upon the individual auditor.

EXTERNAL AUDITING VERSUS INTERNAL AUDITING

External auditing is often called **independent auditing** because it is done by certified public accountants who are independent of the organization being audited. External auditors represent the interests of third-party stakeholders in the organization, such as stockholders, creditors, and government agencies. Because the focus of the external audit is on the financial statements, this type of audit is called a *financial audit*.

The Institute of Internal Auditors defines **internal auditing** as an independent appraisal function established within an organization to examine and evaluate its activities as a service to the organization.[1] Internal auditors perform a wide range of activities on behalf of the organization, including conducting financial audits, examining an operation's compliance with organizational policies, reviewing the organization's compliance with legal obligations, evaluating operational efficiency, detecting and pursuing fraud within the firm, and conducting IT audits.

The characteristic that conceptually distinguishes internal auditors from external auditors is their respective constituencies: while external auditors represent outsiders, internal auditors represent the interests of the organization. Nevertheless, in this capacity, internal auditors often cooperate with and assist external auditors in performing financial audits. This is done to achieve audit efficiency and reduce audit fees. For example, a team of internal auditors can perform tests of computer controls under the supervision of a single external auditor.

The independence and competence of the internal audit staff determine the extent to which external auditors may cooperate with and rely on work performed by internal

---

1.   Institute of Internal Auditors, *Standards of Professional Practice of Internal Auditing* (Orlando, FL.: Institute of Internal Auditors, 1978).

auditors. Some internal audit departments report directly to the controller. Under this arrangement, the internal auditor's independence is compromised, and the external auditor is prohibited by professional standards from relying on evidence provided by the internal auditors. In contrast, external auditors can rely in part on evidence gathered by internal audit departments that are organizationally independent and that report to the board of directors' audit committee. A truly independent internal audit staff adds value to the audit process. Internal auditors can gather audit evidence throughout a fiscal period, which external auditors can then use at year end to conduct more efficient, less disruptive, and less costly audits of the organization's financial statements.

WHAT IS AN INFORMATION TECHNOLOGY (IT) AUDIT?

An IT audit focuses on the computer-based aspects of an organization's information system. This includes assessing the proper implementation, operation, and control of computer resources. Since most modern information systems employ information technology, the IT audit is typically a significant component of all external (financial) and internal audits.

THE ELEMENTS OF AUDITING

To this point, we have painted a broad picture of auditing. Let's now fill in some details. The following definition of auditing is applicable to external auditing, internal auditing, and IT auditing:

> Auditing is a systematic process of objectively obtaining and evaluating evidence regarding assertions about economic actions and events to ascertain the degree of correspondence between those assertions and established criteria and communicating the results to interested users.[2]

This seemingly obtuse definition contains several important points that are examined below.

A SYSTEMATIC PROCESS.   Conducting an audit is a systematic and logical process that applies to all forms of information systems. While important in all audit settings, a systematic approach is particularly important in the IT environment. The lack of physical procedures that can be visually verified and evaluated injects a high degree of complexity into the IT audit. Therefore, a logical framework for conducting an audit in the IT environment is critical to help the auditor identify all-important processes and data files.

MANAGEMENT ASSERTIONS AND AUDIT OBJECTIVES.   The organization's financial statements reflect a set of **management assertions** about the financial health of the entity. The task of the auditor is to determine whether the financial statements are fairly presented. To accomplish this, the auditor establishes **audit objectives**, designs procedures, and gathers evidence that corroborate or refute management's assertions. These assertions fall into five general categories:

---

2.   AAA Committee on Basic Auditing Concepts, "A Statement of Basic Auditing Concepts," *Accounting Review*, supplement to vol. 47, 1972.

- The **existence or occurrence** assertion affirms that all assets and equities contained in the balance sheet exist and that all transactions in the income statement actually occurred.
- The **completeness** assertion declares that no material assets, equities, or transactions have been omitted from the financial statements.
- The **rights and obligations** assertion maintains that assets appearing on the balance sheet are owned by the entity and that the liabilities reported are obligations.
- The **valuation or allocation** assertion states that assets and equities are valued in accordance with generally accepted accounting principles and that allocated amounts such as depreciation expense are calculated on a systematic and rational basis.
- The **presentation and disclosure** assertion alleges that financial statement items are correctly classified (e.g., long-term liabilities will not mature within one year) and that footnote disclosures are adequate to avoid misleading the users of financial statements.

Generally, auditors develop their audit objectives and design **audit procedures** based on the preceding assertions. The example in Table 1–1 outlines these procedures.

Audit objectives may be classified into two general categories. Those in Table 1–1 relate to transactions and account balances that directly impact financial reporting. The second category pertains to the information system itself. This includes the audit objectives for assessing controls over manual operations and computer technologies used in transaction processing. In the chapters that follow, we consider both categories of audit objectives and the associated audit procedures.

OBTAINING EVIDENCE.   Auditors seek evidential matter that corroborates management assertions. In the IT environment, this involves gathering evidence relating to the reliability of computer controls as well as the contents of databases that have been

TABLE 1–1

Audit Objectives and Audit Procedures Based on Management Assertions

Management Assertion	Audit Objective	Audit Procedure
Existence or Occurrence	Inventories listed on the balance sheet exist.	Observe the counting of physical inventory.
Completeness	Accounts payable include all obligations to vendors for the period.	Compare receiving reports, supplier invoices, purchase orders, and journal entries for the period and the beginning of the next period.
Rights and Obligations	Plant and equipment listed in the balance sheet are owned by the entity.	Review purchase agreements, insurance policies, and related documents.
Valuation or Allocation	Accounts receivable are stated at net realizable value.	Review entity's aging of accounts and evaluate the adequacy of the allowance for uncorrectable accounts.
Presentation and Disclosure	Contingencies not reported in financial accounts are properly disclosed in footnotes.	Obtain information from entity lawyers about the status of litigation and estimates of potential loss.

processed by computer programs. Evidence is collected by performing tests of controls, which establish whether internal controls are functioning properly, and substantive tests, which determine whether accounting databases fairly reflect the organization's transactions and account balances.

ASCERTAINING THE DEGREE OF CORRESPONDENCE WITH ESTABLISHED CRITERIA. The auditor must determine whether weaknesses in internal controls and misstatements found in transactions and account balances are material. In all audit environments, assessing *materiality* is an auditor judgment. In an IT environment, however, this decision is complicated further by technology and a sophisticated internal control structure.

COMMUNICATING RESULTS.   Auditors must communicate the results of their tests to interested users. Independent auditors render a report to the audit committee of the board of directors or stockholders of a company. The audit report contains, among other things, an **audit opinion**. This opinion is distributed along with the financial report to interested parties both internal and external to the organization. IT auditors often communicate their findings to internal and external auditors, who can then integrate these findings with the non-IT aspects of the audit.

THE STRUCTURE OF AN IT AUDIT

The IT audit is generally divided into three phases: audit planning, tests of controls, and substantive testing. Figure 1–3 illustrates the steps involved in these phases.

AUDIT PLANNING

The first step in the IT audit is **audit planning**. Before the auditor can determine the nature and extent of the tests to perform, he or she must gain a thorough understanding of the client's business. A major part of this phase of the audit is the analysis of audit risk (discussed later). The objective of the auditor is to obtain sufficient information about the firm to plan the other phases of the audit. The risk analysis incorporates an overview of the organization's internal controls. During the review of controls, the auditor attempts to understand the organization's policies, practices, and structure. In this phase of the audit, the auditor also identifies the financially significant applications and attempts to understand the controls over the primary transactions that are processed by these applications.

FIGURE 1–3

Phases of an
IT Audit

The techniques for gathering evidence at this phase include questionnaires, interviewing management, reviewing systems documentation, and observing activities. During this process, the IT auditor must identify the principal exposures and the controls that attempt to reduce these exposures. Having done so, the auditor proceeds to the next phase, where he or she tests the controls for compliance with preestablished standards.

TESTS OF CONTROLS

The objective of the **tests of controls** phase is to determine whether adequate internal controls are in place and functioning properly. To accomplish this, the auditor performs various tests of controls. The evidence-gathering techniques used in this phase may include both manual techniques and specialized computer audit techniques. We shall examine several such methods later in this text.

At the conclusion of the tests-of-controls phase, the auditor must assess the quality of the internal controls. The degree of reliance the auditor can ascribe to internal controls affects the nature and extent of substantive testing that needs to be performed. The relationship between tests of controls and substantive tests is discussed later.

SUBSTANTIVE TESTING

The third phase of the audit process focuses on financial data. This involves a detailed investigation of specific account balances and transactions through what are called **substantive tests**. For example, a customer confirmation is a substantive test sometimes used to verify account balances. The auditor selects a sample of accounts receivable balances and traces these back to their source—the customers—to determine if the amount stated is in fact owed by a bona fide customer. By so doing, the auditor can verify the accuracy of each account in the sample. Based on such sample findings, the auditor is able to draw conclusions about the fair value of the entire accounts receivable asset.

Some substantive tests are physical, labor-intensive activities such as counting cash, counting inventories in the warehouse, and verifying the existence of stock certificates in a safe. In an IT environment, the information needed to perform substantive tests (such as account balances and names and addresses of individual customers) is contained in data files that often must be extracted using **Computer Assisted Audit Tools and Techniques (CAATTs)** software. Later in this text, we will examine the role of CAATTs in performing traditional substantive tests and other data analysis and reporting tasks.

INTERNAL CONTROL

Organization management is required by law to establish and maintain an adequate system of internal control. Consider the following Securities and Exchange Commission statement on this matter:

> The establishment and maintenance of a system of internal control is an important management obligation. A fundamental aspect of management's stewardship responsibility is to provide shareholders with reasonable assurance that the business is adequately controlled. Additionally, management has a responsibility to furnish shareholders and potential investors with reliable financial information

on a timely basis. An adequate system of internal control is necessary to management's discharge of these obligations.[3]

Corporate management has not always lived up to its internal control responsibility. With the discovery that U.S. business executives were using their organizations' funds to bribe foreign officials, internal control issues, formerly of little interest to stockholders, quickly became a matter of public concern. From this scandal came the passage of the **Foreign Corrupt Practices Act of 1977 (FCPA)**. Among its provisions, the FCPA requires companies registered with the SEC to:

1. Keep records that fairly and reasonably reflect the transactions of the firm and its financial position.
2. Maintain a system of internal control that provides reasonable assurance that the organization's objectives are met.

The FCPA has had a significant impact on organization management. With the knowledge that violation of the FCPA could lead to heavy fines and imprisonment, managers have developed a deeper concern for control adequacy.

Since much of the internal control system relates directly to transaction processing, accountants are key participants in ensuring control adequacy. This section deals first with internal control at a conceptual level. It then presents the authoritative control framework defined by SAS 78.

INTERNAL CONTROL IN CONCEPT

The **internal control system** comprises policies, practices, and procedures employed by the organization to achieve four broad objectives:

1. To safeguard assets of the firm.
2. To ensure the accuracy and reliability of accounting records and information.
3. To promote efficiency in the firm's operations.
4. To measure compliance with management's prescribed policies and procedures.[4]

MODIFYING ASSUMPTIONS

Inherent in these control objectives are four modifying assumptions that guide designers and auditors of internal control systems.[5]

MANAGEMENT RESPONSIBILITY.   This concept holds that the establishment and maintenance of a system of internal control is a **management responsibility**. The FCPA supports this postulate.

REASONABLE ASSURANCE.   The internal control system should provide **reasonable assurance** that the four broad objectives of internal control are met. This means that no

---

3. Securities and Exchange Commission, Securities Release 34-13185 (19 January 1977).
4. American Institute of Certified Public Accountants, *AICPA Professional Standards*, vol. 1 (New York: AICPA, 1987) AU Sec. 320.30-35.
5. American Institute of Certified Public Accountants, Committee on Auditing Procedure, Internal Control—Elements of a Coordinated System and Its Importance to Management and the Independent Public Accountant, *Statement on Auditing Standards No. 1*, Sec. 320 (New York: AICPA, 1973).

system of internal control is perfect and the cost of achieving improved control should not outweigh its benefits.

METHODS OF DATA PROCESSING.   The internal control system should achieve the four broad objectives regardless of the data processing method used. However, the techniques used to achieve these objectives will vary with different types of technology.

LIMITATIONS.   Every system of internal control has limitations on its effectiveness. These include (1) the possibility of error—no system is perfect, (2) circumvention—personnel may circumvent the system through collusion or other means, (3) management override—management is in a position to override control procedures by personally distorting transactions or by directing a subordinate to do so, and (4) changing conditions—conditions may change over time so that existing controls may become ineffectual.

EXPOSURES AND RISK

Figure 1–4 portrays the internal control system as a shield that protects the firm's assets from numerous undesirable events that bombard the organization. These include attempts at unauthorized access to the firm's assets (including information); fraud perpetrated by persons both in and outside the firm; errors due to employee incompetence, faulty computer programs, and corrupted input data; and mischievous acts, such as unauthorized access by computer hackers and threats from computer viruses that destroy programs and databases.

The absence or weakness of a control is called an **exposure**. Exposures, which are illustrated as holes in the control shield in Figure 1–4, increase the firm's risk to financial loss or injury from undesirable events. A weakness in internal control may expose the firm to one or more of the following types of risks:

1. Destruction of assets (both physical assets and information).
2. Theft of assets.
3. Corruption of information or the information system.
4. Disruption of the information system.

THE PREVENTIVE-DETECTIVE-CORRECTIVE INTERNAL CONTROL MODEL.   Figure 1–5 illustrates that the internal control shield consists of three levels of control: preventive controls, detective controls, and corrective controls. This is the PDC control model.

PREVENTIVE CONTROLS.   Prevention is the first line of defense in the control structure. **Preventive controls** are passive techniques designed to reduce the frequency of occurrence of undesirable events. Preventive controls force compliance with prescribed or desired actions and thus screen out aberrant events. When designing internal control systems, an ounce of prevention is most certainly worth a pound of cure. Preventing errors and fraud is far more cost-effective than detecting and correcting problems after they occur. The vast majority of undesirable events can be blocked at this first level. For example, a well-designed data entry screen is an example of a preventive control. The logical layout of the screen into zones that permits only specific types of data, such as customer name, address, items sold, and quantity, forces the data entry clerk to enter the required data and prevents necessary data from being omitted. However, not all problems can be anticipated and prevented. Some will elude the most comprehensive network of preventive controls.

FIGURE 1–4

Internal Control
Shield

DETECTIVE CONTROLS.   Detection of problems is the second line of defense. **Detective controls** are devices, techniques, and procedures designed to identify and expose undesirable events that elude preventive controls. Detective controls reveal specific types of errors by comparing actual occurrences to preestablished standards. When the detective control identifies a departure from standard, it sounds an alarm to attract attention to the problem. For example, assume that because of a data entry error, a customer sales order record contains the following data:

Quantity	Price	Total
10	$10	$1,000

Before processing this transaction and posting to the accounts, a detective control should recalculate the total value using the price and quantity. Thus, the error above would be detected.

FIGURE 1–5

Preventive,
Detective, and
Corrective
Controls

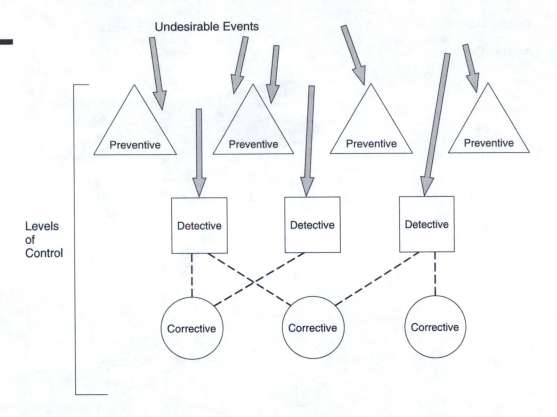

CORRECTIVE CONTROLS.   Corrective actions must be taken to reverse the effects of detected errors. There is an important distinction between detective controls and corrective controls. Detective controls identify undesirable events and draw attention to the problem; **corrective controls** actually fix the problem. For any detected error, there may be more than one feasible corrective action, but the best course of action may not always be obvious. For example, in viewing the preceding error, your first inclination may have been to change the total value from $1,000 to $100 to correct the problem. This presumes that the quantity and price values in the record are correct; they may not be. At this point, we cannot determine the real cause of the problem; we know only that one exists.

Linking a corrective action to a detected error, as an automatic response, may result in an incorrect action that causes a worse problem than the original error. For this reason, error correction should be viewed as a separate control step that should be taken cautiously.

The PDC control framework is a conceptual model that offers little practical guidance for designing control systems. For this, we need a more precise set of objectives. The current authoritative document for specifying internal control objectives and techniques is the *Statement on Auditing Standards No. 78.*[6] We now discuss the key elements of this document.

---

6.   American Institute of Certified Public Accountants, SAS No. 78—Consideration of Internal Control in a Financial Statement Audit: An Amendment to *SAS No. 55* (New York: AICPA, 1995).

STATEMENT ON AUDITING STANDARDS NO. 78

Statement on Auditing Standards No. 78 (SAS 78) conforms to the recommendations of the Committee of Sponsoring Organizations of the Treadway Commission (COSO). Internal control as defined in SAS 78 consists of five components: the control environment, risk assessment, information and communication, monitoring, and control activities.

THE CONTROL ENVIRONMENT

The **control environment** is the foundation for the other four control components. The control environment sets the tone for the organization and influences the control awareness of its management and employees. Important elements of the control environment are:

- The integrity and ethical values of management.
- The structure of the organization.
- The participation of the organization's board of directors and the audit committee, if one exists.
- Management's philosophy and operating style.
- The procedures for delegating responsibility and authority.
- Management's methods for assessing performance.
- External influences, such as examinations by regulatory agencies.
- The organization's policies and practices for managing its human resources.

SAS 78 requires that auditors obtain sufficient knowledge to assess the attitude and awareness of the organization's management, board of directors, and owners regarding internal control. The following paragraphs provide examples of techniques that may be used to obtain an understanding of the control environment:

1. Auditors should assess the integrity of the organization's management and may use investigative agencies to report on the backgrounds of key managers. Some of the "Big Five" public accounting firms employ ex-FBI agents whose primary responsibility is to perform background checks on existing and prospective clients. If cause for serious reservations comes to light about the integrity of the client, the auditor should withdraw from the audit. The reputation and integrity of management are critical factors in determining the organization's auditability. Auditors cannot function properly in an environment in which client management is deemed to be unethical and corrupt.
2. Auditors should be aware of conditions that would predispose the management of an organization to commit fraud. Some of the obvious conditions may be lack of sufficient working capital, adverse industry conditions, bad credit ratings, and the existence of extremely restrictive conditions in bank or indenture agreements. If auditors encounter any such conditions, their examination should give due consideration to the possibility of fraudulent financial reporting. Appropriate measures should be taken, and every attempt should be made to uncover any fraud.
3. Auditors should understand a client's business and industry and should be aware of conditions peculiar to the industry that may affect the audit. Auditors should read industry-related literature and familiarize themselves with the risks that are inherent in the business.

4. Auditors should determine if the organization's board of directors is actively involved in establishing business policy and if it monitors management and organization operations. An independent internal audit group that reports to the audit committee of the board of directors is an excellent environmental control.
5. From organizational charts and job descriptions, auditors can assess whether segregation between organizational functions is adequate. In particular, auditors are concerned with the segregation of duties within and between the accounting function and other functional areas.

RISK ASSESSMENT

Organizations must perform a **risk assessment** to identify, analyze, and manage risks relevant to financial reporting. Risks can arise out of changes in circumstances such as:

- Changes in the operating environment that impose new competitive pressures on the firm.
- New personnel who possess a different or inadequate understanding of internal control.
- New or reengineered information systems that affect transaction processing.
- Significant and rapid growth that strains existing internal controls.
- The implementation of new technology into the production process or information system that impacts transaction processing.
- The introduction of new product lines or activities with which the organization has little experience.
- Organizational restructuring resulting in the reduction and/or reallocation of personnel such that business operations and transaction processing are affected.
- Entering into foreign markets that may impact operations (i.e., the risks associated with foreign currency transactions).
- Adoption of a new accounting principle that impacts the preparation of financial statements.

SAS 78 requires that auditors obtain sufficient knowledge of the organization's risk assessment procedures to understand how management identifies, prioritizes, and manages the risks related to financial reporting.

INFORMATION AND COMMUNICATION

The accounting information system consists of the records and methods used to initiate, identify, analyze, classify, and record the organization's transactions and to account for the related assets and liabilities. The quality of information generated by the AIS impacts management's ability to take actions and make decisions in connection with the organization's operations and to prepare reliable financial statements. An effective accounting information system will:

- Identify and record all valid financial transactions.
- Provide timely information about transactions in sufficient detail to permit proper classification and financial reporting.
- Accurately measure the financial value of transactions so their effects can be recorded in financial statements.
- Accurately record transactions in the time period in which they occurred.

SAS 78 requires that auditors obtain sufficient knowledge of the organization's information system to understand:

- The classes of transactions that are material to the financial statements and how those transactions are initiated.
- The accounting records and accounts that are used in the processing of material transactions.
- The transaction processing steps involved from the initiation of an economic event to its inclusion in the financial statements.
- The financial reporting process used to prepare financial statements, disclosures, and accounting estimates.

MONITORING

Management must determine that internal controls are functioning as intended. **Monitoring** is the process by which the quality of internal control design and operation can be assessed. This may be accomplished by separate procedures or by ongoing activities.

An organization's internal auditors may monitor the entity's activities in separate procedures. They gather evidence of control adequacy by testing controls, then communicate control strengths and weaknesses to management. As part of this process, internal auditors make specific recommendations for improvement to controls.

Ongoing monitoring may be achieved by integrating special computer modules into the information system that capture key data and/or permit tests of controls to be conducted as part of routine operations. Such embedded audit modules (EAMs) allow management and auditors to maintain constant surveillance over the functioning of internal controls.

Another technique for achieving ongoing monitoring is the judicious use of management reports. Timely reports allow managers in functional areas such as sales, purchasing, production, and cash disbursements to oversee and control their operations. By summarizing activities, highlighting trends, and identifying exceptions from normal performance, well-designed management reports provide evidence of internal control function or malfunction. In Chapter 8, we review the Management Reporting System and examine the characteristics of effective management reports.

CONTROL ACTIVITIES

Control activities are the policies and procedures used to ensure that appropriate actions are taken to deal with the organization's identified risks. Control activities can be grouped into two distinct categories: *computer controls*, and *physical controls*.

COMPUTER CONTROLS.   Computer controls constitute a body of material that is of primary concern to us. These controls, which relate specifically to the IT environment and IT auditing, fall into two broad groups: **general controls** and **application controls**. General controls pertain to entity-wide concerns such as controls over the data center, organization databases, systems development, and program maintenance. Application controls ensure the integrity of specific systems such as sales order processing, accounts payable, and payroll applications. Later in the chapter we examine a framework for viewing general and application controls and the risks to which they relate. Subsequent chapters expand upon this framework to explore these issues in detail. However, before pursuing this material further, we need to review more fundamental, but important, physical control issues.

PHYSICAL CONTROLS.   This class of control activities relates primarily to traditional accounting systems that employ manual procedures. However, an understanding of these control concepts also gives insight to the risks and control concerns associated with the IT environment. Our discussion will address the issues pertaining to six traditional categories of physical control activities: transaction authorization, segregation of duties, supervision, accounting records, access control, and independent verification. For each control category, the IT implications will also be reviewed.

Transaction Authorization.   The purpose of **transaction authorization** is to ensure that all material transactions processed by the information system are valid and in accordance with management's objectives. Authorizations may be general or specific. General authority is granted to operations personnel to perform day-to-day operations. An example of general authorization is the procedure to authorize the purchase of inventories from a designated vendor only when inventory levels fall to their predetermined reorder points. This is called a *programmed procedure* (not necessarily in the computer sense of the word). The decision rules are specified in advance, and no additional approvals are required. On the other hand, specific authorizations deal with case-by-case decisions associated with nonroutine transactions. An example of this is the decision to extend a particular customer's credit limit beyond the normal amount. Specific authority is usually a management responsibility.

In an IT environment, transaction authorization may consist of coded rules embedded within computer programs. For example, a program module in a purchases system will determine when, how much, and from which vendor inventories are ordered. Such transactions may be initiated automatically and without human involvement. Within this setting, it may be difficult for auditors to assess whether these transactions are in compliance with management's objectives. For instance, is the organization buying inventory only when it is needed? Are correct quantities being purchased only from approved vendors? Because automated authorization procedures are unobserved by management, control failure may go unnoticed until the firm experiences some adverse symptoms. In the case of purchases authorization, symptoms of a problem may take the form of an inventory stockout or an excessive buildup of inventory. Unfortunately, by the time the problem is recognized, the firm may have incurred substantial financial losses.

In an IT environment, the responsibility for achieving the control objectives of transaction authorization rests directly on the accuracy and consistency (integrity) of the computer programs that perform these tasks. Later in the text, we explore several control techniques that promote computer program integrity. As we shall see, program integrity bears directly on many control issues.

Segregation of Duties.   One of the most important control activities is the segregation of employee duties to minimize incompatible functions. **Segregation of duties** can take many forms, depending upon the specific duties to be controlled. However, the following three objectives provide general guidelines applicable to most organizations. These objectives are illustrated in Figure 1–6.

> *Objective 1.* The segregation of duties should be such that the authorization for a transaction is separate from the processing of the transaction. For example, purchases should not be initiated by the purchasing department until authorized by the inventory control department. This separation of tasks is a control to prevent the purchase of unnecessary inventory by individuals.

> *Objective 2.* Responsibility for the custody of assets should be separate from the recordkeeping responsibility. For example, the department that has physical custody of finished goods inventory (the warehouse) should not keep the official

FIGURE 1-6

Segregation of
Duties Objectives

inventory records. Accounting for finished goods inventory is performed by inventory control, an accounting function. When a single individual or department has responsibility for both asset custody and recordkeeping, the potential for fraud exists. Assets can be stolen or lost, and the accounting records falsified to hide the event.

Objective 3. The organization should be structured so that a successful fraud requires collusion between two or more individuals with incompatible responsibilities. In other words, no single individual should have sufficient access to assets and supporting records to perpetrate a fraud. For most people, the thought of approaching another employee with the proposal to collude in a fraud presents an insurmountable psychological barrier. The fear of rejection and subsequent disciplinary action discourages solicitations of this sort. However, when employees with incompatible responsibilities work together daily in close quarters, the resulting familiarity will tend to erode this barrier. For this reason, the segregation of incompatible tasks should be physical as well as organizational. Indeed, concern about personal familiarity on the job is the justification for establishing rules prohibiting nepotism.

In an IT environment, segregation of duties is not identical to that of the manual environment. Computer programs typically perform tasks that are deemed incompatible in a manual system. For example, a program may be solely responsible for authorizing a purchase, processing the purchase order, and recording the account payable. When the supplier's invoice arrives, the computer will also determine the timing and amount of the payment to be made.

These are several reasons why duties that are separated in a manual system need not be separated in an IT environment. It would be inefficient, contrary to the objectives of automation, and operationally futile to separate incompatible tasks among several different programs simply to emulate traditional manual procedures. The reason for segregating duties in a manual environment is to control against some negative aspect of human behavior. Humans make mistakes and occasionally perpetrate frauds. Segregating duties helps to prevent and detect such acts. Computers do not make mistakes and do not perpetrate frauds. Most so-called computer errors are actually programming errors that are, in fact, human errors. Because they possess unimpeachable integrity, no computer has ever perpetrated a fraud unless programmed to do so by a human. Separating computer processing functions, therefore, serves no purpose.

Segregation of duties still plays a role in the IT environment. However, the IT auditor's attention must be redirected to those activities that threaten application integrity. For example, once the proper functioning of a program is established at system implementation, its integrity must be preserved throughout the application's life cycle. The activities of *program development, program operations*, and *program maintenance* are critical IT functions that must be adequately separated.

Supervision.   Implementing adequate segregation of duties requires that a firm employ a sufficiently large number of employees. Achieving adequate segregation of duties often presents difficulties for small organizations. Obviously, it is impossible to separate five incompatible tasks among three employees. Therefore, in small organizations or in functional areas that lack sufficient personnel, management must compensate for the absence of segregation controls with close **supervision**. For this reason, supervision is often called a *compensating control*.

An underlying assumption of supervision control is that the firm employs competent and trustworthy personnel. Obviously, no company could function for long on the alternative assumption that its employees are incompetent and dishonest. The "competent and trustworthy employee" assumption promotes supervisory efficiency. Firms can thus establish a managerial span of control whereby a single manager supervises several employees. In manual systems, maintaining a span of control tends to be straightforward because both manager and employees are at the same physical location.

In an IT environment, supervisory control must be more elaborate than in manual systems for three reasons. The first relates to the problem of attracting competent employees. The technology of data processing creates an exceedingly complex environment that demands a unique class of employees. Those who design, program, maintain, and operate the firm's computer system must possess highly specialized skills. These individuals operate in a dynamic setting characterized by a high rate of staff turnover. The task of restaffing is complicated further by rapid changes in technology, which tend to frustrate management's ability to assess the competence of prospective employees.

The second reason reflects management's concern over the trustworthiness of data processing personnel in high-risk areas. Some systems professionals serve in positions of authority that permit direct and unrestricted access to the organization's programs and data. The combination of technical skill and opportunity in the hands of an individual, who may be mischievous or corrupt, represents a significant exposure to the organization.

The third reason is management's inability to adequately observe employees in an IT environment. The activities of employees engaged in data processing are frequently hidden from management's direct observation. For example, data processing personnel may be distributed throughout areas and perform their functions remotely via telecommunications links. Supervisory controls must, therefore, be designed into the computer system to compensate for the lack of direct supervision.

Accounting Records.   The traditional **accounting records** of an organization consist of source documents, journals, and ledgers. These records capture the economic essence of transactions and provide an audit trail of economic events. The audit trail enables the auditor to trace any transaction through all phases of its processing from the initiation of the event to the financial statements. Organizations must maintain audit trails for two reasons. First, this information is needed for conducting day-to-day operations. The audit trail helps employees respond to customer inquiries by showing the current status of transactions in process. Second, the audit trail plays an essential role in the financial audit of the firm. It enables external (and internal) auditors to verify selected transactions by tracing them from the financial statements, to the ledger accounts, to the journals, to the source documents, and back to their original source. For reasons of both practical expedience and legal obligation, business organizations must maintain sufficient accounting records to preserve their audit trails.

The obligation to maintain an audit trail exists in an IT environment just as it does in a manual setting. However, automated accounting records and audit trails are very different from those in manual systems. Some computer systems maintain no physical source documents. Journals and ledgers often do not exist in the traditional sense. Instead, records of transactions and other economic events are fragmented across several normalized database tables. Audit trails may take the form of pointers, hashing techniques, indexes, or embedded keys that link record fragments between and among the database tables. To meet their responsibilities, auditors must understand the operational principles of the database management systems in use and the effects on accounting records and audit trails of alternative file structures.

Access Controls.   The purpose of **access controls** is to ensure that only authorized personnel have access to the firm's assets. Unauthorized access exposes assets to misappropriation, damage, and theft. Therefore, access controls play an important part in safeguarding assets. Access to assets can be direct or indirect. Physical security devices, such as locks, safes, fences, and electronic and infrared alarm systems, control against direct access. Indirect access to assets is achieved by gaining access to the records and documents that control their use, ownership, and disposition. For example, an individual with access to all the relevant accounting records can destroy the audit trail that describes a particular sales transaction. Thus, by removing the records of the transaction, including the account receivable balance, the sale may never be billed and the firm will never receive payment for the items sold. The access controls needed to protect accounting records will depend upon the technological characteristics of the accounting system. In a manual system, accounting records are physical and tend to be distributed among several locations. Indirect access control is accomplished by controlling the use of documents and records and by segregating the duties of those who must access and process these records.

In the IT environment, accounting records are often concentrated within the data processing center on mass storage devices. Data consolidation exposes the organization to two forms of threat: (1) computer fraud and (2) losses from disasters.

Fraud.   An individual with the proper skills and unrestricted access to accounting records is in a prime position to perpetrate a fraud. With all the necessary records in one location, the successful perpetrator does not need to gain access to several different places and is thus more likely to achieve his or her objective without detection.

Disasters.   Disasters such as fires in Los Angeles caused by civil unrest, earthquakes in southern California, floods in the Midwest, hurricanes in Florida, the bombing of the World Trade Center, and less spectacular events such as computer hardware failures all can destroy an organization's accounting records. A firm unable to recover its essential records may well be unable to continue in business. For example, if the firm's accounts receivable file is destroyed, it may be unable to determine what its customers owe for goods and services previously provided. Access control in the IT environment includes provisions for the physical security of the computer facilities. With all of its eggs in one basket, the firm must protect the basket well.

Another problem unique to the IT environment is controlling access to computer programs. During the development phase, computer applications come under a great deal of scrutiny and testing intended to expose logic errors. However, concern for application integrity should not cease when systems are implemented. Errors and fraud exposures are more likely to occur after implementation in the operational period of the system's life cycle, called the *maintenance phase*. During this period, which may last for years, a typical application may be modified dozens of times. This is an opportunity for errors to be inserted unintentionally in the application and for the computer criminal to perpetrate a fraud by making an illegal program change.

Access control in an IT environment covers many levels of exposure. Controls that address these exposures include techniques designed to limit personnel access authority, restrict access to computer programs, provide physical security for the data processing center, ensure adequate backup for data files, and provide disaster recovery capability. Some access controls are technological procedures and devices, while others are physical barriers implemented through organizational segregation of duties. But underlying all access control techniques is the fundamental principle of "need to know." Individuals should be granted access to data, programs, and restricted areas only when a need in connection with their assigned tasks has been demonstrated. This principle should never be violated.

Independent Verification.   **Verification procedures** are independent checks of the accounting system to identify errors and misrepresentations. Verification differs from supervision because it takes place after the fact, by an individual who is not directly involved with the transaction or task being verified. Supervision takes place while the activity is being performed, by a supervisor with direct responsibility for the task. Through independent verification procedures, management can assess (1) the performance of individuals, (2) the integrity of the transaction processing system, and (3) the correctness of data contained in accounting records. Examples of independent verifications include:

- Reconciling batch totals at points during transaction processing.
- Comparing physical assets with accounting records.
- Reconciling subsidiary accounts with control accounts.
- Reviewing management reports (both computer and manually generated) that summarize business activity.

The timing of verification depends upon the technology employed in the accounting system and the task under review. Some verifications occur several times an hour; some are done several times a day; and others are performed daily, weekly, monthly, and annually.

Independent verification control is needed in the manual environment because employees sometimes make mistakes or forget to perform necessary tasks. In an IT environment, computer programs perform many routine tasks. Being precise machines, computers will always do what their programs specify; if these programs are accurate and complete, there is no reason to perform an independent check on their functioning as an ongoing operational procedure. Once again, our concern rests with application integrity. In the IT environment, IT auditors perform an independent verification function by evaluating controls over systems development and maintenance activities and occasionally by reviewing the internal logic of programs.

THE IMPORTANCE OF THE INTERNAL CONTROLS

The five components of internal control—the control environment, risk assessment, information and communication, monitoring, and control activities—provide the auditor with important information about the risks of material misrepresentation in financial statements and fraud. Auditors are therefore required to obtain a sufficient knowledge of the internal controls to plan their audits. For example, the internal controls in place affect how the auditor will assess whether an organization has reported all of its liabilities. The auditor must understand how purchases are initiated, processed, and recorded. The internal control structure provides this information and guides the auditor in the planning of specific tests to determine the likelihood and extent of financial statement misrepresentation.

ASSESSING AUDIT RISK AND DESIGNING TESTS OF CONTROLS

Audit risk is the probability that the auditor will render an unqualified (clean) opinion on financial statements that are, in fact, materially misstated. Material misstatements may be caused by errors or irregularities or both. Errors are unintentional mistakes. Irregularities are intentional misrepresentations to perpetrate a fraud or to mislead the users of financial statements. The auditor's objective is to minimize audit risk by performing tests of controls and substantive tests.

AUDIT RISK COMPONENTS

The three components of audit risk are inherent risk, control risk, and detection risk.

INHERENT RISK

Inherent risk is associated with the unique characteristics of the business or industry of the client.[7] Firms in declining industries have greater inherent risk than firms in stable or thriving industries. Auditors cannot reduce the level of inherent risk. Even in a system protected by excellent controls, financial data and, consequently, financial statements can be materially misstated.

To illustrate inherent risk, let's assume that the audit client's financial statements show an accounts receivable balance of $10 million. Unknown to the auditor and the client, several customers with accounts receivable totalling $2 million are about to go out of business. These accounts, which are a material component of the total accounts receivable balance of $10 million, are not likely to be collected. To represent these accounts as an asset in the financial statements would be a material misstatement of the firm's economic position.

CONTROL RISK

Control risk is the likelihood that the control structure is flawed because controls are either absent or inadequate to prevent or detect errors in the accounts.[8] To illustrate

---

7.   Auditing Standards Board, *AICPA Professional Standards* (New York: AICPA, 1994), AU Sec. 312.20.
8.   Ibid.

control risk, consider the following partial customer sales record, which is processed by the sales order system.

Quantity	Unit Price	Total
10 Units	$20	$2,000

Assuming the Quantity and Unit Price fields in the record are correctly presented, then the extended amount (Total) value of $2,000 is in error. Previously in the chapter, we saw than an AIS with adequate controls should prevent or detect such an error. If, however, controls are lacking and the value of Total in each record is not validated before processing, then the risk of undetected errors entering the data files increases.

Auditors reduce the level of control risk by performing tests of internal controls. In the preceding example, the auditor could create test transactions, including some with incorrect Total values, which are processed by the application in a test run. The results of the test will indicate that price extension errors are not detected and are being incorrectly posted to the accounts receivable file.

DETECTION RISK

Detection risk is the risk that auditors are willing to take that errors not detected or prevented by the control structure will also not be detected by the auditor.[9] Auditors set an acceptable level of detection risk (planned detection risk) that influences the level of substantive tests that they perform. For example, more substantive testing would be required when the planned detection risk is 1 percent than when it is 5 percent.

THE RELATIONSHIP BETWEEN TESTS OF CONTROLS AND SUBSTANTIVE TESTS

Tests of controls and substantive tests are auditing techniques used for reducing total audit risk. The relationship between tests of controls and substantive tests varies according to the auditor's risk assessment of the organization. The stronger the internal control structure, the lower the control risk and the less substantive testing the auditor must do. This is because the likelihood of errors in the accounting records is reduced. In other words, when controls are strong, the auditor may limit substantive testing. However, the weaker the internal control structure, the greater the control risk and the more substantive testing the auditor must perform to reduce total audit risk. Evidence of weak controls forces the auditor to extend substantive testing to search for misstatements in financial data caused by control errors as well as business problems inherent to the organization.

Because substantive tests are labor-intensive and time-consuming, they are expensive. Increased substantive testing translates into longer and more disruptive audits and higher audit costs. Thus, management's best interests are served by having a strong internal control structure.

GENERAL FRAMEWORK FOR VIEWING IT RISKS AND CONTROLS

Figure 1–7 presents a framework for viewing areas of IT risks and controls. The areas of greatest potential risk are indicated by the circled numbers, which correspond to the following six topics.

---

9.   Ibid.

FIGURE 1-7   Framework for Viewing IT Risks

1. Operations
2. Data Management Systems
3. New Systems Development
4. Systems Maintenance
5. Electronic Commerce
6. Computer Applications

IT internal controls are divided into the two broad categories of *general controls* and *application controls*.[10] General controls apply to a wide range of risks that systematically threaten the integrity of all applications processed within the IT environment. General controls are topics numbered 1 through 5. Chapters 2 through 6 examine the technologies, the control objectives, and the audit techniques related to each of these areas.

Application controls are narrowly focused on exposures associated with specific systems, such as payroll, accounts receivable, and purchases. Tests of application controls relate to specific audit objects such as verifying the *completeness* of accounts payable. Chapters 7, 8, and 9 deal with the audit objectives, tests of controls, and substantive tests related to revenue and expenditure cycle applications. The issue of computer fraud is examined in Chapter 10.

SUMMARY

This chapter outlined the impact of information technology on the field of auditing. We began by distinguishing between the auditor's traditional attestation responsibility and the emerging field of assurance services. The chapter focused on issues that pertain primarily to attest services but which could also apply to assurance services. The structure of an IT audit, management assertions, audit objectives, tests of controls, and substantive tests were explained. The chapter outlined the key points of SAS 78, which defines internal controls in both manual and IT environments. The final section of the chapter presented a framework for risk assessment that identifies six areas of computer risk. The remainder of the text is based upon this framework.

KEY TERMS

access controls
accounting records
application controls
assurance services
audit objectives
audit opinion
audit planning
audit procedure
audit risk
auditing
completeness

Computer Assisted Audit Tools and Techniques (CAATTs)
control activities
control environment
control risk
corrective controls
detection risk
detective controls
existence or occurrence
exposure
Foreign Corrupt Practices Act of 1977 (FCPA)

---

10.   The Committee of Sponsoring Organizations of the Treadway Commission (New York: 1991), p. 115.

general controls
independent auditing
information technology (IT)
inherent risk
internal auditing
internal control system
management assertions
management responsibility
monitoring
obtaining evidence
presentation and disclosure
preventive controls

reasonable assurance
rights and obligations
risk assessment
segregation of duties
Statement on Auditing Standards No. 78 (SAS 78)
substantive tests
supervision
tests of controls
transaction authorization
valuation or allocation
verification procedures

REVIEW QUESTIONS

1. What is the purpose of an IT audit?
2. Discuss the concept of independence within the context of an audit.
3. What are the conceptual phases of an audit? How do they differ between general auditing and IT auditing?
4. Distinguish between internal and external auditors.
5. What are the four primary elements described in the definition of auditing?
6. Explain the concept of materiality.
7. What tasks do auditors perform during audit planning, and what techniques are used?
8. What are the four broad objectives of internal control?
9. What are the four modifying assumptions that guide designers and auditors of internal control systems?
10. Give an example of a preventive control.
11. Give an example of a detective control.
12. Give an example of a corrective control.
13. What is the objective of SAS 78?
14. What are the five internal control components described in the *Statement on Auditing Standards No. 78*?
15. What are the four broad classes of control activities defined by SAS 78?

16. How do automated authorization procedures differ from manual authorization procedures?
17. Explain why certain duties that are deemed incompatible in a manual system may be combined in an IT environment. Give an example.
18. Explain how the audit trail differs between a manual system and a computer system.
19. What exposures do data consolidation in an IT environment pose?
20. Give some examples of independent verifications in an IT environment.
21. Differentiate between general and application controls.
22. Distinguish between tests of controls and substantive testing.
23. Define audit risk.
24. Distinguish between errors and irregularities. Which do you think concern auditors the most?
25. Distinguish between inherent risk and control risk. How do internal controls affect inherent risk and control risk, if at all? What is the role of detection risk?
26. What is the relationship between tests of controls and substantive tests?

DISCUSSION QUESTIONS

1. Discuss the differences between the attest function and assurance services.
2. A CPA firm has many clients. For some of its clients, it relies very heavily on the work of

the internal auditors, while for others it does not. The amount of reliance affects the fees charged. How can the CPA firm justify the apparent inconsistency of fees charged in a competitive marketplace?

3. Accounting firms are very concerned that their employees have excellent communication skills, both oral and written. Explain why this is so important by giving examples of where these skills would be necessary in each of the three phases of an audit.

4. Discuss how the process of obtaining IT audit evidence is inherently different than in a manual system.

5. Explain the audit objectives of existence or occurrence, completeness, rights and obligations, valuation or allocation, and presentation and disclosure.

6. How has the Foreign Corrupt Practices Act of 1977 had a significant impact on organization management?

7. Discuss the concept of exposure and explain why firms may tolerate some exposure.

8. If detective controls signal errors, why shouldn't they automatically make a correction to the identified error? Why are separate corrective controls necessary?

9. Most accounting firms allow married employees to work for the firm. However, they do not allow an employee to remain working for them if he or she marries an employee of one of their auditing clients. Why do you think this policy exists?

10. Discuss whether a firm with fewer employees than there are incompatible tasks should rely more heavily on general authority than specific authority.

11. An organization's internal audit department is usually considered to be an effective control mechanism for evaluating the organization's internal control structure. The Birch Company's internal auditing function reports directly to the controller. Comment on the effectiveness of this organizational structure.

12. According to SAS 78, the proper segregation of functions is an effective internal control procedure. Comment on the exposure (if any) caused by combining the tasks of paycheck preparation and distribution to employees.

13. Explain whether authorizations are necessary in a computer environment.

14. Explain how an IT environment affects the segregation of functions.

15. Explain how an IT environment affects supervision.

16. Explain how an IT environment affects the firm's obligation to maintain adequate accounting records.

17. Explain how an IT environment affects access control.

18. Explain how an IT environment affects independent verification.

PROBLEMS

1. Audit Committee
CMA 6898 3-3
Micro Dynamics, a developer of database software packages, is a publicly held company whose stock is traded over the counter. The company recently received an enforcement release proceeding through an SEC administrative law judge that cited the company for inadequate internal controls. In response, Micro Dynamics has agreed to establish an internal audit function and strengthen its audit committee.

A manager of the internal audit department has been hired as a result of the SEC enforcement action to establish an internal audit function. In addition, the composition of the audit committee has been changed to include all outside directors. Micro Dynamics has held its initial planning meeting to discuss the roles of the various participants in the internal control and financial reporting process. Participants at the meeting included the company president, the chief financial officer, a member of the audit committee, a partner from Micro Dynamics' external audit firm, and the newly appointed manager of the internal audit department. Comments by the various meeting participants are presented below.

President: "We want to ensure that Micro Dynamics complies with the SEC's enforcement release and that we don't find ourselves in this position again. The internal audit department should help to strengthen our internal control system by correcting the problems. I would like your thoughts on the proper reporting relationship for the manager of the internal audit department."

CFO: "I think the manager of the internal audit department should report to me since much of the department's work is related to financial issues. The audit committee should have oversight responsibilities."

Audit committee member: "I believe we should think through our roles more carefully. The Treadway Commission has recommended that the audit committee play a more important role in the financial reporting process; the duties of today's audit committee have expanded beyond mere rubber-stamp approval. We need to have greater assurance that controls are in place and being followed."

External audit firm partner: "We need a close working relationship among all of our roles. The internal audit department can play a significant role in monitoring the control systems on a continuing basis and should have strong ties to your external audit firm."

Internal audit department manager: "The internal audit department should be more involved in operational auditing, but it also should play a significant monitoring role in the financial reporting area."

Required:
  a. Describe the role of each of the following in the establishment, maintenance, and evaluation of Micro Dynamics' system of internal control.
    i.   Management
    ii. Audit committee
    iii. External auditor
    iv. Internal audit department
  b. Describe the responsibilities that Micro Dynamics' audit committee has in the financial reporting process.

2. Role of Internal Auditor
    CMA 1290 4-Y8
    Leigh Industries has an internal audit department consisting of a director and four staff auditors. The director of internal audit, Diane Bauer, reports to the corporate controller, who receives copies of all internal audit reports. In addition, copies of all internal audit reports are sent to the audit committee of the board of directors and the individual responsible for the area of activity being audited.

    In the past, the company's external auditors have relied on the work of the internal audit department to a substantial degree. However, in recent months, Bauer has become concerned that the objectivity of the internal audit function is being affected by the nonaudit work being performed by the department. This possible loss of objectivity could result in more extensive testing and analysis by the external auditors. The percentage of nonaudit work performed by the internal auditors has steadily increased to about 25 percent of the total hours worked. A sample of five recent nonaudit activities follows.

    *   One of the internal auditors assisted in the preparation of policy statements on internal control. These statements included such things as policies regarding sensitive payments and the safeguarding of assets.
    *   Reconciling the bank statements of the corporation each month is a regular assignment of one of the internal auditors. The corporate controller believes this strengthens the internal control function because the internal auditor is not involved in either the receipt or the disbursement of cash.
    *   The internal auditors are asked to review the annual budget each year for relevance and reasonableness before the budget is approved. At the end of each month, the corporate controller's staff analyzes the variances from budget and prepares explanations of these variances. These variances and explanations are then reviewed by the internal audit staff.
    *   One of the internal auditors has been involved in the design, installation, and initial operation of a new computerized inventory system. The auditor was

primarily concerned with the design and implementation of internal accounting controls and conducted the evaluation of these controls during the test runs.

- The internal auditors are sometimes asked to make the accounting entries for complex transactions as the employees in the accounting department are not adequately trained to handle such transactions. The corporate controller believes this gives an added measure of assurance to the accurate recording of these transactions.

Required:

a. Define objectivity as it relates to the internal audit function.

b. For each of the five nonaudit activities presented, explain whether the objectivity of Leigh Industries' internal audit department has been materially impaired. Consider each situation independently.

c. The director of internal audit reports directly to the corporate controller. Does this reporting relationship affect the objectivity of the internal audit department? Explain your answer.

d. Would your evaluation of the five situations in question (b) change if the director of internal audit reported to the audit committee of the board of directors? Explain your answer.

3. Segregation of Function
CMA 1288 3-22
An effective system of internal control includes the segregation of incompatible duties. Some of the examples presented represent incompatible duties. Comment on the specific exposures (if any) that are caused by the combination of tasks.

a. The treasurer has the authority to sign checks but gives the signature block to the assistant treasurer to run the check-signing machine.

b. The warehouse clerk, who has custodial responsibility over inventory in the warehouse, may authorize disposal of damaged goods.

c. The sales manager, who works on commission based on gross sales, approves credit and has the authority to write off uncollectible accounts.

d. The shop foreman submits time cards and distributes paychecks to employees.

e. The accounting clerk posts to individual account receivable subsidiary accounts and performs the reconciliation of the subsidiary ledger and the general ledger control account.

4. Segregation of Duties
CMA 1288 3-23
Explain why each of the following combinations of tasks should, or should not, be separated to achieve adequate internal control.

a. Approval of bad debt write-offs and the reconciliation of accounts payable subsidiary ledger and the general ledger control account.

b. Distribution of payroll checks to employees and approval of sales returns for credit.

c. Posting of amounts from both the cash receipts and the cash disbursements journals to the general ledger.

d. Distribution of payroll checks to employees and recording cash receipts in the journal.

e. Recording cash receipts in the journal and preparing the bank reconciliation.

5. Internal Control
CMA Adapted 1289 3-4
Oakdale, Inc., is a subsidiary of Solomon Publishing and specializes in the publication and distribution of reference books. Oakdale's sales for the past year exceeded $18 million, and the company employed an average of 65 employees. Solomon periodically sends a member of its internal audit department to audit the operations of each of its subsidiaries, and Katherine Ford, Oakdale's treasurer, is currently working with Ralph Johnson of Solomon's internal audit staff. Johnson has just completed a review of Oakdale's investment cycle and prepared the following report.

General

Throughout the year, Oakdale has made both short-term and long-term investments in securities; all securities are registered in the company's name. According to Oakdale's bylaws, long-term investment activity must be approved by its board of directors, while short-term investment activity may be approved by either the president or the treasurer.

Transactions

Oakdale has a computer link with its broker; thus, all buy and sale orders are transmitted electronically. Only individuals with authorized passwords may initiate certain types of transactions. All purchases and sales of short-term securities in the year were made by the treasurer. In addition, two purchases and one sale of long-term securities were executed by the treasurer. The long-term security purchases were approved by the Board. The president, having on-line authorization access to all transactions, was able to approve a sale of a long-term security. The president is given access to authorize all transactions engaged in by the firm. Because the treasurer is listed with the broker as the company's contact, all revenue from these investments is received by this individual, who then forwards the checks to accounting for processing.

Documentation

Purchase and sales authorizations, along with broker's advices, are maintained in an electronic file with authorized access by the treasurer. Broker's advices are received verbally on the phone, and this advice is noted on a broker advice form. This form is filed by the treasurer. The certificates for all long-term investments are kept in a safe deposit box at the local bank; only the president of Oakdale has access to this box. An inventory of this box was made, and all certificates were accounted for. Certificates for short-term investments are kept in a locked metal box in the accounting office. Other documents, such as long-term contracts and legal agreements, are also kept in this box. There are three keys to the box, held by the president, treasurer, and the accounting manager. The accounting manager's key is available to all accounting personnel, should they require documents kept in this box. Certificates of investments may take up to four weeks to receive after the purchase of the investment. An electronic inventory list is kept perpetually. The data is keyed in by accounting personnel who receive a buy/sale transaction sheet from the treasurer. The president, treasurer, and accounting manager all have passwords to access and update this inventory list. The accounting manager's password is known by two of the accounting supervisors in case the inventory list needs to be updated when the accounting manager is not available. Documentation for two of the current short-term investments could not be located in this box; the accounting manager explained that some of the investments are for such short periods of time that formal documentation is not always provided by the broker.

Accounting Records

Deposits of checks for interest and dividends earned on investments are recorded by the accounting department, but these checks could not be traced to the cash receipts journal maintained by the individual who normally opens, stamps, and logs incoming checks. These amounts are journalized monthly to an account for investment revenue. Electronic payments for investment purchases are authorized by the treasurer. If the amount is in excess of $15,000, an authorization code given by the treasurer or president is necessary.

Each month, the accounting manager and the treasurer prepare the journal entries required to adjust the short-term investment account. There was insufficient backup documentation attached to the journal entries reviewed to trace all transactions; however, the balance in the account at the end of last month closely approximates the amount shown on the statement received from the broker. The amount in the long-term investment account is correct, and the transactions can be clearly traced through the documentation attached to the journal entries. No attempts are made to adjust either account to the lower of aggregate cost or market.

Required:

To achieve Solomon Publishing's objective of sound internal control, the company believes the following four controls are basic for an effective system of accounting control.

- Authorization of transactions
- Complete and accurate recordkeeping
- Physical control
- Internal verification

a. Describe the purpose of each of the four controls listed above.

b. Identify an area in Oakdale's investment procedures that violates each of the four controls listed above.

c. For each of the violations identified, describe how Oakdale can correct it.

6. Internal Control
   CMA 1290 4-2
   Arlington Industries manufactures and sells component engine parts for large industrial

equipment. The company employs over 1,000 workers for three shifts, and most employees work overtime when necessary. Arlington has had major growth in its production and has purchased a mainframe computer to handle order processing, inventory management, production planning, distribution operations, and accounting applications. Michael Cromley, president of Arlington, suspects that there may be internal control weaknesses due to the quick implementation of the computer system. Cromley recently hired Kathleen Luddy as the internal control accountant.

Cromley asked Luddy to review the payroll processing system first. Luddy has reviewed the payroll process, interviewed the individuals involved, and compiled the flowchart shown in the next column. The following additional information concerns payroll processing:

- The personnel department determines the wage rate of all employees at Arlington. Personnel starts the process by sending an authorization form for adding an employee to the payroll to Marjorie Adams, the payroll coordinator. After Adams inputs this information into the system, the computer automatically determines the overtime and shift differential rates for the individual, updating the payroll master files.

- Arlington uses an external service to provide monthly payroll tax updates. The company receives a magnetic tape every month, which the data processing department installs to update the payroll master file for tax calculations.

- Employees at Arlington use a time clock to record the hours worked. Every Monday morning, Adams collects the previous week's time cards and begins the computerized processing of payroll information to produce paychecks the following Friday. Adams reviews the time cards to ensure that the hours worked are correctly totaled; the system will determine whether overtime has been worked or a shift differential is required.

- All the other processes displayed on the flowchart are performed by Adams. The system automatically assigns a sequential number to each payroll check produced.

The checks are stored in a box next to the computer printer to provide immediate access. After the checks are printed, Adams uses an automatic check-signing machine to sign the checks with an authorized signature plate that Adams keeps locked in a safe.

- After the check processing is completed, Adams distributes the checks to the employees, leaving the checks for the second- and third-shift employees with the appropriate shift supervisor. Adams then notifies the data processing department that she is finished with her weekly processing, and data processing makes a backup of the payroll master file to magnetic tape for storage on the tape shelves in the computer room.

Required:

By referring to the information in Problem 6 and the flowchart, identify and describe:

a. Five different areas in Arlington's payroll processing system where the system controls are inadequate.

b. Two different areas in Arlington's payroll processing system where the system controls are satisfactory.

chapter 2

COMPUTER OPERATIONS

This chapter explores several audit issues related to computer operations. The topics covered are divided into the following categories: structuring of the information technology (IT) function, controlling computer center operations, the computer operating system, and the personal computer environment. The chapter opens by reviewing the advantages and potential risks associated with both centralized and distributed IT structures. Control techniques, audit objectives, and audit procedures are examined. Next, computer center risks and controls are considered. The key elements of a disaster recovery plan are presented. The chapter then presents an overview of multiuser operating system features common to networks and mainframes. Fundamental operating system objectives and the risks that threaten system security are reviewed. This material is followed by a discussion of operating system controls and audit techniques. The chapter concludes with a review of the features that characterize the personal computer environment. The primary risks, controls, and audit issues are discussed.

LEARNING OBJECTIVES

After studying this chapter, you should:

- Understand the control and audit issues related to both the centralized and DDP approaches to structuring the IT function.
- Be familiar with computer center controls and the procedures used to test them.
- Understand the role that operating systems play in an organization's internal control structure and be familiar with the risks that threaten operating system security.
- Be familiar with the control techniques used to provide operating system security.
- Understand the audit objectives and audit procedures applicable to an operating system audit.
- Understand the risks unique to the PC environment and the controls that help to reduce them.

STRUCTURING THE INFORMATION TECHNOLOGY FUNCTION

The organization of the information technology (IT) function has implications for the nature of internal controls, which, in turn, has implications for the audit. In this section, we examine some important control issues related to IT structure. We begin by reviewing basic processes and then examine two extreme organizational models—the centralized approach and the distributed approach. The risks, controls, and audit issues related to each model are then discussed. The reader should recognize that most organizational structures fall somewhere between these extremes and embody elements of both.

CENTRALIZED DATA PROCESSING

Under the **centralized data processing** model, all data processing is performed by one or more large computers housed at a central site that serve users throughout the organization. Figure 2–1 illustrates this approach, in which computer services activities are consolidated and managed as a shared organization resource. End users compete for these resources on the basis of need. The computer services function is usually treated as a cost center whose operating costs are charged back to the end users. Figure 2–2 illustrates a centralized computer services structure and shows its primary service areas: database administration, data processing, and systems development and maintenance. A description of the key functions of each of these areas follows.

DATABASE ADMINISTRATION

Centrally organized companies maintain their data resources in a central location that is shared by all end users. In this shared data arrangement, an independent group—**database administration (DBA)**—headed by the database administrator is responsible for the security and integrity of the database.

FIGURE 2–1

Centralized Data
Processing
Approach

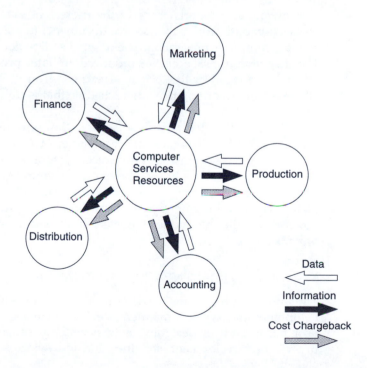

FIGURE 2-2   Organizational Chart of a Centralized Computer Services Function

DATA PROCESSING

The data processing group manages the computer resources used to perform the day-to-day processing of transactions. It consists of the following organizational functions: **data control, data conversion, computer operations**, and the **data library**.

Many organizations have a *data control* group as liaison between the end user and data processing. Data control is responsible for receiving batches of transaction documents for processing from end users and then distributing computer output (documents and reports) back to the users. The *data conversion* function transcribes transaction data from paper source documents to magnetic media (tape or disk) suitable for computer processing. The original source documents are returned to the user. The magnetic transaction files produced are later processed by the central computer, which is managed by the *computer operations* groups. Accounting applications are usually executed according to a strict schedule that is controlled by the central computer's operating system.

The *data library* is a room adjacent to the computer center that provides safe storage for the off-line data files, such as magnetic tapes and removable disk packs. A data librarian, who is responsible for the receipt, storage, retrieval, and custody of data files, controls access to the library. The librarian issues tapes to computer operators in accordance with program requests and takes custody of files when processing is completed. The trend in recent years toward real-time processing and the increased use of direct-access files has reduced or even eliminated the role of the data librarian in many organizations.

SYSTEMS DEVELOPMENT AND MAINTENANCE

The information systems needs of users are met by two related functions: system development and systems maintenance. The former group is responsible for analyzing user needs and for designing new systems to satisfy those needs. The participants in system development activities include systems professionals, end users, and stakeholders.

Systems professionals include systems analysts, database designers, and programmers who design and build the system. Systems professionals gather facts about the user's problem, analyze the facts, and formulate a solution. The product of their efforts is a new information system.

End users are those for whom the system is built. They are the managers who receive reports from the system and the operations personnel who work directly with the system as part of their daily responsibilities.

Stakeholders are individuals inside or outside the firm who have an interest in the system, but are not end users. They include accountants, internal auditors, external auditors, and others who oversee systems development.

Once a new system has been designed and implemented, the systems maintenance group assumes responsibility for keeping it current with user needs. Over the course of the system's life (often several years), as much as 80 or 90 percent of its total cost will be incurred due to maintenance activities.

SEGREGATION OF INCOMPATIBLE IT FUNCTIONS

Segregating incompatible functions is no less important in the IT environment than it is in the manual environment. While the tasks are different, the underlying theory is the same. The following three fundamental objectives of segregation of duties were discussed in Chapter 1:

1. Segregate the task of transaction authorization from transaction processing.
2. Segregate recordkeeping from asset custody.
3. Divide transaction processing tasks among individuals so that the perpetration of a fraud will require collusion between two or more individuals.

In the IT environment, a single application may authorize, process, and record all aspects of a transaction. Thus, the focus of segregation control shifts from the operational level (transaction processing tasks now performed by computer programs) to higher-level organizational relationships within the computer services function. Using the organizational chart in Figure 2–2 as a reference, we shall examine the interrelationships among systems development, systems maintenance, database administration, and computer operations activities.

SEPARATING SYSTEMS DEVELOPMENT FROM COMPUTER OPERATIONS

The segregation of systems development (both new systems development and maintenance) and operations activities is of the greatest importance. The relationship between these groups should be extremely formal, and their responsibilities should not be commingled. Systems development and maintenance professionals should create (and maintain) systems for users. Operations staff should run these systems and have no involvement in their design. These functions are inherently incompatible, and consolidating them invites errors and fraud. With detailed knowledge of the application's logic and control parameters and access to the computer's operating system and utilities, a privileged individual could make unauthorized changes to the application during its execution. Such changes may be temporary ("on the fly") and will disappear without a trace when the application terminates.

SEPARATING DATABASE ADMINISTRATION FROM OTHER FUNCTIONS

Another important organizational control is the segregation of the database administration (DBA) from other computer center functions. The DBA function is responsible for a number of critical tasks pertaining to database security, including creating the database schema and user views, assigning database access authority to users, monitoring database usage, and planning for future expansion. Delegating these responsibilities to others that perform incompatible tasks threatens database integrity. Thus, we see from Figure 2–2 how the DBA function is organizationally independent.

SEPARATING NEW SYSTEMS DEVELOPMENT FROM MAINTENANCE

Some companies organize their in-house systems development function into two groups: systems analysis and programming (see Figure 2–3). The systems analysis group works with the users to produce detailed designs of the new systems. The programming group codes the programs according to these design specifications. Under this approach, the programmer who codes the original programs also maintains the system during the maintenance phase of the systems development life cycle (discussed in Chapter 4). Although a popular arrangement, this approach is associated with two types of control problems: **inadequate documentation** and the potential for **program fraud**.

INADEQUATE DOCUMENTATION.   Poor systems documentation is a chronic problem for many firms. This is particularly true in companies that do not use Computer-Assisted Software Engineering (CASE) tools with automatic documentation features. There are at least two explanations for this phenomenon. First, documenting a system is not as interesting as designing, testing, and implementing it. Systems professionals much prefer to move on to an exciting new project rather than document one that is finished. Pressure from users demanding new systems makes the decision to prematurely move on to something else even easier.

The second reason for inadequate documentation is job security. When a system is poorly documented, it is difficult to interpret, test, and debug. Therefore, the programmer who understands the system (the one who coded it) is in a position of power and becomes relatively indispensable. However, when she or he leaves the firm, a new programmer must maintain the system. The new programmer may need to devote a great deal of time studying the detailed code of the application to glean an understanding of its logic. Depending upon the complexity of the system, the transition period can be costly.

PROGRAM FRAUD.   When the original programmer of a system also has maintenance responsibility, the potential for fraud is increased. Program fraud involves

FIGURE 2–3

Alternative
Organization
of Systems
Development

making unauthorized changes to program modules for the purpose of committing an illegal act. The original programmer may successfully conceal the fraudulent code among the thousands of lines of legitimate code and the hundreds of modules that constitute a system. However, for the fraud to work successfully, the programmer must have continued and unrestricted access to these programs. To control the situation, the programmer must protect the fraudulent code from accidental detection by another programmer (during maintenance) or by the auditor. Therefore, being vested with sole responsibility for maintenance is an important element in the duplicitous programmer's scheme. Through this maintenance authority, the programmer may freely access the system, disabling fraudulent code during audits and then restoring the code when the coast is clear. Frauds of this sort may go on for years without detection.

AN ALTERNATIVE STRUCTURE FOR SYSTEMS DEVELOPMENT

Figure 2–2 presents a superior organizational structure in which the systems development function is separated into two different groups: *new systems development* and *systems maintenance*. The new systems development group is responsible for designing, programming, and implementing new systems projects. Upon successful implementation, responsibility for the system's ongoing maintenance falls to the systems maintenance group. This restructuring has implications that directly address the two control problems just described.

First, documentation standards are improved because the maintenance group requires documentation to perform its maintenance duties. Without complete and adequate documentation, the formal transfer of system responsibility from new systems development to systems maintenance simply cannot occur.

Second, denying the original programmer future access to the program deters program fraud. That the fraudulent code, once concealed within the system, is out of the programmer's control and may later be discovered increases the risk associated with program fraud. The success of this control depends on the existence of other controls that limit, prevent, and detect unauthorized access to programs (such as source program library controls). Organizational separations alone cannot prevent such unauthorized access. However, they are critical to creating the environment in which unauthorized access can be prevented.

SEPARATING THE DATA LIBRARY FROM OPERATIONS

The data library is usually a room adjacent to the computer center that provides safe storage for the off-line data files, such as magnetic tapes and removable disk packs. A data librarian who is responsible for the receipt, storage, retrieval, and custody of data files should control access to the library. The librarian must keep a detailed log of each file, including file name, serial number, contents, creation date, and retention dates. The librarian issues scratch tapes (expired tapes that are going to be overwritten) to computer operators in accordance with system requests. When the program run is complete, the operator returns the file(s) to the librarian for storage.

The separation of the librarian from operations is important for the physical security of off-line data files. However, for many organizations, the volume of tape file usage is insufficient to justify a full-time librarian. The trend in recent years toward real-time and direct access batch systems has reduced the need for sequential tape storage. Thus, firms with modest tape usage—which still may represent several hundred tape volumes—often assign librarian functions to selected operators who perform these tasks on an ad hoc basis in addition to their usual operator functions.

Operators who are assigned library tasks must understand the control importance of this apparently mundane responsibility. Management should maintain strict control over who performs library functions to ensure that these responsibilities are not assumed by other operators during busy periods. This apparently innocuous transgression creates an environment of shared responsibility that inevitably deteriorates into one of no responsibility. In such an environment, data security suffers. The potential exposure can be illustrated through the following three scenarios.

1. Computer centers become very busy at times. Rushed operators, hurrying to start the next job, may forget to return to the library the tapes used by the program that has just completed processing. Lacking a librarian with the formal responsibility to account for the disposition of all tapes, these tapes may remain in a corner of the computer room for days, exposed to physical damage, loss, theft, or corruption.

2. Inexperienced individuals filling in as librarian during busy periods may return a tape to the wrong storage location in the library. When it is needed again, the librarian may not be able to find it. This is analogous to placing an important book in a randomly selected shelf space in a library. How does one go about relocating it?

3. The librarian is directly responsible for implementing the firm's scratch tape policy. The librarian issues expired tapes to operators as scratch tapes for other systems. Inexperienced librarians have been known to issue current tapes, thinking they were scratch tapes. Such an error could result in the destruction of the organization's general ledger or other important accounting files.

AUDIT OBJECTIVES

- To verify that individuals in incompatible areas are segregated in accordance with the level of potential risk and in a manner that promotes a working environment in which formal, rather than casual, relationships exist between incompatible tasks.

AUDIT PROCEDURES

- Obtain and review the corporate policy on computer security. Verify that the security policy is communicated to responsible employees and supervisors.
- Review relevant documentation, including the current organizational chart, mission statement, and job descriptions for key functions, to determine if individuals or groups are performing incompatible functions.
- Review systems documentation and maintenance records for a sample of applications. Verify that maintenance programmers assigned to specific projects are not also the original design programmers.
- Through observation, determine that segregation policy is being followed in practice. Review operations room access logs to determine whether programmers enter the facility for reasons other than system failures.
- Review user rights and privileges to verify that programmers have access privileges consistent with their job description. User rights and privileges are discussed later in the chapter.

THE DISTRIBUTED MODEL

For many years, economies of scale favored large, powerful computers and centralized processing. However, recent developments in small, powerful, and inexpensive systems have changed this picture dramatically. An alternative to the centralized model is the concept of **distributed data processing (DDP)**. The topic of DDP is quite broad, touching upon such related topics as end user computing, commercial software, networking, and office automation. Simply stated, DDP involves reorganizing the computer services function into small IT units that are placed under the control of end users. The IT units may be distributed according to business function, geographic location, or both. All or any of the computer services activities represented in Figure 2–2 may be distributed. The degree to which IT activities are distributed will vary depending upon the philosophy and objectives of the organization's management. Figure 2–4 presents two alternative DDP approaches.

Alternative A is actually a variant of the centralized model; the difference is that terminals (or microcomputers) are distributed to end users for handling input and output. This eliminates the need for the centralized data control and data conversion groups, since the user now performs these tasks. However, systems development, computer operations, and database administration remain centralized.

Alternative B is a radical departure from the centralized model. This alternative distributes all computer services to the end users, where they operate as standalone units. The result is the elimination of the central computer services function from the organizational structure. Notice the interconnections between the distributed units in Figure 2–4. These connections represent a *networking* arrangement that permits

FIGURE 2–4

Two Distributed
Data Processing
Approaches

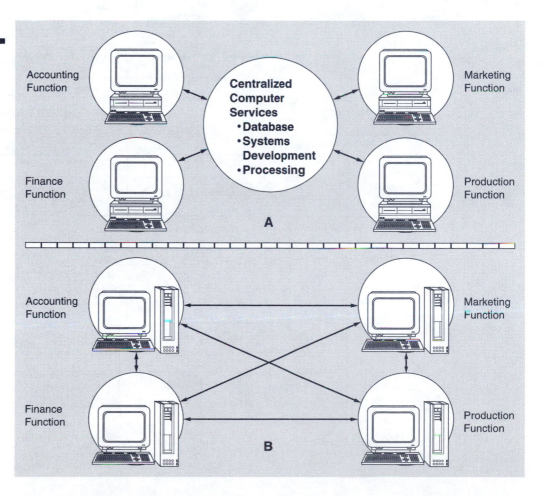

communication and data transfers between the units. Figure 2–5 shows a possible organizational structure following the distribution of all traditional data processing tasks to the end user areas.

RISKS ASSOCIATED WITH DDP

This section discuss the of organizational risks that need to be considered when implementing DDP. The discussion focuses on important issues that carry control implications that auditors should recognize. Potential problems include the inefficient use of resources, the destruction of audit trails, inadequate segregation of duties, an increased potential for programming errors and systems failures, and the lack of standards.

MISMANAGEMENT OF ORGANIZATION-WIDE RESOURCES.   Some argue that when organization-wide resources exceed a threshold amount, say 5 percent of the total operations budget, they should be controlled and monitored centrally. IT services (such as computer operations, programming, data conversion, and database management) represent a significant expenditure for many organizations that needs careful

FIGURE 2–5

Distributed
Organization
with Corporate
Computer
Services Function

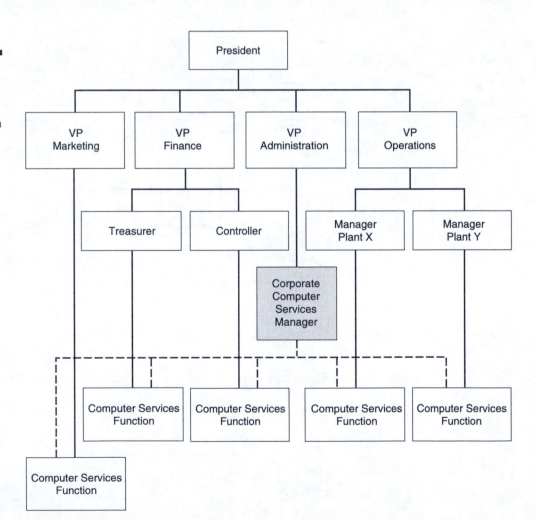

management. Those opposed to DDP argue that distributing responsibility for these resources will inevitably lead to their mismanagement and suboptimal utilization.

HARDWARE AND SOFTWARE INCOMPATIBILITY.   Distributing the responsibility for hardware and software purchases to users may result in uncoordinated and poorly conceived decisions. For example, decision-makers in different organizational units working independently may settle on dissimilar and incompatible operating systems, technology platforms, spreadsheets, word processors, and database packages. Hardware and software incompatibilities can degrade and disrupt the connectivity between units, causing the loss of transactions and the destruction of audit trails.

REDUNDANT TASKS.   Autonomous systems development initiative distributed throughout the firm can result in each user area reinventing the wheel. For example, application programs created by one user, which could be used with little or no change by others, will be redesigned from scratch rather than shared. Likewise, data common to many users may be recreated for each, resulting in a high level of data redundancy. This has implications for data accuracy and consistency.

CONSOLIDATING INCOMPATIBLE ACTIVITIES.   The distribution of the IT services to users may result in the creation of many small units that do not permit the necessary separation of incompatible functions. For example, within a single unit the same person may write application programs, perform program maintenance, enter transaction data into the computer, and operate the computer equipment. This would be a fundamental violation of internal control. However, achieving an adequate segregation of duties may not be possible in some distributed environments.

HIRING QUALIFIED PROFESSIONALS.   End user managers may lack the knowledge to evaluate the technical credentials and relevant experience of candidates applying for a position as a computer professional. Also, if the organizational unit into which a new employee is entering is small, the opportunity for personal growth, continuing education, and promotion may be limited. For these reasons, managers may experience difficulty attracting highly qualified personnel. This problem spills over into the domain of accountants and auditors. The risk of programming errors and system failures increases directly with the level of employee incompetence.

LACK OF STANDARDS.   Because of the distribution of responsibility in the DDP environment, standards for developing and documenting systems, choosing programming languages, acquiring hardware and software, and evaluating performance may be unevenly applied or even nonexistent. Opponents of DDP argue that the risks associated with the design and operation of a data processing system are made tolerable only if such standards are consistently applied. This requires that standards be imposed centrally.

ADVANTAGES OF DDP

This section considers potential advantages of DDP, including cost reductions, improved cost control, improved user satisfaction, and backup.

COST REDUCTIONS.   For many years, achieving economies of scale was the principal justification for the centralized approach. The economics of data processing favored large, expensive, powerful computers. The wide variety of needs that centralized systems must satisfy calls for a computer that is highly generalized and employs a complex operating system. However, the sheer overhead associated with running such a system can diminish the advantages of its raw processing power. Thus, for many users, large, centralized systems represent expensive overkill that they must escape.

Powerful and inexpensive microcomputers and minicomputers that can perform specialized functions have changed the economics of data processing dramatically. In addition, the unit cost of data storage, which was once the justification for consolidating data in a central location, is no longer the prime consideration. Moreover, the move to DDP can reduce costs in two other areas: (1) data can be entered and edited at the user area, thus eliminating the centralized tasks of data preparation and data control; and (2) application complexity can be reduced, which in turn reduces development and maintenance costs.

IMPROVED COST CONTROL RESPONSIBILITY.   End user managers carry the responsibility for the financial success of their operations. This requires that they be properly empowered with the authority to make decisions about resources that influence their overall success. When managers are precluded from making the decisions necessary to achieve their goals, their performance can be negatively influenced. A less aggressive and less effective management may evolve.

If IT capability is critical to the success of a business operation, then management must be given control over these resources. This argument counters the earlier discussion favoring the centralization of organization-wide resources. Proponents of DDP argue that the benefits of improved management attitudes more than outweigh any additional costs incurred from distributing these resources.

IMPROVED USER SATISFACTION.   Perhaps the most often cited benefit of DDP is improved user satisfaction. This derives from three areas of need that too often go unsatisfied in the centralized approach: (1) as previously stated, users desire to control the resources that influence their profitability; (2) users want systems professionals (analysts, programmers, and computer operators) who are responsive to their specific situation; and (3) users want to become more actively involved in developing and implementing their own systems. Proponents of DDP argue that providing more customized support (feasible only in a distributed environment) has direct benefits for user morale and productivity.

BACKUP.   The final argument in favor of DDP is the ability to back up computing facilities to protect against potential disasters such as fires, floods, sabotage, and earthquakes. The only way to back up a central computer site against such disasters is to provide a second computer facility. Later in the chapter we examine disaster recovery planning for such contingencies. The distributed model provides organizational flexibility for providing backup. Each IT unit IPU can be designed with excess capacity. If a disaster destroys a single site, the other sites can use their excess capacity to process the transactions of the destroyed site. This requires close coordination between the end user managers to ensure that they do not implement incompatible hardware and software.

CONTROLLING THE DDP ENVIRONMENT

Careful planning and implementation of controls can mitigate the risks just discussed. This section reviews the controls and audit issues relevant to DDP.

NEED FOR CAREFUL ANALYSIS

DDP carries a certain leading-edge prestige value that, during an analysis of its pros and cons, may overwhelm important considerations of economic benefit and operational feasibility. Some organizations have made the move to DDP without considering fully whether the distributed organizational structure will better achieve their business objectives. Many DDP initiatives have proven to be ineffective, and even counterproductive, because decision-makers saw in these systems virtues that were more symbolic than real. Before taking an irreversible step, decision-makers must assess the true merits of DDP for their organization. Auditors have an opportunity and an obligation to play an important role in this analysis.

IMPLEMENT A CORPORATE IT FUNCTION

The completely centralized model and the distributed model represent extreme positions on a continuum of structural alternatives. The needs of most firms fall somewhere between these end points. For most firms, the control problems we have described can be addressed by implementing a **corporate IT function** such as that illustrated in Figure 2–5.

This function is greatly reduced in size and status from that of the centralized model shown in Figure 2–2. The corporate IT group provides systems development and database management for entity-wide systems in addition to technical advice and expertise to the distributed IT community. This advisory role is represented by the dotted lines in Figure 2–5. Some of the services provided are described below.

CENTRAL TESTING OF COMMERCIAL SOFTWARE AND HARDWARE.   The corporate IT group is better able to evaluate the merits of competing vendor software and hardware. A central, technically astute group such as this can evaluate systems features, controls, and compatibility with industry and organizational standards most efficiently. Test results can then be distributed to user areas as standards for guiding acquisition decisions.

USER SERVICES.   A valuable feature of the corporate group is its user services function. This activity provides technical help to users during the installation of new software and in troubleshooting hardware and software problems. The creation of an electronic bulletin board for users is an excellent way to distribute information about common problems and allows the sharing of user-developed programs with others within the organization. The user services staff in many organizations teaches technical courses for end users and their computer services staff; this raises the level of user awareness and promotes the continued education of technical personnel.

STANDARD-SETTING BODY.   The relatively poor control environment imposed by the DDP model can be improved by establishing some central guidance. The corporate group can contribute to this goal by establishing and distributing to user areas appropriate standards for systems development, programming, and documentation.

PERSONNEL REVIEW.   The corporate group is probably better equipped than users to evaluate the technical credentials of prospective systems professionals. Although the systems professional will actually be part of the user group, the involvement of the corporate group in employment decisions can render a valuable service to the organization.

AUDIT OBJECTIVES

- To verify that distributed IT units employ entity-wide standards of performance that promote compatibility among hardware, software applications, and data.

AUDIT PROCEDURES

- Verify that corporate policies and standards for systems design, documentation, and hardware and software acquisition are published and sent out to distributed IT units.
- Review the current organizational chart, mission statement, and job descriptions for key functions to determine if individuals or groups are performing incompatible duties. Verify that compensating controls such as supervision and management monitoring are employed when segregation of incompatible duties is economically infeasible.
- Review systems documentation to verify that applications, procedures, and databases are designed and functioning in accordance with corporate standards.
- Verify that individuals are granted system access privileges to programs and data in a manner consistent with their job descriptions. User rights and privileges for distributed systems and PC environments are discussed later in the chapter.

THE COMPUTER CENTER

Fires, floods, wind, sabotage, earthquakes, or even power outages can deprive an organization of its data processing facilities and bring to a halt those functions that are performed or aided by the computer. Although the likelihood of such a disastrous event is remote, the consequences to the organization could be serious. If a disaster does occur, the organization not only loses its investment in data processing facilities; more important, it loses its ability to do business.

The objective of this section is to present computer center controls that help create a secure environment. We will begin with a look at controls designed to prevent and detect threats to the computer center. However, no matter how much is invested in control, some disasters simply cannot be anticipated and prevented. What does a company do to prepare itself for such an event? How will it recover? These questions are at the heart of the organization's disaster recovery plan. The second half of this section deals with issues pertaining to the development of a disaster recovery plan.

COMPUTER CENTER CONTROLS

Accountants routinely examine the physical environment of the computer center as part of their annual audit. Exposures in these areas have a great potential impact on information, accounting records, transaction processing, and the effectiveness of other, more conventional, internal controls. The following are some of the control features that contribute directly to the security of the computer center environment.

PHYSICAL LOCATION

The physical location of the computer center directly affects the risk of disaster. To the extent possible, the computer center should be away from human-made and natural hazards, such as processing plants, gas and water mains, airports, high-crime areas, flood plains, and geological faults.

CONSTRUCTION

Ideally, a computer center should be located in a single-story building of solid construction with controlled access (discussed shortly). Utility (power and telephone) and communications lines should be underground. The building windows should not open. An air filtration system should be in place that is capable of excluding pollens, dust, and dust mites.

ACCESS

Access to the computer center should be limited to the operators and other employees who work there. Programmers and analysts who need access to correct program errors should be required to sign in and out. The computer center should maintain accurate records of all such events to verify access control. The main entrance to the computer center should be through a single door, though fire exits with alarms are necessary. To achieve a higher level of security, access should be monitored by closed-circuit cameras and video recording systems.

AIR CONDITIONING

Computers function best in an air-conditioned environment. For mainframe computers, providing adequate air conditioning is often a requirement of the vendor's warranty. Computers operate best in a temperature range of 70 to 75 degrees Fahrenheit and a relative humidity of 50 percent. Logic errors can occur in computer hardware when temperatures depart significantly from this optimal range. Also, the risk of circuit damage from static electricity is increased when humidity drops. High humidity, on the other hand, can cause molds to grow and paper products (such as source documents) to swell and jam equipment.

FIRE SUPPRESSION

The most common threat to a firm's computer equipment is from fire. Half of companies that suffer fires go out of business because of the loss of critical records, such as accounts receivable. The implementation of an effective fire suppression system requires consultation with specialists. However, some of the major features of such a system follow.

1. Automatic and manual alarms should be placed in strategic locations around the installation. These alarms should be connected to permanently staffed fire-fighting stations.
2. There must be an automatic fire extinguishing system that dispenses the appropriate type of suppressant (carbon dioxide or halon) for the location. For example, spraying water and certain chemicals on a computer can do as much damage as the fire.
3. There should be manual fire extinguishers placed at strategic locations.
4. The building should be of sound construction to withstand water damage caused by fire suppression equipment.
5. Fire exits should be clearly marked and illuminated during a fire.

POWER SUPPLY

Commercially provided electrical power presents several problems that can disrupt the computer center operations, including total power failures, brownouts, power fluctuations, and frequency variations. The equipment used to control these problems includes voltage regulators, surge protectors, generators, and batteries. The extent and configuration of control equipment needed will depend on the firm's ability to withstand such disruptions and the power company's record for providing reliable service. This can be an expensive control decision and requires extensive analysis and the advice of experts.

AUDIT OBJECTIVES

- To evaluate the controls governing computer center security. Specifically, the auditor should verify that (1) physical security controls are adequate to reasonably protect the organization from physical exposures; (2) insurance coverage on equipment is adequate to compensate the organization for the destruction of, or damage to, its computer center; and (3) operator documentation is adequate to deal with system failures.

AUDIT PROCEDURES

The following are tests of physical security controls.

TESTS OF PHYSICAL CONSTRUCTION.   The auditor should determine that the computer center is solidly built of fireproof material. There should be adequate drainage under the raised floor to allow water to flow away in the event of water damage from a fire in an upper floor or from some other source. In addition, the auditor should evaluate the physical location of the computer center. The facility should be located in an area that minimizes its exposure from fire, civil unrest, and other hazards.

TESTS OF THE FIRE DETECTION SYSTEM.   The auditor should establish that fire detection and suppression equipment, both manual and automatic, are in place and are tested regularly. The fire detection system should detect smoke, heat, and combustible fumes. The adequacy of these devices can be determined by reviewing official fire marshal records of tests that are stored at the computer center.

TESTS OF ACCESS CONTROL.   The auditor must establish that routine access to the computer center is restricted to authorized employees. Details about visitor access (by programmers and others), such as arrival and departure times, purpose, and frequency of access, can be obtained by reviewing the access log. To establish the veracity of this document, the auditor may covertly observe the process by which access is permitted.

TESTS OF THE BACKUP POWER SUPPLY.   The computer center should perform periodic tests of the backup power supply to ensure that it has sufficient capacity to run the computer and air conditioning. These are extremely important tests, and their results should be formally recorded. As a firm's computer function develops, its backup power needs are likely to grow proportionally. Indeed, without such tests, an organization may be unaware that it has outgrown its backup capacity until it is too late.

TESTS FOR INSURANCE COVERAGE.   The auditor should annually review the organization's insurance coverage on its computer hardware, software, and physical facility. New acquisitions should be listed on the policy and obsolete equipment and software should be deleted. The extent of coverage should reflect management's needs and objectives. For example, the firm may wish to be partially self-insured.

TESTS OF OPERATOR DOCUMENTATION CONTROLS.   Computer operators use a *run manual* to perform certain functions. For example, large batch systems may require special attention from operators. During the course of the day, computer operators may execute dozens of computer programs, each of which processes multiple files and produces multiple reports. To achieve effective data processing operations, the run manual must be sufficiently detailed to guide operators in their tasks. The auditor should review the run manual for completeness and accuracy. Typical contents of a run manual include:

- The name of the system, such as "Purchases System."
- The run schedule (daily, weekly, time of day).
- Required hardware devices (tapes, disks, printers, or special hardware).
- File requirements specifying all the transaction (input) files, master files, and output files used in the system.
- Run time instructions describing the error messages that may appear, actions to be taken, and the name and telephone number of the programmer on call, should the system fail.
- A list of users who receive the output from the run.

The auditor should also verify that other systems documentation, such as systems flowcharts, logic flowcharts, and program code listings, are not part of the operation documentation. Operators should not have access to the operational details of a system's internal logic.

DISASTER RECOVERY PLANNING

Sometimes disastrous events cannot be prevented or evaded. Examples include hurricanes in Florida, widespread flooding in the Midwest, earthquakes in California, and the bombing of public buildings. The survival of a firm affected by such disasters depends on how well and how quickly it reacts. With careful contingency planning, the full impact of a disaster can be absorbed and the organization can still recover.

A **disaster recovery plan (DRP)** is a comprehensive statement of all actions to be taken before, during, and after a disaster, along with documented, tested procedures that will ensure the continuity of operations. Although the details of each plan are unique to the needs of the organization, all workable plans possess common features. The remainder of this section is devoted to a discussion of these essential features: providing second-site backup, identifying critical applications, performing backup and off-site storage procedures, creating a disaster recovery team, and testing the DRP.

PROVIDING SECOND-SITE BACKUP

A necessary ingredient in a DRP is that it provide for duplicate data processing facilities following a disaster. Among the options available are mutual aid pact, empty shell, recovery operations center, and internally provided backup.

MUTUAL AID PACT.   A **mutual aid pact** is an agreement between two or more organizations (with compatible computer facilities) to aid each other with their data processing needs in the event of a disaster. In such an event, the "host" company must disrupt its processing schedule to process the critical applications of the disaster-stricken company. In effect, the host company itself must go into an emergency operation mode (and cut back on the processing of its lower-priority applications) to accommodate the sudden increase in demand for its EDP resources.

Reciprocal agreements of this sort are a popular option. This is partly because they are relatively cost-free (as long as no disaster occurs) and provide some degree of psychological comfort. In fact, plans of this sort tend to work better in theory than in practice. To rely on such an arrangement for substantive relief during a disaster requires a level of faith and untested trust that is uncharacteristic of sophisticated management and its auditors.

THE EMPTY SHELL.   An option that is growing in popularity is the **empty shell** or "cold site" plan. This arrangement usually involves two or more user organizations that buy or lease a building and remodel it into a computer site, but without the computer and peripheral equipment. For example, shells are normally equipped with raised floors and air conditioning. In the event of a disaster, the shell is available and ready to receive whatever hardware the temporary user requires to run its essential data processing systems.

Although an improvement over the mutual aid pact, the empty shell approach has two major problems. First, recovery depends on the timely availability of the necessary computer hardware to restore the data processing function. Management must obtain assurances from hardware vendors that filling the organization's needs will be given priority in the event of a disaster. An unanticipated hardware supply problem at this critical juncture could be a fatal blow.

The second problem with this approach is the potential for competition among users for the shell resources. For example, a widespread natural disaster, such as a flood or earthquake, may destroy the data processing capabilities of several shell members located in the same geographic area. Those affected by the disaster would be faced with a second major problem: how to allocate the limited facilities of the shell among them. The situation is analogous to a sinking ship that has an inadequate number of lifeboats. What equitable criteria should be used for assigning lifeboat seats?

The period of confusion following a disaster is not an ideal time to negotiate such property rights. Therefore, before entering into an arrangement to share the cost of shell facilities, management, accountants, and auditors should consider the potential problems of overcrowding and geographic clustering of members. Quotas—limiting the number of members by size of firm and geographic location—should provide effective control.

THE RECOVERY OPERATIONS CENTER.   A variation on the empty shell approach is the completely equipped **recovery operations center (ROC)** or "hot site." Because of the heavy investment involved, ROCs are typically shared among many companies. These firms either buy shares in or become subscribers to the ROC, paying a monthly fee for rights to its use.

ROCs may be tailor-equipped to serve the needs of their members, or they may be designed to accommodate a wide range of computer systems. The advantage of the ROC option over the empty shell is a vastly reduced initial recovery period. ROC facilities are ready for use. In the event of a major disruption, a subscriber can occupy the premises and, within a few hours, resume processing critical applications.

INTERNALLY PROVIDED BACKUP.   Larger organizations with multiple data processing centers may prefer self-reliance provided by creating internal excess capacity. This permits firms to develop standardized hardware and software configurations, which ensure functional compatibility among their data processing centers and minimize cutover problems in the event of a disaster.

IDENTIFYING CRITICAL APPLICATIONS

Another essential element of a DRP is to identify the firm's critical applications and data files. Recovery efforts must concentrate on restoring those applications that are critical to the short-run survival of the organization. Obviously, over the long term, all applications must be restored to pre-disaster business activity levels. However, the DRP should not attempt to restore the organization's data processing facility to 100 percent capacity. Rather, the plan should focus on short-run survival. In any disaster scenario, it is the firm's short-run survivability that is at risk.

For most organizations, short-term survival requires the restoration of those functions that generate cash flows sufficient to satisfy short-term obligations. For example, assume that the following items affect the cash flow position of a particular firm:

- Customer sales and service
- Fulfillment of legal obligations
- Accounts receivable maintenance and collection
- Production and distribution decisions
- Purchasing functions
- Communications between branches or agencies
- Public relations

The computer applications that support these items directly are critical. Hence, these applications should be so identified and prioritized in the restoration plan.

Application priorities may change over time, and these decisions must be reassessed regularly. Systems are constantly revised and expanded to reflect changes in user requirements. Similarly, the DRP must be updated to reflect new developments and identify critical applications. Up-to-date priorities are important, because they affect other aspects of the strategic plan. For example, changes in application priorities may cause changes in the nature and extent of second-site backup requirements and specific backup procedures.

The task of identifying critical items and prioritizing applications requires the active participation of user departments, accountants, and auditors. Too often, this task is incorrectly viewed as a technical "computer" issue and delegated to systems professionals. Although the technical assistance of a systems professional will be required, this is a business decision and should be made by those best equipped to understand the problem.

PERFORMING BACKUP AND OFF-SITE STORAGE PROCEDURES

All data files, application documentation, and supplies needed to perform critical functions should be specified in the DRP. Backup and storage procedures to safeguard these critical resources should be routinely performed by data processing personnel.

BACKUP DATA FILES.   Databases should be copied daily to tape or disks and secured off-site. In the event of a disruption, reconstruction of the database is achieved by updating the most current backed-up version with subsequent transaction data. Likewise, master files and transaction files should be protected. Techniques for data backup were discussed earlier.

BACKUP DOCUMENTATION.   The system documentation for critical applications should be backed up and stored off-site in much the same manner as data files. The large volumes of material involved and constant application revisions complicate the task. The process can be made more efficient through the use of CASE documentation tools.

BACKUP SUPPLIES AND SOURCE DOCUMENTS.   The firm should provide backup inventories of supplies and source documents used in critical applications. Examples of critical supplies are check stocks, invoices, purchase orders, and any other special-purpose forms that cannot be obtained immediately. The DRP should specify the types and quantities needed of these special items. Because they are such an integral part of the daily operations, these items are often overlooked by disaster contingency planners. At this point, it is worth noting that a copy of the current DRP document should also be stored off-site at a secure location.

CREATING A DISASTER RECOVERY TEAM

Recovering from a disaster depends on timely corrective action. Failure to perform essential tasks (such as obtaining backup files for critical applications) prolongs the recovery period and diminishes the prospects for a successful recovery. To avoid serious omissions or duplication of effort during implementation of the contingency plan, task responsibility must be clearly defined and communicated to the personnel involved.

Figure 2–6 presents an organizational chart depicting the composition of a disaster recovery team. The team members should be experts in their areas and have assigned tasks. Following a disaster, team members will delegate subtasks to their subordinates. It should be noted that traditional control concerns do not apply in this setting. The environment created by the disaster may make it necessary to violate control techniques, such as segregation of duties, access controls, and supervision.

TESTING THE DRP

The most neglected aspect of contingency planning is testing the plans. Nevertheless, DRP tests are important and should be performed periodically. Tests measure the preparedness of personnel and identify omissions or bottlenecks in the plan.

A test is most useful when the simulation of a disruption is a surprise. When the mock disaster is announced, the status of all processing affected by it should be documented. This provides a benchmark for subsequent performance assessments. The plan should be carried through as far as is economically feasible. Ideally, that would include the use of backup facilities and supplies.

The progress of the plan should be noted at key points throughout the test period. At the conclusion of the test, the results can then be analyzed and a DRP performance report prepared. The degree of performance achieved provides input for decisions to modify the DRP or schedule additional tests. The organization's management should seek measures of performance in each of the following areas: (1) the effectiveness of DRP team personnel and their knowledge levels, (2) the degree of conversion success (that is, the number of lost records), (3) an estimate of financial loss due to lost records or facilities, and (4) the effectiveness of program, data, and documentation backup and recovery procedures.

AUDIT OBJECTIVE

* To verify that the organization's disaster recovery plan (DRP) is adequate to meet the needs of the organization and that implementation is feasible and practical.

FIGURE 2-6

Disaster
Recovery
Team

Objective: Prepare backup site for operation and acquire hardware from vendors.

Objective: Provide current versions of all critical applications, data files, and documentation.

Objective: Reestablish the data conversion and data control functions necessary to process critical applications.

AUDIT PROCEDURES

- Verify that management's DRP is a realistic solution for dealing with a catastrophe that could deprive the organization of its computer resources. The following tests focus on areas of greatest concern.

SECOND-SITE BACKUP.   The auditor should evaluate the adequacy of the backup site arrangement. System incompatibility and human nature can both greatly reduce the effectiveness of the mutual aid pact. Auditors should be skeptical of such arrangements for two reasons. First, the sophistication of the computer system can make it difficult to find a potential partner with an identical or even a compatible configuration. Second, most firms do not have the necessary excess capacity to support a disaster-stricken partner while also processing their own work. When it comes to the "crunch," the management of the firm untouched by disaster may have little appetite for the sacrifices that must be made to honor the agreement.

More viable but expensive alternatives to the mutual aid pact are the empty shell and the recovery operation center. These too must be examined carefully. The auditor should be concerned about the number of members in these arrangements and their geographic dispersion. A widespread disaster may create a demand that cannot be satisfied by the backup facility.

CRITICAL APPLICATION LIST.   The auditor should review the list of critical applications to ensure that it is complete. Missing applications can result in failure to recover. However, the same is true for restoring unnecessary applications. To include applications on the critical list that are not needed to achieve short-term survival can misdirect resources and distract attention from the primary objective during the recovery period.

BACKUP CRITICAL APPLICATIONS.   The auditor should verify that copies of critical programs are stored off-site. In the event of a disaster or system failure, the production applications can then be reconstructed from the backup versions.

BACKUP CRITICAL DATA FILES.   The auditor should verify that critical data files are backed up in accordance with the DRP. We discussed data backup procedures in our examination of data resource controls.

BACKUP SUPPLIES, SOURCE DOCUMENTS, AND DOCUMENTATION.   The system documentation, supplies, and source documents needed to restore and run critical applications should be backed up and stored off-site. The auditor should verify that the types and quantities of items specified in the DRP exist in a secure location. Examples of critical supplies are check stock, invoices, purchase orders, and any other special-purpose forms that cannot be obtained immediately.

THE DISASTER RECOVERY TEAM.   The DRP should clearly list the names, addresses, and emergency telephone numbers of the disaster recovery team members. The auditor should verify that members of the team are current employees and are aware of their assigned responsibilities. On one occasion, while reviewing a firm's DRP, the author discovered that a team leader listed in the plan had been deceased for nine months.

OPERATING SYSTEMS

The **operating system** is the computer's control program. It allows users and their applications to share and access common computer resources, such as processors, main memory, databases, and printers. The modern auditor needs to recognize the operating system's role in the overall control picture to properly assess the risks that threaten the accounting system.

If operating system integrity is compromised, controls within individual accounting applications may also be circumvented or neutralized. Because the operating system is common to all users, the larger the computer facility, the greater the scale of potential damage. Thus, with more and more computer resources being shared by an ever-expanding user community, operating system security becomes an important audit issue.

The operating system performs three main tasks. First, it translates high-level languages, such as COBOL, FORTRAN, BASIC, and SQL, into the machine-level language that the computer can execute. The language translator modules of the operating system are called **compilers** and **interpreters**. The control implications of language translators are examined later in the chapter.

Second, the operating system allocates computer resources to users, workgroups, and applications. This includes assigning memory work space (partitions) to applications and authorizing access to terminals, telecommunications links, databases, and printers.

Third, the operating system manages the tasks of job scheduling and multiprogramming. At any point in time, numerous user applications (jobs) are seeking access to the computer resources under the control of the operating system. Jobs are submitted to the system in three ways: (1) directly by the system operator, (2) from various batch-job queues, and (3) through telecommunications links from remote workstations. To achieve efficient and effective use of finite computer resources, the operating system must schedule job processing according to established priorities and balance the use of resources among the competing applications.

To perform these tasks consistently and reliably, the operating system must achieve five fundamental control objectives.[1]

1. The operating system must protect itself from users. User applications must not be able to gain control of, or damage in any way, the operating system, thus causing it to cease running or destroy data.
2. The operating system must protect users from each other. One user must not be able to access, destroy, or corrupt the data or programs of another user.
3. The operating system must protect users from themselves. A user's application may consist of several modules stored in separate memory locations, each with its own data. One module must not be allowed to destroy or corrupt another module.
4. The operating system must be protected from itself. The operating system is also made up of individual modules. No module should be allowed to destroy or corrupt another module.
5. The operating system must be protected from its environment. In the event of a power failure or other disaster, the operating system should be able to achieve a controlled termination of activities from which it can later recover.

OPERATING SYSTEM SECURITY

Operating system security involves policy, procedures, and controls that determine who can access the operating system, which resources (files, programs, printers) they can access, and what actions they can take. The following security components are found in secure operating systems: logon procedure, access tokens, access control list, and discretionary access control.

LOGON PROCEDURE

A formal **logon procedure** is the operating system's first line of defense against unauthorized access. When the user initiates the process, he or she is presented with a dialog box requesting the user's ID and password. The system compares the ID and password to a database of valid users. If the system finds a match, then the logon

---

1. F. M. Stepczyk, "Requirements for Secure Operating Systems," *Data Security and Data Processing*, vol. 5; Study Results: TRW Systems, Inc., (New York: IBM Corporation, 1974), pp. 25–73.

attempt is authenticated. If, however, the password or ID is entered incorrectly, the logon attempt fails and a message is returned to the user. The message should not reveal whether the password or the ID caused the failure. The system should allow the user to reenter the logon information. After a specified number of attempts (usually no more than five), the system should lock out the user from the system.

ACCESS TOKEN

If the logon attempt is successful, the operating system creates an **access token** that contains key information about the user, including user ID, password, user group, and privileges granted to the user. The information in the access token is used to approve all actions attempted by the user during the session.

ACCESS CONTROL LIST

Access to system resources such as directories, files, programs, and printers is controlled by an **access control list** assigned to each resource. These lists contain information that define the access privileges for all valid users of the resource. When a user attempts to access a resource, the system compares his or her ID and privileges contained in the access token with those contained in the access control list. If there is a match, the user is granted access.

DISCRETIONARY ACCESS CONTROL

The central system administrator usually determines who is granted access to specific resources and maintains the access control list. In distributed systems, however, resources may be controlled (owned) by end users. Resource owners in this setting may be granted **discretionary access control**, which allows them to grant access privileges to other users. For example, the controller, who is the owner of the general ledger, grants read-only privileges to a manager in the budgeting department. The accounts payable manager, however, is grated both read and write permission to the ledger. Any attempt by the budgeting manager to add, delete, or change the general ledger will be denied. The use of discretionary access control needs to be closely supervised to prevent security breaches due to its liberal use.

THREATS TO OPERATING SYSTEM INTEGRITY

Operating system control objectives are sometimes not achieved because of flaws in the operating system that are exploited either accidentally or intentionally. Accidental threats include hardware failures that cause the operating system to crash. Operating system failures are also caused by errors in user application programs that the operating system cannot interpret. Accidental system failures may cause whole segments of memory to be "dumped" to disks and printers, resulting in the unintentional disclosure of confidential information.

Intentional threats to the operating system are most commonly attempts to illegally access data or violate user privacy for financial gain. However, a growing form of threat is from destructive programs from which there is no apparent gain. These exposures come from three sources:

1. Privileged personnel who abuse their authority. Systems administrators and systems programmers require unlimited access to the operating system to perform

maintenance and to recover from system failures. Such individuals may use this authority to access users' programs and data files.

2. Individuals, both internal and external to the organization, who browse the operating system to identify and exploit security flaws.

3. An individual who intentionally (or accidentally) inserts a computer virus or other form of destructive program into the operating system.

OPERATING SYSTEM CONTROLS AND AUDIT PROCEDURES

This section of the text describes a variety of operating system controls and the audit procedures associated with them.

CONTROLLING ACCESS PRIVILEGES

User access privileges are assigned to individuals and to entire workgroups authorized to use the system. Privileges determine which directories, files, applications, and other resources an individual or group may access. They also determine the types of actions that can be taken. Recall that the system administrator or the owner of the resource may assign privileges. Management should be concerned that individuals are not granted privileges that are incompatible with their assigned duties. Consider, for example, a cash receipts clerk who is granted the right to access and make changes to the accounts receivable file.

Overall system security is influenced by the way access privileges are assigned. Privileges should, therefore, be carefully administered and closely monitored for compliance with organizational policy and principles of internal control.

AUDIT OBJECTIVES

- To verify that access privileges are granted in a manner that is consistent with the need to separate incompatible functions and is in accordance with organizational policy.

AUDIT PROCEDURES

- Review the organization's policies for separating incompatible functions and ensure that they promote reasonable security.
- Review the privileges of a selection of user groups and individuals to determine if their access rights are appropriate for their job descriptions and positions. The auditor should verify that individuals are granted access to data and programs based on their need to know.
- Review personnel records to determine whether privileged employees undergo an adequately intensive security clearance check in compliance with company policy.
- Review employee records to determine whether users have formally acknowledged their responsibility to maintain the confidentiality of company data.
- Review the users' permitted logon times. Permission should be commensurate with the tasks being performed.

PASSWORD CONTROL

A **password** is a secret code entered by the user to gain access to systems, applications, data files, or a network server. If the user cannot provide the correct password, the operating system will deny access. Although passwords can provide a degree of security, when imposed on nonsecurity-minded users, password procedures can result in end user behavior that actually circumvents security. The most common forms of contra-security behavior include:

- Forgetting passwords and being locked out of the system.
- Failing to change passwords on a frequent basis.
- The post-it syndrome, whereby passwords are written down and displayed for others to see.
- Simplistic passwords that are easily anticipated by a computer criminal.

REUSABLE PASSWORDS.   The most common method of password control is the **reusable password**. The user defines the password to the system once and then reuses it to gain future access. Most operating systems set only basic standards for password acceptability. The quality of the security provided by a reusable password depends on the quality of the password itself. If the password pertains to something personal about the user, such as a child's name, pet's name, birthdate, or hair color, it can be deduced by a computer criminal. Even if the password is derived from nonpersonal data, such as a string of keystrokes (such as A–S–D–F) or the same letter used multiple times, the computer criminal can use a frequency table to run through the most common passwords very quickly. Reusable passwords that contain random letters and digits are more difficult to crack, but are also more difficult for the user to remember.

To improve access control, management should discourage the use of "weak" passwords. Inexpensive software is available that automatically scans password files and notifies the security administrator when weak passwords are detected, thus assuring that only "smart" passwords are used on the network. An alternative to the standard reusable password is the *one-time* password.

ONE-TIME PASSWORDS.   The **one-time password** was designed to overcome the problems just discussed. Under this approach, the user's network password constantly changes. To access the network, the user must provide both a secret reusable personal identification number (PIN) and the current one-time only password for that point in time. The problem, of course, is how to advise the valid user of the current password?

One technology employs a credit-card-sized device (smart card) that contains a microprocessor programmed with an algorithm that generates, and electronically displays, a new and unique password every 60 seconds. The card works in conjunction with special authentication software located on the server. Each user's card is synchronized to the authentication software, so that at any point in time both the smart card and the network software are generating the same password for the same user.

To access the network, the user enters the PIN followed by the current password displayed on the card. The password can be used one time only. If, for example, a computer hacker intercepts the password and PIN during transmission and attempts to use them within the one-minute time frame, access will be denied. Also, if the smart card should fall into the hands of a computer criminal, access cannot be achieved without the PIN.

AUDIT OBJECTIVES

- To ensure that the organization has an adequate and effective password policy for controlling access to the operating system.

AUDIT PROCEDURES

- Verify that all users are required to have passwords.

- Verify that new users are instructed in the use of passwords and the importance of password control.
- Determine that procedures are in place to identify weak passwords. This may involve the use of software for scanning password files on a regular basis.
- Assess the adequacy of password standards such as length and expiration interval.
- Review the account lockout policy and procedures. Most operating systems allow the system administrator to define the action to be taken after a certain number of failed logon attempts. The auditor should determine how many failed logon attempts are allowed before the account is locked. The duration of the lockout also needs to be determined. This could range from a few minutes to a permanent lockout that requires formal reactivation of the account.

CONTROLLING AGAINST VIRUSES AND OTHER DESTRUCTIVE PROGRAMS

Destructive programs such as viruses are responsible for millions of dollars of corporate losses annually. The losses are measured in terms of data corruption and destruction, degraded computer performance, hardware destruction, violations of privacy, and the personnel time devoted to repairing the damage. The discussion that follows outlines some of the more common types of destructive programs.

VIRUS.   A **virus** is a program (usually destructive) that attaches itself to a legitimate program to penetrate the operating system. The virus destroys application programs, data files, and operating systems in a number of ways. One common technique is for the virus to simply replicate itself over and over within the main memory, thus destroying whatever data or programs are resident. One of the most insidious aspects of a virus is its ability to spread throughout the system and to other systems before perpetrating its destructive acts. Typically, a virus will have a built-in counter that will inhibit its destructive role until the virus has copied itself a specified number of times to other programs and systems. The virus thus grows geometrically, which makes tracing its origin extremely difficult.

Microcomputers are a major source of virus penetration. When connected in a network or a mainframe, an infected microcomputer can upload the virus to the host computer. Once in the host, the virus can spread throughout the operating system and to other users.

Due to the heavy dependency on connectivity, the proliferation of microcomputers, and the need for extensive application programming, it may be impossible to eliminate the threat of viruses from the modern business environment. Sometimes, viruses are created internally by disgruntled employees in positions of power; othertimes, they are created outside the organization and are brought inside by unsuspecting users with legitimate access privileges to the system. Understanding how viruses work and how they are passed between systems is critical to their effective control.

Virus programs usually attach themselves to the following types of files:

1. An .EXE or .COM program file.
2. An .OVL (overlay) program file.
3. The boot sector of a disk.
4. A device driver program.

When a virus-infected program is executed, the virus searches the system for uninfected programs and copies itself into these programs. The virus may thus spread to the applications of other users or to the operating system itself.

Personal computers are the most common source of virus infestation. Their proliferation in business and society, combined with their relatively unsophisticated operating systems, has created a fertile environment in which viruses can grow and spread. A major contributing factor to the spread of viruses is the sharing of programs among users. The downloading of public-domain programs from network bulletin boards and the exchange of illegal "bootleg" software are the primary methods of virus transfer. Because of the lack of control features in microcomputer operating systems, microcomputers connected to mainframes pose a serious threat to the mainframe environment as well. For example, an application programmer may develop and test programs on a microcomputer and then upload the finished system to the mainframe. If a virus is in the microcomputer on which the program is developed, it can spread to the mainframe via the new application. When this program is executed, the virus can then spread to other applications on the mainframe.

WORM.   The term **worm** is used interchangeably with virus. A worm is a software program that "burrows" into the computer's memory and replicates itself into areas of idle memory. The worm systematically occupies idle memory until the memory is exhausted and the system fails. Worms differ from viruses in that the replicated worm modules remain in contact with the original worm that controls their growth. The replicated virus modules, on the other hand, grow independently of the initial virus.

LOGIC BOMB.   A **logic bomb** is a destructive program, such as a virus, that is triggered by some predetermined event. Quite often a date (such as Friday the 13th, April Fool's Day, or a birthday) will be the logic bomb's trigger. The famous Michelangelo virus (triggered by his birth date) is an example of a logic bomb. Logic bombs have also been triggered by events of less public prominence, such as the dismissal of an employee. For example, during the customary two-week severance period, a terminated programmer may embed a logic bomb in the system that will activate six months after his or her departure from the firm.

BACK DOOR.   A **back door** (also called a *trap door*) is a software program that allows unauthorized access to a system without going through the normal (front door) logon procedure. Programmers who want to provide themselves with unrestricted access to the programs that they are developing for users create a logon procedure that will accept both the user's private password and their own secret password, thus creating a back door to the system. The purpose of the back door may be to provide easy access to perform program maintenance, or it may be to perpetrate a fraud or insert a virus into the system.

TROJAN HORSE.   A **Trojan horse** is a program whose purpose is to capture IDs and passwords from unsuspecting users. The program is designed to mimic the normal logon procedures of the operating system. When the user enters his or her ID and password, the Trojan horse stores a copy of them in a secret file. At some later date, the author of the Trojan horse uses these IDs and passwords to access the system and masquerade as an authorized user.

Threats from destructive programs can be substantially reduced through a combination of technology controls and administrative procedures. The following examples are relevant to most operating systems.

- Purchase software only from reputable vendors and accept only those products that are in their original, factory-sealed packages.
- Issue an entity-wide policy pertaining to the use of unauthorized software or illegal (bootleg) copies of copyrighted software.

- Examine all upgrades to vendor software for viruses before they are implemented.
- Inspect all public-domain software for virus infection before using.
- Establish entity-wide procedures for making changes to production programs. (This topic is examined in-depth in Chapter 4.)
- Establish an educational program to raise user awareness regarding threats from viruses and malicious programs.
- Install all new applications on a standalone computer and thoroughly test them with antiviral software prior to implementing them on the mainframe or LAN server.
- Routinely make backup copies of key files stored on mainframes, servers, and workstations.
- Wherever possible, limit users to read and execute rights only. This allows users to extract data and run authorized applications, but denies them the ability to write directly to mainframe and server directories.
- Require protocols that explicitly invoke the operating system's logon procedures in order to bypass Trojan horses. A typical scenario is one in which a user sits down to a terminal that is already displaying the logon screen and proceeds to enter his or her ID and password. This, however, may be a Trojan horse rather than the legitimate procedure. Some operating systems allow the user to directly invoke the operating system logon procedure by entering a key sequence such as CTRL + ALT + DEL. The user then knows that the logon procedure on the screen is legitimate.
- Use antiviral software (also called *vaccines*) to examine application and operating system programs for the presence of a virus and remove them from the affected program. Antiviral programs are used to safeguard mainframes, network servers, and personal computers. Most antiviral programs run in the background on the host computer and automatically test all files that are uploaded to the host. However, the software works only on known viruses. If a virus has been modified slightly (mutated), there is no guarantee that the vaccine will work. It is therefore important to maintain the current version of the vaccine.

AUDIT OBJECTIVE

- To verify that effective management policies and procedures are in place to prevent the introduction and spread of destructive programs.

AUDIT PROCEDURES

- Through interviews with operations personnel, determine that they have been educated about computer viruses and are aware of the risky computing practices that can introduce and spread viruses and other malicious programs.
- Review operations procedures to determine if floppy disks are routinely used to transfer data between workgroups.
- Verify that system administrators routinely scan workstations and file servers for viruses.
- Verify that new software is tested on standalone workstations prior to being implemented on the host or network server.

CONTROLLING AUDIT TRAILS

Audit trails are logs that can be designed to record activity at the system, application, and user level. When properly implemented, audit trails provide an important detective control to help accomplish security policy objectives. Many operating systems allow organization management to select the level of auditing to be provided by the system. This determines which events will be recorded in the log. An effective audit policy will capture all significant events without cluttering the log with trivial activity. Each organization needs to decide where the threshold between information and irrelevant facts lies. Audit trails typically consist of two types of audit logs: (1) detailed logs of individual keystrokes and (2) event-oriented logs.

KEYSTROKE MONITORING. **Keystroke monitoring** involves recording both the user's keystrokes and the system's responses. This form of log may be used after the fact to reconstruct the details of an event or as a real-time control to monitor or prevent unauthorized intrusion. Keystroke monitoring is the computer equivalent of a telephone wiretap. Some situations may justify this level of surveillance. In some circumstances, however, keystroke monitoring may be regarded as a violation of privacy. Before implementing this type of control, management and auditors should consider the possible legal, ethical, and behavioral implications.

EVENT MONITORING. **Event monitoring** summarizes key activities related to users, applications, and system resources. Event logs typically record the IDs of all users accessing the system; the time and duration of a user's session; programs that were executed during a session; and the files, databases, printers, and other resources accessed.

AUDIT TRAIL OBJECTIVES

Audit trails can be used to support security objectives in three ways: (1) detecting unauthorized access to the system, (2) facilitating the reconstruction of events, and (3) promoting personal accountability.

DETECTING UNAUTHORIZED ACCESS.   Detecting unauthorized access can occur in real time or after the fact. The primary objective of real-time detection is to protect the system from outsiders who are attempting to breach system controls. A real-time audit trail can also be used to report on changes in system performance that may indicate infestation by a virus or worm. Depending upon how much activity is being logged and reviewed, real-time detection can impose a significant overhead on the operating system, which can degrade operational performance. After-the-fact detection logs can be stored electronically and reviewed periodically or as needed. When properly designed, they can be used to determine if unauthorized access was accomplished, or attempted and failed.

RECONSTRUCTING EVENTS.   Audit analysis can be used to reconstruct the steps that led to events such as system failures, security violations by individuals, or application processing errors. Knowledge of the conditions that existed at the time of a system failure can be used to assign responsibility and to avoid similar situations in the future. Audit trail analysis also plays an important role in accounting control. For example, by maintaining a record of all changes to account balances, the audit trail can be used to reconstruct accounting data files that were corrupted by a system failure.

PERSONAL ACCOUNTABILITY.   Audit trails can be used to monitor user activity at the lowest level of detail. This capability is a preventive control that can be used to influence behavior. Individuals are less likely to violate an organization's security policy if they know that their actions are recorded in an audit log.

An audit log can also serve as a detective control to assign personal accountability for actions taken. Serious errors and the abuse of authority are of particular concern. It may be easier to prevent unauthorized intruders from accessing a system than to ensure that authorized users act only in accordance with their assigned authority. For example, an accounts receivable clerk is authorized to access customer records. The audit log may disclose that the clerk has been printing an inordinate number of records, which could indicate that the clerk is selling customer information.

IMPLEMENTING AN AUDIT TRAIL

The information contained in audit logs is useful to accountants in measuring the potential damage and financial loss associated with application errors, abuse of authority, or unauthorized access by outside intruders. Logs also provide valuable evidence for assessing both the adequacy of controls in place and the need for additional controls. Audit logs, however, can generate data in overwhelming detail. Important information can easily get lost among the superfluous details of daily operation. Thus, poorly designed logs can actually be dysfunctional. Protecting exposures with the potential for material financial loss should drive management's decision as to which users, applications, or operations to monitor, and how much detail to log. As with all controls, the benefits of audit logs must be balanced against the costs of implementating them.

AUDIT OBJECTIVES

- To ensure that the auditing of users and events is adequate for preventing and detecting abuses, reconstructing key events that preceded systems failures, and planning resource allocation.

AUDIT PROCEDURES

Most operating systems provide some form of audit manager function to specify the events that are to be audited. The auditor should verify that the event audit trail has been activated according to organizational policy.

- Many operating systems provide an audit log viewer that allows the auditor to scan the log for unusual activity. These can be reviewed on screen or by archiving the file for subsequent review. The auditor can use general-purpose data extraction tools such as ACL for accessing archived log files to search for defined conditions such as:
  - Unauthorized or terminated user
  - Periods of inactivity
  - Activity by user, workgroup, or department
  - Logon and logoff times
  - Failed logon attempts
  - Access to specific files or applications
- The organization's security group has the responsibility to monitor and report on security violations. The auditor should select a sample of security violation cases and evaluate their disposition to assess the effectiveness of the security group.

FAULT TOLERANCE CONTROLS

Fault tolerance is the ability of the system to continue operation when part of the system fails due to hardware failure, application program error, or operator error. Various levels of fault tolerance can be achieved by implementing redundant system components. These include:

- **Redundant arrays of inexpensive disks (RAID).** There are several types of RAID configurations. Essentially, each method involves the use of parallel disks that contain redundant elements of data and applications. If one disk fails, the lost data are automatically reconstructed from the redundant components stored on the other disks.
- **Uninterruptible power supplies.** In the event of a power supply failure, short-term backup power is provided to allow the system to shut down in a controlled manner. This will prevent data loss and corruption that would otherwise result from an uncontrolled system crash.
- **Multiprocessing.** The simultaneous use of two or more processors improves throughput under normal operation. During a processor failure, the redundant processors balance the workload and provide complete backup.

Implementing fault tolerance control ensures that there is no single point of potential system failure. Total failure can occur only in the event of the failure of multiple components.

AUDIT OBJECTIVES

- To ensure that the organization is employing an appropriate level of fault tolerance.

AUDIT PROCEDURES

- Most systems that employ RAID provide a graphical mapping of their redundant disk storage. From this mapping, the auditor should determine if the level of RAID in place is adequate for the organization, given the level of business risk associated with disk failure.
- If the organization is not employing RAID, the potential for a single point of system failure exists. The auditor should review with the system administrator alternative procedures for recovering from a disk failure.
- Determine that copies of boot disks have been made for each server on the network in the event of a boot sector failure. Since boot disks can be used to bypass the normal boot process, they should be secured and access to them restricted to the system administrator.

PERSONAL COMPUTER SYSTEMS

The discussion to this point has dealt with multiuser operating systems. The remainder of the chapter examines risks, controls, and audit issues related to the personal computing environment. The PC environment possesses significant features that characterize and distinguish it from the mainframe and client-server environments. The most important of these features are listed below. In general, PC systems:

- Are relatively simple to operate and program and do not require extensive professional training to use.
- Frequently are controlled and operated by the end users rather than by systems administrators.

- Usually employ interactive data processing rather than batch processing.
- Typically run commercial software applications designed to minimize effort. Usually, data are entered by end users and may be uploaded to a mainframe or network server for further processing.
- Often are used to access data on mainframe and client-server systems that are downloaded for local processing.
- Allow users to develop their own software (such as spreadsheets and databases).

PC OPERATING SYSTEMS

The operating system is booted and resides in the computer's primary memory as long as it is turned on. The operating system has several functions. It controls the CPU, accesses RAM, executes programs, receives input from the keyboard or other input device, retrieves and saves data to and from secondary storage devices, displays data on the monitor, controls the printer, and performs other functions that control the hardware system.

The operating system contains two types of instructions. *System-resident commands* are active in primary memory at all times to coordinate input/output requests and execute programs. *Disk-resident commands* reside on a secondary storage device until a request is made to execute these special-purpose utility programs.

At one time, the most popular operating system for the IBM-compatible computer was *DOS (Disk Operating System)*. Microsoft Corporation sells this product under the name MS-DOS (Microsoft Disk Operating System) and licenses another version, called PC-DOS, to IBM for use in its personal computers. An enormous number of microcomputers ran versions of DOS; as a result, there is an abundance of application software for DOS computers.

DOS was written for the microcomputer technology of the early 1980s. Even though there have been numerous improvements to the software since its introduction, limitations still exist. For example, application programs running on DOS computers have direct access to only 640,000 bytes of primary memory.

Newer operating systems, such as Microsoft Windows 95, have broken the 640,000-byte barrier, providing direct access to millions of bytes of memory. These operating systems take advantage of today's more powerful microprocessor chips, such as the Intel Pentium, which address more memory and run faster than the older microprocessors. Some operating systems employ *multitasking*, which allows more than one task to be executed at a time in a single-user computer. Operating systems that address more memory can run several tasks simultaneously.

The computer's operating system defines the family of software that the computer can use. *Application software* is written for a particular operating system. For example, the user of an IBM-compatible microcomputer with the DOS operating system must select programs from the available software written for that operating system. The user of an IBM-compatible microcomputer with a different operating system, such as OS/2, must select from a different set of software.

PC SYSTEMS CONTROL AND AUDIT

In both mainframe and microcomputer environments, the computer's operating system is an important element of the internal control structure. Mainframes, being multi-user systems, are designed to maintain a separation between end users and permit only authorized users to access data and programs. Unauthorized attempts to access data or programs can be thwarted by the security system. In contrast, PCs provide only minimal security over data files and programs. This control weakness is inherent in the philosophy behind the design of PC operating systems. Intended primarily as single-user systems, they are designed to make computer use easy and to facilitate access, not restrict it. This philosophy, while necessary to promote end user computing, is sometimes at odds with internal control objectives. The data stored on microcomputers that are shared by multiple users are exposed to unauthorized access, manipulation, and destruction. Once a computer criminal gains access to the user's microcomputer, there may be little or nothing in the way of control to prevent him or her from stealing or manipulating the data stored on the internal hard drive.

The advanced technology and power of modern PC systems stand in sharp contrast to the relatively unsophisticated operational environment in which they exist. Controlling this environment rests heavily on physical controls. Some of the more significant risks and possible control techniques are outlined on the following pages.

WEAK ACCESS CONTROL

Security software that provides logon procedures is available for PCs. Most of these programs, however, become active *only* when the computer is booted from the hard drive. A computer criminal attempting to circumvent the logon procedure may do so by forcing the computer to boot from the A: drive, whereby an uncontrolled operating system can be loaded into the computer's memory. Having bypassed the computer's stored operating system and security package, the criminal has unrestricted access to data and programs on the hard disk.

Disk locks are devices that prevent unauthorized individuals from accessing the floppy disk drive of a computer. One form of disk lock is a memory-resident program that prevents the computer from being booted from the A: drive. The lock will also prevent the A: drive from being used to run programs, upload data and programs to the hard disk, or download from the hard disk. This form of disk lock is password-controlled so it can be disabled as needed by an authorized user.

There are risks associated with the use of disk locks. In the event of a hard disk failure that prevents the computer from being booted from the hard disk, users can usually boot the computer from the A: drive and recover the system or, at least, retrieve vital data. However, when a memory-resident disk lock is in place, the user may be denied access to the A: drive. Being unable to boot from either drive thus permanently prevents access to data and programs. An alternative solution is to use a physical disk lock rather than the memory-resident type. This device fits into the A: drive like a floppy disk to prevent its use and is secured with a physical lock and key.

AUDIT OBJECTIVES

- To verify that controls are in place to protect data, programs, and computers from unauthorized access, manipulation, destruction, and theft.

AUDIT PROCEDURES

- The auditor should verify that microcomputers and their files are physically controlled. Desktop computers should be anchored to reduce the opportunity to remove them. Locks should be in place to disable input from the keyboard and the A: drive.

INADEQUATE SEGREGATION OF DUTIES

In PC environments, particularly those of small companies, an employee may have access to multiple applications that process incompatible transactions. For example, a single individual may be responsible for entering all transaction data, including sales orders, cash receipts, invoices, and disbursements. Typically, the general ledger and subsidiary accounts are updated automatically from these input sources. This degree of authority would be similar, in a manual system, to assigning accounts receivable, accounts payable, cash receipts, cash disbursement, and general ledger responsibility to the same person. The exposure is compounded when the operator is also responsible for the development (programming) of the applications that he or she runs. In small-company operations, there may be little that can be done to eliminate these inherent conflicts of duties. However, multilevel password control can reduce the risks.

MULTILEVEL PASSWORD CONTROL.   **Multilevel password control** is used to restrict employees who are sharing the same computers to specific directories, programs, and data files. This technique uses stored authorization tables to further limit an individual's access to read-only, data input, data modification, and data deletion capability. While not a substitute for traditional control techniques such as employee supervision and management reports that detail all transactions and their effects on account balances, multilevel password control can greatly enhance the small organization's control environment.

AUDIT OBJECTIVES

- To verify that adequate supervision and operating procedures exist to compensate for lack of segregation between the duties of users, programmers, and operators.

AUDIT PROCEDURES

- The auditor should verify from organizational charts, job descriptions, and observation that the programmers of applications performing financially significant functions do not also operate those systems. In smaller organizational units where functional segregation is impractical, the auditor should verify that there is adequate supervision over these tasks.
- The auditor should confirm that reports of processed transactions, listings of updated accounts, and control totals are prepared, distributed, and reconciled by appropriate management at regular and timely intervals.
- Where appropriate, the auditor should determine that multilevel password control is used to limit access to data and applications.

INADEQUATE BACKUP PROCEDURES

To preserve the integrity of mission-critical data and programs, organizations need formal backup procedures. Adequate backup of critical files is actually more difficult to achieve in simple environments than it is in sophisticated environments. In mainframe and network environments, backup is controlled automatically by the operating system, using specialized software and hardware. The responsibility of providing backup in the PC environment falls to the user. Often because of lack of computer experience and training, users fail to appreciate the importance of backup procedures until it is too late.

Computer failure, usually disk failure, is the primary cause of significant data loss in the PC environment. If the hard drive of the microcomputer fails, it may be impossible to recover the data stored on the disk. Formal procedures for making backup copies of critical data (and program) files can reduce this threat considerably. There are a number of options available for dealing with this problem.

FLOPPY DISK BACKUP.   Files can be backed up to floppy disks at routine periods during processing and stored away from the computer. In the event of a microcomputer failure, the data file can be reconstructed from the backup disks. This requires a conscious effort on the part of the user. Failure to back up data even one time can result in its loss.

DUAL INTERNAL HARD DRIVES.   Microcomputers can be configured with two physical internal hard disks. One disk can be used to store production data while the other stores the backup files. A batch program, run prior to or immediately after each data processing session, can copy the data file to the backup disk. Thus, backup is almost transparent to the user and involves a minimum of effort. This is a useful technique for the backup of large files that cannot be stored effectively on floppy disks. If one of the internal hard drives fails, the data files can be retrieved from the remaining hard drive.

EXTERNAL HARD DRIVES.   A popular backup option is the external hard drive with removable disk cartridge, which can store more than a gigabyte of data per cartridge. When a cartridge is filled, the user can remove it and insert a new one. Removable drives offer the advantages of unlimited storage capacity, portability, and physical security. This technology does not materially degrade computer performance. With an average data access time of 6 milliseconds, external hard drives compare favorably with internal hard drives, whose access time averages about 10 milliseconds.

External hard drives can be used as an effective and simple backup technique. Dual external drives can be used to store both production and backup files. By using two separate drives, backup can be performed automatically before, during, or after the data processing session. Hence, the user does not need to physically switch cartridges and consciously perform the backup procedures, and the chance for human error is reduced. Also, with both versions of the data file residing on external drives, access control is improved. Both the backup and the original can be removed and stored in separate locations away from the microcomputer.

TAPE BACKUP DEVICES.   The most common type of archive device for PCs is magnetic tape. These may be internal or external devices and provide efficient and inexpensive backup. In normal backup mode, a single tape can store about 1.6 gigabytes of data. In compressed mode, a tape can store up to 3.2 gigabytes.

AUDIT OBJECTIVES

- To verify that backup procedures are in place to prevent data and program loss due to hardware failures.

AUDIT PROCEDURES

- If removable hard drives are used, the auditor should verify that the drives are removed and stored in a secure location when not in use.
- By selecting a sample of backup files, the auditor can verify that backup procedures are being followed. By comparing data values and dates on the backup

disks to production files, the auditor can assess the frequency and adequacy of backup procedures.
- The auditor should verify that application source code is physically secured (such as in a locked safe) and that only the compiled version is stored on the micro-computer.

INADEQUATE SYSTEMS DEVELOPMENT AND MAINTENANCE PROCEDURES

In Chapter 4, we examine control issues surrounding the development and mainte-nance of computer applications. The microcomputer environment lacks both the operating system features and the segregation of duties necessary to provide the nec-essary control. Management must thus compensate for these inherent exposures with other, more conventional control techniques. The following examples help reduce the risk.

USE COMMERCIAL SOFTWARE.   To the extent possible, users should acquire com-mercial software from reputable vendors for their PC accounting applications. Many of the hundreds of packages on the market are general-purpose accounting systems. Oth-ers are special-purpose systems designed to meet the unique needs of specific indus-tries. Commercial software purchased from a reputable vendor will normally be thoroughly tested and is highly reliable.

SOFTWARE SELECTION PROCEDURES.   Even small firms should employ formal soft-ware selection procedures that include the following steps:

- Conduct a formal analysis of the problem and user needs.
- Solicit bids from several vendors.
- Evaluate the competing products in terms of their ability to meet the identified needs. (At this point, it is often wise to seek the help of a professional consultant.)
- Contact current users of prospective commercial packages to get their opinions about the product.
- Make a selection. (The firm should keep in mind the degree of support it will need and should be sure that the vendor is willing and able to provide that support.)

AUDIT OBJECTIVES

- To verify that systems selection and acquisition procedures produce applications that are high quality, free from errors and viruses, and protected from unautho-rized changes.

AUDIT PROCEDURES

REVIEW SYSTEMS SELECTION AND ACQUISITION CONTROLS.   The auditor should verify that commercial software packages employed on microcomputers were pur-chased from reputable vendors. The auditor should review the selection and acquisi-tion procedures to ensure that user needs were fully considered and that the purchased software satisfies those needs.

REVIEW VIRUS CONTROL TECHNIQUES.   Strict adherence to organizational policies and procedures that guard against virus infection is critical to effective virus control. The auditor should verify that such policies and procedures exist and that they are being followed. But policy alone will not deter a resolute perpetrator. The organization must therefore resort to additional technical controls in the form of antivirus software.

The auditor can obtain corroborating evidence of virus control adequacy by performing the following tests:

1. The auditor should verify that the organization follows a policy of purchasing software from reputable vendors only.
2. The auditor should review the organization's policy for using antiviral software. This policy may include the following points:
   - Antiviral software should be installed on all microcomputers and invoked as part of the startup procedure when the computers are turned on. This will ensure that all key sectors of the hard disk are examined before any data are transferred through the network.
   - All upgrades to vendor software should be checked for viruses before they are implemented.
   - All public-domain software should be examined for virus infection before it is used.
   - Current versions of antiviral software should be available to all users.
3. The auditor should verify that only authorized software is loaded on personal computers.

SUMMARY

This chapter explored operations control and audit issues related to the structure of the IT function, control of computer center operations, the computer operating system, and the personal computer environment. It opened by examining the potential risks and controls associated with the centralized and distributed approaches to IT organization. Audit objectives and suggested audit procedures were presented. Computer center risks and controls were then considered. The key elements of a disaster recovery plan and the advantages and disadvantages of various options were examined. The operating system and its role in the overall control structure were presented next. The operating system allows users and their applications to share and access common computer resources, such as processors, main memory, databases, and printers. Operating system integrity impacts all programs that run on the system. If operating system integrity is compromised, controls within individual accounting applications may be neutralized. The operating system discussion began with an overview of multiuser operating system features common to both networks and mainframes. Operating system objectives and the risks that threaten system security were examined. This was followed by a review of operating system controls and audit techniques. The chapter concluded with an analysis of the risks, controls, and audit issues pertinent to the personal computer environment.

KEY TERMS

access control list
access token
audit trails
back door

centralized data processing
compilers
computer operations
corporate IT function

database administration
data control
data conversion
data library
disaster recovery plan (DRP)
discretionary access control
disk locks
distributed data processing (DDP)
empty shell
event monitoring
fault tolerance
inadequate documentation
interpreters
keystroke monitoring
logic bomb
logon procedure

multilevel password control
multiprocessing
mutual aid pact
one-time password
operating system
operating system security
password
program fraud
recovery operations center (ROC)
redundant arrays of inexpensive disks (RAID)
reusable password
tape backup devices
Trojan horse
uninterruptible power supplies
virus
worm

REVIEW QUESTIONS

1. What is distributed data processing?
2. What are the advantages and disadvantages of distributed data processing?
3. What types of tasks become redundant in a distributed data processing system?
4. What are the five control objectives of an operating system?
5. What are the three main tasks performed by the operating system?
6. What are the four techniques that a virus could use to infect a system?
7. What is the purpose of an access control list?
8. What is a vaccine and what are its limitations?
9. What are the primary reasons for separating operational tasks?
10. What problems may occur as a result of combining applications programming and maintenance tasks in one position?
11. What is the role of a data librarian? Why is this role so important?
12. Why is poor systems documentation a prevalent problem?
13. Why is it important to separate the data library from operations?
14. What is the role of a corporate computer services department? How does this differ from other configurations?
15. What are the five control implications of distributed data processing?
16. List the control features that directly contribute to the security of the computer center environment.
17. What techniques are available in the microcomputer environment to reduce access exposure?
18. What is a mitigating control to inadequate segregation of duties in microcomputer environments?
19. What advantage do dual external hard drives offer over dual internal hard drives?

DISCUSSION QUESTIONS

1. What types of incompatible activities are prone to becoming consolidated in a distributed data processing system? How can this be prevented?
2. Why would an operational manager be willing to take on more work in the form of supervising an information system?

3. How can data be "centralized" in a "distributed" data processing system?

4. Should standards be centralized in a distributed data processing environment? Explain.

5. How can human behavior be considered one of the biggest potential threats to operating system integrity?

6. A bank in California has 13 branches spread throughout northern California, each with its own minicomputer where its data are stored. Another bank has 10 branches spread throughout California, with the data being stored on a mainframe in San Francisco. Which system do you think is more vulnerable to unauthorized access? Excessive losses from disaster?

7. Why would a systems programmer create a back door if he or she has access to the program in his or her day-to-day tasks?

8. Explain how a Trojan horse may help to penetrate a security system.

9. Many authorities believe that 90 percent of all computer fraud acts are not prosecuted by the employer. What do you think accounts for this lack of prosecution? Discuss the importance of the establishment of a formal policy for taking disciplinary (or legal) action against security violations.

10. End user computing has become extremely popular in distributed data processing organizations. The end users like it because they feel they can more readily design and implement their own applications. Does this type of environment always foster more efficient development of applications? Explain your answer.

11. Compare and contrast the following disaster recovery options: mutual aid pact, empty shell, recovery operations center, and internally provided backup. Rank them from most risky to least risky, as well as from most costly to least costly.

12. Who should determine and prioritize the critical applications? How is this done? How frequently is it done?

13. What types of output would be considered extremely sensitive in a university setting? Give three examples and explain why the information would be considered sensitive. Discuss who should and should not have access to each type of information.

MULTIPLE-CHOICE QUESTIONS

1. CMA 1289 5-6
   A system with several computers that are connected for communication and data transmission purposes but that permits each computer to process its own data is a
   a. distributed data processing network.
   b. centralized network.
   c. decentralized network.
   d. multidrop network.
   e. hybrid system.

2. CMA (Adapted) 687 5-15
   A major disadvantage of distributed data processing is
   a. the increased time between job request and job completion.
   b. the potential for hardware and software incompatibility among users.
   c. the disruption caused when the mainframe goes down.

   d. that users are not likely to be involved.
   e. that data processing professionals may not be properly involved.

3. Which of the following is NOT a control implication of distributed data processing?
   a. redundancy
   b. user satisfaction
   c. incompatibility
   d. lack of standards

4. Which of the following disaster recovery techniques may be least optimal in the case of a widespread natural disaster?
   a. empty shell
   b. mutual aid pact
   c. internally provided backup
   d. they are all equally beneficial

5. A user's application may consist of several modules stored in separate memory locations,

each with its own data. One module must not be allowed to destroy or corrupt another module. This is an objective of
a. operating system controls.
b. data resource controls.
c. computer center and security controls.
d. application controls.

6. A program that attaches to another legitimate program but does not replicate itself is called a
a. virus.
b. worm.
c. Trojan horse.
d. logic bomb.

7. The identification of users who have permission to access the accounts receivable file is found in the
a. operating system.
b. systems manual.
c. database schema.
d. database file definition.
e. access control list.

8. CMA 686 5-4
An integrated group of programs that supervises and supports the operations of a computer system as it executes users' application programs is called a(n)
a. operating system.
b. RAID.
c. utility program.
d. language processor.
e. object program.

9. Which of the following is NOT a feature of fault tolerance control?
a. uninterruptible power supplies
b. redundant arrays of inexpensive disks (RAID)
c. multiprocessing
d. multiprogramming

PROBLEMS

1. Internal Control
In reviewing the processes, procedures, and internal controls of one of your audit clients, Steeplechase Enterprises, you notice the following practices in place. Steeplechase has recently installed a new EDP system that affects the accounts receivable, billing, and shipping records. A specifically identified computer operator has been permanently assigned to each of the functions of accounts receivable, billing, and shipping. Each of these computer operators is assigned the responsibility of running the program for transaction processing, making program changes, and reconciling the computer log. In order to prevent any one operator from having exclusive access to the tapes and documentation, these three computer operators randomly rotate the custody and control tasks every two weeks over the magnetic tapes and the system documentation. Access controls to the computer room consist of magnetic cards and a digital code for each operator. Access to the computer room is not allowed to either the systems analyst or the computer operations supervisor.

The documentation for the EDP system consists of the following: record layouts, program listings, logs, and error listings.

Once goods are shipped from one of Steeplechase's three warehouses, warehouse personnel forward shipping notices to the accounting department. The billing clerk receives the shipping notice and accounts for the manual sequence of the shipping notices. Any missing notices are investigated. The billing clerk also manually enters the price of the item, and prepares daily totals (supported by adding machine tapes) of the units shipped and the amount of sales. The shipping notices and adding machine tapes are sent to the computer department for data entry.

The computer output generated consists of a two-copy invoice and remittance advice and a daily sales register. The invoices and remittance advice are forwarded to the billing clerk, who mails one copy of the invoice and remittance advice to the customer and files the other copy in an open invoice file, which serves as an accounts receivable document. The daily sales register contains the total of units shipped and sales amounts. The computer operator compares the computer-generated totals to the adding machine tapes.

Required:
Identify the control weaknesses present and make a specific recommendation for correcting each of them.

2. Internal Control
    Gustave, CPA, during its preliminary review of the financial statements of Comet, Inc., found a lack of proper segregation of duties between the programming and operating functions. Comet owns its own computing facilities. Gustave, CPA, diligently intensified the internal control study and assessment tasks relating to the computer facilities. Gustave concluded in its final report that sufficient compensating general controls provided reasonable assurance that the internal control objectives were being met.

Required:
What compensating controls are most likely in place?

3. Operating System Exposures and Controls
    Listed below are some scenarios. For each scenario, discuss the potential consequences and give a prevention technique.
    a. The systems operator opened up a bag of burned microwave popcorn directly under a smoke detector in the computing room where two mainframes, three high-speed printers, and approximately 40 tapes were housed. The extremely sensitive smoke detector triggered the sprinkler system. Three minutes passed before the sprinklers could be turned off.
    b. A system programmer intentionally placed an error into a program that caused the operating system to fail and dump certain confidential information to disks and printers.
    c. Jane, a secretary, was laid off. Her employer gave her three weeks to find another job. After two weeks, Jane realized that finding another job was going to be very tough, and she became bitter. Her son told her about a virus that had infected the computers at school. He had a disk infected with the virus. Jane took the disk to

work and copied the disk onto the network server, which is connected to the company's mainframe. One month later, the company realized that some data and application programs had been destroyed.
    d. Robert discovered a new sensitivity analysis public-domain program on the Internet. He downloaded the software to his microcomputer at home, then took the application to work and placed it onto his networked personal computer. The program had a virus on it that eventually spread to the company's mainframe.
    e. Murray, a trusted employee and a systems engineer, had access to both the computer resource authority table and user passwords. He was recently hired away by the firm's competitor for twice his old salary. After leaving, Murray continued to browse through his old employer's data, such as price lists, customer lists, bids on jobs, and so on. He passed this information on to his new employer.

4. Disaster Recovery Plans
    CMA 689 5-Y5
    The headquarters of Gleicken Corporation, a private company with $3.5 million in annual sales, is located in California. Gleicken provides for its 150 clients an on-line legal software service that includes data storage and administrative activities for law offices. The company has grown rapidly since its inception three years ago, and its data processing department has expanded to accommodate this growth. Because Gleicken's president and sales personnel spend a great deal of time out of the office soliciting new clients, the planning of the EDP facilities has been left to the data processing professionals.
    Gleicken recently moved its headquarters into a remodeled warehouse on the outskirts of the city. While remodeling the warehouse, the architects retained much of the original structure, including the wooden-shingled exterior and exposed wooden beams throughout the interior. The minicomputer distributive processing hardware is situated in a large open area with high ceilings and skylights. The openness makes the data processing area accessible to the rest of the staff and encourages a team approach to problem

solving. Before occupying the new facility, city inspectors declared the building safe; that is, it had adequate fire extinguishers, sufficient exits, and so on.

In an effort to provide further protection for its large database of client information, Gleicken has instituted a tape backup procedure that automatically backs up the database every Sunday evening, avoiding interruption in the daily operations and procedures. All tapes are then labeled and carefully stored on shelves reserved for this purpose in the data processing department. The departmental operator's manual has instructions on how to use these tapes to restore the database, should the need arise. A list of home phone numbers of the individuals in the data processing department is available in case of an emergency. Gleicken has recently increased its liability insurance for data loss from $50,000 to $100,000.

This past Saturday, the Gleicken headquarters building was completely ruined by fire, and the company must now inform its clients that all of their information has been destroyed.

Required:

a. Describe the computer security weaknesses present at Gleicken Corporation that made it possible for a disastrous data loss to occur.

b. List the components that should have been included in the disaster recovery plan at Gleicken Corporation to ensure computer recovery within 72 hours.

c. What factors, other than those included in the plan itself, should a company consider when formulating a disaster recovery plan?

5. Separation of Duties
Arcadia Plastics follows the philosophy of transferring employees from job to job within the company. Management believes that job rotation deters employees from feeling that they are stagnating in their jobs and promotes a better understanding of the company. The computer services personnel typically work for six months as a data librarian, one year as a systems developer, six months as a database administrator, and one year in systems maintenance. At that point, they are assigned to a "permanent" position.

Required:
Discuss the importance of separation of duties within the information systems department. How can Arcadia Plastics have both job rotation and well-separated duties?

6. End User Computing
CMA 1287 5-3
The internal audit department of Hastone Manufacturing Company recently concluded a routine examination of the company's computer facilities. The auditor's report identified as a weakness the fact that there had been no coordination by the data processing services department in the purchase of microcomputer systems for the individual departments of Hastone. Among the 12 microcomputers in the organization, there are three different hardware manufacturers. In addition, there are four to five different software vendors for spreadsheets, word processing, and database applications, along with some networking applications for clusters of microcomputers.

Microcomputers were acquired in the operating departments to allow employees in each department to conduct special analyses. Many of the departments also wanted the capability to download data from the mainframe. Therefore, each operating department had requested guidance and assistance from the data processing services department. Data processing, however, responded that it was understaffed and must devote full effort to its main priority, the mainframe computer system.

In response to the internal audit report, the director of data processing services, Stan Marten, has issued the following memorandum.

TO:	All Employees
FROM:	Stan Marten, Director
REFERENCE:	Microcomputer Standardization

Policies must be instituted immediately to standardize the acquisition of microcomputers and applications software. The first step is to specify the spreadsheet software that should be used by all personnel. From now on, everyone will use Micromate. All microcomputer hardware should be MS-DOS compatible. During the next month, we will also select the standard software for word processing and database applications. You will use only the user packages that are prescribed by the data processing services department. In the future, any new purchases of microcomputers, hardware, or software must be approved by the director of data processing services.

Several managers of other operating departments have complained about Marten's memorandum. Apparently, before issuing this memorandum, Marten had not consulted with any of the microcomputer users regarding their current and future software needs.

Required:

a. When acquiring microcomputers for various departments in an organization, describe the factors related to:
   i. computer hardware that needs to be considered during the initial design and set-up phase of the microcomputer environment.
   ii. operating procedures and system controls that need to be considered.
b. Discuss the benefits of having standardized hardware and software for microcomputers in an organization.
c. Discuss the concerns that the memorandum is likely to create for the microcomputer users at Hastone Manufacturing.

7. End User Computing
   CMA Adapted 688 5-Y6
   List the problems inherent in the use, by others, of spreadsheet models developed by users who are not trained in the procedural controls of system design and development.

8. Internal Control and Fraud
   Stephanie Baskill, an unemployed accounting clerk, lives one block from the Cleaver Manufacturing Company. While walking her dog last year, she noticed some material resource planning manuals in the dumpsters. Curious, she took the manuals home with her. She found that the documentation in the manuals was dated two months ago, so she thought that the information must be fairly current. Over the next month, Stephanie continued to collect all types of manuals from the dumpster during her dog-walking excursions. Cleaver Manufacturing Company was apparently updating all of its documentation manuals and placing them on-line. Eventually, Stephanie found manuals about critical

inventory reorder formulas, the billing system, the sales order system, the payable system, and the operating system. Stephanie went to the local library and read as much as she could about this particular operating system.

To gain access to the organization, she took a low-profile position with Cleaver as a cleaning woman. By snooping through offices and guessing at passwords, watching people who were working late type in their passwords, and ultimately printing out lists of user IDs and passwords using a Trojan horse virus, Stephanie was able to obtain all the necessary passwords she needed to set herself up as a supplier, customer, systems operator, and systems librarian. Further, as a cleaning woman, she had access to all areas in the building.

As a customer, she was able to order enough goods so that the inventory procurement system would automatically trigger a need for a purchase of raw materials. Then, as a supplier, Stephanie would stand ready to deliver the goods at the specified price. She then covered her tracks by adjusting the transaction logs once the bills were paid. Stephanie was able to embezzle, on average, $125,000 a month. About 16 months after she began working at Cleaver, the controller saw her arrive at a very expensive French restaurant one evening, driving a Jaguar. Further, she spoke very good French when she ordered her meal. He told the internal auditors to keep a close watch on her, and they were able to catch her in the act.

Required:

a. What weaknesses in the organization's control structure must have existed to permit this type of embezzlement?
b. What specific control techniques and procedures could have helped prevent or detect this fraud?

9. Internal Control and End User Computing
   CMA 1290 4-3
   The National Commercial Bank has 15 branches and maintains a mainframe computer system at its corporate headquarters. National has recently undergone an examination by the state banking examiners, and the

examiners have some concerns about National's computer operations.

During the last few years, each branch has purchased a number of microcomputers to communicate with the mainframe in the emulation mode. Emulation occurs when a microcomputer attaches to a mainframe computer and, with the use of the appropriate software, can act as if it is one of the mainframe terminals. The branch also uses these microcomputers to download information from the mainframe and, in the local mode, manipulate customer data to make banking decisions at the branch level. Each microcomputer is initially supplied with a word processing application package to formulate correspondence to the customers, a spreadsheet package to perform credit and financial loan analyses beyond the basic credit analysis package on the mainframe, and a database management package to formulate customer market and sensitivity information. National's centralized data processing department is responsible only for mainframe operations; microcomputer security is the responsibility of each branch.

Because the bank examiners believe National is at risk, they have advised the bank to review the recommendations suggested in a letter issued by banking regulatory agencies in 1988. This letter emphasizes the risks associated with end user operations and encourages banking management to establish sound control policies. More specifically, microcomputer end user operations have outpaced the implementation of adequate controls and have taken processing control out of the centralized environment, introducing vulnerability in new areas of the bank.

The letter also emphasizes that the responsibility for corporate policies identifying management control practices for all areas of information processing activities resides with the board of directors. The existence, adequacy, and compliance with these policies and practices will be part of the regular banking examiners' review. The three required control groups for adequate information system security as they relate to National are (1) processing controls, (2) physical and environmental controls, and (3) spreadsheet program development controls.

Required:

For each of the three control groups listed

a. identify three types of controls for microcomputer end user operations where National Commercial Bank might be at risk, and

b. recommend a specific control procedure that National should implement for each type of control you identified. Use the following format for your answer.

Control Types	Recommended Procedures

chapter 3

DATA MANAGEMENT SYSTEMS

This chapter deals with auditing the systems that manage and control the organization's data resource. Data management can be divided into two general approaches: the **flat-file model** and the **database model**. The chapter opens with a description of flat-file data management, which is used in many older (legacy) systems that are still in operation today. Private ownership of data, which characterizes this model, is the root cause of several problems that inhibit data integration. The section then presents a conceptual overview of the database model and illustrates how problems associated with the flat-file model are resolved under this approach. The notions of entity-wide data sharing and centralized control of data lie at the heart of the database philosophy.

The second section describes the key functions and defining features of three common database models: the *hierarchical*, the *network*, and the *relational* models. The three models are presented from the perspective of a centralized IT function. The hierarchical and network models are called *navigational databases* because of their structure and inflexibility. Seen as a marked improvement over flat files, navigational databases were used in the design of many late era legacy systems. Newer accounting information systems, however, make extensive use of the relational model. This flexible approach presents data in a two-dimensional format that is conceptually more pleasing to end users than complex navigational structures. When properly implemented, the relational model effectively supports entity-wide data integration.

The third section examines the role of database technology in the distributed environment. Distributed data processing (DDP) empowers end users with ownership and control of IT resources, including databases. Since data ownership is contrary to traditional database philosophy, DDP presents an operational dilemma of sorts. This section presents techniques for achieving the goals of DDP while maintaining the principles of data sharing and integration. Three alternative configurations are examined: centralized, replicated, and partitioned databases.

The chapter concludes with a discussion of the control and audit issues related to data management. The risks, audit objectives, and audit procedures relevant to flat files, centralized databases, and distributed databases are presented.

LEARNING OBJECTIVES

After studying this chapter, you should:

- Understand the operational problems inherent in the flat-file approach to data management, that gave rise to the database approach.
- Understand the relationships among the fundamental components of the database concept.
- Recognize the defining characteristics of three database models: hierarchical, network, and relational.
- Understand the operational features and associated risks of deploying centralized, partitioned, and replicated database models in the DDP environment.
- Be familiar with the audit objectives and procedures used to test data management controls.

DATA MANAGEMENT APPROACHES

There are two general approaches to data management: the flat-file model and the database model. The differences between the two approaches are both technical and philosophical. The defining features of each are presented below.

THE FLAT-FILE APPROACH

The flat-file approach is most often associated with so-called **legacy systems**. These are large mainframe systems that were implemented in the late 1960s through the 1980s. Organizations today still make extensive use of these systems. Eventually, they will be replaced by modern database management systems, but in the meantime, auditors must continue to deal with legacy-system technologies.

The flat-file model describes an environment in which individual data files are not related to other files. End users in this environment *own* their data files rather than *share* them with other users. Data processing is thus performed by standalone applications rather than integrated systems.

When multiple users need the same data for different purposes, they must obtain separate data sets structured to their specific needs. Figure 3–1 illustrates how customer sales data might be presented to three different users in a durable goods retailing organization. The Accounting function needs customer sales data organized by account number and structured to show outstanding balances. This is used for customer billing, account receivable maintenance, and financial statement preparation. Marketing needs customer sales history data organized by demographic keys. They use this for targeting new product promotions and for selling product upgrades. The Product Service group needs customer sales data organized by products and structured to show scheduled service dates. Such information is used for making after-sales contacts with customers to schedule preventive maintenance and to solicit sales of service agreements.

The data redundancy demonstrated in this example contributes to three significant problems in the flat-file environment: **data storage**, **data updating**, and **currency of information**.

FIGURE 3–1   Flat-File Model

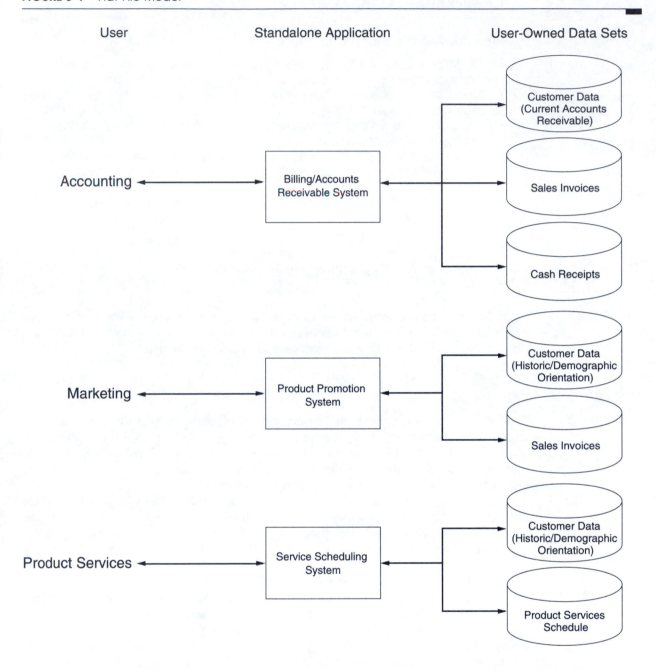

DATA STORAGE

An efficient information system captures and stores data only once and makes this single source available to all users who need it. In the flat-file environment, this is not possible. To meet the private data needs of users, organizations must incur the costs of both multiple collection and multiple storage procedures. Some commonly used data may be duplicated dozens, hundreds, or even thousands of times.

DATA UPDATING

Organizations have a great deal of data stored on master files and reference files that require periodic updating to reflect changes. For example, a change to a customer's name or address must be reflected in the appropriate master files. When users keep separate files, all changes must be made separately for each user. This adds significantly to the task burden and the cost of data management.

CURRENCY OF INFORMATION

In contrast to the problem of performing multiple updates is the problem of failing to update all the user files affected by a change in status. If update information is not properly disseminated, the change will not be reflected in some users' data, resulting in decisions based on outdated information.

TASK-DATA DEPENDENCY

Another problem with the flat-file approach is the user's inability to obtain additional information as his or her needs change, a problem known as **task-data dependency**. The user's information set is constrained by the data that he or she possesses and controls. Users act independently; they do not interact as members of a user community. In this environment, it is very difficult to establish a mechanism for the formal sharing of data. Therefore, new information needs tend to be satisfied by procuring new data files. This takes time, inhibits performance, adds to data redundancy, and drives data management costs even higher.

FLAT FILES LIMIT DATA INTEGRATION

The flat-file approach is a single-view model. Files are structured, formatted, and arranged to suit the specific needs of the *owner* or primary user of the data. Such structuring, however, may exclude data attributes that are useful to other users, thus preventing successful integration of data across the organization. For example, since the Accounting function is the primary user of accounting data, these data are often captured, formatted, and stored to accommodate financial reporting and GAAP. This structure, however, may be useless to the organization's other (non-accounting) users of accounting data, such as the marketing, finance, production, and engineering functions. These users are presented with three options: (1) do not use accounting data to support decisions; (2) manipulate and massage the existing data structure to suit their unique needs; or (3) obtain additional private sets of the data and incur the costs and operational problems associated with data redundancy.

THE DATABASE APPROACH

An organization can overcome the problems associated with flat files by implementing the database approach to data management. This approach centralizes the organization's data into a common database that is *shared* by other users. With the enterprise's data in a central location, all users have access to the data they need to achieve their respective objectives. Access to the data resource is controlled by a **database management system (DBMS)**. The DBMS is a special software system that is programmed to know which data elements each user is authorized to access. The user's program sends requests for data to the DBMS, which validates and authorizes access to the database in accordance with the user's level of authority. If the user requests data that he or she is not authorized to access, the request is denied. Clearly, the organization's procedures

FIGURE 3-2   Database Model

for assigning user authority are an important control issue for auditors to consider. Figure 3–2 provides an overview of the database environment.

The most striking difference between the database model and the flat-file model is the pooling of data into a common database that is shared by all organizational users. With access to the full domain of entity data, changes in user information needs can be satisfied without obtaining additional private data sets. Users are constrained only by the limitations of the data available to the entity and the legitimacy of their need to access it. Through data sharing, the traditional problems associated with the flat-file approach *may* be overcome.

ELIMINATION OF DATA REDUNDANCY

Each data element is stored only once, thereby eliminating data redundancy and reducing data collection and storage costs. For example, customer data exist only once, but are shared by accounting, marketing, and product services users.

SINGLE UPDATE

Because each data element exists in only one place, it requires only a single update procedure. This reduces the time and cost of keeping the database current.

CURRENT VALUES

A single change to a database attribute is automatically made available to all users of the attribute. For example, a customer address change entered by the billing clerk is immediately reflected in the marketing and product services views.

CENTRALIZED DATABASE SYSTEMS

Figure 3–3 presents a breakdown of the database environment into four primary elements: users, the DBMS, the database administrator, and the physical database. Each element is examined separately below.

FIGURE 3-3   Elements of the Database Concept

USERS

Figure 3–3 shows how **users** access the database in two ways. First, access can be achieved via user programs prepared by systems professionals. User programs send data access requests (calls) to the DBMS, which validates the requests and retrieves the data for processing. Under this mode of access, the presence of the DBMS is transparent to the users. Data processing procedures (both batch and real-time) for transactions such as sales, cash receipts, and purchases are essentially the same as they would be in the flat-file environment.

The second method of database access is via direct query, which requires no formal user programs. The DBMS has a built-in query facility that allows authorized users to process data independent of professional programmers. The query facility provides a "friendly" environment for integrating and retrieving data to produce ad hoc management reports. This feature is a most attractive incentive for users to adopt the database approach. The query feature is also an important control issue. Management must ensure that it is not used to achieve unauthorized access to the database.

DATABASE MANAGEMENT SYSTEM

The second element of the database approach depicted in Figure 3–3 is the database management system. The DBMS provides a controlled environment to assist (or prevent) user access to the database and to efficiently manage the data resource. Each DBMS is unique in the way it accomplishes these objectives, but some typical features include:

1. *Program development*. The DBMS contains **application development software**. Both programmers and end users may employ this feature to create applications to access the database.
2. *Backup and recovery*. During processing, the DBMS periodically makes backup copies of the physical database. In the event of a disaster (disk failure, program error, or malicious act) that renders the database unusable, the DBMS can recover to an earlier version that is known to be correct. Although some data loss may occur, without the backup and recovery feature the database would be vulnerable to total destruction.
3. *Database usage reporting*. This feature captures statistics on what data are being used, when they are used, and who uses them. This information is used by the database administrator (DBA) to help assign user authorization and maintain the database. We discuss the role of the DBA later in this section.
4. *Database access*. The most important feature of a DBMS is to permit authorized user access, both direct and via programs, to the database. Figure 3–3 shows the three software modules that facilitate this task. These are the data definition language, the data manipulation language, and the query language.

DATA DEFINITION LANGUAGE

Data definition language (DDL) is a programming language used to define the database to the DBMS. The DDL identifies the names and the relationship of all data elements, records, and files that constitute the database. There are three levels, called *views*, in this definition: the physical internal view, the conceptual view (schema), and the user view (subschema). Figure 3–4 shows the relationship between these views.

INTERNAL VIEW.   The physical arrangement of records in the database is presented through the **internal view**. This is the lowest level of representation, which is one step removed from the physical database. This internal view describes the structures of data records, the linkages between files, and the physical arrangement and sequence of records in a file. There is only one internal view for the database.

CONCEPTUAL VIEW (SCHEMA).   The conceptual view or **schema** describes the entire database. This view represents the database logically and abstractly, rather than the way it is physically stored. There is only one conceptual view for a database.

USER VIEW (SUBSCHEMA).   The **subschema** defines the user view of the database— the portion that an individual user is authorized to access. To a particular user, the user view *is* the database. Unlike the internal and conceptual views, there may be many distinct user views. For example, a user in the personnel department may view the

FIGURE 3–4 Overview of DBMS Operation

Database Management System

database as a collection of employee records and is unaware of the supplier and inventory records seen by the users in the inventory control department.

DBMS OPERATION.   To illustrate the roles of these views, let's look at the typical sequence of events that occurs in accessing data through a DBMS. The following description is hypothetical, and certain technical details are omitted.

1. A user program sends a request for data to the DBMS. The requests are written in a special data manipulation language (discussed later) that is embedded in the user program.
2. The DBMS analyzes the request by matching the called data elements against the user view and the conceptual view. If the data request matches, it is authorized, and processing proceeds to Step 3. If it does not match the views, access is denied.
3. The DBMS determines the data structure parameters from the internal view and passes them to the operating system, which performs the actual data retrieval. Data structure parameters describe the organization and access method for retrieving the requested data. This topic is discussed later.
4. Using the appropriate access method (an operating system utility program), the operating system interacts with the disk storage device to retrieve the data from the physical database.

5. The operating system then stores the data in a main memory buffer area managed by the DBMS.
6. The DBMS transfers the data to the user's work location in main memory. At this point, the user's program is free to access and manipulate the data.
7. When processing is complete, Steps 4, 5, and 6 are reversed to restore the processed data to the database.

DATA MANIPULATION LANGUAGE

Data manipulation language (DML) is the proprietary programming language that a particular DBMS uses to retrieve, process, and store data. Entire user programs may be written in the DML or, alternatively, selected DML commands can be inserted into programs that are written in universal languages, such as PL/1, COBOL, and FORTRAN. Inserting DML commands enables standard programs, which were originally written for the flat-file environment, to be easily converted to work in a database environment. The use of standard language programs also provides the organization with a degree of independence from the DBMS vendor. If the organization decides to switch vendors to one that uses a different DML, it will not be necessary to rewrite all the user programs. By replacing the old DML commands with the new commands, user programs can be modified to function in the new environment.

QUERY LANGUAGE

The query capability of the DBMS permits end users and professional programmers to access data in the database directly without the need for conventional programs. IBM's **Structured Query Language** (SQL, often pronounced *sequel*) has emerged as the standard query language for both mainframe and microcomputer DBMSs. SQL is a fourth-generation, nonprocedural language with many commands that allow users to input, retrieve, and modify data easily. The SELECT command is a powerful tool for retrieving data. The example in Figure 3–5 illustrates the use of the SELECT command to produce a user report from a database called Inventory.

As you can see from this example, SQL is a very efficient data processing tool. Although not a natural English language, SQL requires far less training in computer concepts and fewer programming skills than third-generation languages. In fact, the latest generation of query features require no SQL knowledge at all. Users select data visually by "pointing and clicking" at the desired attributes. This visual user interface then generates the necessary SQL commands automatically. The great advantage of the query feature is that it places ad hoc reporting and data processing capability in the hands of the user/manager. By reducing reliance on professional programmers, the manager's ability to deal with problems that "pop up" is greatly improved.

THE DATABASE ADMINISTRATOR

Refer to Figure 3–3 and note the administrative position of **database administrator (DBA)**. This position does not exist in the flat-file environment. The DBA is responsible for managing the database resource. The sharing of a common database by multiple users requires organization, coordination, rules, and guidelines to protect the integrity of the database.

In large organizations, the DBA function may consist of an entire department of technical personnel under the database administrator. In smaller organizations, DBA responsibility may be assumed by someone within the computer services group. The

FIGURE 3-5   Example of SELECT Command Used to Query an Inventory Database

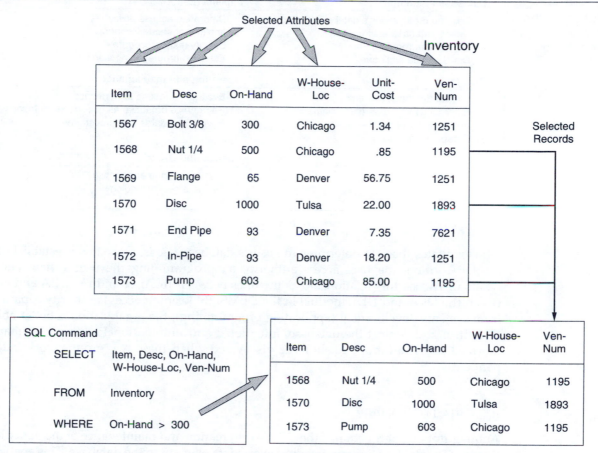

duties of the DBA fall into the following areas:[1] database planning; database design; database implementation, operation, and maintenance; and database growth and change. Table 3–1 presents a breakdown of specific tasks within these broad areas.

ORGANIZATIONAL INTERACTIONS OF THE DBA

Figure 3–6 shows some of the organizational interfaces of the DBA. Of particular importance is the relationship among the DBA, the end users, and the systems professionals of the organization. Refer again to Figure 3–3 during our examination of this relationship.

As information needs arise, users send formal requests for computer applications to the systems professionals (programmers) of the organization. The requests are handled through formal systems development procedures; if they have merit, they result in programmed applications. Figure 3–3 shows this relationship as the line from the user block to the systems development block. The user requests also go to the DBA,

---

1.   Adapted from F.R. McFadden and J.A. Hoffer, *Database Management*, 3d ed. (Redwood City, CA: Benjamin/Cummings Publishing, 1991), p. 343.

TABLE 3-1

Functions of the
Database
Administrator

Database Planning:		Implementation:
Develop organization's database strategy		Determine access policy
Define database environment		Implement security controls
Define data requirements		Specify tests procedures
Develop data dictionary		Establish programming standards
Design:		**Operation and maintenance:**
Logical database (schema)		Evaluate database performance
External users' views (subschemas)		Reorganize database as user needs demand
Internal view of database		Review standards and procedures
Database controls		
		Change and Growth:
		Plan for change and growth
		Evaluate new technology

who evaluates these to determine the user's database needs. Once this is established, the DBA grants the user access authority by programming the user's view (subschema). We see this relationship as the lines between the user and the DBA and between the DBA and DDL module in the DBMS. By keeping access authority separate from systems development (application programming), the organization is better able to control and protect the database. Intentional and unintentional attempts at unauthorized access are more likely to be discovered when these two groups work independently.

THE DATA DICTIONARY

Another important function of the DBA is the creation and maintenance of the **data dictionary**. The data dictionary describes every data element in the database. This enables

FIGURE 3-6

Organizational
Interactions of
the Database
Administrator

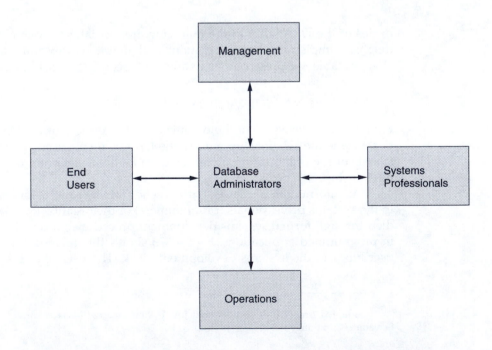

all users (and programmers) to share a common view of the data resource, thus greatly facilitating the analysis of user needs. The data dictionary may be in both paper form and on-line. Most DBMSs employ special software for managing the data dictionary.

THE PHYSICAL DATABASE

The fourth major element of the database approach as presented in Figure 3–3 is the **physical database**. This is the lowest level of the database and the only level that exists in physical form. The physical database consists of magnetic spots on magnetic disks. The other levels of the database (the user view, conceptual view, and internal view) are abstract representations of the physical level.

At the physical level, the database forms a logical collection of records and files that constitute the firm's data resource. This section deals with the data structures used in the physical database. Table 3–2 contains a list of file processing operations that data structures must support.[2] The efficiency with which the DBMS performs these tasks is a major determinant of its overall success, and depends in great part on how a particular file is structured.

DATA STRUCTURES

Data structures are the bricks and mortar of the database. The data structure allows records to be located, stored, and retrieved, and enables movement from one record to another. Data structures have two fundamental components: organization and access method.

The **organization** of a file refers to the way records are physically arranged on the secondary storage device. This may be either *sequential* or *random*. The records in sequential files are stored in contiguous locations that occupy a specified area of disk space. Records in random files are stored without regard for their physical relationship to other records of the same file. Random files may have records distributed throughout a disk.

The **access method** is the technique used to locate records and to navigate through the database. For our purposes, it is sufficient to deal with access methods at the conceptual level only. However, at a technical level, they exist as computer programs (also called *access methods*) that are provided as part of the operating system. During database processing, the access method program, responding to requests for data from the user's application, locates and retrieves or stores the records. The tasks carried out by the access method are completely transparent to the user's application.

TABLE 3–2

Typical File Processing Operations

1.	Retrieve a record from the file based on its primary key value.
2.	Insert a record into a file.
3.	Update a record in the file.
4.	Read a complete file of records.
5.	Find the next record in a file.
6.	Scan a file for records with common secondary keys.
7.	Delete a record from a file.

---

2.   *Ibid.*, p. 287.

No single structure is best for all processing tasks. Selecting one, therefore, involves a trade-off between desirable features. The criteria that influence the selection of the data structure include:

1. Rapid file access and data retrieval.
2. Efficient use of disk storage space.
3. High throughput for transaction processing.
4. Protection from data loss.
5. Ease of recovery from system failure.
6. Accommodation of file growth.

In Chapter 7, we introduce data extraction software for performing substantive tests of details. At that time, we examine a number of data structures used in both flat-file and database environments.

THREE DBMS MODELS

A data model is an abstract representation of the data about entities, including resources (assets), events (transactions), and agents (personnel or customers, etc.) and their relationships in an organization. The purpose of a data model is to represent entity attributes in a way that is understandable to users.

Each DBMS is based upon a particular conceptual model. Three common models are the hierarchical, the network, and the relational models. Because of certain conceptual similarities, we shall examine the hierarchical and network models first. These are termed **navigational models** because of explicit links or paths among their data elements. We shall then review the defining features of the relational model, which is based on implicit linkages between data elements.

DATABASE TERMINOLOGY

Before introducing these models formally, we need to review some important database terms and concepts.

DATA ELEMENT.   A **data element** is a single item of data, such as customer's name, account balance, or address.

ENTITY.   An **entity** is an individual resource, event, or agent about which we choose to collect data. Examples of entities are inventories, sales activities, customers, and employees.

RECORD TYPE.   When we group together data elements that logically pertain to an entity, they form a **record type**. For example, the data elements describing the *sales* event could form the *sales order* record type. A record type is a multiple occurrence (one or more) of a particular type of record. This approximates a file in conventional terminology. A single occurrence of a record type is equivalent to a record.

RECORD ASSOCIATIONS.   Record types exist in relation to other record types. This is called a **record association**. There are three basic record associations: one-to-one, one-to-many, and many-to-many.

One-to-One Association.   Figure 3–7(a) shows the **one-to-one (1:1) association**. This means that for every occurrence in Record Type X, there is zero or one occurrence in Record Type Y. For example, for every occurrence (employee) in the employee record type, there is only one (or zero for new employees) occurrence in the year-to-date earnings record type. Note the direction of the arrowhead on the line between the record types. This shows the nature (a single arrowhead is a 1:1 association) and the direction of the association.

One-to-Many Association.   Figure 3–7(b) shows the **one-to-many (1:M) association**. For every occurrence in Record Type X, there are zero, one, or many occurrences in Record Type Y. To illustrate, for every occurrence (customer) in the customer record type, there are zero, one, or many sales orders in the sales order record type. Note the double arrowhead notation representing a 1:M association and the direction of the association.

Many-to-Many Association.   Figure 3–7(c) illustrates a **many-to-many (M:M) association**, which is a two-way relationship. For each occurrence of Record Types X and Y, there is zero, one, or many occurrences of Record Types Y and X, respectively. An M:M association often exists between a firm's inventory records and its vendor records. One or more vendors may supply a particular inventory item. At the same time, one vendor may supply more than one item class of inventory.

THE HIERARCHICAL MODEL

The earliest database management systems were based on the **hierarchical data model**. This was a popular method of data representation because it reflected, more or less faithfully, many aspects of an organization that are hierarchical in relationship. Figure 3–8 presents a data structure diagram showing a portion of a hierarchical

FIGURE 3–7   Record Associations

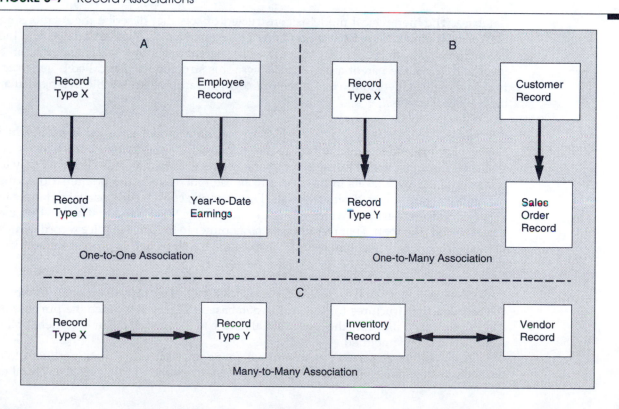

FIGURE 3-8   Hierarchical Data Model

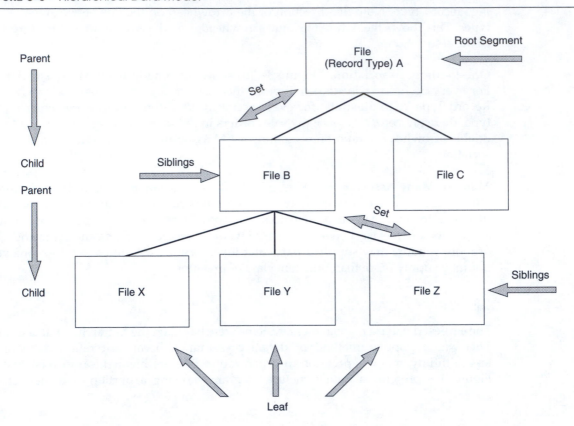

database. The hierarchical model is constructed of sets that describe the relationship between two linked files. Each set contains a *parent* and a *child*. Notice that File B, at the second level, is both the child in one set and the parent in another set. Files at the same level with the same parent are called *siblings*. This structure is also called a *tree structure*. The highest level in the tree is the *root* segment, and the lowest file in a particular branch is called a *leaf*.

NAVIGATIONAL DATABASES.   The hierarchical data model is called a *navigational database* because traversing the files requires following a predefined path. This is established through explicit linkages (pointers) between related records. The only way to access data at lower levels in the tree is from the root and via the pointers down the navigational path to the desired records. For example, consider the partial database in Figure 3–9. To retrieve an invoice line item record, the DBMS must first access the customer record (the root). That record contains a pointer to the sales invoice record, which points to the invoice line item record. We examine the steps in this process in more detail below.

DATA INTEGRATION IN THE HIERARCHICAL MODEL.   Figure 3–10 on page 92 shows the detailed file structures for the partial database in Figure 3–9. Since the purpose of this example is to illustrate the navigational nature of the model, the data content of the records has been simplified.

Assume that a user wishes to retrieve, for inquiry purposes, data pertinent to a particular sales invoice (Number 1921) for a customer John Smith (Account Number

FIGURE 3–9

Portion of a
Hierarchical
Database

1875). The user provides the query application with the primary key (Cust# 1875), which searches the *customer* file for a corresponding key value. Upon matching the key, it directly accesses John Smith's record. Notice the customer record contains only summary information. The current balance figure represents the total dollar amount owed ($1,820) by John Smith. This is the difference between the sum of all sales to this customer minus all cash received in payment on account. The supporting details about these transactions are in lower-level sales invoice and cash receipts records.

From a menu, the user selects the option "List Invoices." From this input, the query application reads the pointer value stored in the customer record, which directs it to the specific location (the address) where the first invoice for customer John Smith resides. These invoice records are arranged as a linked-list, with each record containing a pointer to the next one in the list. The application will follow each of the pointers and retrieve each record in the list. The sales invoice records contain only summary information pertaining to sales transactions. Additional pointers in these records show the locations of supporting detail records (the specific items sold) in the invoice *line item* file. The application then prompts the user to enter the key value sought (Invoice Number 1921) or select it from a menu. Upon entering this input, the application reads the pointer to the first line item record. Starting with the head (first) record, the application retrieves the entire list of line items for Invoice Number 1921. In this example, there are only two records associated with the invoice—item numbers 9215 and 3914. The sales invoice and line item records are then displayed on the user's computer screen.

LIMITATIONS OF THE HIERARCHICAL MODEL.   The hierarchical model presents an artificially constrained view of data relationships. Based on the proposition that all business relationships are hierarchical (or can be represented as such), this model does not always reflect reality. The following rules, which govern the hierarchical model, reveal its operating constraints:

1. A parent record may have one or more child records. For example, in Figure 3–9, customer is the parent of both sales invoice and cash receipts.
2. No child record can have more than one parent.

The second rule is often restrictive and limits the usefulness of the hierarchical model. Many firms need a view of data associations that permit multiple parents, such as that represented by Figure 3–11(a). In this example, the sales invoice file has two natural parents: the customer file and the salesperson file. A specific sales order is the product

FIGURE 3–10 Data Integration in a Hierarchical Database

of both the customer's purchase event and a salesperson's selling event. Management, wishing to integrate sales activity with customer service and employee performance evaluation, will need to view sales order records as the logical child of both parents. This relationship, although logical, violates the single parent rule of the hierarchical model. Since complex relationships cannot be depicted, data integration is restricted.

Figure 3–11(b) shows the most common way of resolving this problem. By duplicating the sales invoice file (and the related line item file), we create two separate hierarchical representations. Unfortunately, we achieve this improved functionality at the cost of increased data redundancy. The network model, which we examine next, deals with this problem more efficiently.

THE NETWORK MODEL

Like the hierarchical model, the **network model** is a navigational database with explicit linkages between records and files. The distinction is that the network model permits a child record to have multiple parents. For example, referring to Figure 3–12, Invoice Number 1 is the child of Salesperson Number 1 and Customer Number 5. Pointer fields in both parent records explicitly define the path to the invoice (child) record. This invoice record has two links to related (sibling) records. The first is a salesperson (SP) link to Invoice Number 2. This record resulted from a sale by Salesperson Number 1 to Customer Number 6. The second pointer is the customer (C) link to Invoice Number 3. This represents the second sale to Customer Number 5, which was processed this time by Salesperson Number 2. Under this data structure, management can track and report sales information pertaining to customers and sales staff.

The structure can be accessed at either of the root level records (salesperson or customer) by entering the appropriate primary key data (SP # or Cust #). Beyond this, the access process is similar to that described for the hierarchical model.

THE RELATIONAL MODEL

E.F. Codd originally proposed the principles of the **relational model** in the late 1960s.[3] The formal model has its foundations in relational algebra and set theory, which

FIGURE 3–11

Multiple Parent Association

(a)   (b)

Natural Relationship

Hierarchical Representation with Data Redundancy

---

3.   C.J. Date, *An Introduction to Database Systems*, vol. 1, 4th ed. (Reading, MS: Addison-Wesley, 1986), p. 99.

FIGURE 3-12   Linkages in a Network Database

provide the theoretical basis for most of the data manipulation operations used. The most apparent difference between the relational model and the navigational models is the way in which data associations are represented to the user. The relational model portrays data in the form of two-dimensional tables. Figure 3–13 presents an example of a database table called Customer.

Across the top of the table are **attributes** (data elements) forming columns. Intersecting the columns to form rows in the table are **tuples**. A tuple is a normalized array of data that is similar, but not precisely equivalent, to a record in a flat-file system. Properly designed tables possess the following characteristics:

1. All occurrences at the intersection of a row and a column are a single value. No multiple values (repeating groups) are allowed.
2. The attribute values in any column must all be of the same class.
3. Each column in a given table must be uniquely named. However, different tables may contain columns with the same name.
4. Each row in the table must be unique in at least one attribute. This attribute is the primary key.

The table should be normalized. Each attribute in the row should be dependent on (uniquely defined by) the primary key and independent of the other attributes.

DATA INTEGRATION IN THE RELATIONAL MODEL.   In the previous section, we saw how navigational databases use explicit linkages (pointers) between records to establish relationships. The linkages in the relational model are implicit. To illustrate this distinction, compare the file structures of the relational tables in Figure 3–14 on page 96 with those of the hierarchical example in Figure 3–10. The conceptual relationship between files is the same, but note the absence of explicit pointers in the relational tables.

FIGURE 3–13

A Relational
Table Called
Customer

Cust # (Key)	Name	Address	Current Balance
1875	J. Smith	18 Elm St.	1820.00
1876	G. Adams	21 First St.	2400.00
1943	J. Hobbs	165 High St.	549.87
2345	Y. Martin	321 Barclay	5256.76
•	•	•	•
•	•	•	•
•	•	•	•
5678	T. Stem	432 Main St.	643.67

Table Name = Customer

Attributes

Tuples (Records)

Relations are formed by an attribute that is common to both tables in the relation. For example, the primary key of the Customer table (Cust #) is also an embedded foreign key in both the Sales Invoice and Cash Receipts tables. Similarly, the primary key in the Sales Invoice table (Invoice #) is a foreign key in the Line Item table. Note that the Line Item table uses a composite primary key comprising two fields—Invoice # and Item #. Both fields are needed to identify each record in the table uniquely, but only the invoice number portion of the key provides the logical link to the Sales Invoice table.

Linkages between records in related tables are established through logical operations of the DBMS rather than via explicit addressees that are structured into the database. For example, if a user wants to view all the invoices for Customer 1875, the system would search the Sales Invoice table for records with a foreign key value of 1875. We see from Figure 3–14 that there is only one—Invoice 1921. To obtain the line item details for this invoice, a search is made of the Line Item table for records with a foreign key value of 1921. Two records are retrieved.

The nature of the association between two tables determines the method used for assigning foreign keys. Where the association is one-to-one, it does not matter which table's primary key is embedded in the other as a foreign key. In one-to-many associations, the primary key on the "one" side is embedded as the foreign key on the "many" side. For example, one customer may have many invoice and cash receipts records. Therefore, Cust # is embedded in the records of the Sales Invoice and Cash Receipts tables. Similarly, there is a one-to-many association between the Sales Invoice and Line

FIGURE 3-14   Data Integration in the Relational Model

Item tables. Many-to-many associations between tables do not use embedded foreign keys. Instead, a separate link table containing keys for the related tables needs to be created. In Chapter 7, we examine the design of relational tables in more detail.

DATABASES IN A DISTRIBUTED ENVIRONMENT

Chapter 2 presented the concept of distributed data processing (DDP). The physical structure of the organization's data is an important consideration in planning a distributed system. In addressing this issue, the planner has two basic options: the databases can be centralized or they can be distributed. Distributed databases fall into two categories: partitioned databases and replicated databases. This section examines issues, features, and trade-offs that need to be evaluated in deciding the disposition of the database.

CENTRALIZED DATABASES

The first approach involves retaining the data in a central location. Remote IT units send requests for data to the central site, which processes the requests and transmits the data back to the requesting IT unit. The actual processing of the data is performed at the remote IT unit. The central site performs the functions of a file manager that services the data needs of the remote sites. The centralized database approach is illustrated in Figure 3–15. A fundamental objective of the database approach is to maintain data currency. This can be a challenging task in a DDP environment.

DATA CURRENCY IN A DDP ENVIRONMENT

During data processing, account balances pass through a state of **temporary inconsistency** where their values are incorrectly stated. This occurs during the execution of a transaction. To illustrate, consider the computer logic for recording the credit sale of $2,000 to customer Jones.

	INSTRUCTION	DATABASE VALUES	
		AR-Jones	AR-Control
	START		
1	Read AR-SUB account (Jones)	1500	
2	Read AR-Control account		10000
3	Write AR-SUB account (Jones) + $2000	3500	
4	Write AR-Control account + $2000		12000
	END		

FIGURE 3–15

Centralized
Database

Immediately after the execution of Instruction Number 3, and before the execution of Instruction Number 4, the AR-Control account value is temporarily inconsistent by the sum of $2,000. Only after the completion of the entire transaction is this inconsistency resolved. In a DDP environment, such temporary inconsistencies can result in the corruption of data. To illustrate the potential for damage, let's look at a slightly more complicated example. Using the same computer logic as before, consider the processing of two separate transactions from two remote IT units: Transaction 1 (T1) is the sale of $2,000 on account to customer Jones from IT unit at Site A; Transaction 2 (T2) is the sale of $1,000 on account to customer Smith from IT unit at Site B. The following logic shows the possible interweaving of the two processing tasks and the potential effect on data currency.

| | | INSTRUCTION | DATABASE VALUES Central Site | | |
IT UNIT A	IT UNIT B		AR-Jones	AR-Smith	AR-Control
T1	T2	START			
1		Read AR-SUB account (Jones)	1500		
	1	Read AR-SUB account (Smith)		3000	
2		Read AR-Control account			10000
3		Write AR-SUB account (Jones) + $2000	3500		
	2	**Read AR-Control account**			10000
4		Write AR-Control account + $2000			12000
	3	Write AR-SUB account (Smith) + $1000		4000	
	4	Write AR-Control account + $1000			11000
		END			

Notice that IT unit B seized the AR-Control data value of $10,000 when it was in an inconsistent state. By using this value to process its transaction, IT unit B effectively erased Transaction T1, which had been processed by IT unit A. Therefore, instead of $13,000, the new AR-Control balance is misstated at $11,000.

DATABASE LOCKOUT

To achieve data currency, simultaneous access to individual data elements by multiple IT units must be prevented. The solution to this problem is to employ a **database lockout**, which is a software control (usually a function of the DBMS) that prevents multiple simultaneous accesses to data. The previous example can be used to illustrate this technique. Immediately upon receiving the access request from IT unit A for AR-Control (T1, Instruction Number 2), the central site DBMS should place a lock on AR-Control to prevent access from other IT units until Transaction T1 is complete. When IT unit B requests AR-Control (T2, Instruction Number 2), it is placed on "wait" status until the lock is removed. When site A's transaction has been posted, IT unit B is granted access to AR-Control and can then complete Transaction T2.

DISTRIBUTED DATABASES

Distributed databases can be either partitioned or replicated. We examine both approaches in the following pages.

PARTITIONED DATABASES

The **partitioned database approach** splits the central database into segments or partitions that are distributed to their primary users. The advantages of this approach are:

- Having data stored at local sites increases users' control.
- Transaction processing response time is improved by permitting local access to data and reducing the volume of data that must be transmitted between IT units.
- Partitioned databases can reduce the potential effects of a disaster. By locating data at several sites, the loss of a single IT unit cannot terminate all data processing by the organization.

The partitioned approach, which is illustrated in Figure 3–16, works best for organizations that require minimal data sharing among their IT units. The primary user manages data requests from other sites. To minimize data access from remote users, the organization needs to carefully select the host location. Identifying the optimum host requires an in-depth analysis of user data needs.

THE DEADLOCK PHENOMENON.   In a distributed environment, it is possible for multiple sites to lock out each other from the database, thus preventing each from processing its transactions. For example, Figure 3–17 illustrates three IT units and their mutual data needs. Notice that Site 1 has requested (and locked) Data A and is waiting for the removal of the lock on Data C to complete its transaction. Site 2 has a lock on C and is waiting for E. Finally, Site 3 has a lock on E and is waiting for A. A **deadlock** occurs here because there is mutual exclusion to the data resource, and the transactions are in a "wait" state until the locks are removed. This can result in transactions being incompletely processed and corruption of the database. A deadlock is a permanent condition that must be resolved by special software that analyzes each deadlock condition to determine the best solution. Because of the implication for transaction processing, accountants should be aware of the issues pertaining to deadlock resolutions.

FIGURE 3–16

The Partitioned
Database
Approach

Site 1
Primary User of
Data A and B

A, B

Site 3
Primary User of
Data E and F

E, F

Requests for Data

Site 2
Primary User of
Data C and D

C, D

FIGURE 3-17

The Deadlock
Condition

Deadlock Resolution.   Resolving a deadlock usually involves terminating one or more transactions to complete processing of the other transactions in the deadlock. The preempted transactions must then be reinitiated. In preempting transactions, the dead-lock resolution software attempts to minimize the total cost of breaking the deadlock. Some of the factors that are considered in this decision are:

1. *The resources currently invested in the transaction.* This may be measured by the number of updates that the transaction has already performed and that must be repeated if the transaction is terminated.
2. *The transaction's stage of completion.* In general, deadlock resolution software will avoid terminating transactions that are close to completion.
3. *The number of deadlocks associated with the transaction.* Because terminating the transaction breaks all deadlock involvement, the software should attempt to ter-minate transactions that are part of more than one deadlock.

REPLICATED DATABASES

Replicated databases are effective in companies where there exists a high degree of data sharing but no primary user. Since common data are replicated at each IT unit site, the data traffic between sites is reduced considerably. Figure 3–18 illustrates the repli-cated database model.

The primary justification for a replicated database is to support read-only queries. With data replicated at every site, data access for query purposes is ensured, and lock-outs and delays due to data traffic are minimized. The problem with this approach is maintaining current versions of the database at each site. Since each IT unit processes only its transactions, common data replicated at each site are affected by different transactions and reflect different values. Using the data from the earlier example, Figure 3–19 illustrates the effect of processing credit sales for Jones at site A and Smith

FIGURE 3–18

Replicated
Database
Approach

Database Replicated at Each Site

at site B. After the transactions are processed, the value shown for the common AR-Control account is inconsistent ($12,000 at IT unit A and $11,000 at IT unit B) and incorrect at both sites.

CONCURRENCY CONTROL

Database concurrency is the presence of complete and accurate data at all user sites. System designers need to employ methods to ensure that transactions processed at each site are accurately reflected in the databases of all the other sites. Because of the implication for the accuracy of accounting records, the concurrency problem is a matter of concern for auditors.

A commonly used method for **concurrency control** is to serialize transactions by time-stamping. This involves labeling each transaction by two criteria. First, special

FIGURE 3–19

Replicated
Databases
Updated
Independently

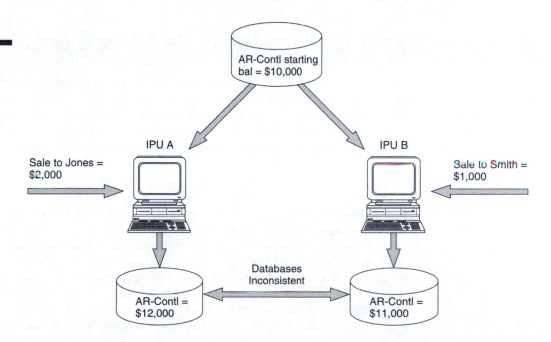

software groups transactions into classes to identify potential conflicts. For example, read-only (query) transactions do not conflict with other classes of transactions. Similarly, accounts payable and accounts receivable transactions are not likely to use the same data and do not conflict. However, multiple sales order transactions involving both read and write operations will potentially conflict.

The second part of the control process is to time-stamp each transaction. A system-wide clock is used to keep all sites, some of which may be in different time zones, on the same logical time. Each time stamp is made unique by incorporating the site's ID number. When transactions are received at each IT unit site, they are examined first by class for potential conflicts. If conflicts exist, the transactions are entered into a serialization schedule. An algorithm is used to schedule updates to the database based on the transaction time stamp and class. This method permits multiple interleaved transactions to be processed at each site with the effect of being executed serially.

DISTRIBUTED DATABASES AND THE ACCOUNTANT

The decision to distribute databases is one that should be entered into thoughtfully. There are many issues and trade-offs to consider. Some of the most basic questions to be addressed are:

- Should the organization's data be centralized or distributed?
- If data distribution is desirable, should the databases be replicated or partitioned?
- If replicated, should the databases be totally replicated or partially replicated?
- If the database is to be partitioned, how should the data segments be allocated among the sites?

The choices involved in each of these questions impact the organization's ability to maintain data integrity. The preservation of audit trails and the accuracy of accounting records are key concerns. Clearly, these are decisions that the modern auditor should understand and influence intelligently.

CONTROLLING AND AUDITING DATA MANAGEMENT SYSTEMS

Controls over data management systems fall into two general categories: access controls and backup controls. **Access controls** are designed to prevent unauthorized individuals from viewing, retrieving, corrupting, or destroying the entity's data. **Backup controls** ensure that in the event of data loss due to unauthorized access, equipment failure, or physical disaster the organization can recover its database.

ACCESS CONTROLS

Users of flat files maintain exclusive ownership of their data. In spite of the data integration problems associated with this model, it creates an environment in which unauthorized access to data can be effectively controlled. When not in use by the owner, a flat file is closed to other users and may be taken off-line and physically secured in the data library. In contrast, the need to integrate and share data in the database environment means that databases must remain on-line and open to all potential users.

In the shared database environment, access control risks include corruption, theft, misuse, and destruction of data. These threats originate from both unauthorized intruders and authorized users who exceed their access privileges. Several control features are now reviewed.

USER VIEWS

The **user view** or subschema is a subset of the total database that defines the user's data domain and provides access to the database. Figure 3–20(a) illustrates the role of the user view. In a centralized database environment, the database administrator (DBA) has primary responsibility for user view design but works closely with users and systems designers in this task. Access privileges to the database, as defined in their views, should be commensurate with the users' legitimate needs.

Although user views can restrict user access to a limited set of data, they do not define task privileges such as read, delete, or write. Often, several users may share a single user view but have different authority levels. For example, users Smith, Jones, and Adams in Figure 3–20(a) all may have access to the same set of data: account number, customer name, account balance, and credit limit. Let's assume that all have read authority, but only Jones has authority to modify and delete the data. Effective access control requires more additional security measures, discussed next.

DATABASE AUTHORIZATION TABLE

The **database authorization table** contains rules that limit the actions a user can take. This technique is similar to the access control list used in the operating system. Each user is granted certain privileges that are coded in the authority table, which is used to verify the user's action requests. For example, Figure 3–20(a) shows that Jones, Smith, and Adams have access to the same data attributes via a common user view, but the authorization table in Figure 3–20(b) shows that only Jones has the authority to modify and delete the data. Each row in the authority table indicates the level of action (read, insert, modify, or delete) that individuals can take based on their entering the correct password.

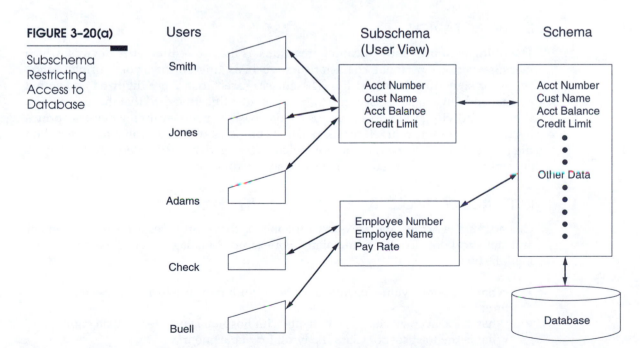

FIGURE 3–20(a)

Subschema Restricting Access to Database

FIGURE 3–20(b)

Database
Authorization
Table

Dept	Accounts Rec			Billings	
User	Jones	Smith	Adams	Check	Buell
Password	Bugs	Dog	Katie	Lucky	Star
Authority:					
Read	Y	Y	Y	Y	Y
Insert	Y	N	Y	Y	N
Modify	Y	N	N	Y	N
Delete	Y	N	N	N	N

USER-DEFINED PROCEDURES

A **user-defined procedure** allows the user to create a personal security program or routine to provide more positive user identification than a single password. Thus, in addition to a password, the security procedure asks a series of personal questions (such as the user's mother's maiden name), which only the legitimate user should know.

DATA ENCRYPTION

Many database systems use encryption procedures to protect highly sensitive data, such as product formulas, personnel pay rates, password files, and certain financial data. **Data encryption** uses an algorithm to scramble selected data, thus making it unreadable to an intruder "browsing" the database. In addition to protecting stored data, encryption is used for protecting data that are transmitted over communications lines. We examine encryption more fully in Chapter 5.

BIOMETRIC DEVICES

The ultimate in user authentication procedures is the use of **biometric devices**, which measure various personal characteristics, such as fingerprints, voice prints, retina prints, or signature characteristics. These user characteristics are digitized and stored permanently in a database security file or on an identification card that the user carries. When an individual attempts to access the database, a special scanning device captures his or her biometric characteristics, which it compares with the profile data stored on file or the ID card. If the data do not match, access is denied. Biometric technology is currently being used to secure ATM cards and credit cards.

INFERENCE CONTROLS

One advantage of the database query capability is that it provides users with summary and statistical data for decision-making. For example, managers might ask the following questions:

- What is the total value for inventory items with monthly turnover less than three?
- What is the average charge to patients with hospital stays greater than eight days?
- What is the total cost of Class II payroll for department XYZ?

Answers to these types of questions are needed routinely for resource management, facility planning, and operations control decisions. Legitimate queries sometimes involve access to confidential data. Thus, individual users may be granted summary and statistical query access to confidential data to which they normally are denied direct access.

To preserve the confidentiality and integrity of the database, **inference controls** should be in place to prevent users from inferring, through query features, specific data values that they otherwise are unauthorized to access. Inference controls attempt to prevent three types of compromises to the database.[4]

1. *Positive compromise*—the user determines the specific value of a data item.
2. *Negative compromise*—the user determines that a data item does not have a specific value.
3. *Approximate compromise*—the user is unable to determine the exact value of an item but is able to estimate it with sufficient accuracy to violate the confidentiality of the data.

Let's use the payroll database table presented in Figure 3–21 to illustrate how inference techniques are used to compromise a database. The salary field in the table is the confidential data being sought. Assuming that no inference controls are in place, a user wanting to determine the salary of Mary Swindle, a staff lawyer, could make the following queries:

Q. How many lawyers are female?
A. One.
Q. What is the average salary of all who are female and lawyers?
A. $65,000.

Since she is the only female lawyer, Mary Swindle's salary is explicitly provided by the query system through this statistical feature. This sort of compromise may be prevented by implementing the following inference control rule that places restrictions on the size of the query set to which the system will respond:

The system will not respond to queries where fewer than two records satisfy the query.

However, a determined and creative user may easily circumvent this control with the following queries:

Q. What is the total salary for the payroll database?
A. $555,000.
Q. What is the total salary for all not lawyers and not female?
A. $490,000.

Swindle's salary can be calculated in this example by subtracting $490,000 from $555,000. Preventing this compromise requires further restrictions on the query set size. This may be accomplished with the following additional inference control rule:

---

4.   R. Weber, *EDP Auditing Conceptual Foundations and Practice*, 2d ed. (New York: McGraw-Hill, 1988), p. 564.

FIGURE 3–21

Payroll Database
Containing
Confidential
Data

Payroll Database

Empl#	Name	Job Title	Salary	Sex	Other Data	
5439	Jim Jones	Consultant	50,000	Male	•	•
9887	Sam Smith	Lawyer	60,000	Male	•	•
8765	Mary Swindle	Lawyer	65,000	Female	•	•
4462	Bob Haub	Manager	60,000	Male	•	•
7742	Joan Hess	Consultant	50,000	Female	•	•
5532	Ben Huber	Lawyer	62,000	Male	•	•
8332	John Enis	Lawyer	63,000	Male	•	•
9662	Jim Hobbs	Consultant	70,000	Male	•	•
3391	Joe Riley	Manager	75,000	Male	•	•

The system will not respond to queries where greater than $(n - 2)$ records satisfy the query (where n is the number of records in the database).

Under this rule, neither query would have been satisfied.

AUDIT OBJECTIVES

- To verify that database access authority and privileges are granted to users in accordance with their legitimate needs.

AUDIT PROCEDURES

RESPONSIBILITY FOR AUTHORITY TABLES AND SUBSCHEMAS.   The auditor should verify that database administration (DBA) personnel retain exclusive responsibility for creating authority tables and designing user views. Evidence may come from three sources: (1) by reviewing company policy and job descriptions, which specify these technical responsibilities; (2) by examining programmer authority tables for access privileges to data definition language (DDL) commands; and (3) through personal interviews with programmers and DBA personnel.

APPROPRIATE ACCESS AUTHORITY.   The auditor can select a sample of users and verify that their access privileges stored in the authority table are consistent with their organizational functions.

BIOMETRIC CONTROLS.   The auditor should evaluate the costs and benefits of biometric controls. Generally, these would be most appropriate where highly sensitive data are accessed by a very limited number of users.

INFERENCE CONTROLS.   The auditor should verify that database query controls exist to prevent unauthorized access via inference. The auditor can test controls by simulating access by a sample of users and attempting to retrieve unauthorized data via inference queries.

ENCRYPTION CONTROLS.   The auditor should verify that sensitive data, such as passwords, are properly encrypted. Printing the file contents to hard copy can do this.

BACKUP CONTROLS

Data can be corrupted and destroyed by malicious acts from external hackers, disgruntled employees, disk failure, program errors, fires, floods, and earthquakes. To recover from such disasters, organizations must implement policies, procedures, and techniques that systematically and routinely provide backup copies of critical files.

BACKUP CONTROLS IN THE FLAT-FILE ENVIRONMENT

The backup technique employed will depend on the media and the file structure. Sequential files (both tape and disk) use a backup technique called grandparent-parent-child (GPC). This backup technique is an integral part of the master file update process. Direct access files, on the other hand, need a separate backup procedure. Both methods are outlined below.

GPC BACKUP TECHNIQUE.   Figure 3–22 illustrates the **grandparent-parent-child (GPC)** backup technique that is used in sequential file batch systems. The backup procedure begins when the current master file (the parent) is processed against the transaction file to produce a new updated master file (the child). With the next batch of transactions, the child becomes the current master file (the parent), and the original parent becomes the backup (grandparent) file. The new master file that emerges from the update process is the child. This procedure is continued with each new batch of transactions, creating generations of backup files. When the desired number of backup copies is reached, the oldest backup file is erased (scratched). If the current master file is destroyed or corrupted, processing the most current backup file against the corresponding transaction file can reproduce it.

The systems designer determines the number of backup master files needed for each application. Two factors influence this decision: (1) the financial significance of the system and (2) the degree of file activity. For example, a master file that is updated several times a day may require 30 or 40 generations of backup, while a file that is updated only once each month may need only four or five backup versions. This decision is important, because certain types of system failures can result in the destruction of large numbers of backup versions within the same family of files.

The author was witness to one system failure that destroyed, through accidental erasure, over 150 master files in only a few hours. The destruction began by erasing the most current master file (parent) in each application being processed. Then, one by one, the older generations were systematically scratched. Some systems lost as many as 20 backup copies. In fact, the accounts payable system had only one backup version left when the error was finally detected and stopped. Reconstruction of files after such a disaster requires locating the most current remaining backup version and methodically

FIGURE 3–22

Grandparent-
Parent-Child-
Approach

reprocessing the batches of past transactions until the current version of the master file is reproduced. This will also recreate all the intermediate generations of the master file. When using the GPC approach for financial systems, management and auditors should be involved in determining the needed number of backup files. Insufficient backup can result in the total destruction of accounting records. Most operating systems permit the creation of up to 256 generations for each application.

DIRECT ACCESS FILE BACKUP. Data values in direct access files are changed in place through a process called *destructive replacement*. Therefore, once a data value is changed, the original value is destroyed, leaving only one version (the current version) of the file. To provide backup, direct access files must be copied before being updated. Figure 3–23 illustrates this process.

The timing of the **direct access backup** procedures will depend upon the processing method being used. Backup of files in batch systems is usually scheduled prior to the update process. Real-time systems pose a more difficult problem. Since transactions are being processed continuously, the backup procedure takes place at specified intervals throughout the day (for example, every 15 minutes).

If the current version of the master file is destroyed through a disk failure or corrupted by a program error, it can be reconstructed with a special recovery program from the most current backup file. In the case of real-time systems, transactions

FIGURE 3–23

Backup of Direct
Access Files

Real-Time Processing System

Real-time systems use timed backup. Transactions processed between backup runs will have
to be reprocessed after restoration of the master file.

Batch Processing System

In a batch processing system using direct access files, the master file is backed up before
the update run.

processed since the last backup and prior to the failure will be lost and will need to be
reprocessed to restore the master file to current status.

OFF-SITE STORAGE.   As an added safeguard, backup files created under both the GPC and direct access approaches should be stored off-site in a secure location. **Off-site storage** was discussed in Chapter 2 in the section dealing with disaster recovery planning.

AUDIT OBJECTIVE

- To verify that backup controls in place are effective in protecting data files from physical damage, loss, accidental erasure, and data corruption through system failures and program errors.

AUDIT PROCEDURES

SEQUENTIAL FILE (GPC) BACKUP.   The auditor should select a sample of systems and determine from the system documentation that the number of GPC backup files specified for each system is adequate. If insufficient backup versions exist, recovery from some types of failure may be impossible.

BACKUP TRANSACTION FILES.   The auditor should verify through physical observation that transaction files used to reconstruct the master files are also retained. Without corresponding transaction files, reconstruction is impossible.

DIRECT ACCESS FILE BACKUP.   The auditor should select a sample of applications and identify the direct access files being updated in each system. From system documentation and through observation, the auditor can verify that each of them was copied to tape or disk before being updated.

OFF-SITE STORAGE.   The auditor should verify the existence and adequacy of off-site storage. This audit procedure may be performed as part of the review of the disaster recovery plan or computer center operations controls.

BACKUP CONTROLS IN THE DATABASE ENVIRONMENT

Since data sharing is a fundamental objective of the database approach, this environment is particularly vulnerable to damage from individual users. One unauthorized procedure, one malicious act, or one program error can deprive an entire user community of its information resource. Also, because of data centralization, even minor disasters such as a disk failure can effect many or all users. When such events occur, the organization needs to reconstruct the database to pre-failure status. This can be done only if the database was properly backed up in the first place. Most mainframe DBMSs have a backup and recovery system similar to the one illustrated in Figure 3–24. This system provides four backup and recovery features: database backup, a transaction log, checkpoints, and a recovery module. Each of these is described below.

BACKUP.   The backup feature makes a periodic backup of the entire database. This is an automatic procedure that should be performed at least once a day. The backup copy should then be stored in a secure remote area.

TRANSACTION LOG (JOURNAL).   The **transaction log** feature provides an audit trail of all processed transactions. It lists transactions in a transaction log file and records the resulting changes to the database in a separate database change log.

CHECKPOINT FEATURE.   The **checkpoint** facility suspends all data processing while the system reconciles the transaction log and the database change log against the

FIGURE 3–24

Database
Backup and
Recovery

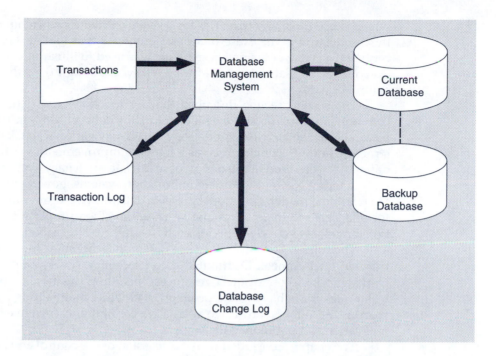

database. At this point, the system is in a "quiet state." Checkpoints occur automatically several times an hour. If a failure occurs, it is usually possible to restart the processing from the last checkpoint. Thus, only a few minutes of transaction processing must be repeated.

RECOVERY MODULE.   The **recovery module** uses the logs and backup files to restart the system after a failure.

AUDIT OBJECTIVE

•   To verify that controls over the data resource are sufficient to preserve the integrity and physical security of the database.

AUDIT PROCEDURE

The auditor should verify that backup is performed routinely and frequently to facilitate the recovery of lost, destroyed, or corrupted data without excessive reprocessing. Production databases should be copied at regular intervals (perhaps several times an hour). A balance must be sought between the inconvenience of frequent backup activities and the business disruption caused by excessive reprocessing that is needed to restore the database after a failure. The auditor should verify that automatic backup procedures are in place and functioning, and that copies of the database are stored off-site for further security.

SUMMARY

Data management can be divided into two general approaches: the flat-file model and the database model. The chapter began with a description of flat-file data management, which is used in many older (legacy) systems. Private ownership of data characterizes this model and is the cause of several problems that inhibit data integration. A conceptual overview of the database model was used to illustrate how the problems associated with the flat-file model can be resolved through data sharing and centralized control of data.

The second section described the key functions and defining features of three common database models: the hierarchical, the network, and the relational models. The hierarchical and network models are called navigational databases because of their structure and inflexibility. Seen as a marked improvement over flat files, navigational databases were used in the design of many late era legacy systems that are still in operation today. Newer accounting information systems, however, make extensive use of the relational model. This model presents data in a two-dimensional format that is easy for end users to understand and work with. When properly implemented, the relational model effectively supports entity-wide data integration.

The third section examined the database technology and applications in the distributed environment. Distributed data processing (DDP) empowers end users with ownership and control of IT resources, including databases. This section presented techniques for achieving the goals of DDP while maintaining the principles of data sharing and integration. Three alternative configurations were examined: centralized, replicated, and partitioned databases.

The chapter concluded with a discussion of the control and audit issues related to data management. The risks, audit objectives, and audit procedures relevant to flat files, centralized databases, and distributed databases were presented.

KEY TERMS

access controls
access method
application development software
attributes
backup controls
biometric devices
checkpoint
concurrency control
currency of information
data definition language (DDL)
data dictionary
data element
data encryption
data manipulation language (DML)
data storage
data structures
data updating
database administrator (DBA)
database authorization table
database lockout
database management system (DBMS)
database model
deadlock

direct access backup
entity
flat-file model
grandparent-parent-child (GPC)
hierarchical data model
inference controls
internal view
legacy systems
many-to-many (M:M) association
navigational models
network model
off-site storage
one-to-many (1:M) association
one-to-one (1:1) association
organization
partitioned database approach
physical database
record association
record type
recovery module
relational model
replicated databases
schema (conceptual view)

Structured Query Language (SQL)
subschema (user view)
task-data dependency
temporary inconsistency
transaction log

tuples
user views
user-defined procedure
users

Review Questions

1. What are the four primary elements of the database approach?
2. What types of problems does data redundancy cause?
3. What flat-file data management problems are solved as a result of using the database concept?
4. What are four ways in which database management systems provide a controlled environment to manage user access and the data resources?
5. Explain the relationship between the three levels of the data definition language. As a user, which level would you be most interested in?
6. What is the internal view of a database?
7. What is SQL?
8. What is a data dictionary and what purpose does it serve?
9. What are the two fundamental components of data structures?
10. What are the criteria that influence the selection of the data structure?
11. Discuss and give an example of one-to-one, one-to-many, and many-to-many record associations.

12. Why is a hierarchical database model considered to be a navigational database? What are some limitations of the hierarchical database model?
13. What is a partitioned database and what are its advantages? Specify any disadvantages.
14. What is a replicated database and why is concurrency control difficult to manage in this setting?
15. What is time-stamping and why is it useful?
16. Explain the grandparent-parent-child backup technique. Is it used for sequential files or direct access techniques? Why? How many generations can be backed up?
17. Distinguish between data access and access privileges. Give an example by designing and explaining a database authorization table.
18. What are inference controls? Why are they needed?
19. What are the four basic backup and recovery features necessary in a DBMS? Briefly explain each.

Discussion Questions

1. In the flat-file data management environment, users are said to own their data files. What is meant by this "ownership" concept?

2. Discuss the potential aggravations you might face as a student as a result of your university using a traditional data management environment, that is, different databases for the registrar, library, parking, and so on.

3. Discuss why control procedures over access to the database become more crucial under the database concept than in the flat-file data management environment. What role does the DBMS play in helping to control the database environment?

4. What is the relationship between a schema and a subschema?

5. Discuss the two ways in which users can access the database in a database environment.

6. How are special database commands inserted into conventional application programs? Why is this necessary?

7. Why might it be advantageous for an organization to use DML commands written in COBOL versus a proprietary programming language?

8. SQL has been said to place power in the hands of the user. What is meant by this statement?

9. Discuss the importance of the role of the database administrator. Why wasn't such a role necessary in the traditional data management environment? What tasks are performed by the DBA?

10. As users determine new computer application needs, requests must be sent to both the system programmers and the DBA. Why is it important that these two groups perform separate functions, and what are these functions?

11. How can data be centralized in a distributed data processing system?

12. In a distributed data processing system, why can temporary inconsistencies result in permanent damage to accounting records? Explain with an example.

13. Explain the deadlock phenomenon. Discuss how it could occur with a phone-in mail order system that locks the inventory records until the order is complete.

14. Which database method would be most appropriate for ticket sales at 30 different outlets to an assigned seating concert? Why?

15. Why is it risky to allow programmers to create user subschemas and assign access authority to users? What unethical technique do programmers sometimes use when they are not allowed to assign access authority to users?

16. Is access control of greater concern in the flat-file or database file environment?

17. How can passwords actually circumvent security? What actions can be taken to minimize this?

MULTIPLE-CHOICE QUESTIONS

1. CMA 1289 5-7
   The database approach to systems and the resulting concept of database management systems have several unique characteristics not found in traditional (flat-file) systems, specifically file-oriented systems. Which one of the following statements does not apply to database-oriented systems?
   a. Database systems have data independence; that is, the data and the programs are maintained separately, except during processing.
   b. Database systems contain a data definition language that helps describe each schema and subschema.
   c. The database administrator is the part of the software package that instructs the operating aspects of the program when data are retrieved.
   d. A primary goal of database systems is to minimize data redundancy.
   e. Database systems increase user interface with the system through increased accessibility and flexibility.

2. CMA 685 5-30
   One of the first steps in the creation of a database is to
   a. define common variables and fields used throughout the firm.
   b. increase the secondary storage capacity.
   c. obtain software that will facilitate data retrieval.
   d. integrate the accounting system into the database.
   e. study the need for a larger central processing unit.

3. CMA 685 5-33
   If a database has integrity, the
   a. software was implemented after extensive acceptance testing.
   b. database has only consistent data.

c. database is secure from accidental entry.

d. database and the system have been reviewed by an external auditor.

e. incidence of failure for the database is within statistically acceptable limits.

4. CMA 687 5-14

The installation of a database management system is not likely to have any direct impact on

a. data redundancy within files.

b. sharing of common data.

c. inconsistencies within common data fields.

d. the logic needed to solve a problem in an application program.

e. the internal control of data accuracy and access.

5. CMA 1287 5-3

The increased use of database processing systems makes managing data and information a major information service function. Because the databases of an organization are used for many different applications, they are coordinated and controlled by a database administrator. The functions of a database administrator are

a. data input preparation, database design, and database operations.

b. database design, database operation, and database security.

c. database design, database operation, and equipment operations.

d. database design, software support, and database security.

e. database operations, hardware support, and software support.

6. CMA 689 5-8

A disk storage unit may be preferred over a magnetic tape drive system because the disk storage unit

a. is a cheaper medium for data storage.

b. offers random access to data files.

c. offers sequential access to data files.

d. can be measured in bytes per inch.

e. has nine tracks.

7. CIA 1186 III-33

In an inventory system on a database management system, one stored record contains part number, part name, part color, and part weight. These individual items are called

a. fields.

b. stored files.

c. bytes.

d. occurrences.

8. CIA 1187 III-28

Which of the following is a characteristic of a database system?

a. Data within the system exist separately from programs.

b. Database processing is inherently simple.

c. A database system is relatively inexpensive to purchase or develop.

d. Database processing was developed to meet microcomputer requirements.

9. CMA 1289 5-6

A system with several computers that are connected for communication and data transmission purposes but that permits each computer to process its own data is a

a. distributed data processing network.

b. centralized network.

c. decentralized network.

d. multidrop network.

e. hybrid system.

10. For those instances where individual users may be granted summary and statistical query access to confidential data to which they normally are denied access, which type of control is MOST suitable?

a. user-defined procedures

b. data encryption

c. inference controls

d. biometric devices

11. CMA 685 5-31

The identification of users who have permission to access data elements in a database is found in the

a. operating system.

b. systems manual.

c. database schema.

d. database authority table.

e. application programs.

12. A checkpoint or restart procedure is primarily designed to recover from

a. programming errors.

b. data input errors.

c. computer operator errors.

d. hardware failures.

e. All of the above.

PROBLEMS

1. **DBMS versus Flat-File Processing**
The Werner Manufacturing Corporation has a flat-file processing system. The information processing facility is very large. Different applications, such as order processing, production planning, inventory management, accounting systems, payroll, and marketing systems, use separate tape and disk files. The corporation has recently hired a consulting firm to investigate the possibility of switching to a database management system. Prepare a memo to the top management team at Werner explaining the advantages of a DBMS. Also, discuss the necessity of a database administrator and the job functions this person would perform.

2. **Database Design**
Design a relational database system for a large costume rental store. The store has approximately 3,200 customers each year. It is stocked with over 500 costumes in various sizes. The rental costumes and other items that may be purchased by the customer (e.g., make-up and teeth) are purchased from approximately 35 different suppliers. Design the necessary database files. Make sure they are in third normal form, and indicate the necessary linkages.

3. **Database Design**
Sears Roebuck, the most well-known and oldest mail-order retailer in the country, recently discontinued its mail-order operations. Other mail-order marketers are beginning to use information systems to trim printing and postage costs of their catalogs. They also want to more effectively target their customers. Explain how an appropriately designed coding system for inventory items (see Chapter 7) incorporated in a database management system with SQL capabilities could allow more cost-efficient and effective mail-order operations. Sketch the necessary database files.

4. **System Configuration**
It is estimated that the "Year 2000" problem will cost billions of dollars to fix. Do you think the cost will be greater for centralized or distributed data processing environments?

5. **System Configuration**
First State Bank provides full banking services to its customers through
   a. automatic teller machines.
   b. checking and saving accounts.
   c. certificate of deposits.
   d. loans.
   e. electronic payroll.
   f. electronic payment of customer's bills.
The bank has 11 branch offices that cover a 30-mile radius. The main office maintains a mainframe computer that serves the branch offices.

   The competitive nature of the banking industry requires that customer satisfaction be considered. Customers want prompt and accurate servicing of transactions. Thus, accuracy and speed are crucial to the success of First State Bank.

   How would you suggest the databases and data communications facilities be configured for First State Bank?

6. **Database Authorization Table**
The following information is stored in two relational database files:
Employee Master File
   Social security number
   Name
   Address
   Date hired
   Hourly wage rate
   Marital status
   Number of exemptions
Weekly Payroll File
   Social security number
   Hours worked
   Deductions
   Bonuses

Required:
   a. Bogey works in personnel and Bacall works in payroll. Prepare a database authorization table that you think is appropriate for Bogey and Bacall for these two files.
   b. Discuss any potential exposure if the right prevention devices are not in place or if Bogey and Bacall collude.

chapter 4

SYSTEMS DEVELOPMENT AND MAINTENANCE ACTIVITIES

One of the most valuable assets of the modern business organization is a responsive, user-oriented information system. A well-designed system can increase productivity, reduce inventories, eliminate nonvalue-added activities, improve customer service and management decisions, and coordinate activities throughout the organization.

This chapter begins by describing the roles of the participants involved in developing an organization's information system, including systems professionals, users, and stakeholders. Then it outlines the key activities that constitute the systems development life cycle (SDLC). These include *systems planning, systems analysis, conceptual design, system selection, detailed design, system implementation*, and *systems maintenance*. This multistage procedure is used to guide systems development in many organizations. Finally, SDLC risks, controls, and audit issues are discussed.

LEARNING OBJECTIVES

After studying this chapter, you should:

- Be able to identify the seven stages in the SDLC.
- Be familiar with common problems that can lead to failure in the systems development process.
- Understand the importance of strategic system planning.
- Have a general understanding of how accountants participate in the SDLC.
- Be able to identify the basic features of both the structured and object-oriented approaches to systems design.
- Be able to identify and discuss the major steps involved in a cost-benefit analysis of proposed information systems.
- Understand the advantages and disadvantages of the commercial software option, and be able to discuss the decision-making process used to select commercial software.
- Understand the purpose of a system walkthrough.
- Be familiar with the different types of system documentation and the purposes they serve.

PARTICIPANTS IN SYSTEMS DEVELOPMENT

The participants in systems development can be classified into three broad groups: systems professionals, end users, and stakeholders.

Systems professionals are systems analysts, systems engineers, and programmers. These individuals actually build the system. They gather facts about problems with the current system, analyze these facts, and formulate a solution to solve the problems. The product of their efforts is a new system.

End users are those for whom the system is built. There are many users at all levels in an organization. These include managers, operations personnel, accountants, and internal auditors. In some organizations, it is difficult to find someone who is not a user. During systems development, systems professionals work with the primary users to obtain an understanding of the users' problems and a clear statement of their needs.

Stakeholders are individuals either within or outside the organization who have an interest in the system but are not end users. These include accountants, internal and external auditors, and the internal steering committee that oversees systems development.

WHY ARE ACCOUNTANTS AND AUDITORS INVOLVED WITH SDLC?

The SDLC process is of interest to accountants and auditors for two reasons. First, the creation of an information system entails significant financial transactions. Conceptually, systems development is like any manufacturing process that produces a complex product through a series of stages. Such transactions must be planned, authorized, scheduled, accounted for, and controlled. Accountants are as concerned with the integrity of this process as they are with any manufacturing process that has financial resource implications.

The second and more pressing concern for accountants and auditors is with the nature of the products that emerge from the SDLC. The quality of accounting information rests directly on the SDLC activities that produce accounting information systems (AIS). These systems are used to deliver accounting information to internal and external users. The accountant's responsibility is to ensure that the systems employ the proper accounting conventions and rules, and possess adequate controls. Therefore, accountants are concerned with the quality of the process that produces AIS. For example, a sales order system produced by a defective SDLC may suffer from serious control weaknesses that introduce errors into the financial accounting records.

HOW ARE ACCOUNTANTS INVOLVED IN THE SDLC?

Accountants are involved in systems development in three ways. First, accountants are users. All systems that process financial transactions impact the accounting function in some way. Like all users, accountants must provide a clear picture of their problems and needs to the systems professional. For example, accountants must specify accounting techniques to be used, internal control requirements (such as audit trails), and special algorithms (such as depreciation models).

Second, accountants participate in systems development as members of the development team. Their involvement often extends beyond the development of strictly AIS applications. Systems that do not process financial transactions directly may still draw from accounting data. The accountant may be consulted to provide advice or to determine if the proposed system constitutes an internal control risk.

Third, accountants are involved in systems development as auditors. Accounting information systems must be auditable. Some computer audit techniques require special features that need to be designed into the system. The auditor/accountant has a stake in such systems and should be involved early in their design.

INFORMATION SYSTEMS ACQUISITION

Organizations usually acquire information systems in two ways: (1) they develop customized systems in-house through formal systems development activities and (2) they purchase commercial systems from software vendors. This section of the text discusses these two alternatives.

IN-HOUSE DEVELOPMENT

Many organizations require systems that are highly tuned to their unique operations. These firms design their own information systems through in-house systems development activities. In-house development requires maintaining a full-time systems staff of analysts and programmers who identify user information needs and satisfy their needs with custom systems.

PURCHASE COMMERCIAL SYSTEMS

A growing number of systems are purchased from software vendors. Faced with many competing packages, each with unique features and attributes, management must choose the system and the vendor that best serves the needs of the organization. Making the optimal choice requires that this be an informed decision.

TRENDS IN COMMERCIAL SOFTWARE

Four factors have stimulated the growth of the commercial software market: (1) the relatively low cost of general commercial software as compared to customized software; (2) the emergence of industry-specific vendors who target their software to the needs of particular types of businesses; (3) a growing demand from businesses that are too small to afford an in-house systems development staff; and (4) the trend toward downsizing of organizational units and the resulting move toward the distributed data processing environment, which has made the commercial software option more appealing to larger organizations. Indeed, organizations that maintain their own in-house systems development staff will often purchase commercial software when the need permits. Commercial software packages fall into three basic groups: turnkey systems, backbone systems, and vendor-supported systems.

TURNKEY SYSTEMS

Turnkey systems are completely finished and tested systems that are ready for implementation. These are often general-purpose systems or systems customized to a specific industry. Turnkey systems are usually sold only as compiled program modules, and users have limited ability to customize them to their specific needs. Some turnkey systems have software options that allow the user to customize input, output, and some processing through menu choices. Other turnkey system vendors will sell their customers the source code if program changes are desired. For a fee, the user or the vendor can then customize the system by reprogramming the original source code. Some examples of turnkey systems are described below.

GENERAL ACCOUNTING SYSTEMS.   **General accounting systems** are designed to serve a wide variety of user needs. By mass-producing a standard system, the vendor is able to reduce the unit cost of these systems to a fraction of in-house development costs. Powerful systems of this sort can be obtained for under $2,000.

To provide as much flexibility as possible, general accounting systems are designed in modules. This allows users to purchase the modules that meet their specific needs. Typical modules include accounts payable, accounts receivable, payroll processing, inventory control, general ledger, financial reporting, and fixed asset.

SPECIAL-PURPOSE SYSTEMS.   Some software vendors create **special-purpose systems** that target selected segments of the economy. For example, the medical field, the banking industry, and government agencies have unique accounting procedures, rules, and conventions that general-purpose accounting systems do not always accommodate. Software vendors have thus developed standardized systems to deal with industry-specific procedures.

OFFICE AUTOMATION SYSTEMS.   **Office automation systems** are computer systems that improve the productivity of office workers. Examples of office automation systems include word processing packages, database management systems, spreadsheet programs, and desktop publishing systems.

BACKBONE SYSTEMS

Backbone systems provide a basic system structure on which to build. Backbone systems come with all the primary processing modules programmed. The vendor designs and programs the user interface to suit the client's needs. Some systems such as SAP offer a vast array of modules for dealing with almost every conceivable business process. By selecting the appropriate modules, the customer can create a highly customized system. Customizing a commercial system, however, is expensive and time-consuming. A fully functional SAP system may take a year or more to install and cost anywhere from $10 to $80 million.

VENDOR-SUPPORTED SYSTEMS

Vendor-supported systems are hybrids of custom systems and commercial software. Under this approach, the vendor develops (and maintains) custom systems for its clients. The systems themselves are custom products, but the systems development service is commercially provided. This option is popular in the health care and legal services industries. Since the vendor serves as the organization's in-house systems development staff, the client organization must rely on the vendor to provide custom programming and on-site maintenance of systems. Much of each client's system may be developed from scratch, but by using an object-oriented approach, vendors can produce common modules that can be reused in other client systems. This approach helps to reduce development costs charged to the client firms.

ADVANTAGES OF COMMERCIAL SOFTWARE

IMPLEMENTATION TIME

Custom systems often take a long time to develop. Months or even years may pass before a custom system can be developed through in-house procedures. Unless the organization successfully anticipates future information needs and schedules application development accordingly, it may experience long periods of unsatisfied need. However, commercial software can be implemented almost immediately upon recognizing a need. The user does not have to wait.

COST

A single user must wholly absorb in-house development costs. However, since the cost of commercial software is spread across many users, the unit cost is reduced to a fraction of the cost of a system developed in-house.

RELIABILITY

Most reputable commercial software packages are thoroughly tested before their release to the consumer market. Any system errors not discovered during testing are likely to be uncovered by user organizations shortly after release and corrected. Although no system is certified as being free from errors, commercial software is less likely to have errors than an equivalent in-house system.

DISADVANTAGES OF COMMERCIAL SOFTWARE

INDEPENDENCE

Purchasing a vendor-supported system makes the firm dependent on the vendor for maintenance. The user runs the risk that the vendor will cease to support the system or even go out of business. This is perhaps the greatest disadvantage of vendor-supported systems.

THE NEED FOR CUSTOMIZED SYSTEMS

The prime advantage of in-house development is the ability to produce applications to exact specifications. This advantage also describes a disadvantage of commercial software. Sometimes, the user's needs are unique and complex, and commercially available software is either too general or too inflexible.

MAINTENANCE

Business information systems undergo frequent changes. Remember the iceberg effect of systems maintenance discussed in the last chapter. If the user's needs change, it may be difficult or even impossible to modify commercial software. On the other hand, in-house development provides users with proprietary applications that can be economically maintained.

THE SYSTEMS DEVELOPMENT LIFE CYCLE

Both the in-house development and the commercial package options have advantages and disadvantages. They are not, however, mutually exclusive propositions. A company may satisfy some of its information needs by purchasing commercial software and develop other systems in-house. Both approaches are enhanced by formal procedures that lend structure to the decision-making process. The systems development life cycle described next is generally associated with in-house development, but many of its phases, particularly those involving needs analysis and system specification, can be effectively employed even when the final system is purchased from an outside vendor.

The objectives and sequence of **systems development life cycle (SDLC)** activities are logical and generally accepted by experts in the systems community. However, the number and the names of specific stages within this process are matters of some disagreement. Different authorities have proposed SDLC models with as few as 4 and as many as 14 specific activities. From an auditing point of view, the number of actual stages is of no particular importance. We are concerned about the substance and the consistent application of this process, however it is defined. The SDLC in Figure 4–1 is a seven-stage process consisting of two major phases: new systems development and maintenance.

NEW SYSTEMS DEVELOPMENT

The first six stages of the SDLC describe the activities that all new systems should undergo. **New systems development** involves five conceptual steps that can apply to any problem-solving process: identify the problem, understand what needs to be done, consider alternative solutions, select the best solution, and, finally, implement the solution. Each stage in the SDLC produces a set of required documentation that together constitutes a body of audit evidence about the overall quality the SDLC. Each of the stages is briefly outlined below.

SYSTEMS PLANNING

The objective of **systems planning** is to link individual system projects or applications to the strategic objectives of the firm. In fact, the basis for the systems plan is the organization's business plan, which specifies where the firm plans to go and how it will get there. Figure 4–2 presents the relationship between these plans and the strategic objectives of the firm. There must be congruence between the individual projects and the

FIGURE 4-1   Systems Development Life Cycle

Required Documentation

FIGURE 4–2

Relationship
between Systems
Plans and
Organizational
Objectives

business plan, or the firm may fail to meet its objectives. Effective systems planning provides this goal congruence.

WHO SHOULD DO SYSTEMS PLANNING?

Most firms that take systems planning seriously establish a systems steering committee to provide guidance and review the status of system projects. The composition of the **steering committee** may include the chief executive officer, the chief financial officer, the chief information officer, senior management from user areas, the internal auditor, and senior management from computer services. External parties, such as management consultants and the firm's external auditors, may also supplement the committee. Typical responsibilities for a steering committee include:

1. Resolving conflicts that arise from new systems.
2. Reviewing projects and assigning priorities.
3. Budgeting funds for systems development.
4. Reviewing the status of individual projects under development.
5. Determining at various checkpoints throughout the SDLC whether to continue with the project or terminate it.

Systems planning occurs at two levels: strategic systems planning and project planning.

STRATEGIC SYSTEMS PLANNING

Strategic systems planning involves the allocation of systems resources at the macro level. It usually deals with a time frame of three to five years. This process is very similar to budgeting resources for other strategic activities, such as product development, plant expansions, market research, and manufacturing technology.

Technically, strategic systems planning is not part of the SDLC because the SDLC pertains to specific applications. The strategic systems plan is concerned with the allocation of such systems resources as employees (the number of systems professionals to be hired), hardware (the number of workstations, minicomputers, and mainframes to be purchased), software (the funds to be allocated to new systems projects and for systems maintenance), and telecommunications (the funds allocated to networking and EDI). It is important that the strategic plan avoid excessive detail. The plan must allow systems specialists to make informed decisions by considering such relevant factors as price, performance measures, size, security, and control.

WHY PERFORM STRATEGIC SYSTEMS PLANNING?   Perhaps no aspect of a firm's business activities is as volatile and unpredictable as information systems planning. Who can look five years into the future and accurately predict the state of systems technology? Because of this volatility, any long-term plans a firm makes are likely to change. How, therefore, can a firm do strategic systems planning? Why should it?

There are three justifications for strategic systems planning:

1. A plan that changes constantly is better than no plan at all. Strategic planning charts the path the firm will follow to reach its information systems goal. Even if it means making many midcourse adjustments, planning is superior to simply wandering in the wilderness.
2. Strategic planning reduces the crisis component in systems development. A formal plan is a model for identifying and prioritizing user needs. It allows management to consider the future needs, recognize problems in their early stages, and even anticipate needs before the symptoms of underlying problems emerge. In the absence of a plan, the trigger that stimulates systems development is the recognition of a problem. Often, problems reach a crisis level before they receive attention, which adversely affects the quality of the solution.
3. Strategic systems planning provides authorization control for the SDLC. The strategic systems plan lays out authorization rules to ensure that decisions to develop specific systems are congruent with the objectives of the firm. Investing in the wrong systems can be just as damaging to a firm as investing in the wrong plant and equipment.

PROJECT PLANNING

The purpose of **project planning** is to allocate resources to individual applications within the framework of the strategic plan. This involves identifying areas of user needs, preparing proposals, evaluating each proposal's feasibility and contribution to the business plan, prioritizing individual projects, and scheduling the work to be done. The product of this phase consists of two formal documents: the project proposal and the project schedule.

The **project proposal** provides management with a basis for deciding whether or not to proceed with the project. The formal proposal serves two purposes. First, it summarizes the findings of the study conducted to this point into a general recommendation for a new or modified system. This enables management to evaluate the perceived problem along with the proposed system as a feasible solution. Second, the proposal outlines the linkage between the objectives of the proposed system and the business objectives of the firm. It shows that the proposed new system complements to the strategic direction of the firm.

The **project schedule** represents management's commitment to the project. The project schedule is a budget of the time and costs for all the phases of the SDLC. A project team selected from systems professionals, end users, and other specialists such as accountants and internal auditors will complete these phases. The composition of the team and the competence and dedication of its members are critical to the success of the new system.

THE AUDITOR'S ROLE IN SYSTEMS PLANNING

Auditors routinely examine the systems planning phase of the SDLC. History has shown that careful systems planning is a cost-effective control technique in the systems development process. Planning greatly reduces the risk of producing unneeded, unwanted, inefficient, and ineffective systems. Both internal and external auditors are interested in ensuring that adequate systems planning takes place.

SYSTEMS ANALYSIS

We now move on to the second phase in the SDLC. **Systems analysis** is actually a two-step process involving first a survey of the current system and then an analysis of the user's needs. A business problem must be fully understood by the systems analyst before he or she can formulate a solution. An incomplete or defective analysis will lead to an incomplete or defective solution. Therefore, systems analysis is the foundation for the rest of the SDLC. The deliverable from this phase is a formal systems analysis report, which presents the findings of the analysis and recommendations for the new system.

THE SURVEY STEP

Most systems are not developed from scratch. Usually, some form of information system and related procedures are currently in place. The analyst often begins the analysis by determining what elements, if any, of the current system should be preserved as part of the new system. This involves a rather detailed **system survey**. Facts pertaining to preliminary questions about the system are gathered and analyzed. As the analyst obtains a greater depth of understanding of the problem, he or she develops more specific questions for which more facts must be gathered. This process may go on through several iterations. When all the relevant facts have been gathered and analyzed, the analyst arrives at an assessment of the current system. Surveying the current system has both disadvantages and advantages.

DISADVANTAGES OF SURVEYING THE CURRENT SYSTEM.   Perhaps the most compelling argument against a current system survey centers on a phenomenon known as the "current physical tar pit."[1] This is the tendency on the part of the analyst to be "sucked in" and then "bogged down" by the task of surveying the current dinosaur system.

Some argue that current system surveys stifle new ideas. By studying and modeling the old system, the analyst may develop a constrained notion about how the new system should function. The result is an improved old system rather than a radically new approach.

ADVANTAGES OF SURVEYING THE CURRENT SYSTEM.   There are three advantages to studying the current system. First, it is a way to identify what aspects of the old system should be kept. Some elements of the system may be functionally sound and can provide the foundation for the new system. By fully understanding the current system, the analyst can identify those aspects worth preserving or modifying for use in the new system.

Second, when the new system is implemented, the users must go through a conversion process whereby they formally break away from the old system and move to the new one. The analyst must determine what tasks, procedures, and data will be phased out with the old system and which will continue. To specify these conversion procedures, the analyst must know not only what is to be done by the new system but

---

1.   W. Keuffel, "House of Structure," *Unit Review* 9 (February, 1991): 36.

also what was done by the old one. This requires a thorough understanding of the current system.

Finally, by surveying the current system, the analyst may determine conclusively the cause of the reported problem symptoms. Perhaps the root problem is not the information system at all; it may be a management or employee problem that can be resolved without redesigning the information system. We may not be able to identify the root cause of the problem if we discard the existing system without any investigation into the symptoms.

GATHERING FACTS.   The survey of the current system is essentially a fact-gathering activity. The facts gathered by the analyst are pieces of data that describe key features, situations, and relationships of the system. System facts fall into the following broad classes.

Data Sources.   These include external entities, such as customers or vendors, as well as internal sources from other departments.

Users.   These include both managers and operations users.

Data Stores.   Data stores are the files, databases, accounts, and source documents used in the system.

Processes.   Processing tasks are manual or computer operations that represent a decision or an action triggered by information.

Data Flows.   Data flows are represented by the movement of documents and reports between data sources, data stores, processing tasks, and users.

Controls.   These include both accounting and operational controls and may be manual procedures or computer controls.

Transaction Volumes.   The analyst must obtain a measure of the transaction volumes for a specified period of time. Many systems are replaced because they have reached their capacity. Understanding the characteristics of a systems transaction volume and its rate of growth are important elements in assessing capacity requirements for the new system.

Error Rates.   Transaction errors are closely related to transaction volume. As a system reaches capacity, error rates increase to an intolerable level. Although no system is perfect, the analyst must determine the acceptable error tolerances for the new system.

Resource Costs.   The resources used by the current system include the costs of labor, computer time, materials (such as invoices), and direct overhead. Any resource costs that disappear when the current system is eliminated are called *escapable costs*. Later, when we perform a cost-benefit analysis, escapable costs will be treated as benefits of the new system.

Bottlenecks and Redundant Operations.   The analyst should note points where data flows come together to form a bottleneck. At peak-load periods, these can result in delays and promote processing errors. Likewise, delays may be caused by redundant operations, such as unnecessary approvals or sign-offs. By identifying these problem areas during the survey phase, the analyst can avoid making the same mistakes in the design of the new system.

FACT-GATHERING TECHNIQUES. Systems analysts employ several techniques to gather the previously cited facts. Commonly used techniques include observation, task participation, personal interviews, and reviewing key documents.

Observation. Observation involves passively watching the physical procedures of the system. This allows the analyst to determine what gets done, who performs the task, when they do it, how they do it, why they do it, and how long it takes.

Task Participation. Participation is an extension of observation, whereby the analyst takes an active role in performing the user's work. This allows the analyst to experience first-hand the problems involved in the operation of the current system. For example, the analyst may work on the sales desk taking orders from customers and preparing sales orders. The analyst can determine that documents are improperly designed, that insufficient time exists to perform the required procedures, or that peak-load problems cause bottlenecks and processing errors. With hands-on experience, the analyst can often envision better ways to perform the task.

Personal Interviews. Interviewing is a method of extracting facts about the current system and user perceptions about the requirements for the new system. The instruments used to gather these facts may be open-ended questions or formal questionnaires.

Open-ended questions allow users to elaborate on the problem as they see it and offer suggestions and recommendations. Answers to these questions tend to be difficult to analyze, but they give the analyst a feel for the scope of the problem. The analyst in this type of interview must be a good listener and able to focus on the important facts. Examples of open-ended questions are: "What do you think is the main problem with our sales order system?" and "How could the system be improved?"

Questionnaires are used to ask more specific, detailed questions and to restrict the user's responses. This is a good technique for gathering objective facts about the nature of specific procedures, volumes of transactions processed, sources of data, users of reports, and control issues.

Reviewing Key Documents. The organization's documents are another source of facts about the system being surveyed. Examples of these include the following:

- Organizational charts
- Job descriptions
- Accounting records
- Charts of accounts
- Policy statements
- Descriptions of procedures
- Financial statements
- Performance reports
- System flowcharts
- Source documents
- Transaction listings
- Budgets
- Forecasts
- Mission statements

Following the fact-gathering phase, the analyst formally documents his or her impressions and understanding about the system. This will take the form of notes, system flowcharts, and data flow diagrams.

THE ANALYSIS STEP

Systems analysis is an intellectual process that is commingled with fact gathering. The analyst is simultaneously analyzing as he or she gathers facts. The mere recognition of a problem presumes some understanding of the norm or desired state. It is therefore difficult to identify where the survey ends and the analysis begins.

SYSTEMS ANALYSIS REPORT.   The event that marks the conclusion of the systems analysis phase is the preparation of a formal **systems analysis report**. This report presents to management or the steering committee the survey findings, the problems identified with the current system, the user's needs, and the requirements of the new system. Figure 4–3 contains a possible format for this report. The primary purpose for conducting a systems analysis is to identify user needs and specify requirements for the new system. The report should set out in detail what the system must do rather than how to do it. The requirements statement within the report establishes an understanding between systems professionals, management, users, and other stakeholders. This document constitutes a formal contract that specifies the objectives and goals of the system. The systems analysis report should establish in clear terms the data sources, users, data files, general processes, data flows, controls, and transaction volume capacity.

FIGURE 4–3

Outline of
Main Topics
in a Systems
Analysis Report

Systems Analysis Report

  I. Reasons for System Analysis
    A. Reasons specified in the system project proposal
    B. Changes in reasons since analysis began
    C. Additional reasons

 II. Scope of Study
    A. Scope as specified by the project proposal
    B. Changes in scope

III. Problems Identified with Current System
    A. Techniques used for gathering facts
    B. Problems encountered in the fact-gathering process
    C. Analysis of facts

IV. Statement of User Requirements
    A. Specific user needs in key areas, such as:
       1. Output requirements
       2. Transaction volumes
       3. Response time
    B. Nontechnical terms for a broad-based audience, including:
       1. End users
       2. User management
       3. Systems management
       4. Steering committee

 V. Resource Implications
    A. Preliminary assessment of economic effect
    B. Is economic feasibility as stated in proposal reasonable?

VI. Recommendations
    A. Should the project continue?
    B. Has analysis changed feasibility, strategic impact,
       or priority of the project?

The systems analysis report does not specify the detailed design of the proposed system. For example, it does not specify processing methods, storage media, record structures, and other details needed to design the physical system. Rather, the report remains at the objectives level to avoid placing artificial constraints on the conceptual design phase. Several possible designs may serve the user's needs, and the development process must be free to explore all of these.

THE AUDITOR'S ROLE IN SYSTEMS ANALYSIS

The firm's auditors (both external and internal) are stakeholders in the proposed system. In Chapter 7, we will see how certain CAATTs (such as the embedded audit module and the integrated test facility) must be designed into the system during the SDLC. Often, advanced audit features cannot be easily added to existing systems. Therefore, the accountant/auditor should be involved in the needs analysis of the proposed system to determine if it is a good candidate for advanced audit features and, if so, which features are best suited for the system.

CONCEPTUAL SYSTEMS DESIGN

The purpose of the **conceptual design** phase is to produce several alternative conceptual systems that satisfy the system requirements identified during systems analysis. By presenting users with a number of plausible alternatives, the systems professional avoids imposing preconceived constraints on the new system. The user will evaluate these conceptual models and settle on the alternatives that appear most plausible and appealing. These alternative designs then go to the systems selection phase of SDLC, where their respective costs and benefits are compared and a single optimum design is chosen.

By keeping systems design conceptual throughout these phases of the SDLC, we minimize the investment of resources in alternative designs that, ultimately, will be rejected. The conceptual system that emerges proceeds to the final phases of the SDLC, where it is designed in detail and implemented.

This section describes two approaches to conceptual systems design: the structured approach and the object-oriented approach. The structured approach develops each new system from scratch from the top down. Object-oriented design builds systems from the bottom up through the assembly of reusable modules rather than creating each system from scratch. This approach is still an emerging concept in AIS, but it promises to be a dominant force in the future.

THE STRUCTURED DESIGN APPROACH

The **structured design** approach is a disciplined way of designing systems from the top down. It consists of starting with the "big picture" of the proposed system that is gradually decomposed into more and more detail until it is fully understood. Under this approach, the business process under design is usually documented by data flow and structure diagrams. Figure 4–4 shows the use of these techniques to depict the top-down decomposition of a hypothetical business process.

We can see from these diagrams how the systems designer follows a top-down approach. The designer starts with an abstract description of the system and, through successive steps, redefines this view to produce a more detailed description. In our example, Process 2.0 in the context diagram is decomposed into an intermediate level DFD. Process 2.3 in the intermediate DFD is further decomposed into an elementary DFD. This decomposition could involve several levels to obtain sufficient details. Let's

FIGURE 4-4   Top-Down Decomposition of the Structured Design Approach

assume that three levels are sufficient in this case. The final step transforms Process 2.3.3 into a structure diagram that defines the program modules that will constitute the process.

HOW MUCH DESIGN DETAIL IS NEEDED?   The conceptual design phase should highlight the differences between critical features of competing systems rather than their similarities. Therefore, system designs at this point should be general. The designs should identify all the inputs, outputs, processes, and special features necessary to distinguish one alternative from another. Figure 4–5 presents two alternative conceptual designs for a purchasing system. These designs lack the details needed to implement the system. For instance, they do not include such necessary components as:

- Database record structures.
- Processing details.
- Specific control techniques.
- Formats for input screens and source documents.
- Output report formats.

The designs do, however, possess sufficient detail to demonstrate how the two systems are conceptually different in their functions. To illustrate, let's examine the general features of each system.

Option A is a traditional batch purchasing system. The initial input for the process is the purchase requisition from inventory control. When inventories reach their predetermined reorder points, new inventories are ordered according to their economic order quantity. Transmittal of purchase orders to suppliers takes place once a day via the U.S. mail.

In contrast, Option B employs EDI technology. The trigger to this system is a purchase requisition from production planning. The purchases system determines the quantity and the vendor and then transmits the order on-line via EDI software to the vendor.

Both alternatives have pros and cons. A benefit of Option A is its simplicity of design, ease of implementation, and lower demand for systems resources than Option B. A negative aspect of Option A is that it requires the firm to carry inventories. On the other hand, Option B may allow the firm to reduce or even eliminate inventories. This benefit comes at the cost of more expensive and sophisticated system resources. It is premature, at this point, to attempt to evaluate the relative merits of these alternatives. This is done formally in the next phase in the SDLC. At this point, system designers are concerned only with identifying plausible system designs.

THE OBJECT-ORIENTED APPROACH

The **object-oriented design** approach is to build information systems from reusable standard components or **objects**. This approach may be equated to the process of building an automobile. Car manufacturers do not create each new model from scratch. New models are actually built from standard components that also go into other models. For example, each model of car produced by a particular manufacturer may use the same type of engine, gearbox, alternator, rear axle, radio, and so on. Some of the car's components will be industry-standard products that are used by other manufacturers. Such things as wheels, tires, spark plugs, and headlights fall into this category. In fact, it may be that the only component actually created from scratch for a new car model is the body.

The automobile industry operates in this fashion to stay competitive. By using standard components, car manufacturers minimize production and maintenance costs. At the same time, they can remain responsive to consumer demands for new products and preserve manufacturing flexibility by mixing and matching components according to the customer's specification.

The concept of reusability is central to the object-oriented approach to systems design. Once created, standard modules can be used in other systems with similar needs. Ideally, the organization's systems professionals will create a library (inventory) of modules that can be used by other system designers within the firm. The benefits of

FIGURE 4-5   Alternative Conceptual Designs for a Purchasing System this approach include reduced time and cost for development, maintenance, and testing and improved user support and flexibility in the development process.

THE AUDITOR'S ROLE IN CONCEPTUAL SYSTEMS DESIGN

The auditor is a stakeholder in all financial systems and, thus, has an interest in the conceptual design stage of the system. The auditability of a system depends in part on its design characteristics. Some computer auditing techniques require systems to be designed with special audit features that are integral to the system. These audit features must be specified at the conceptual design stage.

SYSTEM EVALUATION AND SELECTION

The next phase in the SDLC is the procedure for selecting the one system from the set of alternative conceptual designs that will go to the detailed design phase. The **systems evaluation and selection** phase is an optimization process that seeks to identify the best system. This decision represents a critical juncture in the SDLC. At this point, there is a great deal of uncertainty about the system, and a poor decision here can be disastrous. The purpose of a formal evaluation and selection procedure is to structure this decision-making process and thereby reduce both uncertainty and the risk of making a poor decision. The evaluation and selection process involves two steps:

1. Perform a detailed feasibility study.
2. Perform a cost-benefit analysis.

PERFORM A DETAILED FEASIBILITY STUDY

The following discussion outlines four aspects of project feasibility that need to be considered. Each competing project will be assessed in the same manner. The projects deemed feasible are then compared on a cost-benefit basis. The selected system will then advance to the detailed design phase.

Technical feasibility is concerned with whether the system can be developed under existing technology or if new technology is needed. As a general proposition, the technology in the marketplace is far ahead of most firms' ability to apply it. Therefore, from an availability viewpoint, technical feasibility is not usually an issue. For most firms, the real issue is their desire and ability to apply available technology. Given that technology is the physical basis for most of the system's design features, this aspect bears heavily on the overall feasibility of the competing system.

Legal feasibility identifies any conflicts between the conceptual system and the company's ability to discharge its legal responsibilities. In previous chapters, we have studied the need to comply with the control requirement laid down in the Foreign Corrupt Practices Act of 1977 and SAS 78. In addition, many regulations and statutes deal with invasion of privacy and the confidentiality of stored information. The decision-maker must be certain the proposed system falls inside all legal boundaries.

Operational feasibility shows the degree of compatibility between the firm's existing procedures and personnel skills and the operational requirements of the new system. Implementing the new system may require adopting new procedures and retraining operations personnel. The question that must be answered is, can adequate procedural changes be made, sufficient personnel retrained, and new skills obtained to make the system operationally feasible?

Schedule feasibility relates to the firm's ability to implement the project within an acceptable time. This feasibility factor impacts both the scope of the project and whether it will be developed in-house or purchased from a software vendor. If the project, as conceptually envisioned, cannot be produced internally by the target date, then its design, its acquisition method, or the target date must be changed.

PERFORM A COST-BENEFIT ANALYSIS

Cost-benefit analysis helps management determine whether (and by how much) the benefits received from a proposed system will outweigh its costs. This technique is frequently used for estimating the expected financial value of business investments. However, in this case, the investment is an information system, and the costs and benefits are more difficult to identify and quantify than those of traditional capital projects. Although imperfect for this setting, cost-benefit analysis is employed because of its simplicity and the absence of a clearly better alternative. In spite of its limitations, cost-benefit analysis, combined with feasibility factors, is a useful tool for comparing competing systems designs.

There are three steps in the application of cost-benefit analysis: identify costs, identify benefits, and compare costs and benefits. We discuss each of these steps below.

IDENTIFY COSTS.   One method of identifying costs is to divide them into two categories: one-time costs and recurring costs. *One-time costs* include the initial investment to develop and implement the system. *Recurring costs* include operating and maintenance costs that recur over the life of the system. Table 4–1 shows a breakdown of typical one-time and recurring costs.

One-Time Costs
Hardware Acquisition.   This includes the cost of mainframe, minicomputers, microcomputers, and peripheral equipment, such as tape drives and disk packs. The cost figures for items can be obtained from the vendor.

Site Preparation.   This involves such frequently overlooked costs as building modifications (for example, adding air conditioning or making structural changes), equipment installation (which may include the use of heavy equipment), and freight charges. Estimates of these costs can be obtained from the vendor and the subcontractors who do the installation.

TABLE 4–1

One-Time and
Recurring Costs

ONE-TIME AND RECURRING COSTS
One-Time Costs
Hardware acquisition
Site preparation
Software acquisition
Systems design
Programming and testing
Data conversion from old system to new system
Training personnel
Recurring Costs
Hardware maintenance
Software maintenance contracts
Insurance
Supplies
Personnel

Software Acquisition.   These costs apply to all software purchased for the proposed system, including operating system software (if not bundled with the hardware), network control software, and commercial applications (such as accounting packages). Estimates of these costs can be obtained from vendors.

Systems Design.   These are the costs incurred by systems professionals performing the planning, analysis, and design functions. Technically, such costs incurred up to this point are "sunk" and irrelevant to the decision. The analyst should estimate only the costs needed to complete the detailed design.

Programming and Testing.   Programming costs are based on estimates of the personnel-hours required to write new programs and modify existing programs for the proposed system. System testing costs involve bringing together all the individual program modules for testing as an entire system. This must be a rigorous exercise if it is to be meaningful. The planning, testing, and analysis of the results may demand many days of involvement from systems professionals, users, and other stakeholders of the system. The experience of the firm in the past is the best basis for estimating these costs.

Data Conversion.   These costs arise in the transfer of data from one storage medium to another. For example, the accounting records of a manual system must be converted to magnetic form when the system becomes computer-based. This can represent a significant task. The basis for estimating conversion costs is the number and size of the files to be converted.

Training.   These costs involve educating users to operate the new system. In-house personnel could do this in an extensive training program provided by an outside organization at a remote site or through on-the-job training. The cost of formal training can be easily obtained. The cost of an in-house training program includes instruction time, classroom facilities, and lost productivity.

Recurring Costs

Hardware Maintenance.   This involves the cost of upgrading the computer (increasing the memory), as well as preventive maintenance and repairs to the computer and peripheral equipment. The organization may enter into a maintenance contract with the vendor to minimize and budget these costs. Estimates for these costs can be obtained from vendors and existing contracts.

Software Maintenance.   These costs include upgrading and debugging operating systems, purchased applications, and in-house developed applications. Maintenance contracts with software vendors can be used to specify these costs fairly accurately. Estimates of in-house maintenance can be derived from historical data.

Insurance.   This covers such hazards and disasters as fire, hardware failure, vandalism, and destruction by disgruntled employees.

Supplies.   These costs are incurred through routine consumption of such items as printer ribbons and paper, magnetic disks, magnetic tapes, and general office supplies.

Personnel Costs.   These are the salaries of individuals who are part of the information system. Some employee costs are direct and easily identifiable, such as the salaries of operations personnel exclusively employed as part of the system under analysis. Some personnel involvement (such as the database administrator and computer room personnel) is common to many systems. Such personnel costs must be allocated on the basis of expected incremental involvement with the system.

IDENTIFY BENEFITS.   The next step in the cost-benefit analysis is to identify the benefits of the system. These may be both tangible and intangible.

Tangible Benefits.   Tangible benefits are benefits that can be measured and expressed in financial terms. Table 4–2 lists several types of tangible benefits.

Tangible benefits fall into two categories: those that increase revenue and those that reduce costs. For example, assume a proposed EDI system will allow the organization to reduce inventories and at the same time improve customer service by reducing stockouts. The reduction of inventories is a cost-reducing benefit. The proposed system will use fewer resources (inventories) than the current system. The value of this benefit is the dollar amount of the carrying costs saved by the annual reduction in inventory. The estimated increase in sales due to better customer service is a revenue-increasing benefit.

When measuring cost savings, it is important to include only escapable costs in the analysis. Escapable costs are directly related to the system, and they cease to exist when the system ceases to exist. Some costs that appear to be escapable to the user are not truly escapable and, if included, can lead to a flawed analysis. For example, data processing centers often "charge back" their operating costs to their user constituency through cost allocations. The charge-back rate they use for this includes both fixed costs (allocated to users) and direct costs created by the activities of individual users. Figure 4–6 illustrates this technique.

Assume the management in User Area B proposes to acquire a computer system and perform its own data processing locally. One benefit of the proposal is the cost savings derived by escaping the charge-back from the current data processing center. Although the user may see this as a $400,000 annual charge, only the direct cost portion ($50,000) is escapable by the organization as a whole. Should the proposal be approved, the remaining $350,000 of the charge-back does not go away. The remaining users of the current system must now absorb this cost.

Intangible Benefits.   Table 4–3 lists some common categories of **intangible benefits**. Although intangible benefits are often of overriding importance in information system decisions, they cannot be easily measured and quantified. For example, assume that a proposed point-of-sale system for a department store will reduce the average time to process a customer sales transaction from 11 minutes to 3 minutes. The time saved can be quantified and produces a tangible benefit in the form of an operating cost saving.

TABLE 4–2

Tangible Benefits

TANGIBLE BENEFITS
Increased Revenues
Increased sales within existing markets
Expansion into other markets
Cost Reduction
Labor reduction
Operating cost reduction (such as supplies and overhead)
Reduced inventories
Less expensive equipment
Reduced equipment maintenance

FIGURE 4-6

DP Center Cost
Charge-Back to
User Areas

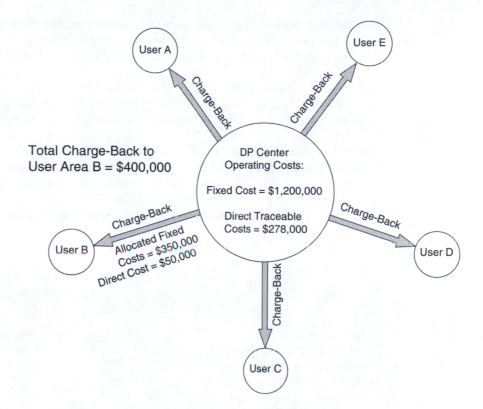

Total Charge-Back to
User Area B = $400,000

DP Center
Operating Costs:

Fixed Cost = $1,200,000

Direct Traceable
Costs = $278,000

Charge-Back

Allocated Fixed
Costs = $350,000
Direct Cost = $50,000

User A

User E

User B

User D

User C

An intangible benefit is improved customer satisfaction; no one likes to stand in long lines to pay for purchases. But what is the true value of this intangible benefit to the organization? Increased customer satisfaction may translate into increased sales. More customers will buy at the store—and may be willing to pay slightly more to avoid long checkout lines. But how do we quantify this translation? Assigning a value is often highly subjective.

Systems professionals draw upon many sources in attempting to quantify intangible benefits and manipulate them into financial terms. Some common techniques include customer (and employee) opinion surveys, statistical analysis, expected value techniques, and simulation models. Though systems professionals may succeed in quantifying some of these intangible benefits, more often they must be content to simply state the benefits as precisely as good judgment permits.

TABLE 4-3

Intangible
Benefits

INTANGIBLE BENEFITS
Increased customer satisfaction
Improved employee satisfaction
More current information
Improved decision making
Faster response to competitor actions
More efficient operations
Better internal and external communications
Improved planning
Operational flexibility
Improved control environment

Because they defy precise measurement, intangible benefits are sometimes exploited for political reasons. By overstating or understating these benefits, a system may be pushed forward by its proponents or killed by its opponents.

COMPARE COSTS AND BENEFITS.   The last step in the cost-benefit analysis is to compare the costs and benefits identified in the first two steps. The two most common methods used for evaluating information systems are net present value and payback.

The Net Present Value Method.   Under the **net present value method**, the present value of the costs is deducted from the present value of the benefits over the life of the system. Projects with a positive net present value are economically feasible. When comparing competing projects, the optimal choice is the project with the greatest net present value. Figure 4–7 illustrates the net present value method by comparing two competing designs.

The example is based on the following data:

	Design A	Design B
Project completion time	1 year	1 year
Expected useful life of system	5 years	5 years
One-time costs (thousands)	$300	$140
Recurring costs (thousands)		
incurred in beginning of Years 1 through 5	$45	$55
Annual tangible benefits (thousands)		
incurred in end of Years 1 through 5	$170	$135

If costs and tangible benefits alone were being considered, then Design A would be selected over Design B. However, the value of intangible benefits, along with the design feasibility scores, must also be factored into the final analysis.

The Payback Method.   The **payback method** is a variation of break-even analysis. The break-even point is reached when total costs equal total benefits. Figure 4–8(a) and (b) illustrates this approach using the data from the previous example.

FIGURE 4–7

Net Present
Value Method
of Cost-Benefit
Analysis

Year Time	Beginning End Year Outflows	Inflows	Beginning Year Time	End Year Outflows	Inflows
0	$(3,000,000)		0	$(140,000)	
1	(45,000)	170,000	1	(55,000)	135,000
2	(45,000)	170,000	2	(55,000)	135,000
3	(45,000)	170,000	3	(55,000)	135,000
4	(45,000)	170,000	4	(55,000)	135,000
5	(45,000)	170,000	5	(55,000)	135,000
PV Out	$(479,672)		PV Out	$(369,599)	
PV In	$628,428		PV In	$499,089	
NPV	$148,810		NPV	$139,490	
Interest Rate	8.00%				

FIGURE 4–8(a)

Discounted
Payback
Method of
Cash Flow
Analysis

Payback Method of Cash Flow Analysis

FIGURE 4–8(b)

Discounted
Payback
Method of
Cost-Benefit
Analysis

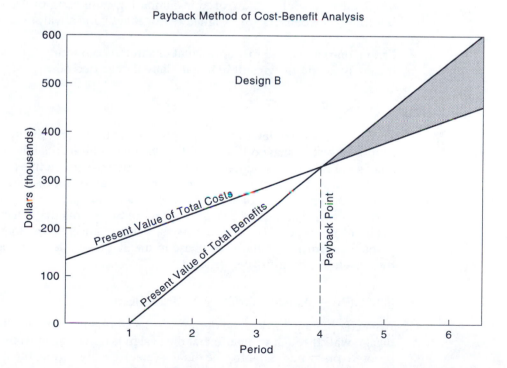

Payback Method of Cost-Benefit Analysis

The total-cost curve consists of the one-time costs plus the present value of the recurring costs over the life of the project. The total benefits curve is the present value of the tangible benefits. The intersection of these lines represents the number of years into the future when the project breaks even, or pays for itself. The shaded area between the benefit curve and the total-cost curve represents the present value of future profits earned by the system.

In choosing an information system, payback speed is often a decisive factor. With brief product life cycles and rapid advances in technology, the effective lives of information systems tend to be short. Using this criterion, Design B, with a payback period of four years, would be selected over Design A, whose payback will take four and one-half years. The length of the payback period often takes precedence over other considerations represented by intangible benefits.

PREPARE SYSTEMS SELECTION REPORT

The deliverable product of the systems selection process is the **systems selection report**. This formal document consists of a revised feasibility study, a cost-benefit analysis, and a list and explanation of intangible benefits for each alternative design. On the basis of this report, the steering committee will select a single system that will go forward to the next phase of the SDLC—detailed design.

THE AUDITOR'S ROLE IN EVALUATION AND SELECTION

The primary concern for auditors is that the economic feasibility of the proposed system is measured as accurately as possible. Specifically, the auditor should ensure that:

1. Only escapable costs are used in calculations of cost savings benefits.
2. Reasonable interest rates are used in measuring present values of cash flows.
3. One-time and recurring costs are completely and accurately reported.
4. Realistic useful lives are used in comparing competing projects.
5. Intangible benefits are assigned reasonable financial values.

Errors, omissions, and misrepresentations in the accounting for such items can distort the analysis and may result in a materially flawed decision.

DETAILED DESIGN

The purpose of the **detailed design** phase is to produce a detailed description of the proposed system that both satisfies the system requirements identified during systems analysis and is in accordance with the conceptual design. In this phase, all system components (user views, database tables, processes, and controls) are meticulously specified. At the end of this phase, these components are presented formally in a detailed design report. This report constitutes a set of blueprints that specify input screen formats, output report layouts, database structures, and process logic. These completed plans then proceed to the final phase in the SDLC—systems implementation—where the system is physically constructed.

PERFORM A SYSTEM DESIGN WALKTHROUGH

After completing the detailed design, the development team usually performs a system design **walkthrough** to ensure that the design is free from conceptual errors that could become programmed into the final system. Many firms have formal, structured walkthroughs conducted by a **quality assurance group**. This is an independent group of programmers, analysts, users, and internal auditors. The job of this group is to simulate the operation of the system to uncover errors, omissions, and ambiguities in the design. Most system errors emanate from poor designs rather than programming mistakes. Detecting and correcting errors in the design phase thus reduces costly reprogramming later.

REVIEW SYSTEM DOCUMENTATION

The **detailed design report** documents and describes the system to this point. This report includes:

- Designs of all screen outputs, reports, and operational documents.
- Entity relationship (ER) diagrams describing the data relations in the system.
- Third normal form designs for database tables, specifying all data elements.
- An updated data dictionary describing each data element in the database.
- Designs for all screen inputs and source documents for the system.
- Context diagrams for the overall system.
- Low-level data flow diagrams of specific system processes.
- Structure diagrams for the program modules in the system, including a pseudocode description of each module.

The quality control group scrutinizes these documents, and any errors detected are recorded in a walkthrough report. Depending on the extent of the system errors, the quality assurance group will make a recommendation. The system design will be either accepted without modification, accepted subject to modification of minor errors, or rejected because of material errors.

At this point, a decision is made either to return the system for additional design or to proceed to the next phase—systems implementation. Assuming the design goes forward, the documents in the design report constitute the blueprints that guide programmers and system designers in constructing the physical system.

SYSTEM IMPLEMENTATION

In the **system implementation** stage of the systems development process, database structures are created and populated with data, applications are coded and tested, equipment is purchased and installed, employees are trained, the system is documented, and the new system is installed. The implementation process engages the efforts of designers, programmers, database administrators, users, and accountants. The activities in this phase entail extensive costs and will often consume more personnel-hours than all other phases of the SDLC combined.

POST-IMPLEMENTATION REVIEW

One of the most important steps in the implementation stage actually takes place some months later in a *post-implementation review*. The review is conducted by an independent team to measure the success of the system and of the process after the dust has settled. Although systems professionals strive to produce systems that are on budget, on time, and meet user needs, this does not always happen. The post-implementation review of the newly installed system can provide insight into ways to improve the process for future systems. The following discussion provides the auditor with valuable evidence regarding the adequacy of the SDLC in general and the risks associated with a particular system.

SYSTEMS DESIGN ADEQUACY.   The physical features of the system should be reviewed to see if they meet user needs. The reviewer should seek answers to the following types of questions:

- Does the output from the system possess such characteristics of information as relevance, timeliness, completeness, accuracy, and so on?
- Is the output in the format most useful and desired by the user (such as tables, graphs, electronic, hard copy, and so on)?
- Are the databases accurate, complete, and accessible?
- Were data lost, corrupted, or duplicated by the conversion process?
- Are input forms and screens properly designed and meeting user needs?
- Are the users using the system properly?
- Does the processing appear to be correct?
- Can all program modules be accessed and executed properly, or does the user ever get stuck in a loop?
- Is user documentation accurate, complete, and easy to follow?
- Does the system provide the user adequate help and tutorials?

ACCURACY OF TIME, COST, AND BENEFIT ESTIMATES.   The task of estimating time, costs, and benefits for a proposed system is complicated by uncertainty. This is particularly true for large projects involving many activities and long timeframes. The more variables in the process, the greater the likelihood for material error in the estimates. History is often the best teacher for decisions of this sort. Therefore, a review of actual performance compared to budgeted amounts provides critical input for future budgeting decisions. From such information, we can learn where mistakes were made and how to avoid them next time. The following questions provide some insight:

- What were the areas of significant departures from budget?
- Were departures from budget controllable (internal) in the short run or noncontrollable (for example, supplier problems)?
- Were estimates of the number of lines of program code accurate?
- Was the degree of rework due to design and coding errors acceptable?
- Were actual costs in line with budgeted costs?
- Are users receiving the expected benefits from the system?
- Do the benefits seem to have been fairly valued?

DOCUMENTING THE SYSTEM

The system's **documentation** provides the auditor with essential information about how the system works. The documentation requirements of three groups—systems designers and programmers, computer operators, and end users—are of particular importance.

DESIGNER AND PROGRAMMER DOCUMENTATION.   Systems designers and programmers need documentation to debug errors and perform maintenance on the system. This group is involved with the system on a highly technical level, which requires both general and detailed information. Some of this is provided through data flow diagrams (DFDs), entity relation (ER) diagrams, and structure diagrams. In addition, system flowcharts, program flowcharts, and program code listings are important forms of documentation. The *system flowchart* shows the relationship of input files, programs, and output files. However, it does not reveal the logic of individual programs that constitute the system. The *program flowchart* provides a detailed description of the sequential and logical operation of the program. Each program in the system's flowchart is represented by a separate program flowchart. From these, the programmer can visually review and evaluate the program's logic. The program code should itself be documented with comments that describe each major program segment.

OPERATOR DOCUMENTATION.   Computer operators use documentation called a **run manual**, which describes how to run the system. The typical contents of a run manual include:

- The name of the system, such as Purchases System.
- The run schedule (daily, weekly, time of day, and so on).
- Required hardware devices (tapes, disks, printers, or special hardware).
- File requirements specifying all the transaction (input) files, master files, and output files used in the system.
- Run-time instructions describing the error messages that may appear, actions to be taken, and the name and telephone number of the programmer on call, should the system fail.
- A list of users who receive the output from the run.

For security and control reasons, system flowcharts, logic flowcharts, and program code listings should not be part of the operator documentation. Operators should not have access to the details of a system's internal logic. We will discuss this point more fully later.

USER DOCUMENTATION.   Users need documentation describing how to use the system. User tasks include such things as entering input for transactions, making inquiries of account balances, updating accounts, and generating output reports. The nature of user documentation will depend upon the user's degree of sophistication with computers and technology. Thus, before designing user documentation, the systems professional must assess and classify the user's skill level. The following is one possible classification scheme:

- Novices
- Occasional users
- Frequent light users
- Frequent power users

   Novices have little or no experience with computers and are embarrassed to ask questions. Novices also know little about their assigned tasks. User training and documentation for novices must be extensive and detailed.

   Occasional users once understood the system but have forgotten some essential commands and procedures. They require less training and documentation than novices.

   Frequent light users are familiar with limited aspects of the system. Although functional, they tend not to explore beneath the surface and lack depth of knowledge. This group knows only what it needs to know and requires training and documentation for unfamiliar areas.

   Frequent power users understand the existing system and will readily adapt to new systems. They are intolerant of detailed instructions that waste their time. They like to find shortcuts and use macro commands to improve performance. This group requires only abbreviated documentation.

With these classes in mind, user documentation often takes the form of a user handbook, as well as on-line documentation. The typical **user handbook** will contain the following items:

- An overview of the system and its major functions
- Instructions for getting started
- Descriptions of procedures with step-by-step visual references
- Examples of input screens and instructions for entering data
- A complete list of error message codes and descriptions
- A reference manual of commands to run the system
- A glossary of key terms
- Service and support information

On-line documentation will guide the user interactively in the use of the system. Some commonly found on-line features include tutorials and help features.

Tutorials.   On-line **tutorials** can be used to train the novice or the occasional user. The success of this technique is based on the tutorial's degree of realism. Tutorials should not restrict the user from access to legitimate functions.

Help Features.   On-line **help features** range from simple to sophisticated. A simple help feature may be nothing more than an error message displayed on the screen. The user must "walk through" the screens in search of the solution to the problem. More sophisticated help is context-related. When the user makes an error, the system will send the message, "Do you need help?" The help feature analyzes the context of what the user is doing at the time of the error and provides help with that specific function (or command).

THE ROLE OF AUDITORS

As the preceding discussion has already suggested, the role of auditors (internal and external) in the detailed design and implementation phases should be significant. Most system failures are due to poor designs and improper implementation. Being a stakeholder in all financial systems, auditors should lend their expertise to this process to guide and shape the finished system. Specifically, auditors may get involved in the following ways.

PROVIDE TECHNICAL EXPERTISE.   The detailed design phase involves precise specifications of procedures, rules, and conventions to be used in the system. In the case of an AIS, these specifications must comply with GAAP, GAAS, SEC regulations, and IRS codes. Failure to so comply can lead to legal exposure for the firm. For example, choosing the correct depreciation method or asset valuation technique requires a technical background not necessarily possessed by systems professionals. The accountant may provide this expertise to the systems design process.

SPECIFY DOCUMENTATION STANDARDS.   In the implementation phase, the auditor plays a role in specifying system documentation. Since financial systems must periodically be audited, they must be adequately documented. The auditor should actively encourage adherence to effective documentation standards.

VERIFY CONTROL ADEQUACY. The applications that emerge from the SDLC must possess controls that are in accordance with the provisions of SAS 78. This requires the auditor's involvement at both the detailed design and implementation phases. Controls may be both programmed and manual procedures. Some controls are part of the daily operation of the system, while others are special actions that precede, follow, or oversee routine processing.

SYSTEMS MAINTENANCE

Once a system is implemented, it enters the second phase in its life cycle—maintenance. **Systems maintenance** involves changing systems to accommodate changes in user needs. Sometime the change is trivial, such as modifying the system to produce a new report or changing the length of a data field. Maintenance can also be extensive, such as making major changes to an application's logic and the user interface. The systems maintenance period can last from five to ten years, depending upon the organization. Systems in highly competitive business environments see much shorter system life spans. When it is no longer feasible for the organization to continue to maintain an aging system, it is scrapped, and a new systems development life cycle begins.

Maintenance represents a significant resource outlay compared to initial development costs. Over a system's life span, as much as 80 to 90 percent of its total cost may be incurred in the maintenance phase. We review the auditing implications of maintenance in the next section.

CONTROLLING AND AUDITING THE SDLC

In this chapter we have reviewed the highly technical and complex processes that constitutes the SDLC. Before proceeding, it is useful to place this material in perspective with regard to audit objectives. Simply stated, the purpose of a financial audit is to provide an expert opinion regarding the fair presentation of the financial statements. To render such an opinion, the expert auditor must perform certain audit tests. Naturally, the accuracy of the financial data in the client's databases bears directly on the auditor's opinion. In a CBIS environment, financial data are processed (accessed, stored, and updated) by computer applications. The accuracy and integrity of these programs directly affects the accuracy of the client's financial data. A materially flawed financial application can corrupt financial data, which are then incorrectly reported in the financial statements.

Chapter 6 reviews several techniques for testing application controls. If audit evidence shows that computer applications process data correctly and accurately, the auditor can form the basis for reducing the amount of substantive testing that needs to be performed. Since the client organization could, however, have hundreds of financially significant applications, testing application controls can prove to be a highly technical and time-consuming activity. Auditors, therefore, seek efficient and effective ways to limit the application testing.

The systems development and maintenance process is common to all applications. A properly functioning systems development process ensures that only needed applications are created, that they are properly specified, that they possess adequate controls, and that they are thoroughly tested before being implemented. The systems maintenance process ensures that only legitimate changes are made to applications and that such changes are also tested before being implemented. Together, these processes establish the accuracy of new applications and preserve their integrity throughout the period under review.

If the auditor can verify that these processes are effectively controlled, he or she can limit the extent of application testing that needs to be done. If, however, audit evidence shows SDLC controls to be weak and inconsistently applied, application testing and substantive testing cannot be reduced. In some situations, it may even be necessary to expand the scope of the audit. With this perspective in place, let's now examine the controls, audit objectives, and audit procedures related to these important processes.

CONTROLLING NEW SYSTEMS DEVELOPMENT

The first six controllable activities discussed below deal with the authorization, development, and implementation of the original system. The last two controllable activities pertain to systems maintenance activities.

SYSTEMS AUTHORIZATION ACTIVITIES

All systems must be properly authorized to ensure their economic justification and feasibility. As with all material transactions, authorizing the development of a new information system should be a formal step in the process. Typically, this requires that each new system request be submitted in writing by users to systems professionals who have both the expertise and authority to evaluate and approve (or reject) the request.

USER SPECIFICATION ACTIVITIES

Users must be actively involved in the systems development process. Their involvement should not be stifled because the proposed system is technically complex. Regardless of the technology involved, the user can and should provide a detailed written description of the logical needs that must be satisfied by the system. The creation of a user specification document often involves the joint efforts of the user and systems professionals. However, it is most important that this document remain a statement of user needs. It should describe the user's view of the problem, not that of the systems professionals.

TECHNICAL DESIGN ACTIVITIES

The technical design activities translate the user specifications into a set of detailed technical specifications of a system that meets the user's needs. The scope of these activities includes systems analysis, general systems design, feasibility analysis, and detailed systems design. The adequacy of these activities is measured by the quality of the documentation that emerges from each phase. Documentation is both a control and evidence of control and is critical to the system's long-term success. Specific documentation requirements were discussed previously.

INTERNAL AUDIT PARTICIPATION

The internal auditor plays an important role in the control of systems development activities, particularly in organizations whose users lack technical expertise. The internal auditor can serve as a liaison between users and the systems professionals to ensure an effective transfer of knowledge. An internal audit group, astute in computer technology and with a solid grasp of the business problems of users, can make a valuable contribution to all aspects of the SDLC process. The auditor should become involved at the inception of the process to make conceptual suggestions regarding system requirements and controls. Auditor involvement should continue throughout all phases of the development process and into the maintenance phase.

PROGRAM TESTING

All program modules must be thoroughly tested before they are implemented. Figure 4–9 shows a program-testing procedure involving the creation of hypothetical master files and transactions files that are processed by the modules being tested. The results of the tests are then compared against predetermined results to identify programming and logic errors. For example, in testing the logic of the accounts receivable update module illustrated in Figure 4–9, the programmer might create an accounts receivable master file record for John Smith with a current balance of $1,000 and a sales order transaction record for $100. Before performing the update test, the programmer concludes that a new balance of $1,100 should be created. To verify the module's internal logic, the programmer compares the actual results obtained from the run with the predetermined results. This is a very simple example of a program test. Actual testing would be extensive and involve many transactions that test all aspects of the module's logic.

Creating meaningful test data is an extremely time-consuming aspect of program testing. This activity can, however, provide future benefits. As we shall see in Chapter 7, application auditing sometimes involves program testing. To facilitate future testing, test data prepared during the implementation phase should be retained for reuse. This will give the auditor a frame of reference for designing and evaluating future audit tests. For example, if a program has undergone no maintenance changes since its original implementation, the test results from the audit should be identical to the original

FIGURE 4–9

Program-Testing
Procedures

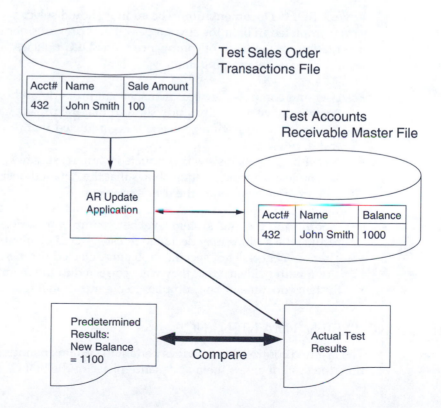

test results. Having a basis for comparison, the auditor can thus quickly verify the integrity of the program code. On the other hand, if changes have occurred, the original test data can provide evidence regarding these changes. The auditor can thus focus attention upon those areas.

USER TEST AND ACCEPTANCE PROCEDURES

Just before implementation, the individual modules of the system must be tested as a unified whole. A test team comprising user personnel, systems professionals, and internal audit personnel subjects the system to rigorous testing. Once the test team is satisfied that the system meets its stated requirements, the system is formally accepted by the user department(s).

The formal testing and acceptance of the system by the user is considered by many auditors to be the most important control over the SDLC. This is the last point at which the user can determine that the system adequately meets his or her needs. Although discovering a major flaw at this juncture can be costly, discovering the flaw later, during operation, can be devastating. The user's acceptance of the new system should be formally documented.

AUDIT OBJECTIVES

- To ensure that (1) SDLC activities are applied consistently and in accordance with management's policies; (2) the system as originally implemented was free from material errors and fraud; (3) the system was judged to be necessary and justified at various checkpoints throughout the SDLC; and (4) system documentation is sufficiently accurate and complete to facilitate audit and maintenance activities.

AUDIT PROCEDURES

Review SDLC Documentation. The auditor should select a sample of completed projects (completed in both the current period and previous periods) and review the documentation for evidence of compliance with SDLC policies. Specific points for review should include determining that:

- User and computer services management properly authorized the project.
- A preliminary feasibility study showed that the project had merit.
- A detailed analysis of user needs was conducted that resulted in alternative general designs.
- A cost-benefit analysis was conducted using reasonably accurate figures.
- The project's documentation shows that the detailed design was an appropriate and accurate solution to the user's problem.
- Test results show that the system was thoroughly tested at both the individual module and the total system level before implementation. (To confirm these test results, the auditor may decide to retest selected elements of the application.)
- There is a checklist of specific problems detected during the conversion period, along with evidence that they were corrected in the maintenance phase.
- Systems documentation complies to organizational requirements and standards.

CONTROLLING SYSTEMS MAINTENANCE

The last two controllable activities pertain to systems maintenance. Upon implementation, the system enters the maintenance phase of the SDLC. This is the longest period in the SDLC, often spanning several years. It is important to recognize that systems do not remain static throughout this period. Rather, they may undergo substantial changes that constitute a financial outlay many times their original cost. If an application has undergone maintenance (and even if it has not), its integrity may have been compromised since implementation. The auditor's review may, therefore, extend into the maintenance phase to determine that application integrity is still intact.

In this section, we see how uncontrolled program changes can increase a firm's exposure to financial misstatement due to programming errors. Some programming errors are subtle, resulting in the creation and distribution of incorrect information that goes undetected by the user. Other forms of errors are more apparent and result in system failures that can disrupt data processing and even bring operations to a halt. In addition to these exposures, program fraud may take root in an environment of poorly controlled maintenance and can go undetected for years.

MAINTENANCE AUTHORIZATION, TESTING, AND DOCUMENTATION

The benefits achieved from controlling new system development can be quickly lost during system maintenance if control does not continue into that phase. Access to systems for maintenance purposes increase the possibility of systems errors. Logic may be corrupted either by the accidental introduction of errors or intentional acts to defraud. To minimize the potential exposure, all maintenance actions should require, as a minimum, four controls: formal authorization, technical specification of the changes, retesting the system, and updating the documentation. In other words, maintenance activities should be given essentially the same treatment as new development. The extent of the change and its potential impact on the system should govern the degree of control applied. When maintenance causes extensive changes to program logic, additional controls, such as involvement by the internal auditor and the implementation of user test and acceptance procedures, may be necessary.

SOURCE PROGRAM LIBRARY CONTROLS

In spite of the preceding maintenance procedures, application integrity can be jeopardized by individuals who gain unauthorized access to programs. The remainder of this section deals with control techniques and procedures for preventing and detecting unauthorized access to application programs.

In larger computer systems, application program source code is stored on magnetic disks called the *source program library (SPL)*. Figure 4–10 illustrates the relationship between the SPL and other key components of the operating environment.

To execute a production application, it must first be compiled and linked to create a load module that the computer can process. As a practical matter, load modules are secure and free from the threat of unauthorized modification. Program changes (both authorized maintenance and unauthorized changes) are accomplished by first making changes to the source code stored on the SPL and then recompiling and linking the program to create a new load module that incorporates the changed code. Therefore, the SPL is a sensitive area, which, to preserve application integrity, must be properly controlled.

THE WORST-CASE SITUATION: NO CONTROLS

Figure 4–10 shows the SPL without controls. This arrangement has the potential to create the following two serious forms of exposure (see list below figure on next page).

FIGURE 4-10 Uncontrolled Access to the Source Program Library

1. Access to programs is completely unrestricted. Programmers and others can access any programs stored in the library, and there is no provision for detecting an unauthorized intrusion.
2. Because of these control weaknesses, programs are subject to unauthorized changes. Hence, there is no basis for relying on the effectiveness of other controls (maintenance authorization, program testing, and documentation). In other words, with no provision for detecting unauthorized access to the SPL, program integrity cannot be verified.

Control is always in conflict with operational flexibility and efficiency. For these reasons, systems professionals who must work daily within this environment sometimes oppose controlling the SPL. To achieve a mutually acceptable control-flexibility trade-off between the needs of systems professionals and auditors, both must understand the exposures that are created when control features are not employed or are routinely circumvented. In spite of the exposure just described, the no-controls approach is often the choice (perhaps inadvertently) that management makes.

A CONTROLLED SPL ENVIRONMENT

To control the SPL, protective features and procedures must be explicitly addressed, and this requires the implementation of an *SPL management system (SPLMS)*. Figure 4–11 illustrates the use of this technique. The black box surrounding the SPL signifies the SPLMS. This software is used to control four routine but critical functions: (1) storing programs on the SPL, (2) retrieving programs for maintenance purposes, (3) deleting obsolete programs from the library, and (4) documenting program changes to provide an audit trail of the changes.

FIGURE 4-11   Source Program Library under the Control of SPL Management Software

You may have recognized the similarities between the SPL management system and a database management system. This is a valid analogy, the difference being that SPL software manages program files and DBMSs manage data files. SPLMSs may be supplied by the computer manufacturer as part of the operating system or may be purchased through software vendors. Some organizations, to provide special control features, develop their own SPL software.

The mere presence of an SPLMS does not guarantee program integrity. Again, we can draw an analogy with the DBMS. To achieve data integrity, the DBMS must be properly used; control does not come automatically, it must be planned. Likewise, an SPL requires specific planning and control techniques to ensure program integrity. The control techniques discussed below address only the most vulnerable areas and should be considered minimum control.

PASSWORD CONTROL.   Assigning passwords provides one form of access control over the SPL. This is similar to password controls used in a DBMS to protect data files. Every financially significant program stored in the SPL can be assigned a separate password. As previously discussed, passwords have drawbacks. When more than one person is authorized to access a program, preserving the secrecy of a shared password is a problem. As more authorized personnel have a need to know the password, the potential for losing control of the password increases. Since responsibility for the secrecy of a shared password lies with the group rather than with an individual, personal accountability is reduced, and individuals within the group may take less care in protecting the password.

SEPARATE TEST LIBRARIES.   Figure 4–11 illustrates an improvement on the shared password approach through the creation of separate password-controlled libraries (or directories) for each programmer. Under this concept, programs are copied into the programmer's library for maintenance and testing. Direct access to the production SPL is limited to an authorized librarian who must approve all requests to modify, delete, and copy programs. Further, passwords to access programs can be changed regularly and disclosed only on a need-to-know basis.

A relatively cost-free enhancement to this control feature is the implementation of program naming conventions. The name assigned a program clearly distinguishes it as being either a test or a production program. When a program is copied from the production SPL to the programmer's library, it is given a temporary "test" name. When the program is returned to the SPL, it is renamed with its original production name. This technique greatly reduces the risk of accidentally running an untested version of a program in place of the production program.

AUDIT TRAIL AND MANAGEMENT REPORTS.   An important feature of SPL management software is the creation of reports that enhance management control and the audit function. The most useful of these are program modification reports, which describe in detail all program changes (additions and deletions) to each module. These reports should be part of the documentation file of each application to form an audit trail of program changes over the life of the application. During an audit, these reports can be reconciled against program maintenance requests to verify that only changes requested and authorized were actually implemented. For example, if a programmer attempted to use a legitimate maintenance action as an opportunity to commit program fraud, the unauthorized changes to the program code would be presented in the program modification report. These reports can be produced as hard copy and on disk and can be governed by password control, thus limiting access to management and auditors.

PROGRAM VERSION NUMBERS.   The SPLMS assigns a version number automatically to each program stored on the SPL. When programs are first placed in the libraries (upon implementation), they are assigned a version number of zero. With each modification to the program, the version number is increased by one. For instance, after five authorized maintenance changes, the production program will be designated version 05, as illustrated in Figure 4–11. This feature, when combined with audit trail reports, provides evidence for identifying unauthorized changes to program modules. An unauthorized change is signaled by a version number on the production load module that cannot be reconciled to the number of authorized changes. For example, if ten changes were authorized but the production program shows version 12, then one of two possibilities explain this discrepancy: (1) authorized changes occurred that are unsupported by documentation or (2) unauthorized changes were made to the program, which incremented the version numbers.

CONTROLLING ACCESS TO MAINTENANCE COMMANDS.   SPL management systems use powerful maintenance commands to alter or eliminate program passwords, alter the program version (modification) number, and temporarily modify a program without generating a record of the modification. There are legitimate technical reasons why systems designers and administrators need these commands. However, if not controlled, maintenance commands open the possibility of unrecorded, and perhaps unauthorized, program modifications. Hence, access to the maintenance commands themselves should be password-controlled, and the authority to use them should be controlled by management or the security group.

AUDIT OBJECTIVES

- To detect unauthorized program maintenance (which may have resulted in significant processing errors or fraud) and to determine that (1) maintenance procedures protect applications from unauthorized changes, (2) applications are free from material errors, and (3) program libraries are protected from unauthorized access.

We will examine each of these objectives in turn, focusing on the tests of controls that are necessary to achieve the objective. The discussion will assume that the organization employs source program library (SPL) software to control program maintenance. It should be noted that without SPL software, it can be difficult to achieve these audit objectives. The procedures described below are illustrated in Figure 4–12.

AUDIT PROCEDURES: IDENTIFYING UNAUTHORIZED CHANGES

To establish that program changes were authorized, the auditor should examine the audit trail of program changes for a sample of applications that have undergone maintenance. The auditor can confirm that authorization procedures were followed by performing the following tests of controls.

FIGURE 4–12   Auditing SPL Software System

RECONCILE PROGRAM VERSION NUMBERS.   The permanent file of the application should contain program change authorization documents that correspond to the current version number of the production application. In other words, if the production application is in its tenth version, there should be ten program change authorizations in the permanent file as supporting documentation. Any discrepancies between version numbers and supporting documents may indicate that unauthorized changes were made.

CONFIRM MAINTENANCE AUTHORIZATION.   The program maintenance authorization documents should indicate the nature of the change requested and the date of the change. It should also be signed and approved by the appropriate management from both computer services and the user departments. The auditor should confirm the facts contained in the maintenance authorization and verify the authorizing signatures with the managers involved.

AUDIT PROCEDURES: IDENTIFYING APPLICATION ERRORS

The auditor can determine that programs are free from material errors by performing three types of tests of controls: reconciling the source code, reviewing the test results, and retesting the program.

RECONCILE THE SOURCE CODE.   Each application's permanent file should contain the current program listing and listings of all changes made to the application. These documents describe in detail the application's maintenance history. In addition, the nature of the program change should be clearly stated on the program change authorization document. The auditor should select a sample of applications and reconcile each program change with the appropriate authorization documents. The modular approach to systems design (creating applications that comprise many small discrete program modules) greatly facilitates this testing technique. The reduced complexity of these modules enhances the auditor's ability to identify irregularities that indicate errors, omissions, and potentially fraudulent programming code.

REVIEW TEST RESULTS.   Every program change should be thoroughly tested before being implemented. Program test procedures should be properly documented by test objectives, test data, and processing results, which support the programmer's decision to implement the change. The auditor should review this record for each significant program change to establish that testing was sufficiently rigorous to identify any errors.

RETEST THE PROGRAM.   The auditor can retest the application to confirm its integrity. We examine several techniques for application testing in Chapter 6.

AUDIT PROCEDURES: TESTING ACCESS TO LIBRARIES

The existence of a secure program library is central to preventing errors and program fraud. One method is to assign library access rights exclusively to individuals who act as librarians. Their function is to retrieve applications from the program libraries for maintenance and to restore the modified programs to the library. In this arrangement, programmers perform program maintenance and testing in their own "private" libraries but do not have direct access to the program library.

The auditor should establish that the program library and private libraries are protected from unauthorized access by performing the following tests of controls.

REVIEW PROGRAMMER AUTHORITY TABLES.   The auditor can select a sample of programmers and review their access authority. The programmer's authority table will specify the libraries a programmer may access. These authorizations should be matched against the programmer's maintenance authority to ensure that no irregularities exist.

TEST AUTHORITY TABLE.   The auditor should simulate the programmer's access privileges and then violate the authorization rules by attempting to access unauthorized libraries. Any such attempts should be denied by the operating system.

SUMMARY

One of the most valuable assets of the modern business organization is a responsive, user-oriented information system. A well-designed system can increase productivity, reduce inventories, eliminate nonvalue-added activities, improve customer service and management decisions, and coordinate activities throughout the organization.

This chapter examined the purpose, control, and audit of the systems development life cycle. It began by describing the roles of the participants involved in systems development, including systems professionals, users, and stakeholders. Then it outlined the key activities associated with SDLC. This process consists of two primary sets of activities: new systems development and maintenance. The former, which is used to guide the development of information systems in many organizations, includes *systems planning, systems analysis, conceptual design, system selection, detailed design*, and *system implementation*. A properly functioning systems development process ensures that only needed applications are created, that they are properly specified, that they possess adequate controls, and that they are thoroughly tested before being implemented. Upon implementation, new systems enter the *systems maintenance* phase, where they remain until they are terminated and ultimately replaced. The systems maintenance process ensures that only legitimate changes are made to applications and that such changes are also tested before being implemented.

The systems development and maintenance process is common to all applications. Together, they establish the accuracy of new applications and preserve their integrity throughout the period under review.

The auditor's objective in testing controls over these processes is to establish application integrity and thus limit the tests of application controls and substantive testing that needs to be done.

KEY TERMS

backbone systems
bottlenecks and redundant operations
conceptual design
controls
data flows
data sources
data stores
detailed design
detailed design report
documentation

end users
error rates
frequent light users
frequent power users
general accounting systems
help features
intangible benefits
legal feasibility
net present value method
new systems development

novices
object-oriented design
objects
observation
occasional users
office automation systems
operational feasibility
payback method
personal interviews
processes
project planning
project proposal
project schedule
quality assurance group
resource costs
reviewing key documents
run manual
schedule feasibility
special-purpose systems
stakeholders
steering committee
strategic systems planning

structured design
system implementation
system survey
systems analysis
systems analysis report
systems development life cycle (SDLC)
systems evaluation and selection
systems maintenance
systems planning
systems professionals
systems selection report
tangible benefits
task participation
technical feasibility
transaction volumes
turnkey systems
tutorials
user handbook
users
vendor-supported systems
walkthrough

REVIEW QUESTIONS

1. Distinguish between systems professionals, end users, and stakeholders.
2. What is the role of the accountant in the SDLC? Why might accountants be called on for input into the development of a nonaccounting information system?
3. What are the three problems that account for most system failures?
4. Why is it often difficult to obtain competent and meaningful user involvement in the SDLC?
5. Who should sit on the systems steering committee? What are their typical responsibilities?
6. Why is strategic systems planning not technically considered to be part of the SDLC?
7. What is strategic systems planning, and why should it be done?
8. What is the purpose of project planning, and what are the various steps?
9. Discuss the various feasibility measures that should be considered. Give an example of each.
10. What are the broad classes of facts that need to be gathered in the system survey?

11. What are the primary fact-gathering techniques?
12. What are the relative merits and disadvantages of a current systems survey?
13. Distinguish between data sources, data stores, and data flows.
14. What are some of the key documents that may be reviewed in a current systems survey?
15. What is the purpose of a systems analysis, and what type of information should be included in the systems analysis report?
16. What is the primary objective of the conceptual systems design phase?
17. What are two approaches to conceptual systems design?
18. How much design detail is needed in the conceptual design phase?
19. What is an object, and what are its characteristics in the object-oriented approach? Give two examples.
20. What is the auditor's primary role in the conceptual design of the system?
21. Who should be included in the group of independent evaluators performing the detailed feasibility study?

22. What makes the cost-benefit analysis more difficult for information systems than most other investments an organization may make?

23. Classify each of the following as either one-time or recurring costs:
    a. training personnel
    b. initial programming and testing
    c. systems design
    d. hardware costs
    e. software maintenance costs
    f. site preparation
    g. rent for facilities
    h. data conversion from old system to new system
    i. insurance costs
    j. installation of original equipment
    k. hardware upgrades

24. Distinguish between turnkey and backbone systems. Which is more flexible?

25. Discuss the relative merits of in-house programs versus commercially developed software.

26. Why is modular programming preferable to free coding?

27. Why should test data be saved after it has been used?

28. Explain the importance of documentation by the systems programmers.

29. What documents not typically needed by other stakeholders do accountants and auditors need for the new system?

DISCUSSION QUESTIONS

1. Comment on the following statement: "The maintenance stage of the SDLC involves making trivial changes to accommodate changes in user needs."

2. Discuss how rushing the system's requirements stage may delay or even result in the failure of a systems development process. Conversely, discuss how spending too long in this stage may result in "analysis paralysis."

3. Is a good strategic plan detail-oriented?

4. Distinguish between a problem and a symptom. Give an example. Are these usually noticed by upper-, middle-, or lower-level managers?

5. What purposes does the systems project proposal serve? How are these evaluated and prioritized? Is the prioritizing process objective or subjective?

6. Most firms underestimate the cost and time requirements of the SDLC by as much as 50 percent. Why do you think this occurs? In what stages do you think the underestimates are most dramatic?

7. A lack of support by top management has led to the downfall of many new systems projects during the implementation phase. Why do you think management support is so important?

8. Many new systems projects grossly underestimate transaction volumes simply because they do not take into account how the new, improved system can actually increase demand. Explain how this can happen and give an example.

9. Compare and contrast the structured design approach and the object-oriented approach. Which do you believe is most beneficial? Why?

10. Do you think legal feasibility is an issue for a system that incorporates the use of machines to sell lottery tickets?

11. Intangible benefits are usually extremely difficult to quantify accurately. Some designers argue that if you understate them, then conservative estimates are produced. Any excess benefits will be greatly welcomed but not required for the new system to be a success. What are the dangers of this viewpoint?

12. If a firm decides early on to go with a special-purpose system, such as SAP, based upon the recommendations of the external audit firm, should the SDLC be bypassed?

13. During a test data procedure, why should the developers bother testing "bad" data?

14. If the system is behind schedule and if each program module is tested and no problems are found, is it necessary to test all modules in conjunction with one another? Why or why not?

15. Run manuals for computer operators are similar in theory to the checklists that airplane pilots use for takeoffs and landings. Explain why these are important.

16. Who conducts the post-implementation review? When should it be conducted? If an outside consulting firm were hired to design and implement the new system, or a canned software package were purchased, would a post-implementation review still be useful?

17. Discuss the importance of involving accountants in the detailed design and implementation phases. What tasks should they perform?

MULTIPLE-CHOICE QUESTIONS

1. CMA 1282 5-9
   The role of an information system steering committee should be to
   a. initiate all computer applications, set computer applications priorities, control access to the computer room, and keep the computer file library.
   b. prepare control totals, maintain systems documentation, and perform follow-up on errors.
   c. assign duties to systems personnel, prepare and monitor system implementation plans, and prepare flowcharts of systems applications.
   d. review systems project proposals, long-range systems plans, and the performance of the systems department and approve major acquisitions in consideration of overall plans.
   e. decide on specific information needs, prepare detailed plans for systems evaluations, set priorities for writing programs, and decide which equipment will be purchased.

2. CIA 582 IV-8
   Many people believe that a data processing department should have a long-range plan. Which of the following is NOT likely to appear in a long-range plan?
   a. organizational goals and objectives
   b. detailed flowcharts for each computer program that will be developed

   c. schedule of the development of each project
   d. identification of the hardware, personnel, and financial resources that will be required
   e. forecast of future hardware developments

3. CIA 584 II-36
   In reviewing a feasibility study for a new computer system, the auditor should ascertain that the study
   a. considered costs, savings, controls, profit improvement, and other benefits analyzed by application area.
   b. provided the preliminary plan for converting existing manual systems and clerical operations.
   c. provided management with assurance from qualified, independent consultants that the use of a computer system appeared justified.
   d. included a report by the internal audit department that evaluated internal control features for each planned application.

4. CMA 686 5-2
   The most important factor in planning for a system change is
   a. having an auditor as a member of the design team.
   b. using state-of-the-art techniques.
   c. concentrating on software rather than hardware.

d. involving top management and people who use the system.

e. selecting a user to lead the design team.

5. CMA 678 5-5

In the context of a feasibility study, technical feasibility refers to whether

a. a proposed system is attainable, given the existing technology.

b. the systems manager can coordinate and control the activities of the systems department.

c. an adequate computer site exists for the proposed system.

d. the proposed system will produce economic benefits exceeding its costs.

e. the system will be used effectively within the operating environment of an organization.

6. CMA 1281 5-13

The stage of a systems study that would include up-to-date organizational charts; a description of the present system; complete flowcharts for the present system; forms and layouts of all input and output documents (along with samples) used in the present system; and summaries of interviews, review sessions, and personal observations regarding the present system is

a. problem definition.

b. problem analysis.

c. system design.

d. program analysis.

e. documentation and maintenance.

7. CMA 678 5-4

A systems survey is being conducted to obtain an accurate perspective on the existing system and to identify weaknesses that can be corrected by the new system. Which one of the following steps is not considered part of this systems survey?

a. Interviews are conducted with operating people and managers.

b. The complete documentation of the system is obtained and reviewed.

c. Measures of processing volume are obtained for each operation.

d. Equipment sold by various computer manufacturers is reviewed in terms of capability, cost, and availability.

e. Work measurement studies are conducted to determine the time required to complete various tasks or jobs.

8. Which of the following is NOT a one-time cost?

a. site preparation

b. insurance

c. software acquisition

d. data conversion

9. Which of the following is NOT an advantage of commercial software?

a. independence

b. cost

c. reliability

d. implementation time

10. CMA 1287 5-6

The process of developing specifications for hardware, software, personnel hours, data resources, and information products required to develop a system is referred to as

a. systems analysis.

b. systems feasibility study.

c. systems maintenance.

d. system implementation.

e. systems design.

11. CMA 689 5-4

The analysis tool for the systems analyst and steering committee to use in selecting the best systems option is

a. cost-benefit analysis.

b. systems design.

c. decision tree analysis.

d. user selection.

e. pilot testing.

12. CMA 1289 5-8

In determining the need for system changes, several types of feasibility studies can be made. The most commonly recognized feasibility studies are

a. legal, environmental, and economic.

b. environmental, operational, and economic.

c. technical, economic, legal, and practical.

d. practical, technical, and operational.

e. technical, operational, and economic.

13. CMA 1290 4-13

The technique that recognizes the time value of money by discounting the after-tax cash

flows for a project over its life to time period zero using the company's minimum desired rate of return is called the
a. net present value method.
b. capital rationing method.
c. payback method.
d. average rate of return method.
e. accounting rate of return method.

14. CMA 691 (Adapted)
Fitzgerald Company is planning to acquire a $250,000 computer that will provide increased efficiencies, thereby reducing annual operating costs by $80,000. The computer will be depreciated by the straight-line method over a five-year life with no salvage value at the end of five years. Assuming a 40 percent income tax rate, the machine's payback period is
a. 3.13 years.
b. 3.21 years.
c. 3.68 years.
d. 4.81 years.
e. 5.21 years.

Questions 15 and 16 are based on the following information and deal with a critique of the cost-benefit analysis portion of the feasibility study.

When management decides to implement a management information system in a segment of the company, the decision is often based upon a feasibility study conducted by the systems department. Listed below are terms and examples of them used in the section of the study dealing with the cost-benefit analysis:

Terms	Examples
Tangible cost	Development cost
Intangible cost	Imputed interest
Tangible benefits	Cost displacement
Intangible benefits	Improved decisions

The feasibility study identifies the major benefits of the new management information system. Many of the benefits are intangible, such as improved decision-making capability and effectiveness, better customer relations, and improved employee morale.

15. CMA Adapted 679 5-9
The estimated category that ordinarily would have the greatest uncertainty as to its precise value is
a. the tangible costs.
b. the intangible costs.

c. the tangible benefits.
d. the intangible benefits.
e. none of the above because they are equally precise.

16. CMA Adapted 679 5-10
Which one of the following statements best describes what is usually true regarding the estimates included in feasibility studies?
a. Development time and cost are usually less than estimated; benefits are stated accurately.
b. Development time and cost are usually less than estimated; benefits are usually greater than estimated.
c. Development cost and benefits are usually greater than estimated; development time is usually less than estimated.
d. Development time and cost are usually greater than estimated; benefits are usually less than estimated.
e. Development time, cost, and benefits are usually greater than estimated.

17. CMA 691 4-29
Errors are most costly to correct during
a. programming.
b. conceptual design.
c. analysis.
d. detailed design.
e. implementation.

18. CMA 1287 5-6
The process of developing specifications for hardware, software, personnel hours, data resources, and information products required to develop a system is referred to as
a. systems analysis.
b. systems feasibility study.
c. systems maintenance.
d. system implementation.
e. systems design.

19. CMA 678 5-2
When designing a computer-based information system, the initial step in the systems design process is to determine
a. the required output.
b. the source documents that serve as the basis for input.
c. the processing required.
d. the decisions for which data will be required.

e. the file information required during processing.

20. CMA 1282 5-12
Characteristics of an accounting application that might influence the selection of data entry devices and media for a computerized accounting system are
a. timing of feedback needs relative to input, need for documentation of an activity, and the necessity for reliability and accuracy.
b. cost considerations, volume of input, complexity of activity, and liquidity of assets involved.
c. need for documentation, necessity for accuracy and reliability, volume of output, and cost considerations.
d. relevancy of data, volume of input, cost considerations, volume of output, and timing of feedback needs relative to input.
e. type of file used, reliability of manufacturer's service, volume of output, and cost considerations.

21. CIA 1187 III-32
User acceptance is part of which phase of the system development life cycle?
a. implementation
b. general systems design
c. program specification and implementation planning
d. detailed systems design

PROBLEMS

1. Systems Planning
A new systems development project is being planned for the Reindeer Christmas Supplies Company. The invoicing, cash receipts, and accounts payable modules are all going to be updated. The controller, Kris K. Ringle, is a little anxious about this project. The last systems development project that affected his department was not very successful, and the employees in the accounting department did not accept the new system very well at first. He feels that the systems personnel did not interact sufficiently with the users of the systems in the accounting department. Prepare a memo from Ringle to the head of the information systems department, Sandy Klaus. In this memo, provide some suggestions for including the accounting personnel in the systems development project. Give some very persuasive arguments why prototyping would be helpful to the workers in the accounting department.

2. Problem Identification
The need for a new information system may be manifest in various symptoms. In the early stages of a problem, these symptoms seem innocuous and go unrecognized. As the underlying source of the problem grows in seventy, so do its symptoms, until they are alarmingly apparent. Classify each of the following as a problem or a symptom. If it is a symptom, give two examples of a possible underlying problem. If it is a problem, give two examples of a possible symptom that may be detected.
a. declining profits
b. defective production process
c. low-quality raw materials
d. shortfall in cash balance
e. declining market share
f. shortage of employees in the accounts payable department
g. shortage of raw material due to a drought in the Midwest
h. inadequately trained workers
i. decreasing customer satisfaction

3. Systems Analysis
The following article describes the tremendous growth experienced by the Minnesota Twins as a result of winning the 1991 World Series.

Copyright 1992
Information Access Company;
Copyright BPI Communications 1992

Amusement Business
September 7, 1992

SECTION: VOL. 104; No. 36; Pg. 16; ISSN: 0003-2344

HEADLINE: Minnesota Twins' President Bell: World Series costly but worth it; Jerry Bell; Sports

BYLINE: Waddell, Ray

MINNEAPOLIS—Winning a World Series can create untold amounts of good will in a community and bring in lots of ancillary income, but there are also major expenses involved in winning Major League Baseball's highest honor.

As winners of the 1991 World Series, the Minnesota Twins should know. Twins' President Jerry Bell would rather talk about the plus side of the equation.

"The biggest advantage of winning a World Series—other than the thrills and good feeling it brings to a community—is it enhances ticket sales for the year you win the Series and for the ensuing year," Bell told AB.

"An old-timer once told me that you have to win the World Series every 10 years to keep the fans happy. I think you have to be more competitive than that."

A Series championship has a direct financial impact in other areas as well. "We added 18 new corporate sponsors this year, and a lot of those who signed on for the year have agreed to come back next year," Bell said.

And then there are the souvenir stands. "Novelties have been great," he said. "We own two stores in this area and they have done really well this year. They sell tickets as well."

The Twins host about 70–78 promotions a year, not all of them giveaways. "We host Family Days where we have $1 off tickets and we work with the concessionaires," Bell said. "Another promotion involves Super America convenience markets when two kids get in free with one adult. We do that about 12 or 13 times a season. We also have a number of premium and group giveaways."

Group sales are extremely important to the Twins, Bell said. "We're always one of the leaders in group sales in the Major League," he said. "We place a lot of emphasis on group sales and the Metrodome helps us in that regard."

The fact that the stadium is covered reduces the risk of offering group discounts in a large geographic region. "If we get 100 people from South Dakota on Saturday, we know we're going to play the game, and that's really important," Bell said.

The team's season ticket base has increased by more than 2,500 over last year, topping 12,000 for the first time in Twins' history. "We could do better if we had more (premium) baseball seats."

Price of Glory

There are lots of costs involved in winning the World Series."Our costs were $1 million out of pocket to be in the World Series," Bell said. "That's three or four more weeks of baseball operations, hotels, charter flights, and all of the extras. We took our whole staff to Atlanta last year—of course we lost all three games. We had parties all week. It was very expensive, but it was worth it."

The costs carried over into 1992. "We had increased costs with our players," Bell said. "You want to keep a World Series team together. We only lost a couple of players."

"But winning the World Series is not all just money in the bank," Bell continued. "The organization doesn't really get any money out of the Series until the fifth game—it goes to the league until then."

The [television] network [broadcasting the games] pays the league in advance and that money is divided among all the teams. "The impact of winning seems more here than in a lot of places," Bell said. "With the smaller communities, there is more excitement and the people get more caught up in it than in the larger cities."

The Twins have been a tenant of the Metrodome in all of the "Dome's 10 years of existence. "It's a lease agreement situation," said Bell, a former manager of the Metrodome. "We have a long-term agreement."

New radio and television deals could be on the horizon for the Twins. "Things could change in a year," Bell said. "We have local flagship radio, over-the-air television, and cable television, and now we're studying taking it in-house. It's definitely something to watch."

The Twins already produce and sell ads for their program.

Anytime Box Office

"We've started something that we're pretty excited about," Bell said. "We've been testing an automatic ticket machine that we think will revolutionize the way tickets are sold—it's just a matter of when."

Twins automatic ticket booths are placed in grocery stores. "They have a television touch screen that is continuously showing Twins highlights," Bell said. "If you want to purchase tickets to an upcoming Twins game, you touch the screen and an announcer comes on and tells you how to buy tickets. What I think is the neatest feature of all is, after you select your seat, a picture comes up on your view of the field—it shows you where your tickets are and says, 'Do you like the view?' You have a chance to pick another ticket."

The service charge is 10 percent, with a maximum service payment set. "We bought our ticketing system and have operated our own ticketing for years," Bell said. "We want to give our fans as much service as they want."

The Twins now have three automatic ticket machines in three Rainbow Food Stores. "Our objective is to have 25–30 installed," Bell said. "Forty-four million people go through Rainbow Food Stores every year."

The Twins' attendance for 1991 was 2.3 million; the team is currently at approximately 2.1 million for this year, up 340,000 over this time last year. "We're still in the race," Bell said. "We have three more games with Oakland in Oakland that could be the deciding factor."

Required:
a. Would you categorize this system as a financial transaction processing system, a marketing system, or a strategic information system?
b. Discuss the five feasibility aspects during the development process and how you think they affected the decision process.
c. Who are the end users of this system?

4. Systems Development and Implementation
Kruger Designs hired a consulting firm three months ago to redesign the information system used by the architects. The architects will be able to use state-of-the-art CAD programs to help in designing the products. Further, they will be able to store these designs on a network server where they and other architects may be able to call them back up for future designs with similar components. The consulting firm has been instructed to develop the system without disrupting the architects. In fact, top management believes that the best route is to develop the system and then to "introduce" it to the architects during a training session. Management does not want the architects to spend precious billable hours guessing about the new system or putting work off until the new system is working. Thus, the consultants are operating in a backroom under a shroud of secrecy.

Required:
a. Do you think that management is taking the best course of action for the announcement of the new system? Why?
b. Do you approve of the development process? Why?

5. Systems Analysis
Consider the following dialogue between a systems professional, Joe Pugh, and a manager of a department targeted for a new information system, Lars Meyer:

Pugh: The way to go about the analysis is to first examine the old system, such as reviewing key documents and observing the workers perform their tasks. Then we can determine which aspects are working well and which should be preserved.

Meyer: We have been through these types of projects before and what always ends up happening is that we do not get the new system we are promised; we get a modified version of the old system.

Pugh: Well, I can assure you that will not happen this time. We just want a thorough understanding of what is working well and what is not.

Meyer: I would feel much more comfortable if we first started with a list of our requirements. We should spend some time up-front determining exactly what we want the system to do for my department. Then you systems people can come in and determine what portions to salvage if you wish. Just don't constrain us to the old system!

Required:
a. Obviously these two workers have different views on how the systems analysis phase should be conducted. Comment on whose position you sympathize with the most.
b. What method would you propose they take? Why?

6. Systems Design and Selection
The DIA has been plagued with problems prior to and since its opening. After reading the following article, discuss where you think

problems went wrong in either the conceptual design and/or the system selection stages.

Modern Materials Handling
April 15, 1996

HEADLINE: Reengineering for the 21st century; contains related articles about the Denver Airport and the Gulf War; the 1990s 50th Anniversary Issue

SECTION: Vol. 51; No. 5; Pg. 90; ISSN: 0026-8038

A major materials handling story of the 1990s was the 16-month delay in the opening of the new Denver International Airport due to problems with the high-tech baggage handling system. Considered to be an enormous technological leap even by today's high-tech standards, the system design called for a series of complicated and highly variable routings of individually-powered baggage carriers.

Designers, however, grossly underestimated the difficulties of dealing with the high level of complexity in the system design. Unrealistic schedules, software problems, and the lack of a backup system all contributed to a string of delays. Not until a $50 million backup system based on conventional conveyor technology was built and the initial scope of the automated system greatly scaled back was the airport able to open on February 28, 1995.

Although disastrous from a public relations perspective, the experience at Denver will prove invaluable in terms of the lessons learned about developing large-scale, technologically-advanced systems. Gaining a better understanding of the kinds of extraordinary challenges that are routinely encountered in dealing with complex systems should help today's designers ask more of the right questions up-front instead of after the fact.

7. Systems Design
Robin Alper, a manager of the credit collections department for ACME Building Supplies, is extremely unhappy with a new system that was installed three months ago. Her complaint is that the data flows from the billing and accounts receivable departments are not occurring in the manner originally requested. Further, the updates to the database files are not occurring as frequently as she had envisioned. Thus, the hope that the new system would provide more current and timely information has not materialized. She claims that the systems analysts spent three days interviewing her and other workers. During that time, she and the other workers thought they had clearly conveyed their needs. She feels as if their needs were ignored and their time was wasted.

Required:
What went wrong during the systems design process? What suggestions would you make for future projects?

8. Conceptual Design
Prepare two alternative conceptual designs for both an accounts payable system and an accounts receivable system. Discuss the differences in concept between the different designs. From a cost perspective, which is more economical? From a benefits perspective, which is more desirable? Which design would you prefer and why?

9. Systems Design
Robert Hamilton was hired six months ago as the controller of a small oil and gas exploration and development company, Gusher, Inc., headquartered in Beaumont, Texas. Before working at Gusher, Hamilton was the controller of a larger petroleum company, Eureka Oil Company, based in Dallas. The joint interest billing and fixed asset accounting systems of Gusher are outdated, and many processing problems and errors have been occurring quite frequently. Hamilton immediately realized these problems and informed the president, Mr. Barton, that it was crucial to install a new system. Barton concurred and met with Hamilton and Sally Jeffries, the information systems senior manager. Barton instructed Jeffries to make the new system that Hamilton wished to have a top priority in her department. Basically, he told Jeffries to deliver the system to meet Hamilton's needs as soon as possible.

Jeffries left the meeting feeling overwhelmed since the IS department is currently working on two other very big projects, one for the production department and the other for the geological department. The next day, Hamilton sent a memo to Jeffries indicating the name of a system he had 100 percent confidence in—Amarillo Software—and he also indicated that he would very much like this system to be purchased as soon as possible. He stated that the system had been used with much success during the past four years in his previous job.

When commercial software is purchased, Jeffries typically sends out requests for proposals to at least six different vendors after conducting a careful analysis of the needed requirements. However, due to the air of urgency demonstrated in the meeting with the president and the overworked systems staff, she decided to go along with Hamilton's wishes and sent only one RFP (request for proposal) out, which went to Amarillo Software. Amarillo promptly returned the completed questionnaire. The purchase price ($75,000) was within the budgeted amount. Jeffries contacted the four references provided and was satisfied with their comments. Further, she felt comfortable since the system was for Hamilton, and he had used the system for four years.

The plan was to install the system during the month of July and try it for the August transaction cycle. Problems were encountered, however, during the installation phase. The system processed extremely slowly on the hardware platform owned by Gusher. When Jeffries asked Hamilton how the problem had been dealt with at Eureka, he replied that he did not remember having had such a problem. He called the systems manager from Eureka and discovered that Eureka had a much more powerful mainframe than Gusher. Further investigation revealed that Gusher has more applications running on its mainframe than Eureka did, since Eureka used a two-mainframe distributed processing platform.

Further, the data transfer did not go smoothly. A few data elements being stored in the system were not available as an option in the Amarillo system. Jeffries found that the staff at Amarillo was very friendly when she called, but they could not always identify the problem over the phone. They really needed to come out to the site and investigate. Hamilton was surprised at the delays between requesting an Amarillo consultant to come out and the time in which he or she actually arrived. Amarillo explained that it had to fly a staff member from Dallas to Beaumont for each trip. The system finally began to work somewhat smoothly in January, after a grueling fiscal year-end close in October. Hamilton's staff viewed the project as an unnecessary inconvenience. At one point, two staff accountants threatened to quit. The extra consulting fees amounted to $35,000. Further, the systems department at Gusher spent 500 more hours during the implementation process than it had expected. These additional hours caused other projects to fall behind schedule.

Required:
Discuss what could have been done differently during the design phase. Why were most of the problems encountered? How might a detailed feasibility study have helped?

10. Cost-Benefit Analysis
    Listed on the following page are some probability estimates of the costs and benefits associated with two competing projects.

Required:
a. Compute the net present value of each alternative. Round the cost projections to the nearest month. What happens to the answer if the probabilities of the recurring costs are incorrect and a more accurate estimate is as follows:

	A		B
.10	$ 75,000	.4	$ 85,000
.55	95,000	.4	100,000
.35	105,000	.2	110,000

b. Repeat Step (a) for the payback method.
c. Which method do you feel provides the best source of information? Why?

chapter 5

ELECTRONIC COMMERCE SYSTEMS

Electronic commerce (EC) involves the electronic processing and transmission of data. It encompasses many diverse activities, including electronic trading of goods and services, on-line delivery of digital products, electronic funds transfer (EFT), electronic trading of stocks, and direct consumer marketing. Electronic commerce, however, is not a new phenomenon. For many years, companies have engaged in electronic data interchange (EDI) over private networks. Today, driven by the Internet revolution, electronic commerce is dramatically expanding and undergoing radical changes. This fast-moving environment is engendering an array of innovative markets and trading communities. While electronic commerce promises enormous opportunities for consumers and businesses, its effective implementation and control are urgent challenges for organization management and auditors.

To properly evaluate the potential exposures and risks in this environment, the modern auditor must be familiar with the technologies and techniques that underlie electronic commerce. Hardware failures, software errors, and unauthorized access from remote locations can expose the organization's accounting system to unique threats. For example, transactions can be lost in transit and never processed, electronically altered or rearranged to change their financial effect, corrupted by transient signals on transmission lines, and diverted to or initiated by the perpetrator of a fraud.

This chapter deals with the technologies, risks, controls, and audit issues associated with electronic commerce. These include private local area networks (LANs), public wide area networks (WANs), electronic data interchange (EDI), and Internet commerce.

LEARNING OBJECTIVES

After studying this chapter, you should:

- Be able to distinguish between LANs and WANs.
- Be familiar with the operational characteristics of the star, ring, bus, hierarchical, and client server topologies.
- Be familiar with the technologies that support electronic commerce, including terminals, modulation and modems, digital transmissions,

multiplexing techniques, the physical transmission path, and the front-end processor.

- Understand the operational features and risks associated with EDI and recognize how these differ from Internet commerce.
- Understand the control techniques used to reduce risk in electronic commerce systems.
- Understand the audit objectives and procedures used to test controls in electronic commerce systems.

NETWORK TOPOLOGIES

A **network topology** is the physical arrangement of components (terminals, servers, and communications links) in a network. In this section, we examine the features of five basic network topologies: star, hierarchical, ring, bus, and client-server. Most networks are a variation on, or combination of, these basic models. However, before proceeding, we must develop a working definition for some of the terms that will be used in the following sections.

LOCAL AREA NETWORKS AND WIDE AREA NETWORKS

One way of distinguishing between types of networks is the geographic area covered by their distributed sites. Networks are usually classified as either *local area networks* (LANs) or *wide area networks* (WANs). **Local area networks** are often confined to a single room in a building, or they may link several buildings within a close geographic area. However, a LAN can cover distances of several miles and connect hundreds of users. LANs are capable of voice and video transmissions, as well as data communications. The nodes connected to a LAN are usually microcomputer-based workstations. Typically, LANs are privately owned and controlled. Over the last decade, they have played a dominant role in the distributed data processing strategy of countless organizations. Their impact on data processing and AIS is certain to grow in the future.

When networks exceed the geographic limitations of the LAN, they are called **wide area networks**. Because of the distances involved and the high cost of interconnections, WANs typically employ common-carrier facilities (such as telephone lines and microwave channels) between remote nodes. Therefore, WANs are often public networks (at least in part) and are thus subject to Federal Communications Commission regulations. The nodes of a WAN can include microcomputer workstations, minicomputers, mainframes, or LANs. The WAN may be used to link together geographically dispersed segments of a single organization or connect multiple organizations in a trading partner arrangement. Later in the chapter, we see how EDI is made financially viable to many organizations because of value-added networks that employ public WANs.

NETWORK INTERFACE CARDS

The workstation's physical connection to the LAN is achieved through a **network interface card (NIC)**, which fits into one of the expansion slots in the microcomputer. This device provides the electronic circuitry needed for inter-node communications. The NIC works with the network control program to send and receive messages, programs, and files across the network.

SERVERS

LAN nodes often share common resources such as programs, data, and printers, which are managed through special-purpose computers called **servers**, as depicted in Figure 5–1. When the server receives requests for resources, the requests are placed in a queue and are processed in sequence.

In a distributed environment, there is often a need to link networks together. For example, users of one LAN may wish to share data with users on a different LAN. A LAN user in one organization may wish to transmit data across the country over a public WAN to a user on a LAN with a different topology. Networks can be linked together via combinations of hardware and software devices called *bridges* and *gateways*. Figure 5–2 illustrates this technique. **Bridges** provide a means for linking LANs of the same type, such as an IBM Token Ring to another IBM Token Ring. **Gateways** connect LANs of different types and are also used to link LANs to WANs. With these definitions in mind, we now turn our attention to the five basic network topologies.

STAR TOPOLOGY

The **star topology** shown in Figure 5–3 describes a network of IPUs with a large central computer (the host) at the hub that has direct connections to a periphery of smaller computers. Communications between the nodes in the star are managed and controlled from the host site.

The star topology is often used for a WAN, in which the central computer is a mainframe. The nodes of the star may be microcomputer workstations, minicomputers, mainframes, or a combination. Databases under this approach may be distributed or centralized. A common model is to partition local data to the nodes and centralize the common data. For example, consider a department store chain that issues its own credit cards. Each node represents a store in a different metropolitan area. In Figure 5–3, these are Dallas, St. Louis, Topeka, and Tulsa. The nodes maintain local databases such as records for customers holding credit cards issued in their areas and records of

FIGURE 5–1

LAN with File and Print Servers

FIGURE 5–2

Bridges and
Gateways
Linking LANs
and WANs

local inventory levels. The central site—Kansas City—maintains data common to the entire regional area, including data for customer billing, accounts receivable maintenance, and overall inventory control. Each local node is itself a LAN, with point-of-sales (POS) terminals connected to a minicomputer at the store.

If one or more nodes in a star network fail, communication between the remaining nodes is still possible through the central site. However, if the central site fails, individual nodes can function locally but cannot communicate with the other nodes. Transaction processing in this type of configuration could proceed as follows. Sales are processed in real time at the POS terminals. Local processing includes obtaining credit approval, updating the customer's available credit, updating the inventory records, and recording the transaction in the transaction file (journal).

At the end of the business day, each of the nodes transmits sales and inventory information to the central site in batches. The central site updates the control accounts, prepares customer bills, and determines inventory replenishment for the entire region.

FIGURE 5–3

Star Network

The assumption underlying the star topology is that primary communication will be between the central site and the nodes. However, limited communication between the nodes is possible. For example, assume a customer from Dallas was in Tulsa and made a purchase from the Tulsa store on credit. The Tulsa database would not contain the customer's record and Tulsa would then send the transaction for credit approval to Dallas via Kansas City. The approved transaction would then be returned by Dallas to Tulsa via Kansas City. Inventory and sales journal updates would be performed at Tulsa.

The preceding transaction processing procedure would differ somewhat depending on the database configuration. For example, if local databases are partial replicas of the central database, credit queries could then be made directly from Kansas City. However, this would require keeping the central database current with all the nodes.

HIERARCHICAL TOPOLOGY

A **hierarchical topology** is one in which a host computer is connected to several levels of subordinate smaller computers in a master-slave relationship. This structure is applicable to firms with many organizational levels that must be controlled from a central location. For example, consider a manufacturing firm with remote plants, warehouses, and sales offices, such as the one illustrated in Figure 5–4. Sales orders from the local sales departments are transmitted to the regional level, where they are summarized and uploaded to the corporate level. Sales data, combined with inventory and plant capacity data from manufacturing, are used to compute production requirements for the period, which are downloaded to the regional production scheduling system. At this level, production schedules are prepared and distributed to the local production departments. Information about completed production is uploaded from the production departments to the regional level, where production summaries are prepared and transmitted to the corporate level.

FIGURE 5–4   Hierarchical Topology

RING TOPOLOGY

The **ring topology** illustrated in Figure 5–5 eliminates the central site. All nodes in this configuration are of equal status; thus, responsibility for managing communications is distributed among the nodes. Every node on the ring has a unique electronic address, which is attached to messages such as an address on an envelope. If Node A wishes to send a message to Node D, the message is received, regenerated, and passed on by Nodes B and C until it arrives at its destination. The ring topology is a *peer-to-peer arrangement* in which all nodes are of equal status. This is a popular topology for LANs. The peer nodes manage private programs and databases locally. However, common resources that are shared by all nodes can be centralized and managed by a file server that is also a node on the network ring.

The ring topology may also be used for a WAN, in which case the databases may be partitioned rather than centralized. For example, consider a company with widely separated warehouses, each with different suppliers and customers and each processing its own shipping and receiving transactions. In this case, where there is little common data, it is more efficient to distribute the database than to manage it centrally. However, when one warehouse has insufficient stock to fill an order, it can communicate through the network to locate the items at another warehouse.

BUS TOPOLOGY

The **bus topology** illustrated in Figure 5–6 is the most popular LAN topology. It is so named because the nodes are all connected to a common cable—the bus. Communications and file transfers between workstations are controlled centrally by one or more servers. As with the ring topology, each node on the bus has a unique address, and only

FIGURE 5–5

Ring Topology

FIGURE 5-6

Bus Topology

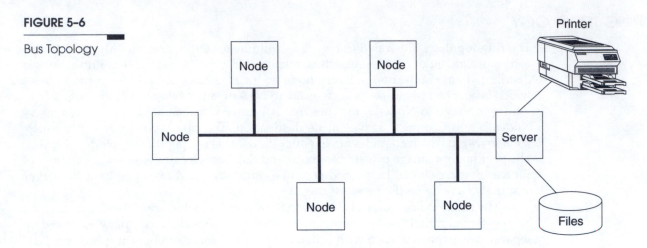

one node may transmit at a time. The technique, which has been used for over two decades, is simple, reliable, and generally less costly to install than the ring topology.

THE CLIENT-SERVER TOPOLOGY

The term *client-server* is often misused to describe any type of network arrangement. In fact, the **client-server topology** has specific characteristics that distinguish it from the other topologies. Figure 5–7 illustrates the approach.

To explain the client-server difference, let's review the features of a traditional distributed system. We have already seen that DDP can result in considerable data

FIGURE 5-7

Client-Server
Topology

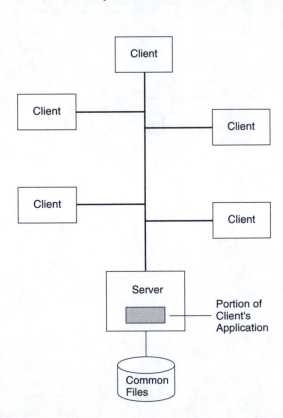

"traffic jams." Users competing for access to shared data files experience queues, delays, and lockouts. A factor influencing the severity of this problem is the data structure (file organization and access methods) in use. For example, assume a user at site A requests a single record from a sequential file located at a central site. To meet this request, the file server at the central site must lock and transmit the entire file to the remote site. The search for the specific record is performed at the remote site by the user's application. When the update is complete, the entire file is then transmitted back to the central site.

The client-server model distributes the processing between the user's (client's) computer and the central file server. Both computers are part of the network, but each is assigned functions that it best performs. For example, the record-searching portion of an application can be placed on the server, and the data manipulation portion can be placed on the client computer. Thus, only a single record, rather than the entire file, must be locked and sent to the client for processing. After processing, the record is returned to the server, which restores it in the file and removes the lock. This approach reduces traffic and allows more efficient use of shared data. Distributing the record-searching logic of the client's application to the server permits other clients to access different records in the same file simultaneously. The client-server approach can be applied to any topology (i.e., ring, star, or bus). Figure 5–7 illustrates the client-server model applied to a bus topology.

ELECTRONIC COMMERCE TECHNOLOGIES

We now turn our attention to the technologies that underlie EC systems. Since we have already examined many of the elements found in local area networks, this discussion emphasizes wide area network technologies. The topics covered in this section follow the diagram in Figure 5–8. The section is divided into the following major topics: terminals, modulation and modems, digital transmission, multiplexers and switching devices, the physical transmission path, and the front-end processor.

TERMINALS

Most users interact with computers via **terminals**, which come in numerous varieties and are produced by scores of vendors. Millions of terminals are installed in this country; the count varies depending on how we define terminal. Technically, any input-output device connected by a communications line to a computer is a terminal.

The simplest way to approach a review of this broad topic is to start with the most basic forms of terminals and then move on to the more complex and powerful types. For this purpose, we shall classify terminals as dumb, smart, or programmable. At the end of this section, we discuss the transmission modes that terminals use for communications.

DUMB TERMINALS

Dumb terminals are so called because they can only send and receive data. All processing capability is centralized in the host computer. The most common examples of dumb terminals are teleprinters and cathode ray tubes (CRTs).

TELEPRINTERS.   The basic dumb terminal consists of a keyboard for data entry and a teleprinter for output. Most computer systems use some form of printer to produce

FIGURE 5–8   Communications System Technology

hard copy output in readable form. Teleprinters may be impact or laser devices. A common type of impact printer is the *dot matrix*, which uses wires to form characters from dots arranged in a matrix. Dot matrix printers can print at speeds of several hundred characters per second. Large *line printers* can attain several thousand lines per second using a metal cylinder with embossed characters as the printing element. *Ink-jet* and *laser printers* produce output of higher quality than is capable with dot matrix and line printers. These devices are also quiet, because they do not impact the paper to print. But laser printers cannot use multipart paper to produce multiple copies of the output simultaneously, as impact printers can. Teleprinters are most useful in batch input-output applications or where interaction between the user and the host computer is minimal.

CATHODE RAY TUBES.   The most common form of terminal is the cathode ray tube (CRT) or video display unit. Used in conjunction with a keyboard, CRTs provide visual display for input-output functions such as data insertions, data deletions, and screen paging through keyboard input. This technology allows the user to view large amounts of data on screen without having to print a hard copy and to access the host computer interactively.

SMART TERMINALS

Smart terminals provide more user features than dumb terminals. For instance, smart terminals can support user applications under the control of the host computer, such as word processing, spreadsheets, and graphics capabilities. Some devices provide local storage of data and permit data editing before transmission. For certain types of data input, smart terminals using pointing devices provide a more efficient alternative than keyboards. For instance, the tasks of making menu choices, selecting icons from a screen, and performing graphics operations can be greatly simplified. Examples of pointing devices include the *electronic mouse, touch-sensitive CRTs*, and the *light pen*.

Smart terminals include a range of optical scanning equipment that read text, graphics, and bar codes and convert them into digital input data. A common example is the optical scanning wand that is used to read product bar codes on food items in supermarkets.

PROGRAMMABLE TERMINALS

The personal computer (PC) is widely used as a **programmable terminal**. A PC workstation may consist of data storage, commercial software, utility programs, CRT, printer, and a processor powerful enough to handle extensive business applications.

TRANSMISSION MODES

The terms *synchronous, asynchronous, simplex, half duplex*, and *full duplex* describe various methods by which terminals (and other devices) attached to a communications line transmit data. The first two terms are associated with the structure and format of the data flow. The last three terms pertain to the direction of the data flow.

The **asynchronous** transmission method is so called because there is no continuous synchronization between the sending and receiving devices. The advantages of asynchronous transmission are that it is simple and inexpensive. The disadvantage is that data transfer rates are slow. This method is used in communications between microcomputers and between microcomputers and mainframes. In contrast, the

synchronous transmission method uses a separate timing signal to keep the receiving end's device in constant synchronization with the transmitting device. The method requires more costly equipment, but is capable of high-speed data transfer. Mainframe-to-mainframe communications use the synchronous transmission method.

The terms *simplex, half duplex*, and *full duplex* characterize transmission by the direction of data flow. Figure 5–9 illustrates the three methods. **Simplex** transmission allows transmission in one direction only. This method is used primarily by output devices. **Half duplex** transmission allows signals to be sent in both directions, but not simultaneously. A transmission can be in only one direction at a time—from terminal to host or vice versa. With **full duplex** transmission, signals can be sent and received simultaneously. This method is the most costly of the three, but permits the greatest volume of data transfer across the network.

MODULATION AND MODEMS

In the early days of data communications, the telephone system provided the technology infrastructure that connected remote locations in a network. However, the system was designed to transmit voice signals, not computer-generated data. Figure 5–10 shows the differences between voice and data signals. Voice signals are represented as oscillating waveforms, and data signals are represented as digital pulses.

The **wave signal** rises from zero to some positive maximum level, then swings back through zero to an equal negative level, and returns to zero to complete 360 degrees of travel, or one *cycle*. Wave signals have three characteristics that can be varied to convey message content: amplitude, frequency, and phase. The **amplitude**, or strength of the signal, is represented by the height of its positive (and negative) peaks relative to zero. Amplitude is measured in *volts*. Signal **frequency** is the number of cycles or oscillations occurring per second. The unit of measure for frequency is the Hertz (Hz). Thus, 1,000 cycles per second is 1000 Hz. The **phase** of the signal is the point in the cycle to which the signal has advanced. This is expressed in degrees. The cycle begins at zero degrees of phase and ends at 360 degrees. The points at one-quarter,

FIGURE 5–9

Simplex, Half Duplex, and Full Duplex Transmission Modes

Printer	Mainframe
	Simplex
Microcomputer	Mainframe
	Half Duplex
Mainframe	Mainframe
	Full Duplex

FIGURE 5–10

Wave and
Digital Signals

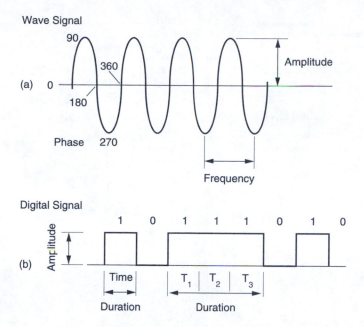

one-half, and three-quarters through the cycle correspond to 90, 180, and 270 degrees, respectively.

Data stored in computers are represented as *binary digits*, or **bits**, which assume a numeric value of either zero or one. To transmit computer data, the bits are converted into a **digital signal** that represents zeros and ones as a series of electrical pulses.

In concept, a digital signal is similar to turning a flashlight on and off to represent ones and zeros, respectively. When the flashlight switch is turned to the on position, an electrical voltage (a pulse) is produced by the battery, which illuminates the bulb to represent a 1 bit. The pulse ends when the switch is turned to the off position. The off condition signifies the presence of a 0 bit. Figure 5–10(b) illustrates a digital signal coding scheme for representing ones and zeros as electric pulses. The time duration of the signal determines the number of ones or zeros being transmitted in a series. In the example, a pulse spanning three time periods is used to represent a series of three 1 bits.

Computers communicate with peripheral devices (such as disk packs, tape drives, printers, and terminal monitors) and with other computers in close proximity through digital signals. However, when data are sent over longer distances to remote locations through the telephone system, the digital signal must be converted to a wave signal. The process of converting from digital to wave form, illustrated in Figure 5–11, is called **modulation**.

Modulation involves mixing an input signal with a base *carrier* frequency to produce an output signal that has the properties needed for transmission. At the receiving end of the transmission path, a reverse modulation process called *demodulation* regenerates the original input signal. The hardware device that performs the *modulator-demodulator* task is called a **modem**. Three basic forms of modulation are commonly used: amplitude modulation, frequency modulation, and phase modulation. These are discussed in Section 1 of the chapter appendix.

DIGITAL TRANSMISSION

Digital transmission is the dominant trend in communications technology. Rather than being transmitted as analog waves, signals are converted to digital values through a

FIGURE 5–11

The Modulation
Process

Transmit Digital
Signal

1 0 1 1 0 1

Modem

1 0 1 1 0 1

Modulated to Create
Analog Signal

Message
Sender

Telephone System

Demodulated to Produce
Digital Signal

1 0 1 1 0 1

Receive Analog
Signal

1 0 1 1 0 1

Modem

Message
Receiver

digitizing process and transmitted as pulses. The advantage of digital technology is its
ability to better suppress line noise and thus reduce **transmission errors**. Voice-grade
transmission circuits suffer from inherent noise from various sources, including adjacent electrical circuits, transient signals, cross-talk, and background or "white" noise,
that can distort analog signals and inject errors into the data. Using special regenera-
tive repeaters, digital systems can provide error-free communications over long distances that would cause analog signals to degenerate.

MULTIPLEXERS AND SWITCHING DEVICES

The communications lines connecting the nodes of a network possess far more
message-carrying capacity than a single node can use. If separate lines were dedicated
to each pair of nodes, they would likely sit idle much of the time. This is not a problem
in most LANs, where distances are short and the cost of a line is relatively small.

However, efficient line utilization is of far greater importance in WANs that employ expensive, long-distance communication paths.

MULTIPLEXER

Long-distance communications lines are extremely expensive to maintain, but have the capacity to carry the signals of many thousands of users simultaneously. To transmit multiple messages simultaneously, each message must be kept separate from the others, or the signals will become commingled and garbled. The effect would be similar to multiple parties talking simultaneously from extensions on the same telephone line. A listener would be unable to distinguish his or her party's message from all the rest.

A **multiplexer** is a device that permits the simultaneous transmission of multiple signals while maintaining a searation between each of them. Figure 5–8 illustrates the role of multiplexers in the communications process. Depending on the communications system, thousands of individual terminal messages can be multiplexed and transmitted over a single long-distance line. At the receiving end, the composite signal is demultiplexed into individual signals, which are then demodulated into digital form.

To achieve message separation over the long-distance line, multiplexers use one of two basic approaches: frequency division multiplexing (FDM) or time division multiplexing (TDM). The FDM method is used to multiplex analog signals, as illustrated in Figure 5–8. Digital systems use the TDM technique.

SWITCHING

Message **switching** is a technique for efficiently connecting the components of a network. Even a relatively small network of, say, 100 components (workstations, printers, file servers, and so on) would require thousands of individual lines if each were to have a direct connection to every other component. The feasible solution to this situation is to use a switched network. Switches are used to establish temporary connections between devices for the duration of the communication session. This is similar to a telephone switchboard operator establishing a connection between two parties by inserting a cord with a connector plug at each end into the jacks of each party's line appearing on the switchboard. When the conversation is over, the operator removes the cords from the switchboard and the path is dropped. Modern-day switches replace the operator and the manual switchboard with a high-speed, computer-controlled device. Two types of switches are used in modern networks: the private branch exchange (PBX) and packet switching.

A **private branch exchange (PBX)**, which is illustrated in Figure 5–12, is used for switching data and voice communications locally within a firm. Increasingly, PBXs are digital devices that are actually special-purpose computers. In addition to switching, they translate the data format of transmitting devices to conform to the requirements of the receiving devices. Thus, a number of devices, including telephones, mainframes, PCs, and fax machines, can be connected to a digital PBX.

Packet switching is used for long-distance communications in WANs. Figure 5–13 illustrates this technique, whereby messages are divided into small packets for transmission. Individual packets of the same message may take different routes to their destination. Each packet contains address and sequencing codes so they can be reassembled into the original complete message at the receiving end. The choice of transmission path is determined according to criteria that achieve optimum utilization of the long-distance lines, including the degree of traffic congestion on the line, the

FIGURE 5-12

Digital PBX
Various Terminal
Devices

shortest path between the end points, and the line status of the path (that is, working, failed, or experiencing errors). The network switches provide a physical connection for the addressed packets only for the duration of the message; the line then becomes available to other users. The international standard for organizing data into packets for public switched networks is X.25.[1]

THE PHYSICAL TRANSMISSION PATH

The physical transmission path is the connection between the transmitting and receiving devices in the network. These include the cables that plug into the back of the end user's microcomputer as well as radio transmissions that carry thousands of signals simultaneously across the country and around the world. Our discussion examines five common transmission media: twisted-pair cable, coaxial cable, fiber optic cable, microwave transmissions, and communications satellites.

TWISTED-PAIR CABLE

A **twisted-pair cable**, illustrated in Figure 5-14(a), consists of hundreds of sets of copper wires that are twisted together in pairs. The twisting is done in an exact pattern

---

1.　The Consultative Committee on International Telephone and Telegraph is a standards-setting body under the auspices of the United Nations. Its search for standards governing international transmissions of data has resulted in the X.25 format. This standard enables LANs and WANs to communicate through packet-switched networks in synchronous mode.

FIGURE 5–13

Message
Packet
Switching

Messages

Messages Are
Divided Into
Small Packets
and Transmitted

Packets Are Reassembled at Their
Destination into Complete Messages

(two twists per foot) to create a better signal transmission than a straight pair of wires can produce. Twisted-pair cables can be shielded or unshielded. Shielded cable is more expensive but provides better protection against signal loss caused by interference from extraneous sources and permits higher data-transmission speeds. Unshielded twisted-pair cables come from the telephone industry and are used as the standard wiring for all business offices. Unshielded twisted-pair cables provide adequate signal paths at lower transmission rates but are more susceptible to cross-talk (noise) between pairs within the cable.

COAXIAL CABLE

Coaxial cable, as illustrated in Figure 5–14(b), has been around since the 1940s. It consists of a central wire conductor covered by insulation and surrounded by a wire mesh shield. The shielding provides the return (ground) path for the signal and prevents interference from other transmissions and noise.

Coaxial cable is often used for the backbone connections between LANs and for linking LANs to WANs. This medium is capable of high-speed transmissions and is especially applicable where electromagnetic interference is a problem.

FIBER OPTIC CABLE

The **fiber optic cable** illustrated in Figure 5–14(c) has a glass core surrounded by a glass cladding. Data, in the form of high-speed pulses of light, travel along the core. The light source for the fiber optic cable is either a laser or a light-emitting diode. Data are conveyed as on and off pulses of light to represent the digital bit stream. Since the light can travel in one direction only, two optical cores (two cables or a single cable with

FIGURE 5-14

Twisted-Pair,
Coaxial, and
Fiber Optic
Cables

Pair of Twisted Wires

Cutaway View of
Twisted-Pair Cable

(a) Twisted-Pair Cable

Copper Wire
Conductor

Insulation

Wire Mesh
Shield

Protective
Sheath

(b) Coaxial Cable

Glass Core

Glass
Cladding

Protective
Sheath

(c) Fiber Optic Cable

two cores) are required to complete a transmit and receive path. Fiber optic cable has several advantages over electromagnetic media.[2]

1. Due to their high frequency range, fiber optic devices have a large capacity for information transmission. A single fiber can carry over 30,000 voice signals.
2. The signals traveling along glass fibers are unaffected by electromagnetic disturbances caused by electric motors, electric sparks, magnetic devices, lightning, and adjacent cables.
3. The signal loss in fiber optic transmissions caused by attenuation is far less than it is in cables that use copper conductors. Two benefits derive from this: repeaters

---

2.   U.D. Black, *Data Communications and Distributed Networks*, 2d ed. (Englewood Cliffs, N.J.: Prentice-Hall, 1987), p. 56.

for fiber optic cables can be placed as far as 50 to 100 miles apart, compared to about 3 miles for copper cables; and these improved signal characteristics translate into much lower error rates in data transmissions.

4. Because light transmissions do not emit an electromagnetic field, this form of transmission is much more secure than microwaves or twisted-pair cables. The electromagnetic field surrounding an electronic transmission contains information that can be selectively retrieved by an intruder with the proper equipment. It is very difficult to tap into a fiber optic cable.

5. Fiber optic technology can operate in environments subject to extreme temperatures and temperature variations.

6. Fiber optic cable is physically small—the thickness of a hair—and requires much less physical space than twisted-pair or coaxial cable.

MICROWAVE TRANSMISSIONS

Microwaves are extremely high-frequency (above 1 gigahertz) radio waves that follow a line-of-sight transmission path. This medium can carry a large amount of traffic from point to point and commonly provides the long-distance (trunk) communication legs for WANs. **Microwave transmissions** are used for over half of the telephone and television trunk traffic in this country.

A disadvantage of this medium is that the microwave transmitter and receiver must be able to "see" each other to permit line-of-sight transmissions. Prominent objects, such as tall buildings and trees, and even the curvature of the earth, can interfere with the signal. For this reason, microwave transmitters and receivers are placed on the tops of tall buildings or on specially constructed towers. To cover long distances, repeater stations located at intermediate points (every 50 miles or so) receive and then retransmit the signal to the next site. Thus, a signal can be relayed from point to point across the country, as illustrated in Figure 5–15. The cost of building and maintaining a string of repeater stations is proportional to the distance to be covered, and for most organizations it is prohibitive. Instead, an organization constructing a WAN will usually lease the long-distance facilities from common carriers such as AT&T.

FIGURE 5–15   Microwave Transmission

COMMUNICATIONS SATELLITES

Communications satellites provide an alternative to ground repeater stations. This technology provides a radio relay station in space, more than 22,000 miles above the transmitting and receiving ends of the signal path. Communications satellites hold a geosynchronous orbit, allowing them to remain positioned over the same point on the earth. Figure 5–16 shows how ground transmitters and receivers can remain in one position since the satellite's movement relative to the earth's is fixed. Communications satellites have the ability to broadcast signals to cover an area of approximately 30 percent of the earth's surface. Thus, a message from a single earth station can be retransmitted to multiple receiving stations across the country and internationally. A practical advantage of this capability is that an organization can achieve database concurrency in a widely distributed system.

THE FRONT-END PROCESSOR

When a mainframe (host) computer is connected to a network, it uses a special-purpose computer called a **front-end processor (FEP)** to manage communications between it and the other nodes or IPUs on the network. Figure 5–8 shows the relationship between the host, the FEP, and the connected nodes. In contrast to the host computer, which is a general-purpose processor, the FEP performs a very specific set of tasks to relieve the workload on the host, including:

- Responding to a host computer's requests to transmit or receive data on the communications lines attached to the FEP.
- Assembling bits into an outgoing message and adding control and synchronization characters to the message.
- Translating the coding schemes of dissimilar devices into a mutually compatible format.
- Managing FEP buffer storage. Messages are temporarily stored in the buffer area before transfer to the host. After transfer is complete, the buffer space must be

FIGURE 5-16   Communications Satellites in Fixed Orbit

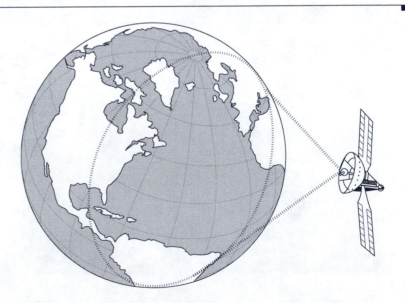

released for additional incoming messages. The efficient management of the limited buffer space is critical to overall network performance.

- Analyzing communications problems by identifying errors, performing diagnostics, testing lines, and selecting alternative paths for failed lines.
- These tasks, if performed by the host, would require valuable CPU time that would be taken away from data processing applications. Without a FEP to offload this work, a typical network could consume a substantial portion of the host's capacity.

NETWORK SOFTWARE

Network software controls communications between the physical devices connected to the network. Its purpose is to perform the following tasks:

1. Establish a communications session between the sender and the receiver.
2. Manage the flow of data across the network.
3. Detect and resolve data collisions between competing nodes.
4. Detect errors in data caused by line failure or signal degeneration.

There are several techniques for managing sessions and controlling transmissions, but most of them are variants of three basic methods: polling, token passing, and carrier sensing.

POLLING

Polling is the most popular technique for establishing a communication session in WANs. One site, designated the "master," polls the other "slave" sites to determine if they have data to transmit. If a slave responds in the affirmative, the master site locks the network while the data are transmitted. The remaining sites must wait until they are polled before they can transmit. The polling technique illustrated in Figure 5–17 is well suited to both the star and the hierarchical topologies. There are two primary advantages to polling. First, polling is *noncontentious*. Because nodes can send data only when requested by the master node, two nodes can never access the network at the

FIGURE 5–17

Polling Method
of Controlling
Data Collisions

same time. Data collisions (the simultaneous transmission of two or more messages that destroy each other) are, therefore, prevented. Second, an organization can set *priorities* for data communications across the network. Important nodes can be polled more often than other, less-important nodes.

TOKEN PASSING

Token passing involves transmitting a special signal—the token—around the network from node to node in a specific sequence. Each node on the network receives the token, regenerates it, and passes it to the next node. Only the node possessing the token is allowed to transmit data.

Token passing can be used with either ring or bus topologies. On a ring topology, the token passing sequence is determined by the order in which the nodes are physically connected. With a bus, the sequence is logical, not physical. The token is passed from node to node in a predetermined order to form a logical ring. Token bus and token ring configurations are illustrated in Figure 5–18. Since nodes are permitted to transmit

FIGURE 5–18

Token Passing Approach to Controlling Data Collisions

only when they possess the token, the node wishing to send data across the network seizes the token upon receiving it. Holding the token blocks other nodes from transmitting and ensures that no data collisions will occur. After the transmitting node sends its message and receives an acknowledgment signal from the receiving node, it releases the token. The next node in sequence then has the option of either seizing the token and transmitting data or passing the token on to the next node in the circuit.

A major advantage of token passing is its *deterministic* access method, which avoids data collisions. This is in contrast to the *random* access approach of carrier sensing (discussed below). IBM's version of token ring is emerging as an industry standard.

CARRIER SENSING

Carrier sensing is a random access technique that detects collisions when they occur. This technique, which is formally labeled *carrier sensed multiple access with collision detection (CSMA/CD)*, is used with the bus topology. The node wishing to transmit "listens" to the bus to determine if it is in use. If it senses no transmission in progress (no carrier), the node transmits its message to the receiving node. This approach is not as fail-safe as token passing. Collisions can occur when two or more nodes, unaware of each other's intent to transmit, do so simultaneously when they independently perceive the line to be clear. When this happens, the network server directs each node to wait a unique and random period of time and then retransmit the message. In a busy network, data collisions are more likely to occur, thus resulting in delays while the nodes retransmit their messages. Proponents of the token passing approach point to its collision-avoidance characteristic as a major advantage over the CSMA/CD model.

Ethernet is the best-known LAN software that uses the CSMA/CD standard. The Ethernet model was developed by the Xerox Corporation in the 1970s. In 1980, Digital Equipment Corporation, in a joint venture with Intel Corporation, published the specifications for a LAN based on the Ethernet model.[3] The greatest advantage of Ethernet is that it is established, reliable, and well understood by network specialists. Ethernet also has a number of economic advantages over token ring: (1) the technology, being relatively simple, is well suited to the less-costly twisted-pair cabling, whereas token ring works best with more expensive coaxial cable; (2) the network interface cards used by Ethernet are much less expensive than those used in the token ring topology; and (3) Ethernet uses a bus topology, which is easier to expand.

NETWORK PROTOCOLS

An important element of network control is achieved through protocols. **Network protocols** are the rules and standards governing the design of hardware and software that permit users of networks manufactured by different vendors to communicate and share data. The general acceptance of protocols within the network community provides both standards and economic incentives for the manufacturers of hardware and software. Products that do not comply with prevailing protocols will have little utility to prospective customers.

The data communications industry borrowed the term *protocol* from the diplomatic community. Diplomatic protocols define the rules by which the representatives of nations communicate and collaborate during social and official functions. These

---

3.   The Ethernet, a Local Area Network Version 1.0. Digital Equipment Corporation, Maynard, Mass.; Intel Corporation, Santa Clara, Calif.; and Xerox Corporation, Stanford, Conn.

formal rules of conduct are intended to avoid international problems that could arise through the misinterpretation of ambiguous signals passed between diplomatic counterparts. The greatest potential for error naturally exists between nations with vastly dissimilar cultures and conventions for behavior. Establishing a standard of conduct through protocols that all members of the diplomatic community understand and practice minimizes the risk of miscommunications between nations of different cultures.

An analogy may be drawn to data communications. A communications network is a community of computer users who also must establish and maintain unambiguous lines of communication. If network members all had homogeneous needs and operated identical systems, this would not be much of a problem; but networks are characterized by heterogeneous systems components. Typically, network users employ hardware devices (PCs, printers, monitors, data storage devices, modems, and so on) and software (user applications, network control programs, and operating systems) that are produced by a variety of vendors. Passing messages effectively from device to device in such a multivendor environment requires ground rules, or protocols.

WHAT FUNCTIONS DO PROTOCOLS PERFORM?

Protocols serve network functions in several ways.[4] First, they facilitate the physical connection between the network devices. Through protocols, devices are able to identify themselves to other devices as legitimate network entities and thus initiate (or terminate) a communications session.

Second, protocols synchronize the transfer of data between physical devices. This involves defining the rules for initiating a message, determining the data transfer rate between devices, and acknowledging message receipt.

Third, protocols provide a basis for error checking and measuring network performance. This is done by comparing measured results against expectations. For example, performance measures pertaining to storage device access times, data transmission rates, and modulation frequencies are critical to controlling the network's function. The identification and correction of errors thus depends on protocol standards that define acceptable performance.

Fourth, protocols promote compatibility among network devices. To successfully transmit and receive data, the various devices involved in a particular session must conform to a mutually acceptable mode of operation, such as synchronous or asynchronous and duplex or half duplex. Without protocols to provide such conformity, messages sent between devices will be distorted and garbled.

Finally, protocols promote network designs that are flexible, expandable, and cost-effective. Users are free to change and enhance their systems by selecting from the best offerings of a variety of vendors. Manufacturers must, of course, construct these products in accordance with established protocols.

INTERNET COMMERCE

Thousands of organizations worldwide are establishing home pages on the Internet to promote their products and solicit sales. By entering the seller's home page address into the Internet communication program from a microcomputer, a potential customer can access the seller's product list, scan the product line, and place an order. Typically,

---

4.   H. M. Kibirige, *Local Area Networks in Information Management* (Westport, CT: Greenwood Press, 1989).

Internet sales are credit card transactions. The customer's order and credit card information are attached to the seller's e-mail file. An employee reviews the order, verifies credit, and enters the transaction into the seller's system for processing in the normal way. Because of the need to review the e-mail file before processing, the turnaround time for processing Internet sales is often longer than for telephone orders. Research is currently underway to develop intelligent agents (software programs) that review and validate Internet orders automatically as they are received.

INTERNET PROTOCOLS

The Internet is a worldwide network of tens of thousands of local networks and on-line services, and millions of single-user microcomputers. The Internet is a cooperative system that has no central controlling site. The basic protocol that permits communication between Internet nodes is **Transfer Control Protocol/Internet Protocol (TCP/IP)**. This protocol controls how individual packets of data are formatted, transmitted, and received. Any computer or network that connects to the Internet must support TCP/IP. However, the following protocols are also used for special tasks:

- HTTP (Hypertext Transfer Protocol) controls web browsers that access the graphical World Wide Web (WWW).
- FTP (File Transfer Protocol) is used to transfer text files, programs, spreadsheets, and databases across the Internet.
- SNMP (Simple Network Mail Protocol) is the most popular protocol for transmitting e-mail messages. Other e-mail protocols are POP (Post Office Protocol) and IMAP (Internet Message Access Protocol).
- SSL (Secure Sockets Layer) is a low-level encryption scheme used to secure transmissions in higher-level (HTTP) format.
- SET (Secure Electronic Transmission) is an encryption scheme developed by a consortium of technology firms and banks (Netscape, Microsoft, IBM, Visa, MasterCard, etc.) to secure credit card transactions. Customers making credit card purchases over the Internet transmit their encrypted credit card number to the merchant, who then transmits the number to the bank. The bank returns an encrypted acknowledgment to the merchant. The customer does not need to worry about an unscrupulous merchant decrypting the customer's credit card number and misusing the information.

As a vehicle for processing business transactions, the potential for commerce on the Internet is almost unlimited. Unlike EDI, which is a formal business arrangement between trading partners, the Internet connects an organization to the thousands of potential business partners with whom the organization shares no formal agreement. In addition to unprecedented business opportunities, risks for both the seller and the buyer accompany Internet commerce. Connecting to the Internet exposes the organization to threats from computer hackers, viruses, and transaction fraud. Later in the chapter we examine controls including password techniques, message encryption, and firewalls that minimize the risk.

ELECTRONIC DATA INTERCHANGE (EDI)

To coordinate sales and production operations and to maintain an uninterrupted flow of raw materials, many organizations enter into a trading partner agreement with their suppliers and customers. This agreement is the foundation for a reengineered and fully automated business process called **electronic data interchange (EDI)**. A general definition of EDI is:

> the intercompany exchange of computer-processible business information in standard format.

The definition reveals several important features of EDI. First, EDI is an intercompany endeavor. A firm cannot engage in EDI on its own. Second, the transaction is processed automatically by the information systems of the trading partners. In a pure EDI environment, there are no human intermediaries to approve or authorize transactions. Third, transaction information is transmitted in a standardized format. Therefore, firms with different internal systems can interface and do business. Figure 5–19 shows an overview of an EDI connection between two companies. Let's assume that the transaction in Figure 5–19 is the purchase of inventory by the customer (Company A) from the supplier (Company B). Company A's purchases system automatically creates an electronic purchase order (PO), which it sends to its translation software. Here, the PO

FIGURE 5–19

Overview of EDI

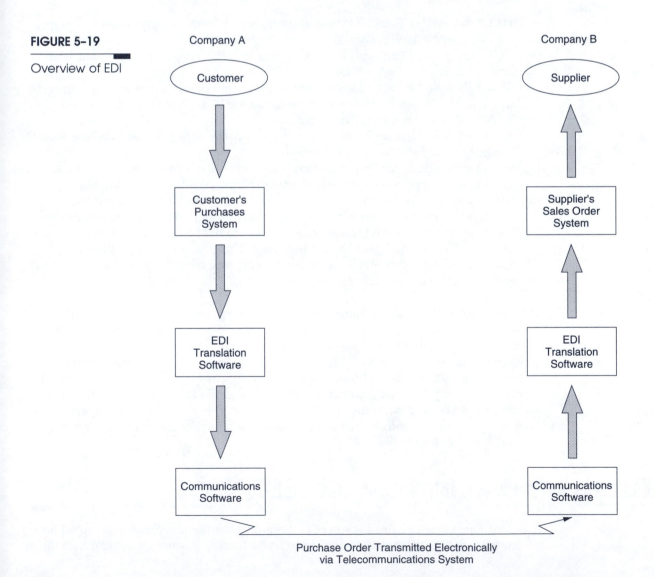

Purchase Order Transmitted Electronically
via Telecommunications System

is converted to a standard format electronic message ready for transmission. The message is transmitted to Company B's translation software, where it is converted to the supplier's internal format. Company B's sales order processing system receives the customer order, which it processes automatically.

Figure 5–19 shows a direct communications link between companies. But many companies choose to use a third-party **value-added network (VAN)** to connect to their trading partners. Figure 5–20 illustrates this arrangement. The originating company transmits its EDI messages to the network rather than directly to the trading partner's computer. The network directs each EDI transmission to its destination and deposits the message in the appropriate electronic mailbox. The messages stay in the mailboxes until the receiving companies connect to the network and retrieve them. The network is called a *value-added network* because it provides service by managing the distribution of the messages between trading partners. VANs can also provide an important degree of control for EDI transactions.

EDI PROTOCOLS

Key to the EDI concept is the use of a standard format for exchanging commerce information between trading partners. Widespread acceptance and growth of EDI did not occur until an acceptable protocol was developed. Over the years, both in the United States and internationally, a number of formats have been proposed. The most popular standard in the United States is the **American National Standards Institute (ANSI)** X.12 format. The standard used internationally is the EDIFACT format. This stands for *EDI For Administration, Commerce, and Transport*. Figure 5–21 presents the X.12 format.

The electronic envelope contains the electronic address of the receiver, communications protocols, and control information. This is the electronic equivalent of a traditional paper envelope. A functional group is a collection of transaction sets (electronic documents) for a particular business application, such as a group of sales

FIGURE 5–20

Value-Added
Network and EDI

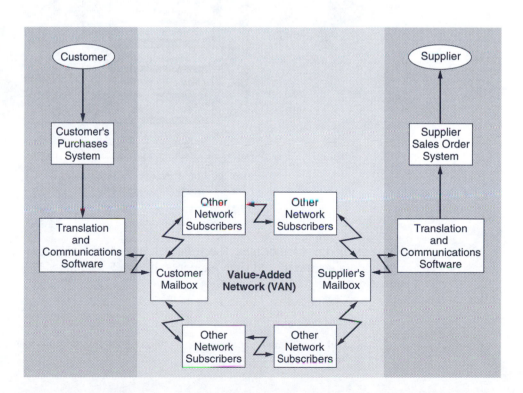

FIGURE 5–21

The X.12 Format

SOURCE: B. K. Stone, *One to Get Ready: How to Prepare Your Company for EDI* (CoreStates, 1988), p. 12.

invoices or purchase orders. The transaction set is the electronic document and comprises data segments and data elements. Figure 5–22 relates these terms to a conventional document.[5]

---

5.   J. M. Cathey, "Electronic Data Interchange: What the Controller Should Know," *Management Accounting* (November 1991): 48.

FIGURE 5–22   Relationship between X.12 Format and a Conventional Source Document

SOURCE: J.M. Cathey, "Electronic Data Interchange: What the Controller Should Know," *Management Accounting* (November 1998): 48.

Each data segment is an information category on the document, such as part number, unit price, or vendor name. The data elements are specific items of data related to a segment. In the example in Figure 5–22, these include such items as REX-446, $127.86, and Ozment Supply.

BENEFITS OF EDI

Although EDI is often associated with the support of just-in-time manufacturing (JIT), its use is not limited to manufacturing firms. EDI has made considerable inroads in a number of industries, including automotive, groceries, retail, health care, and electronics. Following are some common EDI cost savings that justify this approach.

DATA KEYING.   EDI reduces or even eliminates the need for data entry.

ERRORS.   Firms using EDI see reductions in data keying errors, human interpretation and classification errors, and filing (lost document) errors.

REDUCTION OF PAPER.   The use of electronic envelopes and documents reduces drastically the paper forms in the system.

POSTAGE.   Mailed documents are replaced with much cheaper data transmissions.

AUTOMATED PROCEDURES.   EDI automates manual activities associated with purchasing, sales order processing, cash disbursements, and cash receipts.

INVENTORY REDUCTION.   By ordering directly as needed from vendors, EDI reduces the lag time that promotes inventory accumulation.

The benefits of EDI are apparent in the processing of purchases and sales order transactions. On the other hand, using EDI for cash disbursement and cash receipts processing has not seen the same success. The reasons for this are related to the need for intermediary banks in **electronic funds transfer (EFT)** transactions between trading partners. We see this arrangement in Figure 5–23. Purchase invoices are received and automatically approved for payment by the buyer's EDI system. On the payment date, the buyer's system automatically makes an EFT to its originating bank (OBK). The OBK removes funds from the buyer's account and transmits them electronically to the automatic clearing house (ACH) bank. The ACH is a central bank that carries accounts for its member banks. The ACH transfers the funds from the OBK to the receiving bank (RBK), which in turn applies the funds to the seller's account.

Transferring funds by EFT poses no special problem. A check can easily be represented within the X.12 format. The problem arises with the remittance advice information that accompanies the check. Remittance advice information is often quite extensive because of complexities in the transaction. The check may be in payment of multiple invoices or only a partial invoice. There may be disputed amounts because of price disagreements, damaged goods, or incomplete deliveries. In traditional systems, these disputes are resolved by modifying the remittance advice and/or attaching a letter explaining the payment.

Converting remittance information to electronic form can result in very large records. Members of the ACH system are required only to accept and process EFT formats limited to 94 characters of data—a record size sufficient for only very basic messages. Most banks in the ACH system do not support the ANSI standard format for remittances—ANSI 820. Therefore, remittance information must be sent to the seller by separate EDI transmission or conventional mail. The seller must then acquire special software and implement separate procedures to match bank and customer EDI transmissions in applying payments to customer accounts.

Recognizing the void between services demanded and those supplied by the ACH system, many banks have established themselves as **value-added banks (VAB)**, to compete for this market. A VAB can accept electronic disbursements and remittance advices from its clients in any format. It converts EDI transactions to the ANSI X.12 and 820 formats for electronic processing. In the case of non-EDI transactions, the VAB writes traditional checks to the creditor. The services offered by VABs allow their clients to employ a single cash disbursement system that can accommodate both EDI and non-EDI customers. The role of the VAB is expected to expand in the future and compete with VANs for nonfinancial EDI business.

FIGURE 5–23   EFT Transactions between Trading Partners

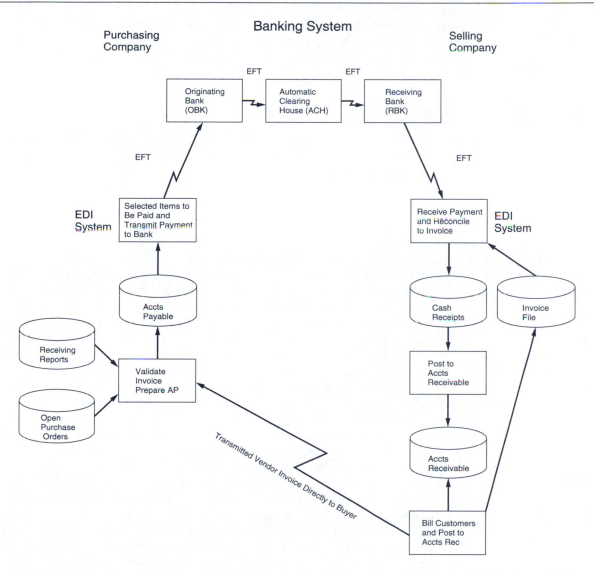

SOURCE: Adapted from B. K. Stone, *One to Get Ready: How to Prepare Your Company for EDI* (CoreStates, 1988), p. 62.

CONTROLLING AND AUDITING ELECTRONIC COMMERCE

Electronic commerce exposes an organization to different types of risks than those faced by traditional systems. These fall into two general categories:

1. *Unauthorized access.* These include, but are not limited to, a computer criminal intercepting a message transmitted between the sender and the receiver, a computer hacker gaining unauthorized access to the organization's network, and a denial-of-service attack from a remote location of the Internet. EDI operations rely on a great deal of mutual access between trading partners. Without proper controls, trading partners may access other partners' data and/or programs from

remote locations to exceed their authority, perpetrate illegal acts, or insert errors into data files.

2. *Equipment failure.* Transmissions between senders and receivers can be disrupted, destroyed, or corrupted by equipment failures in the communications system. Equipment failure can also result in the loss of databases and programs stored on the network server.

CONTROLLING EXPOSURES FROM UNAUTHORIZED ACCESS

Communications channels are accessible to computer criminals, who can perform subversive acts from well outside the physical perimeters of the organization. The following control techniques help reduce the risk.

FIREWALLS

Organizations connected to the Internet or other public networks often implement an electronic "firewall" to insulate their LAN from outside intruders. A **firewall** consists of both software and hardware that provide a focal point for security by channeling all network connections through a control gateway. Firewalls can be used to authenticate an outside user of the network, verify his or her level of access authority, and then direct the user to the program, data, or service requested. In addition to insulating the organization's network from external networks, firewalls can also be used to insulate portions of the organization's network from internal access. For example, a LAN controlling access to financial data can be insulated from other internal LANs. A number of firewall products are on the market. Some of these provide a high level of security, while others are less effective. Firewalls fall into two general types: network-level firewalls and application-level firewalls.

Network-level firewalls provide low cost and low security access control. This type of firewall consists of a **screening router** that examines the source and destination addresses that are attached to incoming message packets. The firewall accepts or denies access requests based on filtering rules that have been programmed into it. Similar to an intelligent PBX, the firewall directs incoming calls to the correct internal receiving node. Network-level firewalls are insecure because they are designed to facilitate the free flow of information rather than restrict it. This method does not explicitly authenticate outside users. Employing a technique called *IP spoofing*, hackers can disguise their message packets to look as if they came from an authorized user and thus gain access to the host's network.

Application-level firewalls provide a high level of customizable network security, but can be extremely expensive. These systems are configured to run security applications called *proxies* that permit routine services such as e-mail to pass through the firewall, but can perform sophisticated functions such as logging or user authentication for specific tasks. An important aspect of this is *one-time password control*, which was discussed in Chapter 2. Application-level firewalls also provide comprehensive transmission logging and auditing tools for reporting unauthorized activity. If an outside user attempts to connect to an unauthorized service or file, the network administrator or security group can be notified immediately.

The highest level of firewall security is provided by a *dual-homed* system. This approach, illustrated in Figure 5–24, has two firewall interfaces. One screens incoming requests from the Internet; the other provides access to the organization's LAN. Direct communication to the Internet is disabled and the two networks are fully isolated. All access is performed by proxy applications that impose separate login procedures.

FIGURE 5-24   Dual-Homed Firewall

Access Attempts from the Internet

The Internet

First Firewall Restricts
Access to Host
Computer Operating
System

HOST

Second Firewall Restricts
Access to Network Server

LAN

Choosing the right firewall involves a trade-off between convenience and security. Ultimately, organization management, in collaboration with accountants and network professionals, must come to grips with what constitutes acceptable risk. The more security provided by the firewall, however, the less convenient it is for authorized users to pass through it. An excessive level of control could, therefore, negatively impact the organization's ability to conduct commerce on the Internet.

CONTROLLING DENIAL-OF-SERVICE ATTACKS

When a user establishes a connection on the Internet through TCP/IP, a three-way handshake takes place. The connecting server sends an initiation code called a *SYN packet* to the receiving server. The receiving server then acknowledges the request by returning a *SYN/ACK packet*. Finally, the initiating host machine responds with an *ACK packet code*. Computer hackers and crackers have devised a malicious act called a *denial-of-service attack*, in which the attacker transmits hundreds of SYN packets to the targeted receiver but never responds with an ACK to complete the connection. As a result, the ports of the receiver's server are clogged with incomplete communication requests that prevent legitimate transactions from being received and processed. Organizations under attack have been prevented from receiving Internet messages for days at a time.

If the target organization could identify the server that is launching the attack, the firewall could be programmed to ignore all communication from that site. Such attacks, however, are difficult to prevent because IP spoofing is used to disguise the source of the messages. IP spoofing programs that randomize the source address of the attacker have been written and publicly distributed over the Internet. Therefore, to the receiving site it appears that the transmissions are coming from all over the Internet.

Denial-of-service attacks can severely hamper an organization's ability to use the Internet to conduct commerce. Although this activity cannot currently be prevented, there are two actions that management and accountants can take to limit the exposure. First, Internet sites with firewalls must engage in a policy of social responsibility. The firewalls at the source sites can be programmed to block messages with noninternal addresses. This would prevent attackers from hiding their locations from the targeted site and would assure the organization's management that no undetected attacks could be launched from its site. This strategy will not, however, prevent attacks from areas of the Internet that do screen outgoing transmissions.

Second, security software is available for the targeted sites that scan for half-open connections. The software looks for SYN packets that have not been followed by an ACK packet. The clogged ports can then be restored to allow legitimate connections to be made

DATA ENCRYPTION

The concept of **encryption** was introduced in Chapter 3 as a means of securing sensitive data in the database. The same principle applies to transmitted messages over a communications line. A computer program transforms a standard (cleartext) message to be transmitted into a coded (ciphertext) form. The receiver of the message must use a decryption program to decode the ciphertext back into its original cleartext form. To control this process and prevent an intruder from capturing and decoding the ciphertext, the encryption program must be provided with a password known as the *encryption key*. Two commonly used methods of encryption are data encryption standard (DES) and public key encryption.

DES ENCRYPTION.   The **data encryption standard (DES)** approach uses a single key known to both the sender and the receiver of the message. Figure 5–25 illustrates this technique. To encode a message, the sender provides the encryption program with the key, which the program uses to produce a ciphertext message. The message enters the communication channel and is transmitted to the receiver's location, where it is stored. When the receiver wishes to read the message, the key must be entered into the decryption program, which transforms the message to cleartext form.

An extension of this technique is to use double encryption. The cleartext message undergoes the encryption process twice. Using two different keys greatly reduces the chances of breaking the cipher. The main problem with the DES approach is that a perpetrator may discover the key (or keys) and decipher the intercepted message. The password control issues discussed in Chapter 2 apply here also. The more individuals who need to know the key, the greater the probability of it falling into the wrong hands. One solution to the problem is public key encryption.

PUBLIC KEY ENCRYPTION.   The **public key encryption** technique uses two different keys: one for encoding the message, the other for decoding it. The encoding key is distributed to all possible users of the network. If this key falls into the hands of a computer criminal, it can be used only to encode messages, not to decode them. The decoding key thus becomes the focal point of control. This key is retained by the security officer in the organization and is distributed only to the user with the authority to decode the message.

MESSAGE SEQUENCE NUMBERING

An intruder in the communications channel may attempt to delete a message from a stream of messages, change the order of messages received, or duplicate a message.

FIGURE 5–25

The Data
Encryption
Standard
Technique

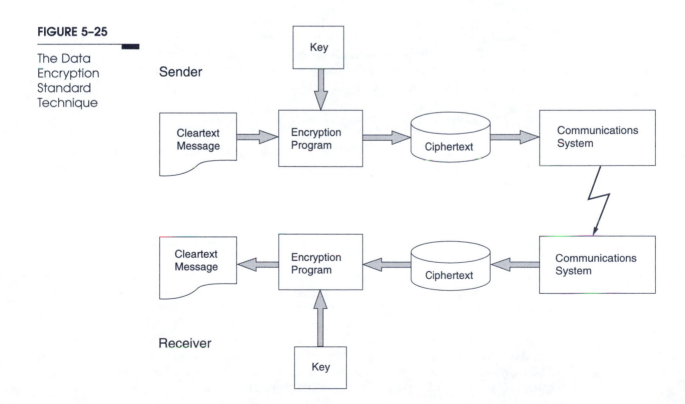

Through **message sequence numbering**, a sequence number is inserted in each message, and any such attempt will become apparent at the receiving end.

MESSAGE TRANSACTION LOG

An intruder may successfully penetrate the system by trying different password and user ID combinations. Therefore, all incoming and outgoing messages, as well as attempted (failed) access, should be recorded in a **message transaction log**. The log should record the user ID, the time of the access, and the terminal location or telephone number from which the access originated.

REQUEST-RESPONSE TECHNIQUE

An intruder may attempt to prevent or delay the receipt of a message from the sender. When senders and receivers are not in constant contact, the receiver may not know that the communications channel has been interrupted and that messages have been diverted. With the **request-response technique**, a control message from the sender and a response from the receiver are sent at periodic, synchronized intervals. The timing of the messages should follow a random pattern that will be difficult for the intruder to determine and circumvent.

CALL-BACK DEVICES

As we have seen, networks can be equipped with security features such as passwords, authentication devices, and encryption. The common weakness to all of these technologies is that they impose the security measure *after* the criminal has connected to the LAN server. Many believe that the key to network security is to keep the intruder off the LAN to begin with.

A **call-back device** requires the dial-in user to enter a password and be identified. The system then breaks the connection to perform user authentication. If the caller is authorized, the call-back device dials the caller's number to establish a new connection. This limits access from only authorized terminals or telephone numbers and prevents an intruder masquerading as a legitimate user.

CONTROLLING EXPOSURES FROM EQUIPMENT FAILURE

This section deals with control techniques designed to limit threats from equipment failure that can disrupt, destroy, or corrupt electrical transactions, databases and computer programs.

LINE ERRORS

The most common problem in data communications is data loss due to **line error**. The bit structure of the message can be corrupted through noise on the communications lines. *Noise* consists of random signals that can interfere with the message signal when they reach a certain level. Electric motors, atmospheric conditions, faulty wiring, defective components in equipment, or noise spilling over from an adjacent communications channel may cause random signals. If not detected, bit structure changes to transmitted data can be catastrophic to the firm. For example, in the case of a database update program, the presence of line errors can result in incorrect transaction values being posted to the accounts. The following two techniques are commonly used to detect and correct such data errors before they are processed.

ECHO CHECK.   The **echo check** involves the receiver of the message returning the message to the sender. The sender compares the returned message with a stored copy of the original. If there is a discrepancy between the returned message and the original, suggesting a transmission error, the message is retransmitted. This technique reduces, by one half, throughput over communications channels. Using full duplex channels, which allow both parties to transmit and receive simultaneously, can increase throughput.

PARITY CHECK.   The **parity check** incorporates an extra bit (the parity bit) into the structure of a bit string when it is created or transmitted. Parity can be both vertical and horizontal (longitudinal). Figure 5–26 illustrates both types of parity. Vertical parity adds the parity bit to each character in the message when the characters are originally coded and stored in magnetic form. For example, the number of 1 bits in the bit structure of each character is counted. If the number is even (say there are four 1 bits in a given eight-bit character) the system assigns the parity bit a value of one. If the number of 1 bits is odd, a 0 parity bit is added to the bit structure.

The concern is that during transmission, a 1 bit will be converted to a 0 bit or vice versa, thus destroying the bit structure integrity of the character. In other words, the original character is incorrectly presented as a different yet valid character. An error of this sort, if it goes undetected, could have a devastating effect on financial numbers. But this error can be detected at the receiving end by a parity check. The 1 bits are again counted by the system and should always equal an odd number. If a 1 bit is added to or removed from the bit structure during transmission, the number of 1 bits for the character will be even, which would signal that an error has occurred.

Vertical parity alone cannot detect an error that changes two bits in the structure simultaneously, thus retaining the parity of the character. Some estimates indicate a 40 to 50 percent chance that line noise will corrupt more than one bit within a character. This problem is greatly reduced by using horizontal parity in conjunction with vertical parity. Referring to Figure 5–26, notice the parity bit following each block of characters. The combination of vertical and horizontal parity provides a higher degree of protection from line errors.

FIGURE 5–26

Vertical and
Horizontal Parity
Using Odd Parity

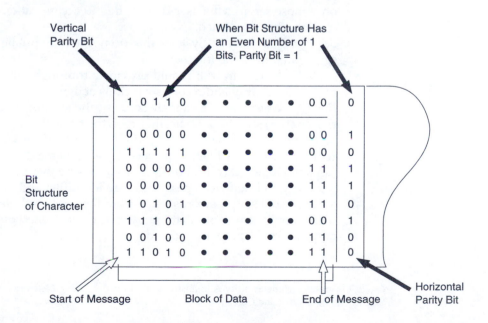

Vertical
Parity Bit

When Bit Structure Has
an Even Number of 1
Bits, Parity Bit = 1

Bit
Structure
of Character

Start of Message   Block of Data   End of Message

Horizontal
Parity Bit

AUDIT OBJECTIVES

- To verify the security and integrity of the electronic commerce transactions by determining that controls (1) can detect and correct message loss due to equipment failure, (2) can prevent and detect illegal access both internally and from the Internet, and (3) will render useless any data that are successfully captured by a perpetrator.

AUDIT PROCEDURES

To achieve these audit objectives, the auditor may perform the following tests of controls:

1. Select a sample of messages from the transaction log and examine them for garbled contents caused by line noise. The auditor should verify that all corrupted messages were successfully retransmitted.
2. Review the message transaction logs to verify that all messages were received in their proper sequence.
3. Test the operation of the call-back feature by placing an unauthorized call from outside the installation.
4. Review security procedures governing the administration of data encryption keys.
5. Verify the encryption process by transmitting a test message and examining the contents at various points along the channel between the sending and receiving locations.
6. Review the adequacy of the firewall in achieving the proper balance between control and convenience based on the organization's business objectives and potential risks. Criteria for assessing the firewall effectiveness include:
   - *Flexibility.* The firewall should be flexible enough to accommodate new services as the security needs of the organization change.
   - *Proxy Services.* Adequate proxy applications should be in place to provide explicit user authentication to sensitive services, applications, and data.
   - *Filtering.* Strong filtering techniques should be designed to deny all services that are not explicitly permitted. In other words, the firewall should specify only those services the user is permitted to access, rather than specifying the services that are denied.
   - *Segregation of Systems.* Systems that do not require public access should be segregated from the Internet.
   - *Audit Tools.* The firewall should provide a thorough set of audit and logging tools that identify and record suspicious activity.
   - *Probe for Weaknesses.* To validate security, the auditor (or a professional security analyst) should periodically probe the firewall for weaknesses just as a computer Internet hacker would do. A number of software products are currently available for identifying security weaknesses.[6]
   - Review password control procedures to ensure that passwords are changed regularly and that weak passwords are identified and disallowed. Reviewing a sample of user passwords taken from the password file can do this. The auditor should also verify that the password file is encrypted and that the encryption key is properly secured.

---

6.   Examples include Security Administrator Tool for Analyzing Networks (SATAN), Internet Security Scanner (ISS), Gabriel, and Courtney.

BACKUP CONTROL FOR NETWORKS

Data backup in networks is accomplished in several different ways depending on the network's complexity. In small networks, a single workstation may be assigned the backup and restore functions for the other nodes. As networks grow to include more nodes and increased data sharing, backup is usually assigned at the network server level. Enterprise-level networks can be very large and include multiple servers. These network environments are likely to control mission-critical data, and a server failure could mark disaster for the organization. Because of the large number of users, enterprise-level networks undergo continuous change to accommodate shifts in user needs. In such a dynamic setting, organization management must be able to centrally monitor and control backup procedures.

Restricting access to backup files in enterprise-level networks is a control issue requiring specific attention. The organization's mission-critical backup data are exposed to the same access threats as its production data. Many backup products provide access control features such as encryption and password management. At the very least, user management should ensure that the backup management package under consideration is compatible with network's existing access control features.

Finally, backup redundancy is advisable in enterprise-level networks. Some top-end products permit dynamic allocation of backup devices and automatic notification of backup status. If an assigned backup device fails, the data are automatically routed to a working device. The backup management system immediately notifies the network administrator of the failure via e-mail or pager.

AUDIT OBJECTIVES

- To verify that backup procedures are sufficient to preserve the integrity and physical security of the databases and other files connected to the network.

AUDIT PROCEDURES

The procedures are similar to those discussed in previous chapters. They include:

- The auditor should verify that backup is performed routinely and frequently to facilitate the recovery of lost, destroyed, or corrupted data.
- Production databases should be copied at regular intervals (perhaps several times an hour). A balance must be sought between the inconvenience of frequent backup activities and the business disruption caused by excessive reprocessing that is needed to restore the database after a failure.
- The auditor should verify that automatic backup procedures are in place and functioning, and that copies of files and databases are stored off-site for further security.

CONTROLLING ELECTRONIC DATA INTERCHANGE

The absence of human intervention in the EDI process presents a unique twist to traditional control problems, including ensuring that transactions are authorized and valid, preventing unauthorized access to data files, and maintaining an audit trail of transactions. Techniques for dealing with these issues follow.

TRANSACTION VALIDATION

Both the customer and the supplier must establish that a transaction being processed is to (or from) a valid trading partner. This can be accomplished at three points in the process.

- Some VANs have the capability of validating passwords and user ID codes for the vendor by matching these against a valid customer file. Any unauthorized trading partner transactions are rejected by the VAN before they reach the vendor's system.
- Before being converted, the translation software can validate the trading partner's ID and password against a validation file in the firm's database.
- Before processing, the trading partner's application software can validate the transaction by referencing the valid customer and vendor files.

ACCESS CONTROL

The degree of access control in the system will be determined by the trading agreement between the trading partners. For EDI to function smoothly, the trading partners must allow a degree of access to private data files that would be forbidden in a traditional environment. For example, before placing an order, the customer's system may need to access the vendor's inventory files to determine if inventories are available. Also, to prevent the vendor from having to prepare an invoice and the customer having to match it against a purchase order, the partners may agree that the prices on the purchase order will be binding on both parties. In such a scenario, the customer must periodically access the vendor's price list file to keep pricing information current. Alternatively, the vendor may need access to the customer's price list to update prices.

To guard against unauthorized access, each company must establish valid vendor and customer files. Inquiries against databases can thus be validated, and unauthorized attempts at access can be rejected. User authority tables can also be established, which specify the degree of access a trading partner is allowed. For example, the partner may be authorized to read inventory or pricing data but not change any values. Again, some VANs can screen and reject unauthorized access attempts by trading partners.

EDI AUDIT TRAIL

The absence of source documents in EDI transactions disrupts the traditional audit trail and restricts the ability of accountants to verify the validity, completeness, timing, and accuracy of transactions. One technique for restoring the audit trail is to maintain a control log, which records the transaction's flow through each phase of the EDI system. Figure 5–27 illustrates how this approach may be employed.

As the transaction is received at each stage in the process, an entry is made into the log. In the customer's system, the transaction log can be reconciled to ensure that all transactions initiated by the purchases system were correctly translated and communicated. Likewise, in the vendor's system, the control log will establish that all messages received by the communications software were correctly translated and processed by the sales order system.

AUDIT OBJECTIVES

- To determine that (1) all EDI transactions are authorized, validated, and in compliance with the trading partner agreement; (2) no unauthorized organizations

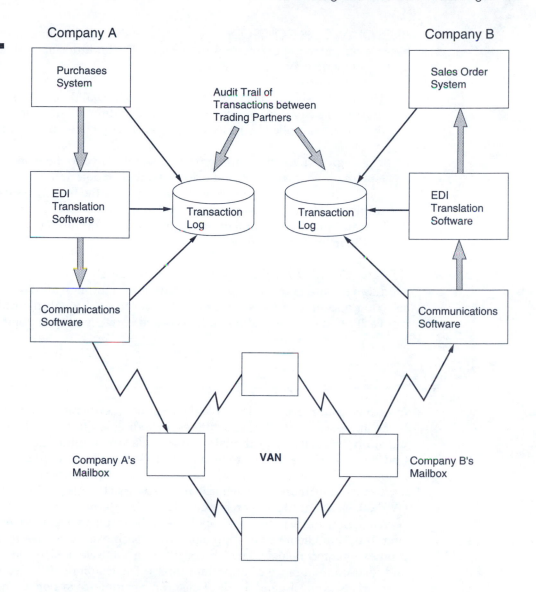

FIGURE 5–27

EDI System using Transaction Control Log for Audit Trail

accessed database records; (3) authorized trading partners have access only to approved data; and (4) adequate controls are in place to ensure a complete audit trail of all EDI transactions.

AUDIT PROCEDURES

To achieve these control objectives, the auditor may perform the following tests of controls.

TESTS OF VALIDATION CONTROLS.   The auditor should establish that trading partner identification codes are verified before transactions are processed. To accomplish this, the auditor should (1) review agreements with the VAN facility to validate transactions and ensure that information regarding valid trading partners is complete and correct and (2) examine the organization's valid trading partner file for accuracy and completeness.

TESTS OF ACCESS CONTROLS.   Security over the valid trading partner file and databases is central to the EDI control framework. The auditor can verify control adequacy in the following ways:

1. The auditor should determine that access to the valid vendor or customer file is limited to authorized employees only. The auditor should verify that access to this file is controlled by password and authority tables and that the data are encrypted.
2. The degree of access a trading partner should have to the firm's database records (such as inventory levels and price lists) will be determined by the trading agreement. The auditor should reconcile the terms of the trading agreement against the trading partner's access privileges stated in the database authority table.
3. The auditor should simulate access by a sample of trading partners and attempt to violate access privileges.

TESTS OF AUDIT TRAIL CONTROLS.   The auditor should verify that the EDI system produces a transaction log that tracks transactions through all stages of processing. By selecting a sample of transactions and tracing these through the process, the auditor can verify that key data values were recorded correctly at each point.

SUMMARY

Electronic commerce (EC) involves the electronic processing and transmission of data. It encompasses many diverse activities, including electronic trading of goods and services, on-line delivery of digital products, electronic funds transfer (EFT), electronic trading of stocks, and direct consumer marketing. This chapter dealt with the technologies, risks, controls, and audit issues associated with electronic commerce. The topics discussed included private local area networks (LANs), public wide area networks (WANs), electronic data interchange (EDI), and Internet commerce. The chapter began with a review of basic network topologies. The respective features of star, hierarchical, ring, bus, and client-server topologies were each examined. We then turned to communications technologies, which constitute a vital element of network architecture, and focused on a range of important topics. The chapter concluded with a discussion of the risks, controls, and audit of electronic commerce systems. The risks associated with electronic commerce can be divided into two general areas: risks from unlawful access and risks from equipment failure. Various controls for dealing with these risks were examined. Audit objectives and suggested audit procedures were presented.

KEY TERMS

American National Standards Institute (ANSI)
amplitude
asynchronous
bits
bridges
bus topology
call-back device

carrier sensing
client-server topology
coaxial cable
communications satellites
data encryption standard (DES)
digital signal
dumb terminals

echo check
electronic data interchange (EDI)
electronic funds transfer (EFT)
encryption
fiber optic cable
firewall
frequency
front-end processor (FEP)
full duplex
gateways
half duplex
hierarchical topology
line error
local area networks
message sequence numbering
message transaction log
microwave transmissions
modem
modulation
multiplexer
network interface card (NIC)
network protocols
network topology
packet switching
parity check

phase
polling
private branch exchange (PBX)
programmable terminal
protocols
public key encryption
request-response technique
ring topology
screening router
servers
simplex
smart terminals
star topology
switching
synchronous
terminals
token passing
Transfer Control Protocol/Internet Protocol
 (TCP/IP)
transmission errors
twisted-pair cable
value-added banks (VAB)
value-added network (VAN)
wave signal
wide area networks

REVIEW QUESTIONS

1. Distinguish between the terms *network*, and *network topologies*.
2. List five basic network topologies.
3. Bridges and gateways are becoming more and more important. Explain what they are.
4. What purpose does a network interface card serve?
5. Does the star topology foster centralized or distributed data processing? Explain your answer.
6. How do the bus and ring topologies differ?
7. In the client-server mode, which end does the searching of the file, which end does the processing, and what part of the database needs to be locked?
8. Distinguish between dumb and smart terminals.
9. Give three examples of where you might see a dumb terminal being used.
10. Give some examples of point devices. What is the most commonly used pointing device?
11. What are the three characteristics of wave signals?
12. What are modulation and demodulation? Why has the modem become a necessity in telecommunications?
13. Distinguish between baud and bit rates of transmission. How can multilevel modulations increase the baud per second transmission level?
14. Discuss the different transmission modes and their relative advantages.
15. What is a multiplexer?
16. What is message switching and packet switching?
17. Why does the addition of a front-end processor allow a primary or host CPU to become efficient?

18. Explain what data collision is, and discuss three basic methods of avoiding collisions. What are their relative merits?

19. What types of threats are faced when using the Internet for business transactions?

20. What are some of the ways in which EDI can generate cost savings for a firm?

21. What are the roles of VABs and VANs in EDI?

22. What is a firewall?

23. Distinguish between network-level and application-level firewalls.

24. What are the most common forms of contra-security behavior?

25. What is a three-way handshake?

26. What are denial-of-service attacks? Can they be thwarted?

27. How does public key encryption work?

28. Categorize each of the following as either an equipment failure control or an unauthorized access control:
   a. Message authentication
   b. Parity check
   c. Call-back device
   d. Echo check
   e. Line error
   f. Data encryption
   g. Request-response technique

29. Will a vertical parity check always catch a data transmission error? Why or why not?

30. At what three points in an electronic data interchange transaction and validation process can authorization and validation be accomplished?

DISCUSSION QUESTIONS

1. Differentiate between a LAN and a WAN. Do you have either or both at your university or college?

2. Explain whether the new trend in digital transmission will cause manufacturers of modems to worry about becoming obsolete.

3. Discuss the paradox of networking.

4. As the information superhighway progresses and electronic data interchange increases in popularity, interfaces between organizational computers are becoming a necessity. Discuss what steps are being taken to foster these types of interfaces.

5. Electronic funds transfers are widely used by payroll departments and individuals to pay their personal bills, so why are they so infrequently used by businesses for cash disbursements?

6. EDI systems tied into inventory control models in conjunction with just-in-time inventory systems have been said to be very beneficial in many ways; however, a mistake made by one firm in over-ordering can mushroom into overproduction for many firms. Explain how this can happen.

7. Does every organization that has a LAN need a firewall?

8. Are one-time passwords foolproof?

9. Why might an individual launch a denial-of-service attack on a company's Internet connection?

10. Discuss the various ways in which data encryption may be used. Which provides the most control?

11. Why is the request-response technique important? Discuss the reasons an intruder may wish to prevent or delay the receipt of a message.

12. Is backup redundancy inefficient?

13. Discuss how the widespread use of laptop and notebook computers is making data encryption standards more easily penetrable.

14. Discuss the unique control problems that EDI creates.

15. "In an EDI system, only the customer needs to verify that the order being placed is from a valid supplier and not vice versa." Do you agree with this statement? Why or why not?

16. Discuss how EDI creates an environment in which sensitive information, such as inventory amounts and price data, is no longer private. What potential dangers exist if the

proper controls are not in place? Give an example.

17. President Clinton wanted to require manufacturers of data encryption software to give the CIA and FBI their decryption algorithms. Do you agree with this type of policy? What are the issues?

MULTIPLE-CHOICE QUESTIONS

1. CMA 687 5-13

   An organization employs multiple central processors to serve multiple real-time applications and multiple classes of users. Data processing jobs are completed by the processor that is best designed to perform the job efficiently. The processors are at different locations and are connected by data communication lines. The organization is employing a systems configuration referred to as a(n)
   a. simplex system.
   b. duplex system.
   c. distributed processing system.
   d. communications (front-end) processor system.
   e. applications system.

2. CMA 1289 5-6

   A system with several computers that are connected for communication and data transmission purposes but that permits each computer to process its own data is a
   a. distributed data processing network.
   b. centralized network.
   c. decentralized network.
   d. multidrop network.
   e. hybrid system.

3. CIA (Adapted) 581 IV-28

   A distinguishing feature of a smart terminal is that it
   a. combines people and machines that work together to get intelligent responses.
   b. can often be programmed to carry out special tasks.
   c. must be on-line to a computer to be used.
   d. is used effectively to store and edit data before transmission.
   e. eliminates the need for batch processing.

4. CMA 686 5-8

   Remote batch processing avoids the need for having
   a. terminals at each user location.
   b. printers at each user location.
   c. a central processing unit at each user location.
   d. input controls at each user location.
   e. well-designed and executed procedures at each user location.

5. CMA 687 5-10

   A modem is a device that
   a. is used to aid in backup procedures.
   b. traces the execution of steps by a program.
   c. packs data in a disk file.
   d. speeds up on-line printing.
   e. allows computer signals to be sent over a telephone line.

6. Which statement below about the client-server model is correct? The client-server model
   a. is best suited to the token-ring topology because the random-access method used by this topology detects data collisions.
   b. distributes both data and processing tasks to the server node. The client-server model can use the bus or ring topology.
   c. is most effective when used as a bus topology because its deterministic access method avoids collisions and prevents data loss during transmissions.
   d. is more efficient than the bus or ring topologies because it transmits an entire file of records to the requesting node rather than only a single record.
   e. is not used in conjunction with either the bus or ring topologies.

7. Hackers can disguise their message packets to look as if they came from an authorized user and gain access to the host's network using a technique called
   a. spoofing.
   b. spooling.
   c. dual-homed.
   d. screening.

8. Transmitting numerous SYN packets to a targeted receiver, but not responding to an ACK, is

    a. a DES message.
    b. the request-response technique.
    c. a denial-of-service attack.
    d. a call-back device.

PROBLEMS

1. System Configuration

A local newspaper in Austin, Texas, receives its stories from two main sources—its own reporters and the wire services. Each of the reporters has a microcomputer on his or her desk. The writer types in the story and carries the story on diskette over to the editor's desk. The editor makes cuts and sends the story back to the writer for revision. The diskette is then sent back to the editor for final approval. After final approval, the story is sent to the printer for typesetting. Stories that come in over wire are first marked up by a reporter and typed in. From there, they follow much the same process as internally generated stories. When two reporters are collaborating on a story, they must pass the diskette back and forth between themselves. Writers reporting from the field must come back to the office to prepare the stories for editorial review. In rare instances, they may dictate a very important story over the phone.

    Discuss the weaknesses in this system. What type of communication system would you suggest for this newspaper?

2. Data Communications Configuration

The big accounting firms have begun to prepare their working papers using electronic spreadsheets. They also use electronic mail capabilities that allow them to transmit these spreadsheets over telecommunication lines. Considering that the staff accountants who prepare the working papers are usually at the client's office and the manager in charge of the job may be at another site or at the accounting firm's main office, what type of data communication configuration is being employed? What are any potential advantages and disadvantages of this method?

3. Distributed Data Processing

CMA Adapted 1286 5-2

Vincent Maloy, director of special projects and analysis for Milok Company, is responsible for preparing corporate financial analyses and monthly projections, and for reviewing and presenting to upper management the financial impacts of proposed strategies. Data for these financial analyses and projections are obtained from reports developed by Milok's systems department and generated from its mainframe computer. Additional data are obtained through terminals via a data inquiry system. Reports and charts for presentations are then prepared by hand and typed. Maloy has tried to have final presentations generated by the computer but has not always been successful.

    The systems department has developed a package using a terminal emulator to link a microcomputer to the mainframe computer. This allows the microcomputer to become part of the current data inquiry systems and enables data to be downloaded to the microcomputer's disk. The data are in a format that allows printing or further manipulation and analyses using commercial software packages, such as spreadsheet analysis. The special projects and analysis department has been chosen to be the first users of this new computer terminal system.

    Maloy questioned whether the new system could do more for his department than implementing the program modification requests that he has submitted to the systems department. He also believes that his people would have to become programmers.

    Lisa Brandt, a supervisor in Maloy's department, has decided to prepare a briefing for Maloy on the benefits of integrating microcomputers with the mainframe computer. She has used the terminal inquiry system extensively and has learned to use spreadsheet software to prepare special analyses, sometimes with multiple alternatives. She also tried the new package while it was being tested.

Required:

a. Identify five enhancements to current information and reporting that Milok Company should be able to realize by integrating microcomputers with its mainframe computer.

b. Explain how the utilization of computer resources would be altered as a result of integrating microcomputers with the company's mainframe computer.

c. Discuss what security of the data is gained or lost by integrating microcomputers with the company's mainframe computer.

4. Distributed Data Processing
CMA Adapted 1288-5Y6
In the last two decades, there has been a transition from a centralized mainframe computer environment to a distributed network where an organization has the ability to share computer processing. One of the fastest-growing segments of the computer industry is the local area network, which is said to be the wave of the future. LANs permit the transfer of information between microcomputers, word processors, data storage devices, printers, voice devices, and telecommunication devices. Current opinion holds that the flow of organizational communications has been enhanced by the transition from the optimization of computers experienced in the traditional distributed network to the optimization of human resources in the LAN environment.

Required:

a. Describe the reasons why an organization would choose a distributed network over the traditional centralized computer environment.

b. Compare and contrast the characteristics of a traditional distributed computer network with those of a local area network as they are related to the
   i. utilization of computer hardware.

ii. user interaction and the sharing of electronic information.

c. Identify and explain three problems that can result from the use of local area networks.

d. Explain the hardware characteristics associated with a computer modem as they relate to distributed information processing.

5. Electronic Data Interchange
The purchase order for one firm is the source document for the sales order of another firm. Consider the following purchase order and sales order data elements stored for two firms. Discuss any differences that may be problematic in transferring information between the two firms.

Purchasing Firm:

GH BETTIS
A Division of Galveston-Houston Corp.
1200 Post Oak Blvd.
P.O. Box 4768
Houston, TX 77637-9877

Data Elements
  Vendor Number
  Vendor Name
  Vendor Address
  Vendor City
  Vendor State
  Vendor Country
  Vendor Zip Code
  Purchase Order No.
  Date
  Shipment Destination Code
  Vendor Part No.
  Item Description
  Quantity Ordered
  Unit Price
  Total

Selling Firm:

Oakland Steel Company
469 Lakeland Blvd.
Chicago, IL 60613-8888

Data Elements
  Customer Number
  Customer Name
  Customer Address
  Customer City
  Customer State

Customer Country
Customer Zip Code
Purchase Order No.
Sales Order No.
Date
Shipping Company
Vendor Part No.
Item Description
Quantity Ordered
Unit Price
Total
Discount Offered
Tax
Freight Charges

6. Access Control
    Design a well-controlled system in terms of access controls for a major insurance company that equips each salesperson (life, property, and investments) with a laptop. Each salesperson must transmit sales data daily to corporate headquarters. Further, the salespeople use their laptops to connect to the company's e-mail system.

7. Input Controls and Telecommunications
    CMA 686 5-2
    Intex Corporation is a multinational company with approximately 100 subsidiaries and divisions, referred to as reporting units. Each reporting unit operates autonomously and maintains its own accounting information system. Each month, the reporting units prepare the basic financial statements and other key financial data on prescribed forms. These statements and related data are either mailed or telexed to corporate headquarters in New York City for entry into the corporate database. Top and middle management at corporate headquarters use the database to plan and direct corporate operations and objectives.

    Under the current system, the statements and data are to be received at corporate headquarters by the twelfth working day following the end of the month. The reports are logged, batched, and taken to the data processing department for coding and entry into the database. Approximately 15 percent of the reporting units are delinquent in submitting their data, and three to four days are required

to receive all of the data. After the data are loaded into the system, data verification programs are run to check footings, cross-statement consistency, and dollar range limits. Any errors in the data are traced and corrected, and reporting units are notified of all errors by form letters. Intex Corporation has decided to upgrade its computer communications network. The new system would allow a more timely receipt of data at corporate headquarters and would provide numerous benefits to each of the reporting units.

The systems department at corporate headquarters is responsible for the overall design and implementation of the new system. It will use current computer communications technology by installing smart computer terminals at all reporting units. These terminals will provide two-way computer communications and serve as microcomputers that can use spreadsheet and other applications software. As part of the initial use of the system, the data collection for the corporate database would be performed through these terminals.

The financial statements and other financial data currently mailed or telexed would be entered by terminals. The required forms would initially be transmitted (downloaded) from the headquarters computer to the terminals of each reporting unit and stored permanently on disk. Data would be entered on the forms appearing on the reporting unit's terminal and stored under a separate file for transmission after the data are checked.

The data edit program would also be downloaded to the reporting units so the data could be verified at the unit location. All corrections would be made before transmitting the data to headquarters. The data would be stored on disk in proper format to maintain a unit file. Data would either be transmitted to corporate headquarters immediately or retrieved by the computer at corporate headquarters as needed. Therefore, data arriving at corporate headquarters would be free from errors and ready to be used in reports.

Charles Edwards, Intex's controller, is very pleased with the prospects of the new system. He believes that the data will be received from the reporting units two to three days faster and that data accuracy will be much improved. However, Edwards is concerned about data security and integrity during the transmission of data between the reporting units and corporate headquarters. He has scheduled a meeting with key personnel from the systems department to discuss these concerns.

Required:

Intex could experience data security and integrity problems when transmitting data between the reporting units and corporate headquarters.

a. Identify and explain the data security and integrity problems that could occur.
b. For each problem identified, identify and explain a control procedure that could be employed to minimize or eliminate the problem. Use the following format to present your answer.

Problem Identification and Explanation	Control Procedure and Explanation

8. **Preventive Controls**

Listed below are some scenarios. For each scenario, discuss the possible damages that can occur. Suggest a preventive control.

a. An intruder taps into a telecommunications device and retrieves the identifying codes and personal identification numbers for ATM cardholders. (The user subsequently codes this information onto a magnetic coding device and places this strip on a piece of cardboard.)
b. Due to occasional noise on a transmission line, electronic messages received are extremely garbled.
c. Due to occasional noise on a transmission line, data being transferred is lost or garbled.
d. Important strategic messages are being temporarily delayed by an intruder over the telecommunications lines.
e. Electronic messages are being altered by an intruder before being received by the user.

chapter **6**

COMPUTER ASSISTED AUDIT
TOOLS AND TECHNIQUES

This chapter examines several issues related to the use of Computer Assisted Audit Tools and Techniques (CAATTs) for performing tests of application controls and data extraction. It opens with a description of application controls. These fall into three broad classes: input controls, processing controls, and output controls. The chapter then examines the *black box* and *white box* approaches to testing application controls. The latter approach requires a detailed understanding of the application's logic. Five CAATT approaches used for testing application logic are then examined: the test data method, base case system evaluation, tracing, integrated test facility, and parallel simulation.

LEARNING OBJECTIVES

After studying this chapter, you should:

- Be familiar with the classes of transaction input controls used by accounting applications.
- Understand the objectives and techniques used to implement processing controls, including run-to-run, operator intervention, and audit trail controls.
- Understand the methods used to establish effective output controls for both batch and real-time systems.
- Know the difference between black box and white box auditing.
- Be familiar with the key features of the five CAATTs discussed in the chapter.

APPLICATION CONTROLS

Application controls are programmed procedures designed to deal with potential exposures that threaten specific applications, such as payroll, purchases, and cash disbursements systems. Application controls fall into three broad categories: input controls, processing controls, and output controls.

INPUT CONTROLS

The data collection component of the information system is responsible for bringing data into the system for processing. **Input controls** at this stage are designed to ensure that these transactions are valid, accurate, and complete. Data input procedures can be either source document-triggered (batch) or direct input (real-time).

Source document input requires human involvement and is prone to clerical errors. Some types of errors that are entered on the source documents cannot be detected and corrected during the data input stage. Dealing with these problems may require tracing the transaction back to its source (such as contacting the customer) to correct the mistake. Direct input, on the other hand, employs real-time editing techniques to identify and correct errors immediately, thus significantly reducing the number of errors that enter the system.

CLASSES OF INPUT CONTROL

For presentation convenience and to provide structure to this discussion, we have divided input controls into the following broad classes:

- Source document controls
- Data coding controls
- Batch controls
- Validation controls
- Input error correction
- Generalized data input systems

These control classes are not mutually exclusive divisions. Some control techniques that we shall examine could fit logically into more than one class.

SOURCE DOCUMENT CONTROLS

In systems that use physical source documents to initiate transactions, careful control must be exercised over these instruments. Source document fraud can be used to remove assets from the organization. For example, an individual with access to purchase orders and receiving reports could fabricate a purchase transaction to a nonexistent supplier. If these documents were entered into the data processing stream, along with a fabricated vendor's invoice, the system could process these documents as if a legitimate transaction had taken place. In the absence of other compensating controls to detect this type of fraud, the system would create an account payable and subsequently write a check in payment.

To control against this type of exposure, the organization must implement control procedures over source documents to account for each document, as described below:

USE PRENUMBERED SOURCE DOCUMENTS. Source documents should come prenumbered from the printer with a unique sequential number on each document. Source document numbers permit accurate accounting of document usage and provide an audit trail for tracing transactions through accounting records. We discuss this further in the next section.

USE SOURCE DOCUMENTS IN SEQUENCE.   Source documents should be distributed to the users and used in sequence. This requires that adequate physical security be maintained over the source document inventory at the user site. When not in use, documents should be locked away. At all times, access to source documents should be limited to authorized persons.

PERIODICALLY AUDIT SOURCE DOCUMENTS.   Reconciling document sequence numbers should identify missing source documents. Periodically, the auditor should compare the numbers of documents used to date with those remaining in inventory plus those voided due to errors. Documents not accounted for should be reported to management.

DATA CODING CONTROLS

Coding controls are checks on the integrity of data codes used in processing. A customer's account number, an inventory item number, and a chart of accounts number are all examples of data codes. Three types of errors can corrupt data codes and cause processing errors: transcription errors, single transposition errors, and multiple transposition errors. **Transcription errors** fall into three classes:

- Addition errors occur when an extra digit or character is added to the code. For example, inventory item number 83276 is recorded as 832766.
- Truncation errors occur when a digit or character is removed from the end of a code. In this type of error, the inventory item above would be recorded as 8327.
- Substitution errors are the replacement of one digit in a code with another. For example, code number 83276 is recorded as 83266.

There are two types of **transposition errors**. *Single transposition errors* occur when two adjacent digits are reversed. For instance, 83276 is recorded as 38276. *Multiple transposition errors* occur when nonadjacent digits are transposed. For example, 83276 is recorded as 87236

   Any of these errors can cause serious problems in data processing if they go undetected. For example, a sales order for customer 732519 that is transposed into 735219 will be posted to the wrong customer's account. A similar error in an inventory item code on a purchase order could result in ordering unneeded inventory and failing to order inventory that is needed. These simple errors can severely disrupt operations.

CHECK DIGITS.   One method for detecting data coding errors is a check digit. A **check digit** is a control digit (or digits) added to the code when it is originally assigned that allows the integrity of the code to be established during subsequent processing. The check digit can be located anywhere in the code: as a prefix, a suffix, or embedded someplace in the middle. The simplest form of check digit is to sum the digits in the code and use this sum as the check digit. For example, for the customer account code 5372 the calculated check digit would be:

$$5 + 3 + 7 + 2 = 17$$

By dropping the tens column, the check digit 7 is added to the original code to produce the new code 53727. The entire string of digits (including the check digit) becomes the customer account number. During data entry, the system can recalculate the check digit to ensure that the code is correct. This technique will detect only transcription errors. For example, if a substitution error occurred and the above code were entered as 52727, the calculated check digit would be 6 (5 + 2 + 7 + 2 = 16 = 6), and the error would be detected. However, this technique would fail to identify transposition errors. For example, transposing the first two digits yields the code 35727, which still sums to 17 and produces the check digit 7. This error would go undetected.

There are many check digit techniques for dealing with transposition errors. A popular method is modulus 11. Using the code 5372, the steps in this technique are as follows:

1. *Assign weights.* Each digit in the code is multiplied by a different weight. In this case, the weights used are 5, 4, 3, and 2, shown as follows:

Digit		Weight
5	˘	5 = 25
3	˘	4 = 12
7	˘	3 = 21
2	˘	2 = 4

2. *Sum the products (25 + 12 + 21 + 4 = 62).*
3. *Divide by the modulus.* We are using modulus 11 in this case, giving 62/11 = 5 with a remainder of 7.
4. *Subtract the remainder from the modulus to obtain the check digit (11 − 7 = 4 [check digit]).*
5. *Add the check digit to the original code to yield the new code: 53724.*

Using this technique to recalculate the check digit during processing, a transposition error in the code will produce a check digit other than 4. For example, if the preceding code was incorrectly entered as 35724, the recalculated check digit would be 6.

WHEN SHOULD CHECK DIGITS BE USED?   The use of check digits introduces storage and processing inefficiencies and therefore should be restricted to essential data, such as primary and secondary key fields. All check digit techniques require one or more additional spaces in the field to accommodate the check digit. In the case of modulus 11, if step three above produces a remainder of 1, the check digit of 10 will require two additional character spaces. If field length is a limitation, one way of handling this problem is to disallow codes that generate the check digit 10. This would restrict the range of available codes by about 9 percent.

BATCH CONTROLS

Batch controls are an effective method of managing high volumes of transaction data through a system. The objective of batch control is to reconcile output produced by the system with the input originally entered into the system. This provides assurance that:

- All records in the batch are processed.
- No records are processed more than once.
- An audit trail of transactions is created from input through processing to the output stage of the system.

Batch control is not exclusively an input control technique. Controlling the batch continues through all phases of the system. We are treating this topic here because batch control is initiated at the input stage.

Achieving batch control objectives requires grouping similar types of input transactions (such as sales orders) together in batches and then controlling the batches throughout data processing. Two documents are used to accomplish this task: a batch transmittal sheet and a batch control log. Figure 6–1 shows an example of a batch

FIGURE 6-1

Batch
Transmittal
Sheet

transmittal sheet. The batch transmittal sheet captures relevant information about the batch, such as:

- A unique batch number.
- A batch date.
- A transaction code (indicating the type of transactions, such as a sales order or cash receipt).
- The number of records in the batch (record count).
- The total dollar value of a financial field (batch control total).
- The total of a unique nonfinancial field (hash total).

Usually, the batch transmittal sheet is prepared by the user department and is submitted to data control along with the batch of source documents. Sometimes, the data control clerk, acting as a liaison between the users and the data processing department, prepares the transmittal sheet. Figure 6–2 illustrates the batch control process.

The data control clerk receives transactions from users assembled in batches of 40 to 50 records. The clerk assigns each batch a unique number, date-stamps the documents, and calculates (or recalculates) the batch control numbers, such as the total dollar amount of the batch and a hash total (discussed later). The clerk enters the batch control information in the batch control log and submits the batch of documents, along with the transmittal sheet, to the data entry department. Figure 6–3 shows a sample batch control log.

The data entry group codes and enters the transmittal sheet data onto the transaction file, along with the batch of transaction records. The transmittal data may be added as an additional record in the file or placed in the file's internal trailer label. (We will discuss internal labels later in this section.) The transmittal sheet becomes the batch control record and is used to assess the integrity of the batch during processing.

FIGURE 6-2   Batch Control Process

For example, the data entry procedure will recalculate the batch control totals to make sure the batch is in balance. The transmittal record shows a batch of 50 sales order records with a total dollar value of $122,674.87 and a hash total of 4537838. At various points throughout and at the end of processing, these amounts are recalculated and compared to the batch control record. If the procedure recalculates the same amounts, the batch is in balance.

After processing, the output results are sent to the data control clerk for reconciliation and distribution to the user. The clerk updates the batch control log to record that processing of the batch was completed successfully.

HASH TOTALS.   The term **hash total**, which was used in the preceding discussion, refers to a simple control technique that uses nonfinancial data to keep track of the records in a batch. Any key field, such as a customer's account number, a purchase

FIGURE 6-3

Batch Control Log

End User							Data Processing					
Batch #	Date	Time	Rec By	Control Total	Hash Total	Record Count	Submitted		Returned		Error Code	Reconciled By
							Date	Time	Date	Time		
12 403	12/4/98	9:05	B.R.	122,674.87	4537838	50	12/4/98	9:55	12/4/98	11:05	0	PMR

order number, or an inventory item number, may be used to calculate a hash total. In the following example, the sales order number (SO#) field for an entire batch of sales order records is summed to produce a hash total.

```
        SO#
        14327
        67345
        19983
          •
          •
          •
          •
        88943
        96543
       4537838  (hash total)
```

Let's see how this seemingly meaningless number can be of use. Assume that after this batch of records leaves data control, and price to data input, someone replaced one of the sales orders in the batch with a fictitious record of the same dollar amount. How would the batch control procedures detect this irregularity? Both the record count and the dollar amount control totals would be unaffected by this act. However, unless the perpetrator obtained a source document with exactly the same sales order number (which would be impossible, since they should come uniquely prenumbered from the printer), the hash total calculated by the batch control procedures would not balance. Thus, the irregularity would be detected.

VALIDATION CONTROLS

Input **validation controls** are intended to detect errors in transaction data before the data are processed. Validation procedures are most effective when they are performed as close to the source of the transaction as possible. However, depending on the type of CBIS in use, input validation may occur at various points in the system. For example, some validation procedures require making references against the current master file. CBISs using real-time processing or batch processing with direct access master files can validate data at the input stage. Figure 6–4(a) and (b) illustrate these techniques.

If the CBIS uses batch processing with sequential files, the transaction records being validated must first be sorted in the same order as the master file. Validating at the data input stage in this case may require considerable additional processing. Therefore, as a practical matter, each processing module prior to updating the master file record performs some validation procedures. This approach is shown in Figure 6–5.

The problem with this technique is that a transaction may be partially processed before data errors are detected. Dealing with a partially complete transaction will require special error-handling procedures. We shall discuss error-handling controls later in this section.

There are three levels of input validation controls:

1. Field interrogation
2. Record interrogation
3. File interrogation

FIELD INTERROGATION.   **Field interrogation** involves programmed procedures that examine the characteristics of the data in the field. The following are some common types of field interrogation.

FIGURE 6-4

Validation during
Data Input

(a) Validation in a Real-Time System

(b) Validation in a Batch-Direct Access System

Missing data checks are used to examine the contents of a field for the presence of blank spaces. Some programming languages are restrictive as to the justification (right or left) of data within the field. If data are not properly justified or if a character is missing (has been replaced with a blank), the value in the field will be improperly processed. In some cases, the presence of blanks in a numeric data field may cause a system failure. When the validation program detects a blank where it expects to see a data value, this will be interpreted as an error.

Numeric-alphabetic data checks determine whether the correct form of data is in a field. For example, a customer's account balance should not contain alphabetic data. As with blanks, alphabetic data in a numeric field may cause serious processing errors.

Zero-value checks are used to verify that certain fields are filled with zeros. Some program languages require that fields used in mathematical operations are initiated with zeros prior to processing. This control may trigger an automatic corrective control to replace the contents of the field with zero if it detects a nonzero value.

Limit checks determine if the value in the field exceeds an authorized limit. For example, assume the firm's policy is that no employee works more than 44 hours per week. The payroll system validation program can interrogate the hours-worked field in the weekly payroll records for values greater than 44.

Range checks assign upper and lower limits to acceptable data values. For example, if the range of pay rates for hourly employees in a firm is between 8 and 20 dollars, all payroll records can be checked to see that this range is not exceeded. The purpose of this control is to detect keystroke errors that shift the decimal point one or more places. It would not detect an error where a correct pay rate of, say, 9 dollars is incorrectly entered as 15 dollars.

Validity checks compare actual values in a field against known acceptable values. This control is used to verify such things as transaction codes, state abbreviations, or employee job skill codes. If the value in the field does not match one of the acceptable values, the record is determined to be in error.

FIGURE 6-5

Validation in
Batch Sequential
File System
(Note: For
simplification,
the necessary
re-sorting of the
transaction file
between update
processes is not
shown.)

This is a frequently used control in cash disbursement systems. One form of cash disbursement fraud involves manipulating the system into making a fraudulent payment to a nonexistent vendor. To prevent this, the firm may establish a list of valid vendors with whom it does business exclusively. Thus, before payment of any trade obligation, the vendor number on the cash disbursement voucher is matched against the valid vendor list by the validation program. If the code does not match, payment is denied, and management reviews the transaction.

Check digit controls identify keystroke errors in key fields by testing the internal validity of the code. We discussed this control technique earlier in the section.

RECORD INTERROGATION.   **Record interrogation** procedures validate the entire record by examining the interrelationship of its field values. Some typical tests are discussed below.

Reasonableness checks determine if a value in one field, which has already passed a limit check and a range check, is reasonable when considered along with other data fields in the record. For example, an employee's pay rate of 18 dollars per hour falls within an acceptable range. However, this rate is excessive when compared to the employee's job skill code of 693; employees in this skill class never earn more than 12 dollars per hour.

Sign checks are tests to see if the sign of a field is correct for the type of record being processed. For example, in a sales order processing system, the dollar amount field must be positive for sales orders but negative for sales return transactions. This control can determine the correctness of the sign by comparing it with the transaction code field.

Sequence checks are used to determine if a record is out of order. In batch systems that use sequential master files, the transaction files being processed must be sorted in the same order as the primary keys of the corresponding master file. This requirement is critical to the processing logic of the update program. Hence, before each transaction record is processed, its sequence is verified relative to the previous record processed.

FILE INTERROGATION.   The purpose of **file interrogation** is to ensure that the correct file is being processed by the system. These controls are particularly important for master files, which contain permanent records of the firm and which, if destroyed or corrupted, are difficult to replace.

Internal label checks verify that the file processed is the one the program is actually calling for. Files stored on magnetic tape are usually kept off-line in a tape library. These files have an external label that identifies them (by name and serial number) to the tape librarian and operator. External labeling is typically a manual procedure and, like any manual task, prone to errors. Sometimes, the wrong external label is mistakenly affixed to a file when it is created. Thus, when the file is called for again, the wrong file will be retrieved and placed on the tape drive for processing. Depending on how the file is being used, this may result in its destruction or corruption. To prevent this, the operating system creates an internal header label that is placed at the beginning of the file. An example of a header label is shown in Figure 6–6.

To ensure that the correct file is about to be processed, the system matches the file name and serial number in the header label with the program's file requirements. If the wrong file has been loaded, the system will send the operator a message and suspend processing. It is worth noting that while label checking is generally a standard feature, it is an option that can be overridden by programmers and operators.

Version checks are used to verify that the version of the file being processed is correct. In a grandparent-parent-child approach, many versions of master files and transactions may exist. The version check compares the version number of the files being processed with the program's requirements.

An *expiration date check* prevents a file from being deleted before it expires. In a GPC system, for example, once an adequate number of backup files is created, the oldest backup file is scratched (erased from the disk or tape) to provide space for new files. Figure 6–7 illustrates this procedure.

To protect against destroying an active file by mistake, the system first checks the expiration date contained in the header label (see Figure 6–6). If the retention period has not yet expired, the system will generate an error message and abort the scratch procedure. Expiration date control is an optional measure. The length of the retention period is specified by the programmer and based on the number of backup files that are desired. If the programmer chooses not to specify an expiration date, the control against such accidental deletion is eliminated.

INPUT ERROR CORRECTION

When errors are detected in a batch, they must be corrected and the records resubmitted for reprocessing. This must be a controlled process to ensure that errors are dealt with completely and correctly. There are three common error handling techniques: (1) immediate correction, (2) create an error file, and (3) reject the entire batch.

FIGURE 6–6

Header Label on
Magnetic Tape

IMMEDIATE CORRECTION.   If the system is using the direct data validation approach (refer to 6–4(a) and (b)), error detection and correction can also take place during data entry. Upon detecting keystroke error or an illogical relationship, the system should halt the data entry procedure until the user corrects the error.

CREATE AN ERROR FILE.   When delayed validation is being used, such as in batch systems with sequential files, individual errors should be flagged to prevent them from being processed. At the end of the validation procedure, the records flagged as errors are removed from the batch and placed in a temporary error holding file until the errors can be investigated.

Some errors can be detected during data input procedures. However, as was mentioned earlier, the update module performs some validation tests. Thus, error records may be placed on the error file at several different points in the process, as illustrated by Figure 6–8. At each validation point, the system automatically adjusts the batch control totals to reflect the removal of the error records from the batch. In a separate procedure, an authorized user representative will later make corrections to the error records and resubmit them as a separate batch for reprocessing.

Errors detected during processing require careful handling. These records may already be partially processed. Therefore, simply resubmitting the corrected records to the system via the data input stage may result in processing portions of these transactions twice. There are two methods for dealing with this complexity. The first is to reverse the effects of the partially processed transactions and resubmit the corrected records to the data input stage. The second is to reinsert corrected records to the

FIGURE 6-7   Scratch Tape Approach Using Retention Date

The obsolete backup file of System A is scratched (written over) by System B and used as an output (child) file. Before scratching, the operating system checks the expiration date in the file's header label.

processing stage in which the error was detected. In either case, batch control procedures (preparing batch control records and logging the batches) apply to the resubmitted data, just as they do for normal batch processing.

REJECT THE BATCH.   Some forms of errors are associated with the entire batch and are not clearly attributable to individual records. An example of this type of error is an imbalance in a batch control total. Assume that the transmittal sheet for a batch of sales orders shows a total sales value of $122,674.87, but the data input procedure calculated a sales total of only $121,454.32. What has caused this? Is the problem a missing or changed record? Or did the data control clerk incorrectly calculate the batch control total? The most effective solution in this case is to cease processing and return the entire batch to data control to evaluate, correct, and resubmit.

Batch errors are one reason for keeping the size of the batch to a manageable number. Too few records in a batch make batch processing inefficient. Too many records make error detection difficult, create greater business disruption when a batch is rejected, and increase the possibility of mistakes when calculating batch control totals.

GENERALIZED DATA INPUT SYSTEMS

To achieve a high degree of control and standardization over input validation procedures, some organizations employ a **generalized data input system (GDIS)**. This technique includes centralized procedures to manage the data input for all of the organization's transaction processing systems. The GDIS approach has three advantages. First, it improves control by having one common system perform all data validation. Second, GDIS ensures that each AIS application applies a consistent standard for data

FIGURE 6–8

Use of Error File in
Batch Sequential
File System with
Multiple
Resubmission
Points

validation. Third, GDIS improves systems development efficiency. Given the high degree of commonality in input validation requirements for AIS applications, a GDIS eliminates the need to recreate redundant routines for each new application. Figure 6–9 shows the primary features of this technique. A GDIS has five major components:[1]

1. Generalized validation module
2. Validated data file
3. Error file
4. Error reports
5. Transaction log

GENERALIZED VALIDATION MODULE.   The **generalized validation module (GVM)** performs standard validation routines that are common to many different applications. These routines are customized to an individual application's needs through parameters that specify the program's specific requirements. For example, the GVM may apply a range check to the HOURLY RATE field of payroll records. The limits of the range are 6 dollars and 15 dollars. The range test is the generalized procedure; the dollar limits are the parameters that customize this procedure. The validation procedures for some applications may be so unique as to defy a general solution. To meet the goals of the

1.   Ron Weber, *EDP Auditing: Conceptual foundations and Practice.* 2d ed. (New York: McGraw-Hill, (1988), pp. 424–27.

FIGURE 6–9

Generalized
Data Input
System

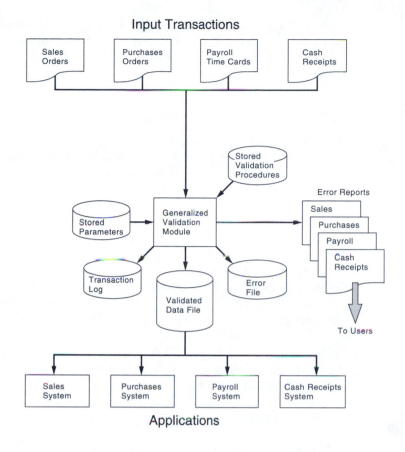

Input Transactions

Applications

generalized data input system, the GVM must be flexible enough to permit special user-defined procedures for unique applications. These procedures are stored, along with generalized procedures, and invoked by the GVM as needed.

VALIDATED DATA FILE.   The input data that are validated by the GVM are stored on a **validated data file**. This is a temporary holding file through which validated transactions flow to their respective applications. The file is analogous to a tank of water whose level is constantly changing, as it is filled from the top by the GVM and emptied from the bottom by applications.

ERROR FILE.   The **error file** in the GDIS plays the same role as a traditional error file. Error records detected during validation are stored in the file, corrected, and then resubmitted to the GVM.

ERROR REPORTS.   Standardized **error reports** are distributed to users to facilitate error correction. For example, if the HOURLY RATE field in a payroll record fails a range check, the error report will display an error message stating the problem so. The report will also present the contents of the failed record, along with the acceptable range limits taken from the parameters.

TRANSACTION LOG.   The **transaction log** is a permanent record of all validated transactions. From an accounting records point of view, the transaction log is equivalent to the journal and is an important element in the audit trail. However, only successful transactions (those that will be completely processed) should be entered in the journal. If a transaction is to undergo additional validation testing during the processing phase (which could result in its rejection), it should be entered in the transaction log only after it is completely validated. This issue is discussed further in the next section under *Audit Trail Controls*.

PROCESSING CONTROLS

After passing through the data input stage, transactions enter the processing stage of the system. **Processing controls** are divided into three categories: run-to-run controls, operator intervention controls, and audit trail controls.

RUN-TO-RUN CONTROLS

Previously, we discussed the preparation of batch control figures as an element of input control. **Run-to-run controls** use batch figures to monitor the batch as it moves from one programmed procedure (run) to another. These controls ensure that each run in the system processes the batch correctly and completely. Batch control figures may be contained in either a separate control record created at the data input stage or an internal label. Specific uses of run-to-run control figures are described below.

RECALCULATE CONTROL TOTALS.   After each major operation in the process and after each run, dollar amount fields, hash totals, and record counts are accumulated and compared to the corresponding values stored in the control record. If a record in the batch is lost, goes unprocessed, or is processed more than once, this will be revealed by the discrepancies between these figures.

TRANSACTION CODES.   The **transaction code** of each record in the batch is compared to the transaction code contained in the control record. This ensures that only the correct type of transaction is being processed.

SEQUENCE CHECKS.   In systems that use sequential master files, the order of the transaction records in the batch is critical to correct and complete processing. As the batch moves through the process, it must be re-sorted in the order of the master file used in each run. The **sequence check** control compares the sequence of each record in the batch with the previous record to ensure that proper sorting took place.

Figure 6–10 illustrates the use of run-to-run controls in a revenue cycle system. This application comprises four runs: (1) data input, (2) accounts receivable update, (3) inventory update, and (4) output. At the end of the accounts receivable run, batch control figures are recalculated and reconciled with the control totals passed from the data input run. These figures are then passed to the inventory update run, where they are again recalculated, reconciled, and passed to the output run. Errors detected in each run are flagged and placed in an error file. The run-to-run (batch) control figures are then adjusted to reflect the deletion of these records.

OPERATOR INTERVENTION CONTROLS

Systems sometimes require operator intervention to initiate certain actions, such as entering control totals for a batch of records, providing parameter values for logical operations, and activating a program from a different point when reentering semi-processed error records. Operator intervention increases the potential for human error. Systems that limit operator intervention through **operator intervention controls**

FIGURE 6-10

Run-to-Run
Controls

are thus less prone to processing errors. Although it may be impossible to eliminate operator involvement completely, parameter values and program start points should, to the extent possible, be derived logically or provided to the system through look-up tables.

AUDIT TRAIL CONTROLS

The preservation of an audit trail is an important objective of process control. In an accounting system, every transaction must be traceable through each stage of processing from its economic source to its presentation in financial statements. In a CBIS environment, the audit trail can become fragmented and difficult to follow. It thus becomes critical that each major operation applied to a transaction be thoroughly documented. The following are examples of techniques used to preserve audit trails in a CBIS.

TRANSACTION LOGS. Every transaction successfully processed by the system should be recorded on a transaction log, which serves as a journal. Figure 6–11 shows this arrangement.

There are two reasons for creating a transaction log. First, the transaction log is a permanent record of transactions. The validated transaction file produced at the data

FIGURE 6-11   Transaction Log to Preserve the Audit Trail

input phase is usually a temporary file. Once processed, the records on this file are erased (scratched) to make room for the next batch of transactions. Second, not all of the records in the validated transaction file may be successfully processed. Some of these records may fail tests in the subsequent processing stages. A transaction log should contain only successful transactions—those that have changed account balances. Unsuccessful transactions should be placed in an error file. The transaction log and error files combined should account for all the transactions in the batch. The validated transaction file may then be scratched with no loss of data.

The system should produce a hard copy transaction listing of all successful transactions. These listings should go to the appropriate users to facilitate reconciliation with input.

LOG OF AUTOMATIC TRANSACTIONS.   Some transactions are triggered internally by the system. An example of this is when inventory drops below a preset reorder point, and the system automatically processes a purchase order. To maintain an audit trail of these activities, all internally generated transactions must be placed in a transaction log.

LISTING OF AUTOMATIC TRANSACTIONS.   To maintain control over automatic transactions processed by the system, the responsible end user should receive a detailed listing of all internally generated transactions.

UNIQUE TRANSACTION IDENTIFIERS.   Each transaction processed by the system must be uniquely identified with a transaction number. This is the only practical means of tracing a particular transaction through a database of thousands or even millions of records. In systems that use physical source documents, the unique number printed on the document can be transcribed during data input and used for this purpose. In real-time systems, which do not use source documents, each transaction should be assigned a unique number by the system.

ERROR LISTING.   A listing of all error records should go to the appropriate user to support error correction and resubmission.

OUTPUT CONTROLS

Output controls ensure that system output is not lost, misdirected, or corrupted and that privacy is not violated. Exposures of this sort can cause serious disruptions to operations and may result in financial losses to a firm. For example, if the checks produced by a firm's cash disbursements system are lost, misdirected, or destroyed, trade accounts and other bills may go unpaid. This could damage the firm's credit rating and result in lost discounts, interest, or penalty charges. If the privacy of certain types of output is violated, a firm could have its business objectives compromised, or it could even become legally exposed. Examples of privacy exposures include the disclosure of trade secrets, patents pending, marketing research results, and patient medical records.

The type of processing method in use influences the choice of controls employed to protect system output. Generally, batch systems are more susceptible to exposure and require a greater degree of control than real-time systems. In this section, we examine output exposures and controls for both methods.

CONTROLLING BATCH SYSTEMS OUTPUT

Batch systems usually produce output in the form of hard copy, which typically requires the involvement of intermediaries in its production and distribution. Figure 6–12 shows the stages in the output process and serves as the basis for the rest of this section.

The output is removed from the printer by the computer operator, separated into sheets and separated from other reports, reviewed for correctness by the data control

FIGURE 6–12

Stages in the
Output Process

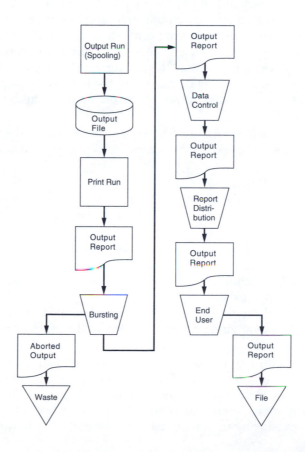

clerk, and then sent through interoffice mail to the end user. Each stage in this process is a point of potential exposure where the output could be reviewed, stolen, copied, or misdirected. An additional exposure exists when processing or printing goes wrong and produces output that is unacceptable to the end user. These corrupted or partially damaged reports are often discarded in waste cans. Computer criminals have successfully used such waste to achieve their illicit objectives.

Below, we examine techniques for controlling each phase in the output process. Keep in mind that not all of these techniques will necessarily apply to every item of output produced by the system. As always, controls are employed on a cost-benefit basis that is determined by the sensitivity of the data in the reports.

OUTPUT SPOOLING.   In large-scale data processing operations, output devices such as line printers can become backlogged with many programs simultaneously demanding these limited resources. This can cause a bottleneck, which adversely affects the throughput of the system. Applications waiting to print output occupy computer memory and block other applications from entering the processing stream. To ease this burden, applications are often designed to direct their output to a magnetic disk file rather than to the printer directly. This is called **output spooling**. Later, when printer resources become available, the output files are printed.

The creation of an output file as an intermediate step in the printing process presents an added exposure. A computer criminal may use this opportunity to perform any of the following unauthorized acts:

- Access the output file and change critical data values (such as dollar amounts on checks). The printer program will then print the corrupted output as if it was produced by the output run. Using this technique, a criminal may effectively circumvent the processing controls designed into the application.
- Access the file and change the number of copies of output to be printed. The extra copies may then be removed without notice during the printing stage.
- Make a copy of the output file to produce illegal output reports.
- Destroy the output file before output printing takes place.

The auditor should be aware of these potential exposures and ensure that proper access and backup procedures are in place to protect output files.

PRINT PROGRAMS.   When the printer becomes available, the print run program produces hard copy output from the output file. Print programs are often complex systems that require operator intervention. Four common types of operator actions are:

1. Pausing the print program to load the correct type of output documents (check stocks, invoices, or other special forms).
2. Entering parameters needed by the print run, such as the number of copies to be printed.
3. Restarting the print run at a prescribed checkpoint after a printer malfunction.
4. Removing printed output from the printer for review and distribution.

Print program controls are designed to deal with two types of exposures presented by this environment: (1) the production of unauthorized copies of output and (2) employee browsing of sensitive data. Some print programs allow the operator to specify more copies of output than the output file calls for, which allows for the possibility of producing unauthorized copies of output. One way to control this is to employ output document controls similar to the source document controls discussed earlier. This is feasible when dealing with prenumbered invoices for billing customers or prenumbered check stock. At the end of the run, the number of copies specified by the output file can be reconciled with the actual number of output documents used. In cases where output documents are not prenumbered, supervision may be the most effective control technique. A security officer can be present during the printing of sensitive output.

To prevent operators from viewing sensitive output, special multipart paper can be used, with the top copy colored black to prevent the print from being read. This type of product, which is illustrated in Figure 6–13, is often used for payroll check printing. The receiver of the check separates the top copy from the body of the check, which contains readable details. An alternative privacy control is to direct the output to a special remote printer that can be closely supervised.

BURSTING.   When output reports are removed from the printer, they go to the **bursting** stage to have their pages separated and collated. The concern here is that the bursting clerk may make an unauthorized copy of the report, remove a page from the report, or read sensitive information. The primary control against these exposures is supervision. For very sensitive reports, bursting may be performed by the end user.

WASTE.   Computer output waste represents a potential exposure. It is important to dispose properly of aborted reports and the carbon copies from multipart paper removed during bursting. Computer criminals have been known to sift through trash cans searching for carelessly discarded output that is presumed by others to be of no value. From such trash, computer criminals may obtain a key piece of information about the firm's market research, the credit ratings of its customers, or even trade secrets that they can sell to a competitor. Computer waste is also a source of technical data, such as passwords and authority tables, which a perpetrator may use to access the firm's data files. Passing it through a paper shredder can easily destroy sensitive computer output.

DATA CONTROL.   In some organizations, the **data control** group is responsible for verifying the accuracy of computer output before it is distributed to the user. Normally, the data control clerk will review the batch control figures for balance; examine the report body for garbled, illegible, and missing data; and record the receipt of the report in data control's batch control log. For reports containing highly sensitive data, the end user may perform these tasks. In this case, the report will bypass the data control group and go directly to the user.

REPORT DISTRIBUTION.   The primary risks associated with report distribution include reports being lost, stolen, or misdirected in transit to the user. A number of control measures can minimize these exposures. For example, when reports are generated, the name and address of the user should be printed on the report. For multicopy reports, an address file of authorized users should be consulted to identify each recipient of the report. Maintaining adequate access control over this file becomes highly important. If an unauthorized individual was able to add his or her name to the authorized user list, he or she would receive a copy of the report.

For highly sensitive reports, the following distribution techniques can be used:

- The reports may be placed in a secure mailbox to which only the user has the key.
- The user may be required to appear in person at the distribution center and sign for the report.
- A security officer or special courier may deliver the report to the user.

FIGURE 6-13   Multipart Check Stock

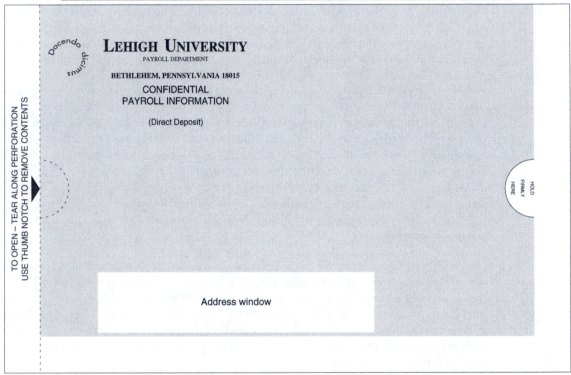

END USER CONTROLS.   Once in the hands of the user, output reports should be re-examined for any errors that may have evaded the data control clerk's review. Users are in a far better position to identify subtle errors in reports that are not disclosed by an imbalance in control totals. Errors detected by the user should be reported to the appropriate computer services management. Such errors may be symptoms of an improper systems design, incorrect procedures, errors inserted by accident during systems maintenance, or unauthorized access to data files or programs.

Once a report has served its purpose, it should be stored in a secure location until its retention period has expired. Factors influencing the length of time a hard copy report is retained include:

- Statutory requirements specified by government agencies, such as the IRS.
- The number of copies of the report in existence. When there are multiple copies, certain of these may be marked for permanent retention, while the remainder can be destroyed after use.
- The existence of magnetic or optical images of reports that can act as permanent backup.

When the retention date has passed, reports should be destroyed in a manner consistent with the sensitivity of their contents. Highly sensitive reports should be shredded.

CONTROLLING REAL-TIME SYSTEMS OUTPUT

Real-time systems direct their output to the user's computer screen, terminal, or printer. This method of distribution eliminates the various intermediaries in the journey from the computer center to the user and thus reduces many of the exposures previously discussed. The primary threat to real-time output is the interception, disruption, destruction, or corruption of the output message as it passes along the communications link. This threat comes from two types of exposures: (1) exposures from equipment failure and (2) exposures from subversive acts, whereby a computer criminal intercepts the output message transmitted between the sender and the receiver. Techniques for controlling communications exposures were discussed previously in Chapter 5.

TESTING COMPUTER APPLICATION CONTROLS

This section examines several techniques for auditing computer applications. Control testing techniques provide information about the accuracy and completeness of an application's processes. These tests follow two general approaches: (1) the black box (around the computer) approach and (2) the white box (through the computer) approach. We first examine the black box approach and then review several white box testing techniques.

BLACK BOX APPROACH

Auditors performing **black box** testing do not rely on a detailed knowledge of the application's internal logic. Instead, they seek to understand the functional characteristics of the application by analyzing flowcharts and interviewing knowledgeable personnel in the client's organization. With an understanding of what the application is supposed to do, the auditor tests the application by reconciling production input transactions processed by the application with output results. The output results are analyzed to verify the application's compliance with its functional requirements. Figure 6–14 illustrates the black box approach.

The advantage of the black box approach is that the application need not be removed from service and tested directly. This approach is feasible for testing applications that are relatively simple. However, complex applications—those that receive input from many sources, perform a variety of operations, or produce multiple outputs—require a more focused testing approach to provide the auditor with evidence of application integrity.

WHITE BOX APPROACH

The **white box approach** relies on an in-depth understanding of the internal logic of the application being tested. The white box approach includes several techniques for testing application logic directly. These techniques use small numbers of specially created test transactions to verify specific aspects of an application's logic and controls. In this way, auditors are able to conduct precise tests, with known variables, and obtain results that they can compare against objectively calculated results. Some of the more common types of tests of controls include the following:

- **Authenticity tests**, which verify that an individual, a programmed procedure, or a message (such as an EDI transmission) attempting to access a system is authentic. Authenticity controls include user IDs, passwords, valid vendor codes, and authority tables.
- **Accuracy tests**, which ensure that the system processes only data values that conform to specified tolerances. Examples include range tests, field tests, and limit tests.
- **Completeness tests**, which identify missing data within a single record and entire records missing from a batch. The types of tests performed are field tests, record sequence tests, hash totals, and control totals.
- **Redundancy tests**, which determine that an application processes each record only once. Redundancy controls include the reconciliation of batch totals, record counts, hash totals, and financial control totals.
- **Access tests**, which ensure that the application prevents authorized users from unauthorized access to data. Access controls include passwords, authority tables, user-defined procedures, data encryption, and inference controls.

FIGURE 6–14

Auditing around
the Computer—
The "Black Box"
Approach

- **Audit trail tests**, which ensure that the application creates an adequate audit trail. This includes evidence that the application records all transactions in a transaction log, posts data values to the appropriate accounts, produces complete **transaction listings**, and generates error files and reports for all exceptions.
- **Rounding error tests**, which verify the correctness of rounding procedures. Rounding errors occur in accounting information when the level of precision used in the calculation is greater than that used in the reporting. For example, interest calculations on bank account balances may have a precision of five decimal places, whereas only two decimal places are needed to report balances. If the remaining three decimal places are simply dropped, the total interest calculated for the total number of accounts may not equal the sum of the individual calculations.

Figure 6–15 shows the logic for handling the rounding error problem. This technique uses an accumulator to keep track of the rounding differences between calculated and reported balances. Note how the sign and the absolute value of the amount in the accumulator determines how the customer account is affected by rounding. To illustrate, the rounding logic is applied on the next page to three hypothetical bank balances. The interest calculations are based on an interest rate of 5.25 percent.

FIGURE 6–15

Rounding Error Algorithm

SOURCE: Adapted from R. Weber, *EDP Auditing Conceptual Foundations and Practice*, 2d ed., (New York: McGraw-Hill, 1988), p. 493.

Record 1

Beginning accumulator balance	.00861
Beginning account balance	2,741.78
Calculated interest	143.94345
New account balance	2,885.72345
Rounded account balance	2,885.72
Adjusted accumulator balance	.01206 (.00345 + .00861)
Adjusted accumulator balance	**2,885.73 (round up 1 cent)**
Ending account balance	.00206 (.01206 − .01)
Ending accumulator balance	

Record 2

Beginning accumulator balance	.00206
Beginning account balance	1,893.44
Calculated interest	99.4056
New account balance	1,992.8456
Rounded account balance	1,992.85
Adjusted accumulator balance	−.00646 (.00206 − .0044)
Ending account balance	**1,992,85 (no change)**
Ending accumulator balance	−.00646

Record 3

Beginning accumulator balance	−.00646
Beginning account balance	7,423.34
Calculated interest	389.72535
New account balance	7,813.06535
Rounded account balance	7,813.07
Adjusted accumulator balance	−.01111 (.00646 − .00464)
Ending account balance	**7,813.06 (round down 1 cent)**
Ending accumulator balance	.00111

Failure to properly account for this rounding difference can result in an imbalance between the total (control) interest amount and the sum of the individual interest calculations for each account. Poor accounting for rounding differences can also present an opportunity for fraud.

Rounding programs are particularly susceptible to so-called salami frauds. **Salami frauds** tend to affect a large number of victims, but the harm to each is immaterial. This type of fraud takes its name from the analogy of slicing a large salami (the fraud objective) into many thin pieces. Each victim assumes one of these small pieces and is unaware of being defrauded. For example, a programmer, or someone with access to the preceding rounding program, can perpetrate a salami fraud by modifying the rounding logic as follows: at the point in the process where the algorithm should increase the customer's account (that is, the accumulator value is > +.01), the program instead adds one cent to another account—the perpetrator's account. Although the absolute amount of each fraud transaction is small, given the thousands of accounts processed, the total amount of the fraud can become significant over time.

Operating system audit trails and audit software can detect excessive file activity. In the case of the salami fraud, there would be thousands of entries into the computer criminal's personal account that may be detected in this way. A clever programmer may disguise this activity by funneling these entries through several intermediate temporary accounts, which are then posted to a smaller number of intermediate accounts and finally to the programmer's personal account. By using many levels of accounts in this way, the activity to any single account is reduced and may go undetected by the audit software. There will be a trail, but it can be complicated. A skilled auditor may also use audit software to detect the existence of unauthorized intermediate accounts used in such a fraud.

COMPUTER AIDED AUDIT TOOLS AND TECHNIQUES FOR TESTING CONTROLS

To illustrate how application controls are tested, this section describes five CAATT approaches: the test data method, base case system evaluation, tracing, integrated test facility, and parallel simulation.

TEST DATA METHOD

The **test data method** is used to establish application integrity by processing specially prepared sets of input data through production applications that are under review. The results of each test are compared to predetermined expectations to obtain an objective evaluation of application logic and control effectiveness. The test data technique is illustrated in Figure 6–16. To perform the test data technique, the auditor must obtain a copy of the current version of the application. In addition, test transaction files and test master files must be created. As illustrated in the figure, test transactions may enter the system from magnetic tape, disk, or via an input terminal. Results from the test run will be in the form of routine output reports, transaction listings, and error reports. In addition, the auditor must review the updated master files to determine that account balances have been correctly updated. The test results are then compared with the auditor's expected results to determine if the application is functioning properly. This comparison may be performed manually or through special computer software.

Figure 6–17 lists selected fields for hypothetical transactions and accounts receivable records prepared by the auditor to test a sales order processing application. The figure also shows an error report of rejected transactions and a listing of the updated accounts receivable master file. Any deviations between the actual results obtained and those expected by the auditor may indicate a logic or control problem.

FIGURE 6–16

The Test Data Technique

FIGURE 6–17   Examples of Test Data and Test Results

Test Transaction File

REC #	CUST #	CUSTOMER NAME	PART #	DESCRIPTION	QNTY	UNIT PRICE	TOTAL PRICE
1	231893	Smith, Joe	AX-612	Water Pump	1	20.00	20.00
2	231893	Azar, Atul	J-912	Gear	3	15.00	45.00
3	245851	Jones, Mary	123-LM	Hose	20	20.00	400.00
4	256519	Lang, Tony	Y-771	Spacer	5	2.00	10.00
5	259552	Tuner, Agnes	U-734	Bushing	5	25.00	120.00
6	175995	Hanz, James	EA-74	Seal	1	3.00	3.00
7	267991	Swindle, Joe	EN-12	Rebuilt Engine	1	1,220.00	1,220.00

Original Test AR Master File

CUST #	CUSTOMER NAME	CUSTOMER ADDRESS	CREDIT LIMIT	CURRENT BALANCE
231893	Smith, Joe	1520 S. Maple, City	1,000.00	400.00
256519	Lang, Tony	18 Etwine St., City	5,000.00	850.00
267991	Swindle, Joe	1 Shady Side, City	3,000.00	2,900.00

Updated Test AR Master File

CUST #	CUSTOMER NAME	CUSTOMER ADDRESS	CREDIT LIMIT	CURRENT BALANCE
231893	Smith, Joe	1520 S. Maple, City	1,000.00	420.00
256519	Lang, Tony	18 Etwine St., City	5,000.00	860.00
267991	Swindle, Joe	1 Shady Side, City	3,000.00	2,900.00

Error Report

REC #	CUST #	CUSTOMER NAME	PART #	DESCRIPTION	QNTY	UNIT PRICE	TOTAL PRICE	EXPLANATION OF ERROR
2	231893	Azar, Atul \ X	J-912	Gear	3	15.00	75.00	CUSTOMER NAME does not correspond to CUST # 231893
3	245851 \ X	Jones, Mary	123-LM	Hose	20	20.00	400.00	Check digit error in CUST # field
5	259552	Tuner, Agnes	U-734	Bushing	5	25.00	120.00 \ X	Price extension error
6	175995 \ X	Hanz, James	EA-74	Seal	1	3.00	3.00	Record out of sequence
7	267991	Swindle, Joe	EN-12	Rebuilt Engine	1	1220.00 \ X	1220.00 \ X	Credit limit error

CREATING TEST DATA

When creating test data, auditors must prepare a complete set of both valid and invalid transactions. If test data are incomplete, auditors might fail to examine critical branches of application logic and error-checking routines. Test transactions should test every possible input error, logical process, and irregularity.

Gaining knowledge of the application's internal logic sufficient to create meaningful test data frequently requires a large investment of time. However, the efficiency of this task can be improved through careful planning during systems development. The auditor should save the test data used to test program modules during the implementation phase of the SDLC for future use. If the application has undergone no maintenance since its initial implementation, current audit test results should equal the test results obtained at implementation. However, if the application has been modified, the auditor can create additional test data that focus on the areas of the program changes.

BASE CASE SYSTEM EVALUATION

There are several variants of the test data technique. When the set of test data in use is comprehensive, the technique is called the **base case system evaluation (BCSE)**. BCSE tests are conducted with a set of test transactions containing all possible transaction types. These are processed through repeated iterations during systems development testing until consistent and valid results are obtained. These results are the base case. When subsequent changes to the application occur during maintenance, their effects are evaluated by comparing current results with base case results.

TRACING

Another type of the test data technique called **tracing** performs an electronic walk-through of the application's internal logic. The tracing procedure involves three steps:

1. The application under review must undergo a special compilation to activate the trace option.
2. Specific transactions or types of transactions are created as test data.
3. The test data transactions are traced through all processing stages of the program, and a listing is produced of all programmed instructions that were executed during the test.

Implementing tracing requires a detailed understanding of the application's internal logic. Figure 6–18 illustrates the tracing process using a portion of the logic for a

FIGURE 6–18

Tracing

Payroll Transaction File

Time Card #	Employee Number	Name	Year	Pay Period	Reg Hrs	OT Hrs
8945	33456	Jones, J.J.	1998	14	40.0	3.0

Payroll Master File

Employee Number	Hourly Rate	YTD Earnings	Dependents	YTD Withhold	YTD FICA
33276	15	12,050	3	3,200	870.02
33456	15	13,100	2	3,600	949.75

Computer Program Logic

```
0001   Read Record from Transaction File
0010   Read Record from Master File
0020   If Employee Number (T) = Employee Number (M)
0030        Wage = (Reg Hrs + (OT Hrs x 1.5) ) x Hourly Rate
0040        Add Wage to YTD Earnings
0050        Go to 0001
0060   Else Go to 0010
```

Trace Listing

0001, 0010, 0020, 0060, 0010, 0020, 0030, 0040, 0050

payroll application. The example shows records from two payroll files—a transaction record showing hours worked and two records from a master file showing pay rates. The trace listing at the bottom of Figure 6–18 identifies the program statements that were executed and the order of execution. Analysis of trace options indicates that Commands 0001 through 0020 were executed. At that point, the application transferred to Command 0060. This occurred because the employee number (the key) of the transaction record did not match the key of the first record in the master file. Then Commands 0010 through 0050 were executed.

ADVANTAGES OF TEST DATA TECHNIQUES

There are three primary advantages of test data techniques. First, they employ through-the-computer testing, thus providing the auditor with explicit evidence concerning application functions. Second, if properly planned, test data runs can be employed with only minimal disruption to the organization's operations. Third, they require only minimal computer expertise on the part of auditors.

DISADVANTAGES OF TEST DATA TECHNIQUES

The primary disadvantage of all test data techniques is that auditors must rely on computer services personnel to obtain a copy of the application for test purposes. This entails a risk that computer services may intentionally or accidentally provide the auditor with the wrong version of the application and may reduce the reliability of the audit evidence. In general, audit evidence collected by independent means is more reliable than evidence supplied by the client.

A second disadvantage of these techniques is that they provide a static picture of application integrity at a single point in time. They do not provide a convenient means of gathering evidence about ongoing application functionality. There is no evidence that the application being tested today is functioning as it did during the year under test.

A third disadvantage of test data techniques is their relatively high cost of implementation, which results in audit inefficiency. The auditor may devote considerable time to understanding program logic and creating test data. In the following section, we see how automating testing techniques can resolve these problems.

THE INTEGRATED TEST FACILITY

The **integrated test facility (ITF)** approach is an automated technique that enables the auditor to test an application's logic and controls during its normal operation. The ITF is one or more audit modules designed into the application during the systems development process. In addition, ITF databases contain "dummy" or test master file records integrated with legitimate records. Some firms create a dummy company to which test transactions are posted. During normal operations, test transactions are merged into the input stream of regular (production) transactions and are processed against the files of the dummy company. Figure 6–19 illustrates the ITF concept.

ITF audit modules are designed to discriminate between ITF transactions and routine production data. This may be accomplished in a number of ways. One of the simplest and most commonly used is to assign a unique range of key values exclusively to ITF transactions. For example, in a sales order processing system, account numbers between 2000 and 2100 can be reserved for ITF transactions and will not be assigned to

FIGURE 6-19

The ITF Technique

actual customer accounts. By segregating ITF transactions from legitimate transactions in this way, routine reports produced by the application are not corrupted by ITF test data. Test results are produced separately on storage media or hard copy output and distributed directly to the auditor. Just as with the test data techniques, the auditor analyzes ITF results against expected results.

ADVANTAGES OF ITF

The ITF technique has two advantages over test data techniques. First, ITF supports ongoing monitoring of controls as required by SAS 78. Second, applications with ITF can be economically tested without disrupting the user's operations and without the intervention of computer services personnel. Thus, ITF improves the efficiency of the audit and increases the reliability of the audit evidence gathered.

DISADVANTAGES OF ITF

The primary disadvantage of ITF is the potential for corrupting the data files of the organization with test data. Steps must be taken to ensure that ITF test transactions do not materially affect financial statements by being improperly aggregated with legitimate transactions. This problem is remedied in two ways: (1) adjusting entries may be processed to remove the effects of ITF from general ledger account balances or (2) data files can be scanned by special software that remove the ITF transactions.

PARALLEL SIMULATION

Parallel simulation requires the auditor to write a program that simulates key features or processes of the application under review. The simulated application is then used to reprocess transactions that were previously processed by the production application. This technique is illustrated in Figure 6–20. The results obtained from the simulation are reconciled with the results of the original production run to establish a basis for making inferences about the quality of application processes and controls.

FIGURE 6-20

Parallel
Simulation
Technique

Auditor reconciles simulation
output with production output.

CREATING A SIMULATION PROGRAM

A simulation program can be written in any programming language. However, because of the one-time nature of this task, it is a candidate for fourth-generation language generators. The steps involved in performing parallel simulation testing are outlined below.

1. The auditor must first gain a thorough understanding of the application under review. Complete and current documentation of the application is required to construct an accurate simulation.
2. The auditor must then identify those processes and controls in the application that are critical to the audit. These are the processes to be simulated.
3. The auditor creates the simulation using a 4GL or **generalized audit software (GAS).**
4. The auditor runs the simulation program using selected production transactions and master files to produce a set of results.
5. Finally, the auditor evaluates and reconciles the test results with the production results produced in a previous run.

Simulation programs are usually less complex than the production applications they represent. Because simulations contain only the application processes, calculations, and controls relevant to specific audit objectives, the auditor must carefully evaluate differences between test results and production results. Differences in output results occur for two reasons: (1) the inherent crudeness of the simulation program and (2) real deficiencies in the application's processes or controls, which are made apparent by the simulation program.

SUMMARY

This chapter examined issues related to the use of Computer Aided Audit Tools and Techniques (CAATTs) for performing tests of application controls and data extraction. The chapter began by describing three broad classes of application controls: input controls, processing controls, and output controls. Input controls, which govern the gathering and insertion of data into the system, attempt to ensure that all data transactions are valid, accurate, and complete. Processing controls attempt to preserve the integrity of individual records and batches of records within the system and must ensure that an adequate audit trail is preserved. The goal of output controls is to ensure that information produced by the system is not lost, misdirected, or subject to privacy violations. Next, the black box and white box approaches to testing application controls were reviewed. The black box technique involves auditing around the computer. The white box approach requires a detailed understanding of the application's logic. Five types of CAATT that are commonly used for testing application logic were then examined: the test data method, base case system evaluation, tracing, integrated test facility, and parallel simulation.

KEY TERMS

access tests
accuracy tests
audit trail tests
authenticity tests
base case system evaluation (BCSE)
batch controls
black box approach
bursting
check digit
completeness tests
data control
error file
error reports
field interrogation
file interrogation
generalized audit software (GAS)
generalized data input system (GDIS)
generalized validation module (GVM)
hash total
input controls
integrated test facility (ITF)

operator intervention controls
output controls
output spooling
parallel simulation
processing controls
record interrogation
redundancy tests
rounding error tests
run-to-run controls
salami frauds
sequence check
test data method
tracing
transaction code
transaction listings
transaction log
transcription errors
transposition errors
validated data file
validation controls
white box approach

REVIEW QUESTIONS

1. What are the broad classes of input controls?
2. Explain the importance of source documents and associated control techniques.
3. Give one example of an error that is detected by a check digit control.
4. What are the primary objectives of a batch control?
5. Classify each of the following as either a field, record, or file interrogation:
   a. Limit check
   b. Validity check
   c. Version check
   d. Missing data check
   e. Sign check
   f. Expiration date check
   g. Numeric-alphabetic data check
   h. Sequence check
   i. Zero-value check
   j. Header label check
   k. Range check
   l. Reasonableness check
6. Compare the three common error-handling techniques discussed in the text.
7. What are the five major components of a GDIS?
8. What are the three categories of processing controls?
9. If all of the inputs have been validated before processing, then what purpose do run-to-run controls serve?
10. What is the objective of a transaction log?
11. How can spooling present an added exposure?

DISCUSSION QUESTIONS

1. The field calls for an "M" for married or an "S" for single. The entry is a "2". What control will detect this error?

2. The firm allows no more than 10 hours of overtime a week. An employee entered "15" in the field. Which control will detect this error?

3. The password was "CANARY"; the employee entered "CAANARY"; which control will detect this error?

4. The inventory item number was omitted on the purchase order. Which control will detect this error?

5. The order entry system will allow a ten percent variation in list price. For example, an item with a list price of $1 could be sold for 90 cents or $1.10 without any system interference. The cost of the item is $3 but the cashier entered $2. Which control would detect this error?

6. How does privacy relate to output control?

7. What are some typical problems with passwords?

8. What are the three categories of processing control?

9. Output controls ensure that output is not lost, misdirected, or corrupted and that privacy is not violated. What are some output exposures, or situations where output is at risk?

10. Input validation includes field interrogation that examines the data in individual fields. List four and indicate what is checked in each.

11. What is record interrogation? Give two examples.

MULTIPLE-CHOICE QUESTIONS

1. CMA 685 5-28
   Routines that use the computer to check the validity and accuracy of transaction data during input are called
   a. operating systems.
   b. edit programs.
   c. compiler programs.
   d. integrated test facilities.
   e. compatibility tests.

2. CMA 686 5-10

An edit of individual transactions in a direct access file processing system usually

a. takes place in a separate computer run.
b. takes place in an on-line mode as transactions are entered.
c. takes place during a backup procedure.
d. is not performed due to time constraints.
e. is not necessary.

3. CMA Adapted 686 5-13

An example of an input control is

a. making sure that output is distributed to the proper people.
b. monitoring the work of programmers.
c. collecting accurate statistics of historical transactions while gathering data.
d. recalculating an amount to ensure its accuracy.
e. having another person review the design of a business form.

4. A control designed to validate a transaction at the point of data entry is

a. recalculation of a batch total.
b. a record count.
c. a check digit.
d. checkpoints.
e. recalculation of hash total.

5. CMA 687 5-8

In a manual system, records of current activity are posted from a journal to a ledger. In a computer system, current records from a(n)

a. table file are updated to a transaction file.
b. index file are updated to a master file.
c. transaction file are updated to a master file.
d. master file are updated to a year-to-date file.
e. current balance file are updated to an index file.

6. CMA 1287 5-1

The primary functions of a computerized information system include

a. input, processing, and output.
b. input, processing, output, and storage.
c. input, processing, output, and control.
d. input, processing, output, storage, and control.
e. collecting, sorting, summarizing, and reporting.

7. CMA 1287 5-16

An employee in the receiving department keyed in a shipment from a remote terminal and inadvertently omitted the purchase order number. The best systems control to detect this error would be a

a. batch total.
b. completeness test.
c. sequence check.
d. reasonableness test.
e. compatibility test.

8. CMA 1287 5-15

In an automated payroll processing environment, a department manager substituted the time card for a terminated employee with a time card for a fictitious employee. The fictitious employee had the same pay rate and hours worked as the terminated employee. The best control technique to detect this action using employee identification numbers would be a

a. batch total.
b. record count.
c. hash total.
d. subsequent check.
e. financial total.

9. CMA 1287 5-17

The reporting of accounting information plays a central role in the regulation of business operations. The importance of sound internal control practices is underscored by the Foreign Corrupt Practices Act of 1977, which requires publicly owned U.S. corporations to maintain systems of internal control that meet certain minimum standards. Preventive controls are an integral part of virtually all accounting processing systems, and much of the information generated by the accounting system is used for preventive control purposes. Which one of the following is NOT an essential element of a sound preventive control system?

a. separation of responsibilities for the recording, custodial, and authorization functions
b. sound personnel practices
c. documentation of policies and procedures
d. implementation of state-of-the-art software and hardware
e. physical protection of assets

10. Which of the following is NOT a test for identifying application errors?
    a. reconciling the source code
    b. reviewing test results
    c. retesting the program
    d. testing the authority table

11. Which of the following is NOT a common type of white box test of controls?
    a. completeness tests
    b. redundancy tests
    c. inference tests
    d. authenticity tests

12. All of the following are examples of source document control except
    a. prenumbering source documents.
    b. limiting access to source documents.
    c. supervising the bursting of source documents.
    d. checking the sequence of numbers to identify missing documents.

13. The correct purchase order number, 123456, was incorrectly recorded as shown in the solutions. All of the following are transcription errors except
    a. 1234567
    b. 12345
    c. 124356
    d. 123457

14. Which of the following is correct?
    a. Check digits should be used for all data codes.
    b. Check digits are always placed at the end of a data code.
    c. Check digits do not affect processing efficiency.
    d. Check digits are designed to detect transcription errors.

15. Which statement is NOT correct? The goal of batch controls is to ensure that during processing
    a. transactions are not omitted.
    b. transactions are not added.
    c. transactions are processed more than once.
    d. an audit trail is created.

16. The data control clerk performs all of the following duties except
    a. maintains the batch control log.
    b. computes (or recomputes) batch control data.

c. reconciles the output results to the batch control log.
d. destroys batch control logs when reconciled.

17. An example of a hash total is
    a. total payroll checks—$12,315.
    b. total number of employees—10.
    c. sum of the social security numbers—12,555,437,251.
    d. none of the above.

18. Which statement is NOT true? A batch control log
    a. is prepared by the user department.
    b. records the record count.
    c. indicates any error codes.
    d. is maintained as a part of the audit trail.

19. Which of the following is an example of a field interrogation?
    a. reasonableness check
    b. sign check
    c. sequence check
    d. numeric/alphabetic check

20. Which of the following is an example of record interrogation?
    a. sequence check
    b. zero value check
    c. limit check
    d. range check

21. Which input validation check would detect a payment made to a nonexistent vendor?
    a. missing data check
    b. numeric/alphabetic check
    c. range check
    d. validity check

22. The employee entered "40" in the "hours worked per day" field. Which check would detect this unintentional error?
    a. numeric/alphabetic data check
    b. sign check
    c. limit check
    d. missing data check

23. A specific inventory record indicates that there are 12 items on hand and a customer purchased two of the items. When recording the order, the data entry clerk mistakenly entered 20 items sold. Which check would detect this error?
    a. numeric/alphabetic data check
    b. sign check

c. sequence check

d. range check

24. Which check is NOT a file interrogation?
   a. header label
   b. expiration date check
   c. sequence check
   d. version check

25. Which statement is NOT correct?
   a. The purpose of file interrogation is to ensure that the correct file is being processed by the system.
   b. File interrogation checks are particularly important for master files.
   c. Header labels are prepared manually and affixed to the outside of the tape or disk.
   d. An expiration date check prevents a file from being deleted before it expires.

26. A computer operator was in a hurry and accidentally used the wrong master file to process a transaction file. As a result, the accounts receivable master file was erased. Which control would prevent this from happening?
   a. header label check
   b. expiration date check
   c. version check
   d. validity check

27. Which of the following is NOT a component of the Generalized Data Input System?
   a. generalized validation module
   b. validated data file
   c. updated master file
   d. error file

28. Advantages of the Generalized Data Input System include all of the following except
   a. control over quality of data input.
   b. automatic calculation of run-to-run totals.
   c. companywide standards for data validation.

d. development of a reusable module for data validation.

29. Run-to-run control totals can be used for all of the following except
   a. to ensure that all data input is validated.
   b. to ensure that only transactions of a similar type are being processed.
   c. to ensure the records are in sequence and are not missing.
   d. to ensure that no transaction is omitted.

30. Methods used to maintain an audit trail in a computerized environment include all of the following except
   a. transaction logs.
   b. unique transaction identifiers.
   c. data encryption.
   d. log of automatic transactions.

31. Risk exposures associated with creating an output file as an intermediate step in the printing process (spooling) include all of the following actions by a computer criminal except
   a. gaining access to the output file and changing critical data values.
   b. using a remote printer and incurring operating inefficiencies.
   c. making a copy of the output file and using the copy to produce illegal output reports.
   d. printing an extra hard copy of the output file.

32. Which statement is NOT correct?
   a. Only successful transactions are recorded on a transaction log.
   b. Unsuccessful transactions are recorded in an error file.
   c. A transaction log is a temporary file.
   d. A hard copy transaction listing is provided to users.

PROBLEMS

1. Input Validation
   Identify the types of input validation techniques for the following inputs to the payroll system. Explain the controls provided by each of these techniques.
   a. Operator access number to payroll file
   b. Add new employee

   c. Employee name
   d. Employee number
   e. Social security number
   f. Rate per hour or salary
   g. Marital status
   h. Number of dependents
   i. Cost center

j. Regular hours worked

k. Overtime hours worked

l. Total employees this payroll period

2. **Processing Controls**
   CMA 691 4-2
   Unless adequate controls are implemented, the rapid advance of computer technology can reduce a firm's ability to detect errors and fraud. Therefore, one of the critical responsibilities of the management team in firms where computers are used is the security and control of information service activities.

   During the design state of a system, information system controls are planned to ensure the reliability of data. A well-designed system can prevent both intentional and unintentional alteration or destruction of data. These data controls can be classified as (1) input controls, (2) processing controls, and (3) output controls.

Required:

For each of the three data control categories listed, provide two specific controls and explain how each control contributes to ensuring the reliability of data. Use the following format for your answer.

Control Category	Specific Controls	Contribution to Data Reliability

3. **Input Controls and Data Processing**
   You have been hired by a catalog company to computerize its sales order entry forms. Approximately 60 percent of all orders are received over the telephone, with the remainder either mailed or faxed in. The company wants the phone orders to be input as they are received. The mail and fax orders can be batched together in groups of 50 and submitted for keypunching as they become ready.

The following information is collected for each order:
- Customer number (if a customer does not have one, one needs to be assigned)
- Customer name
- Address
- Payment method (credit card or money order)
- Credit card number and expiration date (if necessary)
- Items ordered and quantity
- Unit price

Required:

Determine control techniques to make sure that all orders are entered accurately into the system. Also, discuss any differences in control measures between the batch and the real-time processing.

4. Write an essay explaining the following three methods of correcting errors in data entry: immediate correction, creation of an error file, and rejection of the batch.

5. Many techniques can be used to control input data. Write a one-page essay discussing three techniques.

6. The presence of an audit trail is critical to the integrity of the accounting information system. Write a one-page essay discussing three of the techniques used to preserve the audit trail.

7. Write an essay comparing and contrasting the following audit techniques based on costs and benefits:
   - test data method
   - base case system evaluation
   - tracing
   - integrated test facility
   - parallel simulation

chapter 7

CAATTs for Data Extraction and Analysis

This chapter examines the use of CAATTs for data extraction and analysis. Auditors make extensive use of these tools in gathering accounting data for testing application controls and in performing substantive tests. In the previous chapter we studied how CAATTs are used to test application controls directly. The data extraction tools discussed in this chapter are used to analyze the data processed by an application rather than the application itself. By analyzing data retrieved from computer files, the auditor can make inferences about the presence and functionality of controls in the application that processed the data.

Another important use of data extraction software is in performing substantive tests. Most audit testing occurs in the substantive-testing phase of the audit. These procedures are called *substantive tests* because they are used to substantiate dollar amounts in account balances. Substantive tests include, but are not limited to, the following:

1. Determining the correct value of inventory
2. Determining the accuracy of prepayments and accruals
3. Confirming accounts receivable with customers
4. Searching for unrecorded liabilities

In an IT environment, the records needed to perform such tests are stored in computer files and databases. Before substantive tests can be performed, the data need to be extracted from the host system and presented to the auditor in a usable format.

This chapter opens with a review of data structures. Data structures constitute the physical and logical arrangement of data in files and databases. Understanding how data are organized and accessed is central to using data extraction tools. Data extraction software fall into two general categories: embedded audit modules and general audit software. The second section of the chapter describes the features, advantages, and disadvantages of the embedded audit module (EAM) approach. The last section outlines typical functions and uses of generalized audit software (GAS). The section closes with a review of the key features of **ACL**, the leading product in the GAS market.

LEARNING OBJECTIVES

After studying this chapter, you should:

- Understand the components of data structures and how these are used to achieve data processing operations.
- Be familiar with structures used in flat-file systems, including sequential, indexes, hashing, and pointer structures.
- Be familiar with relational database structures and the principles of normalization.
- Understand the features, advantages, and disadvantages of the embedded audit module approach to data extraction.
- Know the capabilities and primary features of generalized audit software.
- Become familiar with the more commonly used features of ACL.

DATA STRUCTURES

Data structures have two fundamental components: organization and access method. **Organization** refers to the way records are physically arranged on the secondary storage device. This may be either *sequential* or *random*. The records in sequential files are stored in contiguous locations that occupy a specified area of disk space. Records in random files are stored without regard for their physical relationship to other records of the same file. Random files may have records distributed throughout a disk. The **access method** is the technique used to locate records and to navigate through the database or file. While several specific techniques are used, in general, they can be classified as either direct access or sequential access methods.

Since no single structure is best for all processing tasks, different structures are used for storing different types of accounting data. Selecting a structure, therefore, involves a trade-off between desirable features. The criteria that influence the selection of the data structure are listed in Table 7–1.

In the following section, we examine several data structures. These are divided between flat-file and database systems. In practice, organizations may employ any of these approaches in various combinations for storing their accounting data.

FLAT-FILE STRUCTURES

Recall from Chapter 3 that the flat-file model describes an environment in which individual data files are not integrated with other files. End users in this environment *own* their data files rather than *share* them with other users. Data processing is thus performed by standalone applications rather than integrated systems. The flat-file

TABLE 7–1

File Processing Operations

1. Retrieve a record from the file based on its primary key.
2. Insert a record into a file.
3. Update a record in the file.
4. Read a complete file of records.
5. Find the next record in the file.
6. Scan a file for records with common secondary keys.
7. Delete a record from a file.

approach is a single view model that characterizes legacy systems. Data files are structured, formatted, and arranged to suit the specific needs of the *owner* or primary user. Such structuring, however, may omit or corrupt data attributes that are essential to other users, thus preventing successful integration of systems across the organization.

SEQUENTIAL STRUCTURE

Figure 7–1 illustrates the **sequential structure**, which is typically called the *sequential access method*. Under this arrangement, for example, the record with key value 1875 is placed in the physical storage space immediately following the record with key value 1874. Thus, all records in the file lie in contiguous storage spaces in a specified sequence (ascending or descending) arranged by their primary key.

Sequential files are simple and easy to process. The application starts at the beginning of the file and processes each record in sequence. Of the file processing operations in Table 7–1, this approach is efficient for Operations 4 and 5, which are, respectively, reading an entire file and finding the next record in the file. Also, when a large portion of the file (perhaps 20 percent or more) is to be processed in one operation, the sequential structure is efficient for record updating (Operation 3 in Table 7–1). An example of this is payroll processing, where 100 percent of the employee records on the payroll file are processed each payroll period. However, when only a small portion of the file (or a single record) is being processed, this approach is not efficient. The sequential structure is not a practical option for the remaining operations listed in Table 7–1. For example, retrieving a single record (Operation 1) from a sequential file requires reading all the records that precede the desired record. On average, this means reading half the file each time a single record is retrieved. The sequential access method does not permit accessing a record directly. Files that require direct access operations need a different data structure. The following data structures address this need.

INDEXED STRUCTURE

An **indexed structure** is so named because, in addition to the actual data file, there exists a separate index that is itself a file of record addresses. This index contains the numeric value of the physical disk storage location (cylinder, surface, and record block) for each record in the associated data file. The data file itself may be organized either sequentially or randomly. Figure 7–2 presents an example of an indexed random file.

FIGURE 7-1   Sequential Storage and Access Method

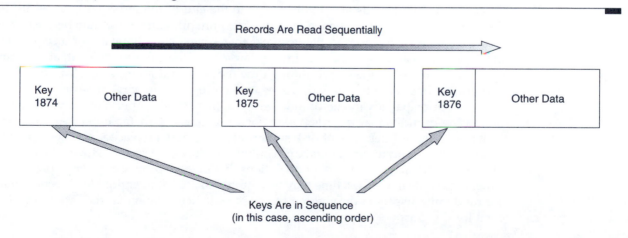

Records Are Read Sequentially

| Key 1874 | Other Data | | Key 1875 | Other Data | | Key 1876 | Other Data |

Keys Are in Sequence
(in this case, ascending order)

FIGURE 7–2   Indexed Random File Structure

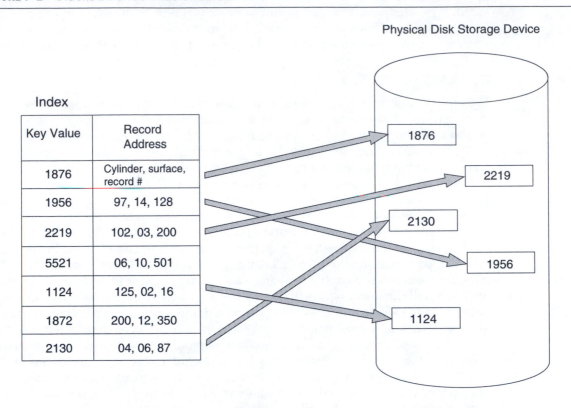

Physical Disk Storage Device

Records in an **indexed random file** are dispersed throughout a disk without regard for their physical proximity to other related records. In fact, records belonging to the same file may reside on different disks. A record's physical location is unimportant as long as the operating system software can find it when needed. This is accomplished by searching the index for the desired key value, reading the corresponding storage location (address), and then moving the disk read-write head to the address location. When a new record is added to the file, the data management software selects a vacant disk location, stores the record, and adds the new address to the index.

The physical organization of the index itself may be either sequential (by key value) or random. Random indexes are easier to maintain, in terms of adding records, because new key records are simply added to the end of the index without regard to their sequence. Indexes in sequential order are more difficult to maintain because new record keys must be inserted between existing keys. One advantage of a sequential index is that it can be searched rapidly. Because of its logical arrangement, algorithms can be used to speed the search through the index to find a key value. This becomes particularly important for large data files with corresponding large indexes.

The principal advantage of indexed random files is in operations involving the processing of individual records (Operations 1, 2, 3, and 6 in Table 7–1). Another advantage is their efficient use of disk storage. Records may be placed wherever there is space without concern for maintaining contiguous storage locations. However, random files are not efficient structures for operations that involve processing a large portion of a file. A great deal of access time may be required to access an entire file of records that are randomly dispersed throughout the storage device. Sequential files are more efficient for this purpose.

The **indexed sequential access method (ISAM)** structure is used for very large files that require routine batch processing and a moderate degree of individual record processing. For instance, the customer file of a public utility company will be processed in batch mode for billing purposes and directly accessed in response to individual customer queries. Because of its sequential organization, the ISAM structure can be searched sequentially for efficient batch processing. Figure 7–3 illustrates how ISAM uses indexes to allow direct access processing.

The ISAM structure is used for files that often occupy several cylinders of contiguous storage on a disk. To find a specific record location, the ISAM file uses a number of indexes that describe in summarized form the contents of each cylinder. For example, in Figure 7–3, we are searching for a record with the key value 2546. The access method goes first to the overall file index, which contains only the highest key value for each cylinder in the file, and determines that Record 2546 is somewhere on Cylinder 99. A quick scan of the surface index for Cylinder 99 reveals that the record is on Surface 3 of Cylinder 99. ISAM indexes do not provide an exact physical address for a single record. However, they identify the disk track where the record in question resides. The last step is to search the identified track sequentially to find the record with key value 2546.

The ISAM structure is moderately effective for Operations 1 and 3 in Table 7–1. Because ISAM must read multiple indexes and search the track sequentially, the average access time for a single record is slower than the indexed sequential or indexed random structures. Direct access speed is sacrificed to achieve very efficient performance in Operations 4, 5, and 6.

FIGURE 7–3   ISAM Used for Direct Access

ISAM – Indexed Sequential Access Method

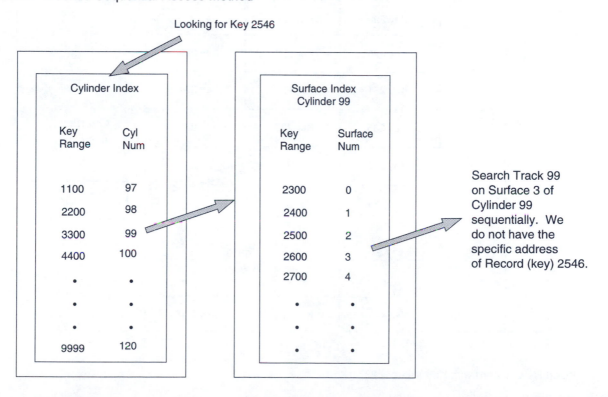

The greatest disadvantage with the ISAM structure is that it does not perform record insertion operations (Operation 2) efficiently. Because the ISAM file is organized sequentially, inserting a new record into the file requires the physical relocation of all the records located beyond the point of insertion. The indexes that describe this physical arrangement must, therefore, also be updated with each insertion. This is extremely time-consuming and disruptive to operations. One method of dealing with this problem is to store new records in an overflow area that is physically separate from the other data records in the file. Figure 7–4 shows how this is done.

An ISAM file has three physical components: the indexes, the prime data storage area, and the overflow area. Rather than inserting a new record directly into the prime area, the data management software places it in a randomly selected location in the overflow area. It then records the address of the location in a special field (called a *pointer*) in the prime area. Later, when searching for the record, the indexes direct the access method to the track location where the record *should* reside. The pointer at that location reveals the record's *actual* location in the overflow area. Thus, accessing a record may involve searching the indexes, searching the track in the prime data area, and finally searching the overflow area. This slows data access time for both direct access and batch processing.

Periodically, the ISAM file must be reorganized by integrating the overflow records into the prime area and then reconstructing the indexes. This involves time, cost, and disruption to operations. Therefore, when a file is highly volatile—(records are added or deleted frequently), the maintenance burden associated with the ISAM approach tends to render it impractical. However, for large, stable files that need both direct access and batch processing, the ISAM structure is a popular option.

FIGURE 7–4   Inserting a Record into an ISAM File

Insert New Record with Key Value = 237

HASHING STRUCTURE

A **hashing structure** employs an algorithm that converts the primary key of a record directly into a storage address. Hashing eliminates the need for a separate index. By calculating the address, rather than reading it from an index, records can be retrieved more quickly. Figure 7–5 illustrates the hashing approach.

This example assumes an inventory file with 100,000 inventory items. The algorithm divides the inventory number (the primary key) into a prime number. Recall that a prime number is one that can be divided only by itself and 1 without leaving a residual value. Therefore, the calculation will always produce a value that can be translated into a storage location. Hence, the residual 6.27215705 becomes Cylinder 272, Surface 15, and Record number 705. The hashing structure uses a random file organization because the process of calculating residuals and converting them into storage locations produces widely dispersed record addresses.

The principal advantage of hashing is access speed. Calculating a record's address is faster than searching for it through an index. This structure is suited to applications that require rapid access to individual records in performing Operations 1, 2, 3, and 6 in Table 7–1.

The hashing structure has two significant disadvantages. First, this technique does not use storage space efficiently. The storage location chosen for a record is a mathematical function of its primary key value. The algorithm will never select some disk locations because they do not correspond to legitimate key values. As much as one-third of the disk pack may be wasted.

The second disadvantage is the reverse of the first. Different record keys may generate the same (or similar) residual, which translates into the same address. This is

FIGURE 7–5

Hashing Technique with Pointer to Relocate the Collision Record

Key Value Being Sought
– 15943

Hashing Technique

Prime #/ Key
= 99997/15943 = 6.27215705

Residual Translates to:
Cylinder 272
Surface 15
Record # 705

15943

Collision Pointer

Relocated Record

Record with Same Hashed Address as 15943

called a *collision* because two records cannot be stored at the same location. One solution to this problem is to randomly select a location for the second record and place a pointer to it from the first (the calculated) location. This technique is represented by the dark arrow in Figure 7–5.

The collision problem slows down access to records. Locating a record displaced in this manner involves first calculating its theoretical address, searching that location, and then determining the actual address from the pointer contained in the record at that location. This has an additional implication for Operation 7 in Table 7–1—deleting a record from a file. If the first record is deleted from the file, the pointer to the second (collision) record will also be deleted and the address of the second record will be lost. This can be dealt with in two ways: (1) After deleting the first record, the collision record can be physically relocated to its calculated address, which is now vacant; or (2) The first record is marked "deleted" but is left in place to preserve the pointer to the collision record.

POINTER STRUCTURES

Figure 7–6 presents the **pointer structure**, which in this example is used to create a *linked-list file*. This approach stores in a field of one record the address (pointer) of a related record. The records in this type of file are spread over the entire disk without

FIGURE 7–6

A Linked-List File

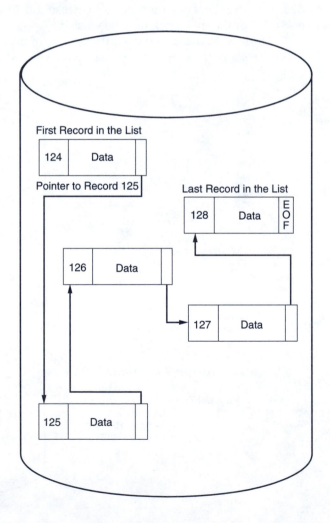

concern for their physical proximity with other related records. The pointers provide connections between the records. In this example, Record 124 points to the location of Record 125, Record 125 points to 126, and so on. The last record in the list contains an end-of-file marker.

Pointers may also be used to link records between files. Figure 7–7 shows an accounts receivable record with three pointers. The first pointer links the AR record to the next AR record within the AR file. The second and third pointers link AR records to sales invoice and remittance advice records, respectively. By accessing an accounts receivable record (for example, Customer 4456), we can locate all sales invoices and remittances pertaining to the account. These records may then be displayed on a computer screen or printed for review. The next transaction record (a sale or cash receipt) to be processed will be added to the end of the appropriate linked-list. The address of the record will then be stored in the preceding record to provide future access.

TYPES OF POINTERS

Figure 7–8 shows three types of pointers: physical address, relative address, and logical key pointers. A **physical address pointer** contains the actual disk storage location (cylinder, surface, and record number) needed by the disk controller. This physical address allows the system to access the record directly without obtaining further information. This method has the advantage of speed, since it does not need to be manipulated further to determine a record's location. However, it also has two disadvantages: First, if the related record is moved from one disk location to another, the pointer must be changed. This is a problem when disks are periodically reorganized or copied. Second, the physical pointers bear no logical relationship to the records they

FIGURE 7–7   Pointers within and between Files

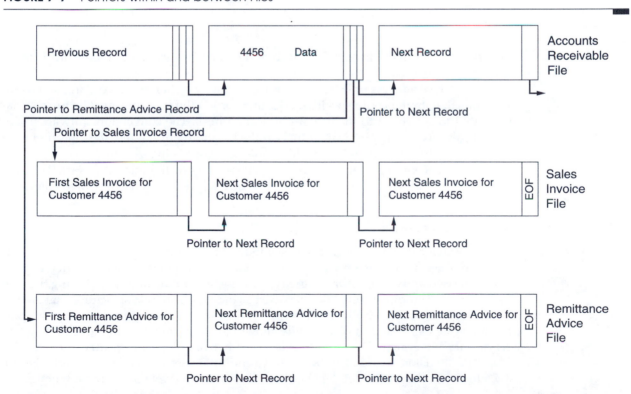

FIGURE 7–8   Types of Pointers

identify. If a pointer is lost or destroyed and cannot be recovered, the record it references is also lost.

A **relative address pointer** contains the relative position of a record in the file. For example, the pointer could specify the 135th record in the file. This must be further manipulated to convert it to the actual physical address. The conversion software calculates this by using the physical address of the beginning of the file, the length of each record in the file, and the relative address of the record being sought.

A **logical key pointer** contains the primary key of the related record. This key value is then converted into the record's physical address by a hashing algorithm.

HIERARCHICAL AND NETWORK DATABASE STRUCTURES

Early hierarchical and network database models employed many of the preceding flat-file techniques as well as new proprietary database structures. A major difference between the two approaches is the degree of process integration and data sharing that can be achieved. Two-dimensional flat files exist as independent data structures that are not linked logically or physically to other files. Database models were designed to support flat-file systems already in place, while allowing the organization to move to new levels of data integration. By providing linkages between logically related files, a third (depth) dimension is added to better serve multiple-user needs. For example, Figure 7–7 illustrates the use of pointers between files in an example of a simple hierarchical database structure. An example of a complex network database structure is illustrated by Figure 7–9.

Figure 7–9 illustrates a many-to-many association between an inventory file and a vendor file. Each vendor supplies many inventory items and each item is supplied by more than one vendor. Notice that each inventory and vendor record exists only once, but there is a separate link record for each item the vendor supplies and for each supplier of a given inventory item. This arrangement of pointers allows us to find all vendors of a given inventory item and all inventories supplied by each vendor.

Link files may also contain accounting data. For example, the link file in Figure 7–9 shows that the price for Inventory Number 1356 from Vendor Number 1 ($10) is not the same price charged by Vendor Number 3 ($12). Similarly, the delivery time (days-lead time) and discount offered (terms) are different. Transaction characteristics such as these can vary between vendors and even between different items from the same vendor. Data that are unique to the item-vendor associations are stored in the unique link file record, as shown in the figure.

RELATIONAL DATABASE STRUCTURES

In the previous section, we saw how hierarchical and network databases use explicit linkages (pointers) between records to establish relationships. The linkages in the

FIGURE 7-9   A Link File in a Many-to-Many Relationship

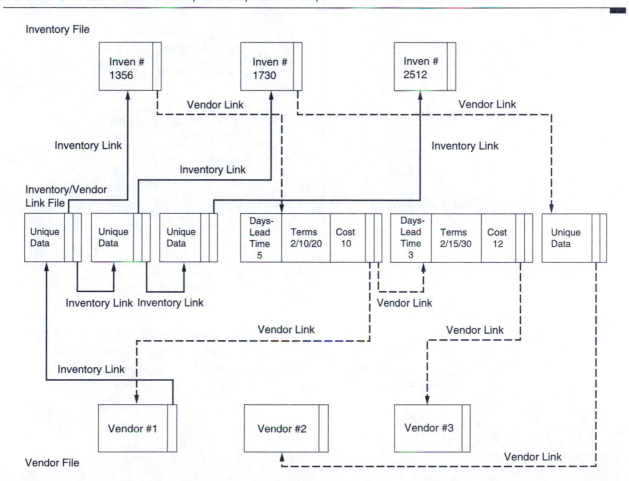

relational model are implicit. Figure 7–10, which was introduced in Chapter 3, illustrates the use of embedded keys to provide a link between related tables. The data structure underlying this model is the *indexed sequential file*.

The **indexed sequential file** structure, illustrated in Figure 7–11, uses an index in conjunction with a sequential file organization. This structure allows both direct access to individual records and batch processing of the entire file. Multiple indexes can be used to create a cross-reference called an **inverted list** that allows even more flexible access to data. In Figure 7–11, two indexes are shown. One contains the employee number (primary key) for uniquely locating records in the file. The second index contains record addresses arranged by year-to-date earnings. Using this non-unique field as a secondary key permits all employee records to be viewed in ascending or descending order according to earnings. Alternatively, individual records with selected earnings balances can be displayed. Indexes may be created for each attribute in the table, allowing data to be viewed from multiple perspectives to produce multiple user views.

FIGURE 7–10   Linkages between Relational Tables

FIGURE 7–11   Indexed Sequential file

Emp # Index			Employee Table						YTD Earnings Index	

Key Value	Record Address		Emp #	Name	Address	Skill Code	YTD Earnings		Key Value	Address
101	1	→	101	J. Smith	15 Main St.	891	15000		20000.00	3
102	2	→	102	S. Buell	107 Hill Top	379	10000		19000	4
103	3	→	103	T. Hill	40 Barclay St.	891	20000		18000	5
104	4	→	104	M. Green	251 Ule St.	209	19000		15000	1
105	5	→	105	H. Litt	423 Rauch Ave.	772	18000		10000	2

USER VIEWS

A **user view** is the set of data that a particular user needs to achieve his or her assigned tasks. For example, a general ledger clerk's view consists of the organization's chart of accounts; a sales manager's view might include detailed customer sales data organized by product, region, and salesperson; and a production manager's view may include finished goods inventory on hand, available manufacturing capacity, and vendor lead times.

A problem arises in meeting diverse user needs when the collection, summarization, storage, and reporting of transaction and standing data are dominated by a single view that is inappropriate for entity-wide purposes. Traditionally, the accountant's view has dictated the set of financial data used by organizations. However, modern managers need both financial and nonfinancial information in formats and at levels of aggregation that differ from those often accommodated by traditional accounting systems. The trend today is to capture data in sufficient detail and diversity to sustain multiple user views. The tables that support the user views are called **base tables**; to be effective, they must be properly **normalized**. In the next section, we examine the relationship between user views, their underlying base tables, and the process of data normalization.

CREATING USER VIEWS FROM NORMALIZED BASE TABLES

The process of creating a user view begins by designing the output reports, documents, and input screens needed by the user. This usually involves an extensive analysis of user information needs. Once the analysis is complete, the designer can derive the set of data attributes (the conceptual user view) necessary to support these views. Because they are the physical representation of the conceptual user view, reports, documents, and computer screens are called *physical views*. They help the designer understand key relationships among the data.

The discussion that follows is based on the physical views of three users. The first view is for a purchasing agent who needs information about inventory items to be ordered and the suppliers of the inventory. Figure 7–12 depicts the inventory status report that conveys this information.

The second user view is for a sales manager who needs a breakdown of daily sales activity organized by customer and product. Figure 7–13 shows the sales report containing this information. The third view, for the general ledger department, presents a listing of journal vouchers summarizing the day's business activity. The journal voucher report is portrayed in Figure 7–14 on page 266.

FIGURE 7–12   Inventory Status Report

Ajax Manufacturing Co.
Inventory Status Report

Part Number	Description	Quantity On Hand	Reorder Point	Order Quantity	Supplier Number	Name	Address	Telephone
1	Bracket	100	150	500	22 24 27	Ozment Sup Buell Co. B&R Sup	123 Main St. 2 Broadhead Westgate Mall	555-7895 555-3436 555-7845
2	Gasket	440	450	1000	22 24 28	Ozment Sup Buell Co. Harris Manuf	123 Main St. 2 Broadhead 24 Linden St.	555-7895 555-3436 555-3316
3	Brace	10	10	50	22 24 28	Ozment Sup Buell Co. Harris Manuf	123 Main St. 2 Broadhead 24 Linden St.	555-7895 555-3436 555-3316
.	.	.	.	.	.	.	.	.
.	.	.	.	.	.	.	.	.
.	.	.	.	.	.	.	.	.

Keep in mind that, at this point, the physical views are at the design stage (on paper) only. By working backward from these, and applying normalization principles, conceptual user views will be derived from which we will design a set of base tables. Once this is done, physical tables can be created and transformed into physical reports and documents. We begin this process with the inventory status report in Figure 7–12.

THE IMPORTANCE OF DATA NORMALIZATION

Correctly designed database tables are critical to the success of the DBMS. Poorly designed tables can cause operational problems that restrict, or even deny, users access to the information they need. **Data normalization** is a process that promotes effective database design by grouping data attributes into tables that comply to specific conditions. There are several possible levels of normalization. Usually, designers of accounting databases normalize tables to the level called **third normal form (3NF)**.

Tables that have not been normalized are associated with three types of problems called *anomalies*: the update anomaly, the insertion anomaly, and the deletion anomaly. One or more of these anomalies will exist in tables that are normalized at lower levels such as *first normal form* (1NF) and *second normal form* (2NF), but tables in 3NF are free of anomalies. To demonstrate the three anomalies and their implications, the physical view in Figure 7–15 is represented as a single unnormalized table called Inventory. This table contains the set of data attributes needed by the purchasing agent. The primary key of the table is Part Num.

UPDATE ANOMALY.   The **update anomaly** results from data redundancy in an unnormalized table. To illustrate, notice that Supplier Number 22 provides each of the three inventory items (Part Num 1, 2, 3) shown in Figure 7–15. The data attributes pertaining to Supplier Number 22 (Name, Address, and Tele Num) are thus repeated in every record of every inventory item that Supplier Number 22 provides. Any change in the supplier's name, address, or telephone number must be made to each of these records in the table. In our simple example, this means three different updates. To better appreciate the implications of the update anomaly, consider a more realistic

FIGURE 7-13 Sales Report

Sales Report

Customer Number: 19321
Customer Name : Jon Smith
Address   : 520 Main St., City

Invoice #	Date	Invoice Total	Part Num	Quantity	Unit Price	Ext'd Price
12390	11/11/98	$850	2	5	$20	$100
			1	10	50	500
			3	25	10	250
12912	11/21/98	$300	4	10	$30	$300

Customer Total: $1,150

* * * * * * * * * * * * * * * * * * * * * * * * * *

Customer Number: 19322
Customer Name : Mary Smith
Address   : 2289 Elm St., City

Invoice #	Date	Invoice Total	Part Num	Quantity	Unit Price	Ext'd Price
12421	11/13/98	$1,000	6	10	$20	$200
			1	2	50	100
			5	7	100	700
12901						
	11/20/98	$500	4	10	$30	$300
			2	10	20	200

Customer Total: $1,500

* * * * * * * * * * * * * * * * * * * * * * * * * *

Next Customer

•
•
•

Next Customer

situation where the vendor supplies 10,000 different items of inventory. Any update to an attribute must then be made 10,000 times.

INSERTION ANOMALY.   To demonstrate the effects of the **insertion anomaly**, assume that a new vendor has entered the marketplace. The organization does not yet purchase from the vendor, but may wish to do so in the future. In the meantime, the organization wants to add the vendor to the database. This is not possible because the primary key for the inventory record is Part Num. Since the vendor does not supply the organization with any inventory items, it cannot be added to the database.

DELETION ANOMALY.   The **deletion anomaly** involves the unintentional deletion of data from a table. To illustrate, assume that Supplier Number 27 provides the company

FIGURE 7–14

Journal
Voucher
Report

Journal Voucher Report

JV #	Date	Title	Acct #	Debit	Credit
1	9/20/01	Cash Acct Rec Sales	101 103 401	1000 2000	 3000
2	9/20/01	Cost of Goods Sold Inventory	501 108	2500	 2500
• • •	• • •	• • •	• • •	• • •	• • •

with only one item: Part Number 1. If the organization discontinues this inventory item and deletes it from the table, the data pertaining to Supplier Number 27 will also be deleted. Although the company may wish to retain the supplier's information for future use, the current table design prevents it from doing so.

The presence of the deletion anomaly is less conspicuous, but potentially more serious than the update and insertion anomalies. A flawed database design that prevents the insertion of records or requires the user to perform excessive updates attracts attention quickly. However, the deletion anomaly may go undetected, and the user may be unaware of the loss of important data until it is too late. A poorly structured database can result in the unintentional loss of critical accounting records and the destruction of the audit trail. Hence, the design of database tables carries internal control significance that accountants must recognize.

THE NORMALIZATION PROCESS

Simply stated, eliminating the three anomalies involves a process that systematically splits unnormalized complex tables into smaller tables that meet two conditions:

FIGURE 7–15 Unnormalized Database Table

Inventory Table

Nonkey Attributes

Primary
Key

Part Num	Description	Quantity On Hand	Reorder Point	EOQ	Supplier Number	Name	Address	Tele Num
1	Bracket	100	150	500	22	Ozment Sup	123 Main St.	555-7895
1	Bracket	100	150	500	24	Buell Co.	2 Broadhead	555-3436
1	Bracket	100	150	500	27	B&R Sup	Westgate Mall	555-7845
2	Gasket	440	450	1000	22	Ozment Sup	123 Main St.	555-7895
2	Gasket	440	450	1000	24	Buell Co.	2 Broadhead	555-3436
2	Gasket	440	450	1000	28	Harris Manuf	24 Linden St.	555-3316
3	Brace	10	10	50	22	Ozment Sup	123 Main St.	555-7895
3	Brace	10	10	50	24	Buell Co.	2 Broadhead	555-3436
3	Brace	10	10	50	28	Harris Manuf	24 Linden St.	555-3316

1. All nonkey attributes in the table are dependent on the primary key.
2. All nonkey attributes are independent of the other nonkey attributes.

While it is possible to represent simple user views with a single 3NF table, complex views require more than one table. The user view in Figure 7–15, for example, cannot be represented by a single table that meets the 3NF conditions above.

Two distinct sets of data are contained in the unnormalized table in Figure 7–15: data about inventory and data about suppliers. The nonkey attributes of Name, Address, and Tele Num are not dependent on (defined by) the table's primary key (Part Num). Rather, these attributes are dependent on the nonkey attribute—Supplier Number. The solution is to remove the supplier data from the table and place them in a separate table, which we will call Supplier. The two new base tables, Inventory and Supplier, are presented in Figure 7–16, along with a third table, Part/Supplier, which is explained next.

When an unnormalized table is split into two or more normalized tables, the normalized tables must then be linked together by one or more common attributes called *embedded foreign keys*. The degree of association between the tables (i.e., 1:1, 1:M, or M:M) determines how the foreign keys are assigned. The concept of associations and the rules for embedding keys were explained in Chapter 3. As you will recall, when the association is one-to-one, it does not matter which table's primary key is embedded in the other as a foreign key. In one-to-many associations, the primary key on the "one"

FIGURE 7–16   Normalized Database Tables

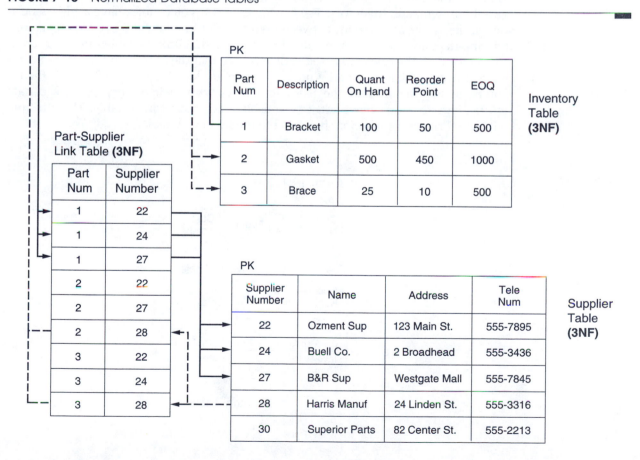

side is embedded as the foreign key on the "many" side. Embedded keys are not used to link tables that have a many-to-many association. Instead, a separate link table, containing keys for the related tables, is created.

In Figure 7–16, the link table (Part/Supplier) contains the primary keys for the records in the Inventory table (Part Num) and the related Supplier table (Supplier Number). Via the link table, every inventory record can be linked to each supplier of the item, and all suppliers can be linked to the inventory items that they supply. For example, by searching the Inventory table for Part Num 1, we see that suppliers 22, 24, and 27 supply this item. Searching in the opposite direction, supplier 28 provides part numbers 2 and 3. Each unique occurrence of a supplier/inventory relation is represented by a separate record in the link table. For example, if supplier 24 provides 500 different items, 500 link records are needed to depict these relations.

All three tables in Figure 7–16 are in 3NF and, as a result, the three anomalies have been eliminated. First, the update anomaly is resolved because data about each supplier exist in only one location—the Supplier table. Any change in the data about an individual supplier is made only once, regardless of how many items it furnishes the company. Second, the insert anomaly is solved, because new vendors can be added to the supplier table even if they are not currently supplying the organization with inventory. For example, Supplier Number 30 in the table does not supply any inventory items. Finally, the deletion anomaly is eliminated. The decision to delete an inventory item from the database will not result in the unintentional deletion of the supplier data as well, since these data reside independently in different tables.

Applying the same normalization principles to the Sales Report in Figure 7–13, we derive the base tables depicted in Figure 7–17. Four tables emerge: Customer, Invoice, Line-Item, and Inventory. The Customer and Invoice tables have a 1:M association. Similarly, the associations between Invoice and Line-Item and between Inventory and Line-Item are 1:M. The embedded foreign keys that link the tables are assigned in accordance with the rules discussed earlier. Notice that the Line-Item table uses a composite of Invoice Num and Part Num as the primary key. Notice also that both the Inventory Status Report and the Sales Report views use inventory data. The data requirements for both views must be consolidated into a single table. The attribute Unit-Sales Price must therefore be added to the Inventory table.

FIGURE 7–17

Normalized Base Tables for Sales Report

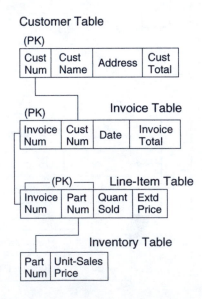

Customer Table

(PK)			
Cust Num	Cust Name	Address	Cust Total

Invoice Table

(PK)			
Invoice Num	Cust Num	Date	Invoice Total

Line-Item Table

(PK)			
Invoice Num	Part Num	Quant Sold	Extd Price

Inventory Table

Part Num	Unit-Sales Price

Figure 7–18 shows the set of base tables and the linkages between them needed to support the three user views in our example. To simplify the illustration, some data attributes are not shown. Notice that the Journal Voucher Report view in Figure 7–14 requires the two tables: General Journal and Chart of Accounts. The view also requires summaries of detailed data that are stored in other tables. These are illustrated with dotted lines. The General Journal table receives summary values for cash payments, credit sales, and invoice total from the Invoice table, to produce the following journal voucher recording total cash and credit sales as shown in Figure 7–14:

	DR	CR
Cash	1000	
Accts Receivable	2000	
Sales		3000

Since the cash payment and credit sales attributes were not in either of the other two views, they must be added to the Invoice table structure. Summaries are required for Quant Sold from the Line-Item table and Unit Cost from the Inventory table to record cost of goods sold per Figure 7–14:

FIGURE 7–18 Base Users and Links for All Views

	DR	CR
Cost of Goods Sold	2500	
Inventory		2500

Unit Cost is also a new attribute that was added to the Inventory table. These summarized values are stored in the General Journal table to produce the Journal Voucher Report.

CREATING THE PHYSICAL BASE TABLES

The base tables created thus far are theoretical (on paper), not physical. The next step is to create the physical tables and, where applicable, populate them with data. This is an involved step that must be carefully planned and executed, and may take many months. To continue with this example, let's assume that the physical tables have been created and are in place. Once this is done, the physical user views can be produced based on available data.

CREATING PHYSICAL USER VIEWS FROM NORMALIZED BASE TABLES

The query function of a relational DBMS allows the system designer to easily create user views from base tables. The designer simply tells the DBMS which tables to use, their primary and foreign keys, and the attributes to select from each table. Older DBMSs require the designer to specify these parameters in SQL or another query language. Newer systems allow this to be done visually. The designer simply points and clicks at the tables and the attributes. From this visual representation, the DBMS generates the SQL commands for the query to produce the view. The SQL commands needed to produce the inventory status report in Figure 7–12 are shown below:

> AS SELECT inventory.part-num, description, quant-on-hand, reorder-point, EOQ, part-supplier.part-num, part-supplier.supplier-number, supplier.supplier-number, name, address, tele-num
>
> FROM inventory, part-supplier, supplier
>
> WHERE inventory.part-num=part-supplier.part-num AND part-supplier.supplier-number=supplier.supplier-number AND quant-on-hand ≤ reorder-point

- The AS SELECT command identifies all the attributes to be contained in the view. When the same attribute appears in more than one table (e.g., part-num) the source table name must also be specified.
- The FROM command identifies the tables used in creating the view.
- The WHERE command specifies how rows in the Inventory, Part-Supplier and Supplier tables are to be matched to create the view. In this case, the three tables are algebraically joined on the primary keys Part Num and Supplier Number.
- Multiple expressions may be linked with the AND, OR, and NOT operators. In this example, the last expression uses AND to restrict the records to be selected with the logical expression *quant-on-hand ≤ reorder-point*. Only records whose quantities on hand have fallen to or below their reorder points will be selected for the view. The user will not see the many thousands of other inventory items that have adequate quantities available.

To view and process data, the user executes the query program. Each time this is done, the query builds a new view with current data. The resulting view is a **virtual table** derived from the base tables. A virtual table does not physically exist as a set of rows and columns. It is a partial representation (subrows and subcolumns) of the actual physical base tables. The user perceives the view as his or her personal database. By restricting the user's access to the view, rather than permitting access to the underlying base tables, the user is limited to authorized data only.

A report program is used to make the view visually attractive and easy to use. Column headings can be added, fields summed, and averages calculated to produce a hard copy or computer screen report that resembles the original user report in Figure 7–12. The report program can suppress unnecessary data from the view, such as repeating groups (duplicated data) and the key values in the Part-Supplier link table. These keys are necessary to build the view but are not needed for the actual report.

AUDITORS AND DATA NORMALIZATION

Database normalization is a technical matter that is usually the responsibility of systems professionals. However, the subject has implications for internal control that make it the concern of auditors also. For example, the update anomaly can generate conflicting and obsolete data values; the insertion anomaly can result in unrecorded transactions and incomplete audit trails; and the deletion anomaly can cause the loss of accounting records and the destruction of audit trails. Although most auditors will never be responsible for normalizing an organization's databases, they should have an understanding of the process and be able to determine whether a table is properly normalized.

Furthermore, in order to extract data from tables to perform audit procedures, the auditor first needs to know how the data are structured. The user's view of the data is often very different from its storage structure. For example, Figure 7–19 demonstrates that extracting purchases order data may involve a number of related tables. The circled numbers relate items in the user view to storage locations in the related base tables.

EMBEDDED AUDIT MODULE

The objective of the **embedded audit module (EAM)** is to identify important transactions while they are being processed and extract copies of them in real time. An EAM is a specially programmed module embedded in a host application to capture predetermined transaction types for subsequent analysis. The approach is illustrated in Figure 7–20.

As the selected transaction is being processed by the host application, a copy of the transaction is stored in an audit file for subsequent review. The EAM approach allows selected transactions to be captured throughout the audit period. Captured transactions are made available to the auditor in real time, at period end, or at any time during the period, thus significantly reducing the amount of work the auditor must do to identify significant transactions for substantive testing.

To begin data capturing, the auditor specifies to the EAM the parameters and materiality threshold of the transactions set to be captured. For example, let's assume that the auditor establishes a $50,000 materiality threshold for transactions processed by a sales order processing system. Transactions equal to or greater than $50,000 will be copied to the audit file. From this set of transactions, the auditor may select a subset to be used for substantive tests. Transactions that fall below this threshold will be ignored by the EAM.

FIGURE 7-19

Normalized
Tables

FIGURE 7–20

Embedded
Audit Module
Technique

While primarily a substantive testing technique, EAMs may also be used to monitor controls on an ongoing basis as required by SAS 78. For example, transactions selected by the EAM can be reviewed for proper authorization, completeness and accuracy of processing, and correct posting to accounts.

DISADVANTAGES OF EAMS

The EAM approach has two significant disadvantages. The first pertains to operational efficiency and the second is concerned with EAM integrity.

OPERATIONAL EFFICIENCY

From the user's point of view, EAMs decrease operational performance. The presence of an audit module within the host application may create significant overhead, especially when the amount of testing is extensive. One approach for relieving this burden from the system is to design modules that may be turned *on* and *off* by the auditor. Doing so will, of course, reduce the effectiveness of the EAM as an ongoing audit tool.

VERIFYING EAM INTEGRITY

The EAM approach may not be a viable audit technique in environments with a high level of program maintenance. When host applications undergo frequent changes, the EAMs embedded within the hosts will also require frequent modifications. The integrity concerns raised earlier regarding application maintenance apply equally to EAMs. The integrity of the EAM directly affects the quality of the audit process. Auditors must therefore evaluate the EAM integrity. This is accomplished in the same way as testing the host application controls.

GENERALIZED AUDIT SOFTWARE

Generalized audit software (GAS) is the most widely used CAATT for EDP auditing. GAS allows auditors to access electronically coded data files and perform various operations on their contents. Some of the more common uses for GAS include:

- Footing and balancing entire files or selected data items.
- Selecting and reporting detailed data contained in files.
- Selecting stratified statistical samples from data files.
- Formatting results of tests into reports.
- Printing confirmations in either standardized or special wording.
- Screening data and selectively including or excluding items.
- Comparing multiple files and identifying any differences.
- Recalculating data fields.

The widespread popularity of GAS is due to four factors: (1) GAS languages are easy to use and require little computer background on the part of the auditor; (2) many GAS products can be used on both mainframe and PC systems; (3) auditors can perform their tests independent of the client's computer service staff; and (4) GAS can be used to audit the data stored in most file structures and formats.

USING GAS TO ACCESS SIMPLE STRUCTURES

Gaining access to flat-file structures is a relatively simple process, as illustrated in Figure 7–21. In this example, an inventory file is read directly by the GAS, which extracts key information needed for the audit, including the quantity on hand, the dollar value, and the warehouse location of each inventory item. The auditor's task is to verify the existence and value of the inventory by performing a physical count of a representative sample of the inventory on hand. Thus, on the basis of a materiality threshold provided by the auditor, the GAS selects the sample records and prepares a report containing the needed information.

USING GAS TO ACCESS COMPLEX STRUCTURES

Gaining access to complex structures, such as a hashed file or other form of random file, may pose a problem for the auditor. Not all GAS products on the market may be capable of accessing every type of file structure. If the CAATT in question is unable to

FIGURE 7–21

Using GAS to Access Simple File Structure

deal with a complex structure, the auditor may need to appeal to systems professionals to write a special program that will copy the records from their actual structure to a flat-file sequential structure for easy retrieval. Figure 7–22 illustrates this approach.

Most DBMSs have utility features that can be used to reformat complex structures into flat files suitable for this purpose. To illustrate the file flattening process, consider the complex database structure presented in Figure 7–23. The database structure uses pointers to integrate three related files—Customer, Sales Invoice, and Line Item—in a hierarchical arrangement. Extracting audit evidence from a structure of this complexity using GAS may be difficult, if not impossible. A simpler flat-file version of this structure is illustrated in Figure 7–24. The single flat file presents the three record types as a sequential structure that can be easily accessed by GAS.

FIGURE 7–22

Using GAS to Access Complex File Structure

Complex File Structure

① Auditor specifies which database records to copy into flat file.

② Database management system produces a flat file of a portion of the data base.

③ Auditor determines the selection criteria used by the GAS.

④ GAS retrieves selected records from the flat file.

FIGURE 7–23 Complex Database Structure

FIGURE 7–24

Flat Version of a
Complex File
Structure

Flat File Structure

AUDIT ISSUES PERTAINING TO THE CREATION OF FLAT FILES

The auditor must sometimes rely on computer services personnel to produce a flat file from the complex file structures. There is a risk that data integrity will be compromised by the procedure used to create the flat file. For example, if the auditor's objective is to confirm accounts receivable, certain fraudulent accounts in the complex structure may be intentionally omitted from the flat-file copy that is created. The sample of confirmations drawn from the flat file may therefore be unreliable. Auditors skilled in programming languages may avoid this potential pitfall by writing their own data extraction routines.

ACL SOFTWARE

Public accounting firms have in the past developed proprietary versions of GAS, which they used in the audits of their clients. More recently, software companies have serviced this market. Among them, ACL is the leader in the industry. ACL was designed as a meta-language for auditors to access most data stored by electronic means and to test them comprehensively. In fact, many of the problems associated with accessing complex data structures have been solved by ACL's Open Data Base Connectivity (ODBC) interface. A student edition of ACL along with sample data files and an instruction manual are stored on the CD that accompanies this text. The remainder of the chapter highlights ACL's more commonly used features. In later chapters, these and other features are demonstrated within the context of specific audit procedures. For a detailed explanation of ACL commands refer to the instruction manual and ACL's extensive on-line help feature.

INPUT FILE DEFINITION

We have already established that a client's system may store data using a number of flat-file or database structures, including sequential files, ISAM files, linked lists, and relational tables. One of ACL's strengths is the ability to read data stored in most formats. ACL uses the **input file definition** feature for this purpose. To create a file definition, the auditor needs to know both where the file physically resides and its field structure layout. Very large files may need to be accessed directly from the mainframe computer. When this is the case, the auditor must obtain access privileges to the directory in which the file resides. Where possible, however, a copy of the file should be stored in a separate test directory or downloaded to the auditor's PC. This usually requires the assistance of systems professionals. The auditor should ensure that he or she secures the correct version of the file, that it is complete, and that the file structure documentation is intact. At this point, the auditor is ready to define the file to ACL. Figure 7–25 illustrates ACL's file definition screen.

FIGURE 7–25

Input File Definition

SOURCE: Courtesy ACL Services Ltd.

The input file definition screen allows the auditor to define important character-istics about the file, including overall record length, the name given to each field, the type of data (i.e., numeric or character) contained in each field, and the starting point and length of each field in the file.[1] This definition is stored under a name defined by the auditor. Since the file in Figure 7–25 contains inventory data, the file definition shall be named *INVNTRY* for this example. Once the file definition is complete, future access to the file is accomplished simply by selecting *INVNTRY* from ACL's file definition menu. ACL automatically retrieves the file and presents it on screen according to its file definition, which is called the **default view**. For example, Figure 7–26 illustrates the default view of the Inventory file after the *INVNTRY* definition is created. As we will see, this view of the data may be changed as needed by the auditor.

CUSTOMIZING A VIEW

A view is simply a way of looking at data in a file; auditors seldom need to use all the data contained in a file. ACL allows the auditor to customize the original view created during file definition to one that better meets his or her audit objectives. New views can be created and reformatted without changing or deleting the data in the underling file. Only the presentation of the data is affected. For example, the inventory file in Figure 7–26 contains a number of fields that are irrelevant to the audit. The key fields of

FIGURE 7–26

View of Inventory File

SOURCE: Courtesy ACL Services Ltd.

---

1.   Refer to "Defining Files and Fields" under the Contents section of ACL's on-line Help feature, for a detailed explanation of this process.

interest to the auditor are not organized in contiguous fields. Instead, they are interspersed with irrelevant data, making review of important data difficult. The auditor can easily delete and/or rearrange the data to facilitate effective usage. Figure 7–27 presents a reorganized view of the inventory data that focuses on critical data elements.

FILTERING DATA

ACL provides powerful options for filtering data that support various audit tests. **Filters** are expressions that search for records that meet the filter criteria. ACL's **expression builder** allows the auditor to use logical operators such as AND, OR, <, >, NOT and others to define and test conditions of any complexity and to process only those records that match specific conditions. For example, the auditor can search an inventory file for records with negative or zero quantity on hand. The expression builder screen and the filter needed for this test is illustrated in Figure 7–28.

When the auditor executes this filter procedure, ACL produces a new view of the inventory file (Figure 7–29) containing only two records that both have negative quantity-on-hand levels. This example demonstrates how auditors use ACL to search for anomalies and unusual conditions in accounting files containing thousands of records that defy review by visually scanning their contents.

STRATIFYING DATA

ACL's stratification feature allows the auditor to view the distribution of records that fall into specified strata. Data can be stratified on any numeric field such as sales price,

FIGURE 7–27

Customized View of Inventory File

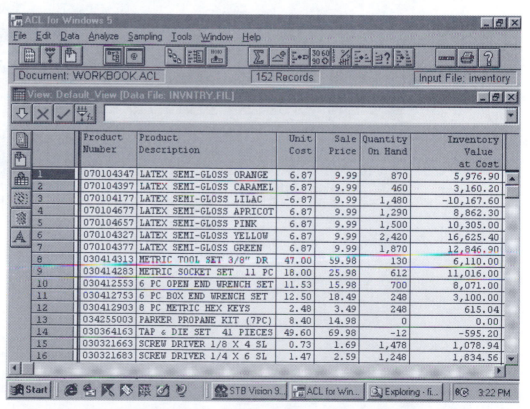

	Product Number	Product Description	Unit Cost	Sale Price	Quantity On Hand	Inventory Value at Cost
1	070104347	LATEX SEMI-GLOSS ORANGE	6.87	9.99	870	5,976.90
2	070104397	LATEX SEMI-GLOSS CARAMEL	6.87	9.99	460	3,160.20
3	070104177	LATEX SEMI-GLOSS LILAC	-6.87	9.99	1,480	-10,167.60
4	070104677	LATEX SEMI-GLOSS APRICOT	6.87	9.99	1,290	8,862.30
5	070104657	LATEX SEMI-GLOSS PINK	6.87	9.99	1,500	10,305.00
6	070104327	LATEX SEMI-GLOSS YELLOW	6.87	9.99	2,420	16,625.40
7	070104377	LATEX SEMI-GLOSS GREEN	6.87	9.99	1,870	12,846.90
8	030414313	METRIC TOOL SET 3/8" DR	47.00	59.98	130	6,110.00
9	030414283	METRIC SOCKET SET 11 PC	18.00	25.98	612	11,016.00
10	030412553	6 PC OPEN END WRENCH SET	11.53	15.98	700	8,071.00
11	030412753	6 PC BOX END WRENCH SET	12.50	18.49	248	3,100.00
12	030412903	8 PC METRIC HEX KEYS	2.48	3.49	248	615.04
13	034255003	PARKER PROPANE KIT (7PC)	8.40	14.98	0	0.00
14	030364163	TAP & DIE SET 41 PIECES	49.60	69.98	-12	-595.20
15	030321663	SCREW DRIVER 1/8 X 4 SL	0.73	1.69	1,478	1,078.94
16	030321683	SCREW DRIVER 1/4 X 6 SL	1.47	2.59	1,248	1,834.56

SOURCE: Courtesy ACL Services Ltd.

FIGURE 7-28

Expression Builder

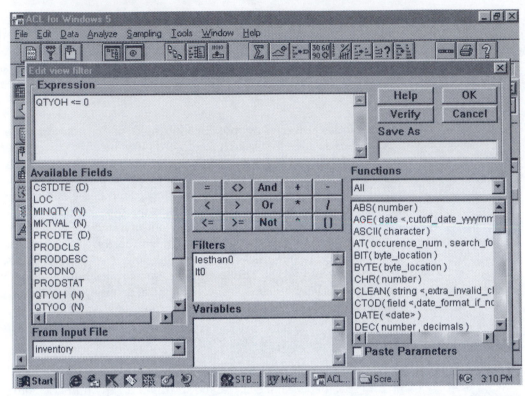

SOURCE: Courtesy ACL Services Ltd.

FIGURE 7-29

View of Filtered
Inventory File

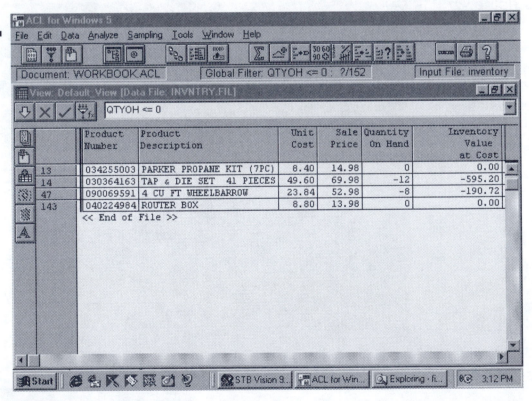

SOURCE: Courtesy ACL Services Ltd.

unit cost, quantity sold, and so on. The data are summarized and classified by strata, which can be equal in size (called *intervals*) or vary in size (called *free*). Figure 7–30 illustrates the results of stratifying the inventory file on the unit-cost field. In this example, inventory value is also calculated for each interval.

The stratified report presented in Figure 7–30 shows unit cost data allocated across ten intervals from $-6.87 to $381.20. If desired, the auditor may choose to change the size and number of intervals or examine only a subset of the file. For example, the first two strata show that they contain a disproportionate number of items. The auditor can obtain a clearer picture of the inventory cost structure by increasing the number of intervals or by reducing the upper limit of the range to $71.

STATISTICAL ANALYSIS

ACL offers many sampling methods for statistical analysis. Two of the most frequently used are **record sampling** and **monetary unit sampling (MUS)**. Each method allows random and interval sampling. The choice of methods will depend on the auditor's strategy and the composition of the file being audited. When records in a file are fairly evenly distributed across strata, the auditor may want an unbiased sample and will thus choose the record sample approach. Using inventory to illustrate, each record, regardless of the dollar amount of the inventory value field, has an equal chance of being included in the sample. On the other hand, if the file is heavily skewed with large value items, the auditor may select MUS, which will produce a sample that includes all the larger dollar amounts.

FIGURE 7–30

Inventory File
Stratified on
Unit Cost

SOURCE: Courtesy ACL Services Ltd.

SUMMARY

This chapter began with a review of data structures, which specify (1) how records are organized in the physical file or database and (2) the access method employed to navigate the file. A number of basic data structures were examined, including sequential, indexed, hashing, and pointers. The chapter then focused on the use of CAATTs for data extraction and analysis. Data extraction can be done by embedded audit modules and general audit software. Audit software supports two types of audit tests: (1) they allow the auditor to make inferences about application control effectiveness, and (2) they provide access to data needed for substantive tests. The second section of the chapter described the features, advantages, and disadvantages of the embedded audit module (EAM) approach. The third section outlined typical functions and uses of generalized audit software (GAS). The section closed with a review of a few features of ACL, the leading product in the GAS market.

KEY TERMS

access method
ACL
base tables
data normalization
data structures
default view
deletion anomaly
embedded audit module (EAM)
expression builder
filters
generalized audit software (GAS)
hashing structure
indexed random file
indexed sequential access method (ISAM)
indexed sequential file
indexed structure

input file definition
insertion anomaly
inverted list
logical key pointer
monetary unit sampling (MUS)
normalized
organization
physical address pointer
pointer structure
record sampling
relative address pointer
sequential structure
third normal form (3NF)
update anomaly
user view
virtual table

REVIEW QUESTIONS

1. What are the two fundamental components of data structures?
2. What are the criteria that influence the selection of the data structure?
3. What are the advantages and disadvantages of using a sequential data structure? Give an example of each.
4. What are the advantages and disadvantages of using an indexed random file structure? An indexed sequential file structure?
5. What are the three physical components of an ISAM file? Explain how a record is searched through these components.
6. What is a pointer? Discuss the three commonly used types of pointers and their relative merits.
7. List the hierarchy of database elements.
8. Discuss and give an example of one-to-one, one-to-many, and many-to-many record associations.

9. Why is a hierarchical database model considered to be a navigational database? What are some limitations of the hierarchical database model?

10. Explain how a separate linking file works in a network model.

11. What is an embedded audit module?

12. Explain what GAS is and why it is so popular with larger public accounting firms. Discuss the independence issue related to GAS.

DISCUSSION QUESTIONS

1. Explain how a hashing structure works and why it is quicker than using an index. Give an example. If it is so much faster, why isn't it used exclusively?

2. Explain how an embedded audit module works and why auditors may choose not to use it.

3. Explain the term "navigational data models." Contrast the hierarchical model and the network model.

4. Explain the three types of anomalies associated with database tables that have not been normalized.

5. Contrast embedded audit modules with generalized audit software.

6. Describe a specific accounting application that could make use of an ISAM file.

7. Explain why auditors should be familiar with the principle of data normalization.

8. How is a virtual table different from a base table?

9. Explain what the term third normal form (3NF) means.

10. Explain how a user view differs from a base table.

11. Explain the following three types of pointers: physical address pointer, relative address pointer, and logical key pointer.

12. Explain why GAS technology is popular with most auditors.

13. Explain the risk associated with using GAS to access complex file structures.

14. Explain the purpose of the input file definition feature of ACL.

15. Assume that an auditor is reviewing a file containing 25 fields of data, only 5 of which are relevant to the auditor's objective. Explain how ACL can help in this situation.

16. Explain the purpose of ACL's filter capability.

17. Distinguish between record sampling and monetary unit sampling (MUS).

MULTIPLE-CHOICE QUESTIONS

1. CIA 1186 III-33
   In an inventory system on a database management system, one stored record contains part number, part name, part color, and part weight. These individual items are called
   a. fields.
   b. stored files.
   c. bytes.
   d. occurrences.

2. CIA 586 III-31
   The use of pointers can save time when sequentially updating a
   a. master file.
   b. database management system.
   c. batch file.
   d. random file.

3. It is appropriate to use a sequential file structure when
   a. records are routinely inserted.
   b. a large portion of the file will be processed in one operation.
   c. records need to be scanned using secondary keys.
   d. single records need to be retrieved.

4. Which statement is NOT correct?
   a. The sequential file structure is appropriate for payroll records.
   b. An advantage of a sequential index is that it can be searched rapidly.
   c. The index sequential access method performs record insertion operations efficiently.
   d. The principal advantage of the hashing structure is speed of access.

5. All of the following statements are true except
   a. indexed random files are dispersed throughout the storage device without regard for physical proximity with related records.
   b. indexed random files use disk storage space efficiently.
   c. indexed random files are efficient when processing a large portion of a file at one time.
   d. indexed random files are easy to maintain in terms of adding records.

6. Which statement is NOT correct? The indexed sequential access method
   a. is used for very large files that need both direct access and batch processing.
   b. may use an overflow area for records.
   c. provides an exact physical address for each record.
   d. is appropriate for files that require few insertions or deletions.

7. Which statement is true about a hashing structure?
   a. The same address could be calculated for two records.
   b. Storage space is used efficiently.
   c. Records cannot be accessed rapidly.
   d. A separate index is required.

8. In a hashing structure,
   a. two records can be stored at the same address.
   b. pointers are used to indicate the location of all records.
   c. pointers are used to indicate the location of a record with the same address as another record.
   d. all locations on the disk are used for record storage.

9. Pointers can be used for all of the following except

   a. to locate the subschema address of the record.
   b. to locate the physical address of the record.
   c. to locate the relative address of the record.
   d. to locate the logical key of the record.

10. An advantage of a physical address pointer is that
    a. it points directly to the actual disk storage location.
    b. it is easily recovered if it is inadvertently lost.
    c. it remains unchanged when disks are reorganized.
    d. all of the above are advantages of the physical address pointer.

11. Pointers are used
    a. to link records within a file.
    b. to link records between files.
    c. to identify records stored in overflow.
    d. all of the above.

12. In a hierarchical model,
    a. links between related records are implicit.
    b. the way to access data is by following a predefined data path.
    c. an owner (parent) record may own just one member (child) record.
    d. a member (child) record may have more than one owner (parent).

13. In a network model
    a. there is one predefined path to a particular record.
    b. many-to-many relationships are supported in a simple network.
    c. management can track and report information by one criterion only.
    d. link files are used to connect records in different files.

14. Which term is NOT associated with the relational database model?
    a. tuple
    b. attribute
    c. collision
    d. relation

15. In the relational database model,
    a. relationships are explicit.
    b. the user perceives that files are linked using pointers.
    c. data are represented on two-dimensional tables.
    d. data are represented as a tree structure.

16. In the relational database model, all of the following are true except
    a. data are presented to users as tables.
    b. data can be extracted from specified rows from specified tables.
    c. a new table can be built by joining two tables.
    d. only one-to-many relationships can be supported.

17. In a relational database,
    a. the user's view of the physical database is the same as the physical database.
    b. users perceive that they are manipulating a single table.
    c. a virtual table exists in the form of rows and columns of a table stored on the disk.
    d. a programming language (COBOL) is used to create a user's view of the database.

18. The update anomaly in unnormalized databases
    a. occurs because of data redundancy.
    b. complicates adding records to the database.
    c. may result in the loss of important data.
    d. often results in excessive record insertions.

19. The most serious problem with unnormalized databases is the
    a. update anomaly.
    b. insertion anomaly.
    c. deletion anomaly.
    d. none of the above.

20. The deletion anomaly in unnormalized databases
    a. is easily detected by users.
    b. may result in the loss of important data.
    c. complicates adding records to the database.
    d. requires the user to perform excessive updates.

PROBLEMS

1. Access Methods
   For each of the following file processing operations, indicate whether a sequential file, indexed random file, indexed sequential access method (ISAM), hashing, or pointer structure works the best. You may choose as many as you wish for each step. Also indicate which would perform the least optimally.
   a. Retrieve a record from the file based upon its primary key value.
   b. Update a record in the file.
   c. Read a complete file of records.
   d. Find the next record in a file.
   e. Insert a record into a file.
   f. Delete a record from a file.
   g. Scan a file for records with secondary keys.

2. File Organization
   For the following situations, indicate the most appropriate type of file organization. Explain your choice.
   a. A local utility company has 80,000 residential customers and 10,000 commercial customers. The monthly billings are staggered throughout the month and, as a result, the cash receipts are fairly uniform throughout the month. For 99 percent of all accounts, one check per month is received. These receipts are recorded in a batch file, and the customer account records are updated biweekly. In a typical month, customer inquires are received at the rate of about 20 per day.
   b. A national credit card agency has 12 million customer accounts. On average, 30 million purchases and 700,000 receipts of payments are processed per day. Additionally, the customer support hot line provides information to approximately 150,000 credit card holders and 30,000 merchants per day.
   c. An airline reservation system assumes that the traveler knows the departing city. From that point, fares and flight times are examined based on the destination. Once a flight is identified as being acceptable to the traveler, then the availability is checked and, if necessary, a seat is reserved. The volume of transactions exceeds one-half million per day.

d. A library system stocks over 2 million books and has 30,000 patrons. Each patron is allowed to check out five books. On average, there are 1.3 copies of each title in the library. Over 3,000 books are checked out each day, with approximately the same amount being returned daily. The check-outs are posted immediately, as well as any returns of overdue books by patrons who wish to pay their fines.

3. Structured Query Language

The vice president of finance has noticed in the aging of the accounts receivable that the amount of overdue accounts is substantially higher than anticipated. He wants to investigate this problem. To do so, he requires a report of overdue accounts containing the attributes shown in the top half of the table below. The bottom half of the table contains the data fields and relevant files in the relational database system. Further, he wants to alert the salespeople of any customers not paying their bills on time. Using the SQL commands given in this chapter, write the code necessary to generate a report of overdue accounts that are greater than $5,000 and over 30 days due. Each customer has an assigned salesperson.

4. Indexed Sequential Access Method

Using the index provided, explain, step-by-step, how the Key 12987 would be found using the indexed sequential access method. Once a surface on a cylinder is located, what is the average number of records that must be searched?

CYLINDER INDEX		SURFACE INDEX CYLINDER	
Key Range	Cylinder Number	Key Range	Surface Number
2,000	44	12,250	0
4,000	45	12,500	1
6,000	46	12,750	2
8,000	47	13,000	3
10,000	48	13,250	4
12,000	49	13,500	5
14,000	50	14,750	6
16,000	51	15,000	7
18,000	52		
20,000	53		

5. Hashing Algorithm

The systems programmer uses a hashing algorithm to determine storage addresses. The hashing structure is 9,997/key. The resulting number is then used to locate the record. The

Problem 3: Structured Query Language

REPORT ATTRIBUTES

Salesperson Name, Salesperson Branch Office, Customer Number, Customer Name, Amount Overdue, Last Purchase Date, Goods Delivered?, Amount of Last Sales Order, Amount of Last Payment, Date of Last Payment

FILES AVAILABLE:

Salesperson Table	Customer Table	Sales Order Table
Salesperson Name	Customer Number	Sales Order Number
Salesperson Number	Customer Name	Customer Number
Commission Rate	Customer Address1	Order Date
Rank	Customer Address2	Amount
Branch	Salesperson Number	Delivery Date
Date of Hire	Last Sales Order Number	
	Year to Date Purchases	
	Account Balance	
	Overdue Balance	
	Amount of Last Payment	
	Date of Last Payment	

first two digits after the decimal point represent the cylinder number, while the second two digits represent the surface number. The fifth, sixth, and seventh digits after the decimal point represent the record number. This algorithm results in a unique address 99 percent of the time. What happens the remainder of the time when the results of the algorithm are not unique? Explain in detail the storage process when Key=3 is processed first, Key=2307 at a later date, and shortly thereafter Key=39.

6. Normalization of Data
   Given below is a table of data for a library. Normalize this data into the third normal form, preparing it for use in a relational database environment. The library's computer is programmed to compute the due date to be 14 days after the check-out date. Document the steps necessary to normalize the data similar to the procedures found in the chapter. Index any fields necessary and show how the databases are related.

7. Normalization of Data
   On the following page is a table of data for a veterinarian practice. Normalize this data into the third normal form, preparing it for use in a relational database environment. Indicate the primary keys and embedded foreign keys in the tables.

8. Normalization of Data
   Prepare the base tables, in third normal form, needed to produce the user view below.

9. Normalization of Data
   Prepare the base tables, in third normal form, needed to produce the user view on the following page.

10. Exposure Identification and Plan of Action
    As the manager of the external audit team, you realize that the embedded audit module writes only "material" invoices to the audit file for the accounts receivable confirmation process. You are immediately concerned that the accounts receivable account may be

Problem 6: Normalization of Data

Student ID Number	Student First Name	Student Last Name	Number of Books Out	Book Call No	Book Title	Date Out	Due Date
678-98-4567	Amy	Baker	3	hf351.j6	Avalanches	09-02-98	09-16-98
678-98-4567	Amy	Baker	4	hf878.k3	Tornadoes	09-02-98	09-16-98
244-23-2348	Ramesh	Sunder	1	i835.123	Politics	09-02-98	09-16-98
398-34-8793	James	Talley	3	k987.d098	Sports	09-02-98	09-16-98
398-34-8793	James	Talley	4	d879.39	Legal Rights	09-02-98	09-16-98
678-98-4567	Amy	Baker	4	p987.t87	Earthquakes	09-03-98	09-17-98
244-23-2348	Ramesh	Sunder	1	q875.i76	Past Heroes	09-03-98	09-17-98

Problem 8: Normalization of Data

USER VIEW									
Part #	Description	QOH	Reorder Point	EOQ	Unit Cost	Ven #	Ven Name	Ven Address	Tel
132	Bolt	100	50	1000	1.50	987	ABC Co.	654 Elm St	555 5498
143	Screw	59	10	100	1.75	987	ABC Co.	654 Elm St	555 5498
760	Nut	80	20	500	2.00	742	XYZ Co.	510 Smit	555 8921
982	Nail	100	50	800	1.00	987	ABC Co.	654 Elm St	555 5498

Problem 7: Normalization of Data

Patient ID Number	Patient Name	Owner ID Number	Owner Last Name	Owner First Name	Address1	Address2	Date	Animal Code	Animal Description	Service Code	Service Description	Service Charge
417	Beau	Magel	Magee	Elaine	23 Elm St	Houston, TX	01/04/99	GR	Golden Retriever	238	Rabies Shot	15.00
417	Beau	Magel	Magee	Elaine	23 Elm St	Houston, TX	01/04/99	GR	Golden Retriever	148	Flea Dip	25.00
417	Beau	Magel	Magee	Elaine	23 Elm St	Houston, TX	01/04/99	GR	Golden Retriever	337	Bloodwork II	20.00
632	Luigi	Cacil	Caciolo	Tony	8 Oak St	Houston, TX	01/09/99	DN	Dalmation	238	Rabies Shot	15.00
632	Luigi	Cacil	Caciolo	Tony	8 Oak St	Houston, TX	01/09/99	DN	Dalmation	500	Kennel-medium	9.00
632	Luigi	Cacil	Caciolo	Tony	8 Oak St	Houston, TX	01/24/99	DN	Dalmation	500	Kennel-medium	9.00
632	Luigi	Cacil	Caciolo	Tony	8 Oak St	Houston, TX	02/01/99	DN	Dalmation	148	Flea Dip	25.00
168	Astro	Jetsl	Jetson	George	3 Air Rd	Sprockley, TX	02/02/99	MX	Canine-mixed	368	Ear Cleaning	17.00

Problem 9: Normalization of Data

USER VIEW

Part #	Description	QOH	Reorder Point	EOQ	Unit Cost	Ven #	Ven Name	Ven Address	Tel
132	Bolt	100	50	1000	1.50	987	ABC Co.	654 Elm St	555 5498
					1.55	750	RST Co.	3415 8th St	555 3421
					1.45	742	XYZ Co.	510 Smit	555 8921
982	Nail	100	50	800	1.00	987	ABC Co.	654 Elm St	555 5498
					1.10	742	XYZ Co.	510 Smit	555 8921
					1.00	549	LMN Co.	18 Oak St.	555 9987

substantially overstated this year and for the prior years in which this EAM was used.

Required:
Explain why you are concerned since all "material" invoices are candidates for confirmation by the customer. Outline a plan for determining if the accounts receivable are overstated.

11. Generalized Audit Software
    CMA 1290 4-Y7
    The internal audit department of Sachem Manufacturing Company is considering buying computer software that will aid in the auditing process. Sachem's financial and manufacturing control systems are completely automated on a large mainframe computer. Melinda Robinson, the director of internal audit, believes that Sachem should acquire computer audit software to assist in the financial and procedure audits that her department conducts. The types of software packages that Robinson is considering are described below.

    - A generalized audit software package that assists in basic audit work, such as the retrieval of live data from large computer files. The department would review this information using conventional audit investigation techniques. More specifically, the department could perform criteria selection, sampling, basic computations for quantitative analysis, record handling, graphical analysis, and the printing of output (confirmations).
    - An integrated test facility package that uses, monitors, and controls dummy test data through existing programs and checks the existence and adequacy of program data entry controls and processing controls.
    - A control flowcharting package that provides a graphical presentation of the data flow of information through a system, pinpointing control strengths and weaknesses.
    - A program (parallel) simulation and modeling package that uses actual data to conduct the same systemized process by using a different computer-logic program developed by the auditor. The package

can also be used to seek answers to difficult audit problems (involving many comparisons and computations) within statistically acceptable confidence limits.

Required:
a. Without regard to any specific computer audit software, explain to the internal auditor the general advantages of using computer audit software to assist with audits.
b. Describe the audit purpose facilitated and the procedural steps to be followed by the internal auditor to use a(n)
   i. generalized audit software package.
   ii. integrated test facility package.
   iii. control flowcharting package.
   iv. program (parallel) simulation and modeling package.

12. Exposure Identification and Plan of Action
    Two years ago an external auditing firm supervised the programming of embedded audit modules for Previts Office Equipment Company. During the audit process this year, the external auditors requested that a transaction log of all transactions be copied to the audit file. The external auditors noticed large gaps in dates and times for transactions being copied to the audit file. When they inquired about this, they were informed that increased processing of transactions had been burdening the mainframe system and that operators frequently had to turn off the EAM to allow the processing of important transactions in a timely fashion. In addition, much maintenance had been performed during the past year on the application programs.

Required:
Outline any potential exposures and determine the courses of action the external auditors should use to proceed.

13. ACL Exercise—Input File Definition
    Following the instructions in the Readme.txt file on the CD that accompanies this text, load ACL onto your computer and download the instruction manual. Read pages 1 through 20 and complete the exercises.

14. ACL Exercise—General
    Complete the exercises on pages 21 through 34 in the ACL instruction manual.

chapter 8

AUDITING THE REVENUE CYCLE

This chapter examines audit procedures associated with the revenue cycle. The chapter is divided into three main sections. It begins with a review of alternative technologies used in both legacy and modern systems. The focus is on the key operational tasks performed under each technological environment. The second section discusses the revenue cycle audit objectives, controls, and tests of controls that an auditor would perform to gather evidence needed to limit the scope, timing, and extent of substantive tests. The last section describes revenue cycle substantive tests in relation to audit objectives. Specific procedures based upon ACL software are illustrated.

LEARNING OBJECTIVES

After studying this chapter, you should:

- Understand the operational tasks associated with the revenue cycle under different levels of technology.
- Understand audit objectives related to the revenue cycle.
- Be familiar with revenue cycle control issues related to alternative technologies.
- Recognize the relationship between revenue cycle audit objectives, controls, and tests of controls.
- Understand the nature of substantive tests in achieving revenue cycle audit objectives.
- Be familiar with common features and functions of ACL that are used to perform substantive tests.

OVERVIEW OF REVENUE CYCLE TECHNOLOGIES

This section examines alternative information technologies used in the revenue cycle. The first of these is a sales order system that employs batch processing and uses sequential files for storing accounting records. This is an example of an early legacy system. This approach characterizes the era of data ownership in which files were designed exclusively for the use of a single user. Data sharing is difficult if not impossible in this setting and results in a great deal of data redundancy and data obsolescence. Although archaic, such systems are still used because they continue to add value for organizations. For years, the anticipation has been that legacy systems would be replaced before the end of the century. That goal is no longer realizable. Instead, many organizations have opted to commit significant resources to repair and modify these systems for the next millennium. Once the investments are made, the pressure to replace legacy systems will be reduced. Odds favor the likelihood that auditors will be dealing with these technologies for some time to come.

Secondly, we review the operational features of a cash receipts system that employs batch processing and uses direct access files. This configuration is found in both modern systems and late-era legacy systems. The direct access file approach offers operational advantages over sequential file processing and permits limited data sharing.

The final example depicts a modern real-time sales order entry and cash receipts system that uses database technology. Modern systems design embraces **reengineering** to radically reshape business processes and workflow. The objective of reengineering is to reduce business-processing costs by identifying and eliminating non-value-added tasks. This involves replacing traditional procedures with procedures that are innovative and sometimes very different from those that previously existed.

You should recognize that the space limitations prohibit a review of all possible configurations of processing technologies, techniques, and file structures. The objective, instead, is to present examples of fundamentally different approaches that are typically found in practice and examine their control and audit implications.

BATCH PROCESSING USING SEQUENTIAL FILES

Figure 8–1 illustrates an automated sales order system that uses batch processing and sequential files. In this basic system, order taking, credit checking, warehousing, and shipping are performed manually. Computer programs process the accounting records. The following discussion outlines the key features of the system.

MANUAL PROCEDURES

OBTAINING AND RECORDING THE CUSTOMERS' ORDERS.   The sales process begins in the sales department with the receipt of a **customer order** indicating the type and quantity of merchandise being requested. At this point, the customer order is not in a standard format and may not be a physical document. Orders may arrive by mail, by telephone, or from a field representative who visited the customer's place of business. When the customer is also a business entity, the order is usually a copy of the customer's purchase order.

The primary objective of this step is to ensure that relevant data about the transaction are transcribed into a standard format that can be processed by the selling entity's system. The document prepared in this procedure is the **sales order**, an example of which is presented in Figure 8–2.

The sales order captures such vital information as the name and address of the customer; the customer's account number; the name, number, and description of the items sold; the quantities and unit prices of each item sold; and other financial information such as taxes, discounts, and freight charges. In manual systems, multiple copies of sales orders are produced to serve different purposes. The number of copies created will vary from system to system, depending on the operations to be supported. The hypothetical system in Figure 8–2 uses sales order copies for credit authorizations, packing slips, stock release documents, and shipping notices. Customer invoicing and ledger posting are performed by the computer system. In an actual system, the various sales order copies would be numbered or color-coded to signify their purpose and

FIGURE 8-1   Batch Processing with Sequential Files

FIGURE 8–2

Sales Order

CHARGE SALE INVOICE

MONTEREY PENINSULA CO-OP
527 River Road
Chicago, IL 60612
(312) 555-0407

INVOICE NUMBER _____

SOLD TO
FIRM NAME _____
ATTENTION OF _____
ADDRESS _____
CITY _____
STATE _____ ZIP _____

INVOICE DATE _____
PREPARED BY _____
CREDIT TERMS_____

CUSTOMER PURCHASE ORDER
NUMBER_____
DATE_____
SIGNED BY_____

SHIPMENT DATE _____
SHIPPED VIA _____
B.O.L. NO._____

QUANTITY ORDERED	PRODUCT NUMBER	DESCRIPTION	QUANTITY SHIPPED	UNIT PRICE	TOTAL
			TOTAL SALE		
			CUSTOMER ACCT. NO.		
			VERIFICATION		

distribution. Copies that are used for more than one purpose, and that go to several locations, sometimes have routing information printed on them.

After preparing the sales order, the sales clerk files one copy of it in the **customer open order file** for future reference. Filling the order and getting the product to the customer may take days or even weeks. Customers frequently contact their suppliers by telephone to check the status of their orders. To facilitate customer inquiries, the open order file is often organized alphabetically by customer name. Although customer name is not an efficient primary key for accessing data, it is often used as a secondary key to cross-reference orders since customers do not always know their account numbers and may not have copies of their invoices handy. In these situations, the customer file enables the clerk to find the sales order and respond to the customer's questions.

APPROVING CREDIT.   The next step in the revenue cycle is transaction authorization, which involves verifying the customer's creditworthiness. The circumstances of the sale will determine the nature of the credit check. For example, a seller may perform a full financial investigation on new customers to establish a line of credit. However, once a credit limit is set, credit checking on subsequent sales may involve nothing more than ensuring that the current sale does not exceed the limit. In our hypothetical system, the **credit authorization** copy of the sales order is sent to the credit department for approval. The returned approval triggers the release of the other sales order copies simultaneously to various departments. The credit copy is filed in the customer open order file until the transaction is completed.

PROCESSING SHIPPING ORDERS.   The sales department sends the **stock release** (also called the *picking ticket*) copy of the sales order to the warehouse. This document identifies the items of inventory that must be located and picked from the warehouse shelves. It also provides formal authorization for the warehouse clerk to release custody of the specified assets. After picking the stock, the clerk initials the stock release copy to indicate that the order is complete and accurate. Any out-of-stock items are noted on the stock release copy. One copy of the stock release travels with the goods to the shipping department, and the other is filed in the warehouse to provide a record of the transaction.

The clerk then adjusts the stock records to reflect the reduction in inventory. The stock records are *not* the formal accounting records for these assets. Assigning the warehouse clerk asset custody and record-keeping responsibility would violate internal control. Updating the inventory accounting records is an automated procedure that is described later.

Before the arrival of the goods and the stock release copy, the shipping department receives the **packing slip** and **shipping notice** copies from the sales department. The packing slip travels with the goods to the customer to describe the contents of the order. These are either placed inside the shipping container or attached to the outside in a special plastic pouch. The shipping notice informs the billing department that the customer's order has been filled and shipped. This document contains such pertinent facts as the date of shipment, items and quantities shipped, the carrier, and freight charges. In some systems, the shipping notice is a separate document prepared by the shipping clerk.

Upon receiving the goods from the warehouse, the shipping clerk reconciles the physical items with the stock release documents, the packing slip, and the shipping notice to verify the correctness of the order. This is an important control because it is the last opportunity to detect errors before shipment. The shipping clerk packages the goods, attaches the packing slip to the container, completes the shipping notice, and prepares a **bill of lading**. The bill of lading is a formal contract between the seller and the shipping company (carrier) to transport the goods to the customer. This document establishes legal ownership and responsibility for assets in transit. Figure 8–3 shows a bill of lading.

The shipping clerk transfers custody of the goods, the packing slip, and two copies of the bill of lading to the carrier, then performs the following tasks:

1. Records the shipment in the shipping log.

FIGURE 8–3

Bill of Lading

UNIFORM STRAIGHT BILL OF LADING — Domestic

Monterey Peninsula Co-op
527 River Road
Chicago, IL 60612
(312) 555-0407

Document No. _____

Shipper No. _____

Carrier No. _____

Date _____

TO:

Consignee _____

Street _____

City/State _____ Zip Code _____

_____
(Name of Carrier)

Route:		Vehicle		
No. Shipping Units	Kind of packaging, description of articles, special marks and exceptions	Weight	Rate	Charges

TOTAL CHARGES $

The agreed or declared value of the property is hereby specifically stated by the shipper to be not exceeding:	IF WITHOUT RECOURSE: The carrier shall not make delivery of this shipment without payment of freight
$ _____ per_____	_____ (Signature of Consignor)
FREIGHT CHARGES Check appropriate box: [ ] Freight prepaid [ ] Collect [ ] Bill to shipper	Signature below signifies that the goods described above are in apparent good order, except as noted. Shipper hereby certifies that he is familiar with all the bill of lading terms and agrees with them.
SHIPPER Monterey Peninsula Co-op	CARRIER
PER	PER DATE

(This bill of lading is to be signed
by the shipper and agent of the
carrier issuing same.)
CONSIGNEE

2. Sends the stock release document and the shipping notice to the billing department as proof of shipment.
3. Files one copy each of the bill of lading and the shipping document.

AUTOMATED PROCEDURES

The computer system described below is an example of a *legacy* system that employs the sequential file structure for its accounting records. Both tapes and disks can be used as the physical storage medium for such systems. However, the use of tapes has declined considerably in recent years. For day-to-day operations, tapes are inefficient because they must be physically mounted on a tape drive and then dismounted when the job ends. This approach is labor intensive and expensive. The constant decline in the cost of disk storage in recent years has eliminated the economic advantage once associated with tapes. Most organizations that still use sequential files store them on disks that are permanently connected (on-line) to the computer system and require no human intervention. The operational features of sequential files described earlier are the same for both tape and disk media. Today, tapes are used primarily as backup devices and for storing archive data. For these purposes, they provide an efficient and effective storage medium for a large system.

KEYSTROKE.   The process begins with the arrival of batches of shipping notices from the shipping department. These documents are copies of the sales orders that contain accurate information about the number of units shipped and information about the carrier. The keystroke clerk converts the shipping notices to magnetic media to produce a transaction file of sales orders. Typically, this is a continuous process. Throughout the day, the keystroke clerks receive and convert batches of shipping notices to magnetic media. The resulting transaction file will thus contain many separate batches of sales orders. **Batch control totals** are calculated for each batch on the file.

EDIT RUN.   Periodically, the batch sales order system is executed. Depending upon the volume of transaction and computer resource constraints, the process make take place only once or several times each day. The edit program is the first run in the batch process. This program validates transactions by testing each record for the existence of clerical or logical errors. Typical tests include field checks, limit tests, range tests, and price times quantity extensions. Recall from Chapter 6 that detected errors are removed from the batch and copied to a separate error file. Later, these are corrected by an authorized person and resubmitted for processing with the next day's business. The edit program recalculates the batch control totals to reflect changes due to the removal of error records. The "clean" transaction file is then passed to the next run in the process.

SORT RUN.   At this point, the sales order file is in no useful sequence. To process a sequential transaction file, it must be placed in the same sequence as the master file that it is updating. Since the first master file to be updated in the systems is accounts receivable, the sort run physically arranges the sales order transaction file sequentially by Account Number, which is one of its secondary keys.

AR UPDATE AND BILLING RUN.   The AR update program posts to accounts receivable by sequentially matching the Account Number key in each sales order record with the corresponding record in the AR-SUB master file. This procedure creates a new AR-SUB master file that incorporates all the changes to the customer accounts that are affected by transaction records. The original AR-SUB master file remains complete and unchanged by the process. The creation of a new and separate master file is a characteristic of sequential file processing. A side benefit of this is the automatic creation of a backup version of the file being updated. Figure 8–4 illustrates this method with some sample records.

Each sales transaction record processed is added to the sales journal file. At the end of the run, these are summarized and an entry is made to the journal voucher file to reflect total sales and total increases to accounts receivable.

To spread the billing task evenly over the month, some firms employ **cycle billing** of their customers. The update program searches the billing date field in the AR-SUB master file for those customers to be billed on that day of the month and prepares statements for the selected accounts. The statements are then mailed to the customer.

SORT AND INVENTORY UPDATE RUNS.   The procedures for the second sort and inventory update runs are similar to those just described. The sort program sorts the sales order file on the other secondary key—Inventory Number. The inventory update program reduces the Quantity On Hand field in the affected inventory records by the Quantity Sold field in each sales order record. A new inventory master file is created in the process. Figure 8–5 illustrates the process.

In addition, the program compares values of the Quantity On Hand and the Reorder Point fields to identify inventory items that need to be replenished. This information is sent to the purchasing department. Finally, a journal voucher is prepared to reflect cost of goods sold and the reduction in inventory.

GENERAL LEDGER UPDATE RUN.   Under the sequential file approach, the general ledger master file is not updated after each batch of transactions. To do so would result in the recreation of the entire general ledger every time a batch of transactions (such as sales orders, cash receipts, purchases, and cash disbursements) is processed. Firms using sequential files typically employ separate end-of-day procedures to update the general ledger accounts. This is the technique depicted in Figure 8–1.

At the end of the day, the general ledger system accesses the journal voucher file. This file contains journal vouchers reflecting all of the day's transactions processed by the organization. The journal vouchers are sorted by general ledger account number and posted to general ledger in a single run, and a new general ledger is created.

The end-of-day procedures will also generate a number of management reports. These may include sales summaries, inventory status reports, transaction listings, journal voucher listings, and budget and performance reports. Quality management reports play a key role in helping management monitor operations to ensure that controls are in place and functioning properly.

BATCH CASH RECEIPTS SYSTEM WITH DIRECT ACCESS FILES

Cash receipts procedures are natural batch systems. Unlike sales transactions, which tend to occur continuously throughout the day, cash receipts are discrete events. Checks and remittance advices arrive from the postal service in batches. Likewise, the deposit of cash receipts in the bank usually happens as a single event at the end of the business day. Because of these characteristics, many firms see no significant benefit from investing in costly real-time cash procedures.

The cash receipts system in Figure 8–6 on page 300 uses direct access files and batch processing. The technology employed in this example is used to automate traditional procedures. The following discussion outlines the main points of this system.

FIGURE 8–4 Update of Accounts Receivable from Sales Orders

Sales Order Transaction File

PK   SK

Order #	Acct Num	Inven Num	Order Date	Ship Date	Carrier Code	Shipping Charges	Qnty Sold	Unit Price	Invoice Amount
3	1	17	12/22	12/24	011	10	25	10	250
1	4	14	12/22	12/24	011	5	10	2	20
2	7	16	12/22	12/24	011	20	100	5	500

Transaction File sorted by secondary key to primary key of master file.

Original Account Receivable Master File

Update Fields

PK

ACCT NUM	Address	Current Balance	Credit Limit	Last Payment Date	Billing Date
1	123 Elm St., City	350	1000	12/8/98	1
2	35 Main S.	600	1500	12/12/98	1
3	510 Barclay Dr. Beth.	1000	1500	12/5/98	1
4	26 Taylo Rd. Alltn.	100	2000	12/16/98	8
5	4 High St., Naz.	800	1000	12/9/98	1
6	850 1st, Beth.	700	2000	12/7/98	8
7	78 Market Alltn.	150	2000	12/17/98	15

New Account Receivable Master File

ACCT NUM	Address	Current Balance	Credit Limit	Last Payment Date	Billing Date
1	123 Elm St., City	600	1000	12/8/98	1
2	35 Main S.	600	1500	12/12/98	1
3	510 Barclay Dr. Beth.	1000	1500	12/5/98	1
4	26 Taylo Rd. Alltn.	120	2000	12/16/98	8
5	4 High St., Naz.	800	1000	12/9/98	1
6	850 1st, Beth.	700	2000	12/7/98	8
7	78 Market Alltn.	650	2000	12/17/98	15

FIGURE 8-5   Update of Inventory from Sales Order

Sales Order Transaction File

Update Fields

PK							Update Fields		
Order #	Acct Num	Inven Num	Order Date	Ship Date	Carrier Code	Shipping Charges	Qnty Sold	Unit Price	Invoice Amount
1	4	14	12/22	12/24	011	5	10	2	20
2	7	16	12/22	12/24	011	20	100	5	500
3	1	17	12/22	12/24	011	10	25	10	250

SK = Inven Num

Transaction File Sorted by Secondary Key to Primary Key of Master File

Original Inventory Master File

PK									
Inven Num	Description	Qnty On Hand	Reorder Point	Qnty On Order	EOQ	Vendor Number	Standard Cost	Total Inven Cost
11		300	100	0	500	25	1	300
12		100	20	0	200	25	2	200
13		200	150	0	500	18	3	600
14		800	100	0	1000	25	2	1600
15		250	300	800	800	18	3	750
16		700	60	0	500	18	4	2800
17		850	200	0	1000	25	1	850

New Inventory Master File

PK									
Inven Num	Description	Qnty On Hand	Reorder Point	Qnty On Order	EOQ	Vendor Number	Standard Cost	Total Inven Cost
11		300	100	0	500	25	1	300
12		100	20	0	200	25	2	200
13		200	150	0	500	18	3	600
14		790	100	0	1000	25	2	1580
15		250	300	800	800	18	3	750
16		600	50	0	500	18	4	2400
17		825	200	0	1000	25	1	825

FIGURE 8-6 Computer-Based Cash Receipts System

UPDATE PROCEDURES

MAIL ROOM.   The mail room separates the checks and remittance advices and prepares a remittance list. These checks and a copy of the remittance list are sent to the cash receipts department. The remittance advices and a copy of the remittance list go to the accounts receivable department.

CASH RECEIPTS DEPARTMENT.   The cash receipts clerk reconciles the checks and the remittance list and prepares the deposit slips. Via terminal, the clerk creates a journal voucher record of total cash received. The clerk files the remittance list and one copy of the deposit slip. At the end of the day, the clerk deposits the cash in the bank.

ACCOUNTS RECEIVABLE DEPARTMENT.   The accounts receivable clerk receives and reconciles the remittance advices and remittance list. Via terminal, the clerk creates the cash receipts transaction file based on the individual remittance advices. The clerk then files the remittance advices and the remittance list.

DATA PROCESSING DEPARTMENT.   At the end of the day, the batch program reconciles the journal voucher with the transaction file of cash receipts, and updates the AR-SUB and the general ledger control accounts (AR-Control and Cash). This process employs the direct access method described earlier. Finally, the system produces a transaction listing that the accounts receivable clerk will reconcile against the remittance list.

REAL-TIME SALES ORDER ENTRY AND CASH RECEIPTS

Figure 8–7 illustrates a reengineered sales order system. Interactive computer terminals now replace many of the manual procedures and physical documents. This system provides real-time input and output with batch updating of only some of the master files.

ORDER ENTRY PROCEDURES

SALES PROCEDURES.   Under real-time processing, sales clerks receiving orders from customers process each transaction separately as it is received. Using a computer terminal connected to an edit/inquiry program, the clerk performs the following tasks in real-time mode:

1. A credit check is performed on-line by accessing the customer credit file. This file contains information such as the customer's credit limit, current balance, date of last payment, and current credit status. Based upon programmed criteria, the customer's request for credit is approved or denied.
2. If credit is approved, the clerk then accesses the inventory master file and checks the availability of the inventory. The system reduces inventory by the quantities of items sold to present an accurate and current picture of inventory on hand and available for sale.
3. The system automatically transmits an electronic stock release record to the warehouse and a shipping notice to the shipping department, and records the sale in the open sales order file. This is a temporary holding for sales orders until they are shipped and can then be billed.

WAREHOUSE PROCEDURES.   The warehouse clerk's terminal immediately produces a hard copy printout of the electronically transmitted stock release document. The clerk

FIGURE 8-7   Real-Time Sales Order Entry and Cash Receipts

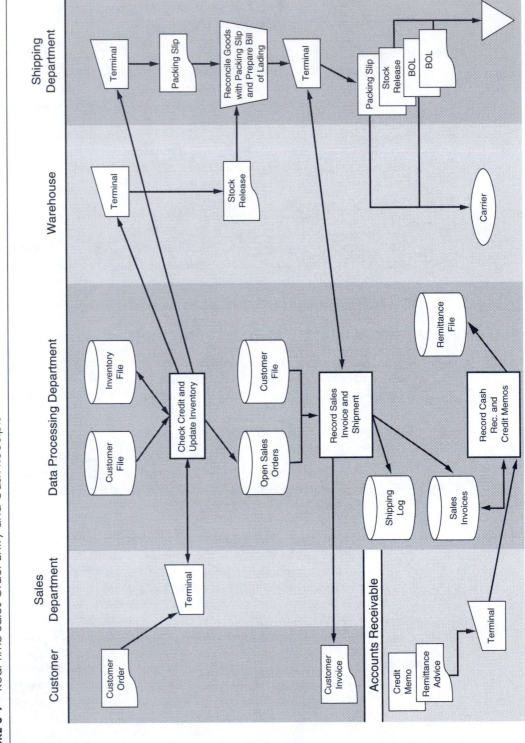

then picks the goods and sends them, along with a copy of the stock release document, to the shipping department.

SHIPPING AND BILLING.   The shipping clerk reconciles the goods, the stock release document, and the hard copy packing slip produced on the terminal. The clerk then selects a carrier and prepares the goods for shipment. From a terminal, the clerk transmits a shipping notice containing invoice, date, and carrier information to create a shipping log record of the event. The transaction record is removed from the open sales order file and added to the sales invoice file. Finally, drawing from data in the customer file, the system automatically prepares the customer's bill.

CASH RECEIPTS PROCEDURES

In open invoice systems, such as this, each invoice is billed and paid individually Cash from customers may be received and processed as just described or may be sent directly to a bank lock-box. In either case, the remittance advices (and credit memos to reflect returns and allowances) are sent to the accounts receivable function, where the clerk enters them into the system via a terminal. Each remittance record is assigned a unique remittance number and added to the remittance file. Placing the remittance number and the current date in the respective fields then closes the corresponding open invoice record.

FEATURES OF REAL-TIME PROCESSING

The system described above is a departure from traditional accounting. A central feature of the system is the use of an **events database**. Traditional accounting records may not exist per se. For instance, in this example the sales invoice file replaces the sales journal and AR-SUB ledger. Total sales is the sum of *all* invoices for the period. Summing the *open* sales invoices (those not closed by cash receipts or credit memos) provides accounts receivable information. In theory, such a system does not even need a general ledger since sales, sales returns, accounts receivable-control, and cost of goods sold can all be derived from the invoices in the events database. Most organizations, however, prefer to maintain a separate general ledger file for efficiency and as a cross check of processing accuracy.

Reengineered sales order processes can significantly reduce operating costs and improve efficiency. The following advantages make this approach an attractive option for many organizations:

1. Real-time processing greatly shortens the cash cycle of the firm. Lags inherent in traditional systems can cause delays of several days between taking an order and billing the customer. A real-time system with remote terminals reduces or eliminates these lags. An order received in the morning may be shipped by early afternoon, thus permitting same-day billing of the customer.

2. Real-time processing can give a firm a competitive advantage in the marketplace. By maintaining current inventory information, sales staff can determine immediately whether inventories are available. In contrast, batch systems do not provide salespeople with current information. As a result, a portion of the order must sometimes be back-ordered, causing customer dissatisfaction. Current information provided through real-time processing enhances the firm's ability to maximize customer service, which translates to increased sales.

3. Manual procedures tend to produce clerical errors, such as incorrect account numbers, invalid inventory numbers, and price-quantity extension miscalculations. These errors may go undetected in batch systems until the source documents reach data processing, by which time the damage may already be done. For example, the firm may find that it has shipped goods to the wrong address, shipped the wrong goods, or promised goods to a customer at the wrong price. Real-time editing permits the identification of many kinds of errors when they occur and greatly improves the efficiency and the effectiveness of operations.

4. Finally, real-time processing reduces the amount of paper documents in a system. Hard copy documents are expensive to produce and clutter the system. The permanent storage of these documents can become a financial and operational burden. Documents in electronic format are efficient, effective, and adequate for most audit trail purposes.

REVENUE CYCLE AUDIT OBJECTIVES, CONTROLS, AND TESTS OF CONTROLS

Chapter 1 introduced the concept of audit objectives for transactions and account balances that are derived from management assertions about financial statement presentation. The assertions are existence or occurrence, completeness, accuracy, rights and obligations, valuation or allocation and presentation and disclosure. Table 8–1 shows how these translate to specific revenue cycle audit objectives.[1]

Achieving these audit objectives requires designing audit procedures to gather evidence that either corroborates or refutes the management assertions. Generally, this involves a combination of tests of controls and substantive tests of details. The specific controls we address here are based on the more extensive discussion of application controls issues contained in Chapter 6. The discussion in this section presumes that the reader is familiar with that material. Recall that computer application controls fall into three broad categories: input controls, process controls, and output controls. Within this framework, we examine application controls, tests of controls, and the audit objectives to which they relate. Substantive tests and their relationship to audit objectives are considered later in the chapter.

INPUT CONTROLS

Input controls are designed to ensure that transactions are valid, accurate, and complete. Control techniques vary considerably between batch and real-time systems. The following input controls relate to revenue cycle operations.

CREDIT AUTHORIZATION PROCEDURES

The purpose of the credit check is to establish the creditworthiness of the customer. Only customer transactions that meet the organization's credit standards are valid and should be processed further. In batch systems with manual credit authorization procedures, the credit department (or credit manager) is responsible for implementing the

---

1.   Adapted from *Montgomery's Auditing*, 12th ed. (New York: Cooper's & Lybrand, L.L.P., 1998) p. 18-4.

TABLE 8–1

Relationship
between
Management
Assertions and
Revenue Cycle
Audit Objectives

Management Assertions	Revenue Cycle Audit Objectives
Existence or Occurrence	Verify that the accounts receivable balance represents amounts actually owed to the organization at the balance sheet date.
	Establish that revenue from sales transactions represent goods shipped and services rendered during the period covered by the financial statements.
Completeness	Determine that all amounts owed to the organization at the balance sheet date are reflected in accounts receivable.
	Verify that all sales for shipped goods, all services rendered, and all returns and allowances for the period are reflected in the financial statements.
Accuracy	Verify that revenue transactions are accurately computed and based on current prices and correct quantities.
	Ensure that the accounts receivable subsidiary ledger, the sales invoice file, and the remittance file are mathematically correct and agree with general ledger accounts.
Rights and Obligations	Determine that the organization has a legal right to recorded accounts receivable. Customer accounts that have been sold or factored have been removed from the accounts receivable balance.
Valuation or Allocation	Determine that accounts receivable balance states its net realizable value.
	Establish that the allocation for uncollectible accounts is appropriate.
Presentation and Disclosure	Verify accounts receivable and revenues reported for the period are properly described and classified in the financial statements.

firm's credit policies. When credit checks are computerized, the organization's credit policy is implemented through decision rules that have been programmed into the system. For routine transactions, this typically involves determining if the current transaction plus the customer's current account receivable balance exceeds a preestablished credit limit. If the credit limit is exceeded by the transaction, it should be rejected by the program and passed to an exception file, where it can be reviewed by management. The credit manager will decide either to disapprove the sale or to extend the credit limit consistent with the manager's authority.

TESTING CREDIT PROCEDURES.   Failure to apply credit policy correctly and consistently has implications for the adequacy of the organization's allowance for uncollectible accounts. The tests described below provide evidence pertaining to the *valuation/allocation* audit objectives and, to a lesser extent, the *accuracy* objective.

The auditor needs, therefore, to determine that effective procedures exist to establish appropriate customer credit limits; communicate this information adequately to the credit policy decision-makers; review credit policy periodically and revise it as necessary; and monitor adherence to current credit policy.

The auditor can verify the correctness of programmed decision rules by using either the *test data* or *integrated test facility (ITF)* approaches to directly test their functionality. This is easily accomplished by creating several "dummy" customer accounts with various lines of credit and then processing test transactions that will exceed some of the credit limits. The auditor can then analyze the rejected transactions to determine if the computer application correctly applied the credit policy.

The integrity of reference data is an important element in testing credit policy controls. A correctly functioning computer application cannot successfully apply credit policy if customer credit limits are excessively high or can be changed by unauthorized personnel. The auditor needs to verify that authority for making line-of-credit changes is limited to authorized credit department personnel. Performing substantive tests of detail to identify customers with excessive credit limits can do this. Substantive tests traditionally follow tests of controls because the results of tests of controls are used to determine the nature, timing, and extent of the substantive tests. In this case, however, substantive tests may be the most efficient way to verify if credit policy is being properly applied.

DATA VALIDATION CONTROLS

Input validation controls are intended to detect transcription errors in transaction data before they are processed. Since errors detected early are less likely to infiltrate the accounting records, validation procedures are most effective when they are performed as close to the source of the transaction as possible. In the batch system depicted in Figure 8–1, data validation occurs only after the goods have been shipped. Extensive error logs, error correction, and transaction resubmission procedures characterize such systems. On the other hand, validity tests performed in real-time, as shown in Figure 8–7, can deal with most errors as they occur. This approach also minimizes human data entry and thus reduces the risk of data entry errors. For example, when the clerk enters the customer's account number, the system automatically retrieves his or her name and mailing address. When the clerk enters the product number and quantity sold, the data entry system automatically retrieves the product description and price, and then calculates the extended price plus tax and shipping charges.

Chapter 6 presented a number of general types of validation tests. Examples that are relevant to the revenue cycle are reviewed below.

Missing data checks are used to examine the contents of a field for the presence of blank spaces. Missing product numbers, missing customer account numbers, or incomplete mailing or billing addresses will cause the transaction to be rejected. When the validation program detects a blank where it expects to see a data value, this will be interpreted as an error.

Numeric-alphabetic data checks determine whether the correct form of data is in a field. For example, an invoice total should not contain alphabetic data. As with blanks, alphabetic data in a numeric field may cause serious processing errors.

Limit checks determine if the value in the field exceeds an authorized limit. For example, an organization may allow its sales personnel to negotiate prices with customers up to a maximum discount percentage. The order entry validation program can interrogate the discount field in the sales order records for values that exceed the threshold.

Range checks assign upper and lower limits to acceptable data values. For example, the actual sales price charged for a product can be compared to a range of acceptable prices. The purpose of this control is to detect keystroke errors that shift the decimal point one or more places.

Validity checks compare actual values in a field against known acceptable values. This control is used to verify such things as product codes, shipping company codes, and state abbreviations in customer addresses. If the value in the field does not match one of the acceptable values, the record is determined to be in error.

Check digit controls identify keystroke errors in key fields by testing their internal validity. This is often used to control data entry errors that would otherwise cause the wrong customer's account to be charged for a transaction.

TESTING VALIDATION CONTROLS.   Data entry errors that slip through edit programs undetected can cause recorded accounts receivable and revenue amounts to be materially misstated. The audit procedures described below provide evidence about the *accuracy* assertion.

The central audit issue is whether the validation programs in the data editing system are functioning correctly and have continued to function as intended throughout the period. Testing the logic of a validation program, however, represents a significant undertaking. The auditor may decide to rely on the quality of other controls to provide the assurance needed to reduce substantive testing. For example, after reviewing systems development and maintenance controls, the auditor may determine that controls over original program design and testing and subsequent changes to programs are effective. This evidence permits the auditor to assess the risk of material program errors at a low level and thus reduce the substantive tests related to the audit objective of accuracy.

If controls over systems development and maintenance are weak, however, the auditor may decide that testing the data editing controls would be more efficient than performing extensive substantive tests of details. In such a case, ITF or the test data approach would enable the auditor to perform explicit tests of the logic. This would require the auditor to gain a familiarity with all of the validation procedures in place. The auditor would need to create a comprehensive set of test transactions that include both valid and erroneous data values that fall within and outside of the test parameters. An analysis of the test results will show the auditor which types of errors, if any, can pass undetected by the validation program. This evidence will help the auditor determine the nature, timing, and extent of subsequent substantive tests.

In addition to direct testing of program logic, the auditor can achieve some degree of assurance by reviewing error listings and error logs. These documents provide evidence of the effectiveness of the data entry process, the types and volume of errors encountered, and the manner in which the errors are corrected and reentered into the system. Error listings and logs do not, however, provide evidence of undetected errors. An analysis of error conditions not present in the listing can be used to guide the auditor in designing substantive tests to perform. For example, assume that the error listing of the sales invoice file contains no price limit errors. This may simply mean that sales personnel strictly adhere to pricing guidelines. On the other hand, it may mean that the validation program does not test for this type of error. To determine whether material price discrepancies exist in the sales invoice file, the auditor can perform substantive tests that compare the actual price charged with the suggested retail price.

BATCH CONTROLS

Batch controls are used to manage high volumes of transaction data through a system. The objective of batch control is to reconcile output produced by the system with the input originally entered into the system. While initiated at the data input stage, batch control continues through all phases of data processing. For example, in the revenue cycle sales invoices are gathered together and enter the system at data entry. After each subsequent processing stage in the system, the batch is reviewed for completeness. An important element of batch control is the batch transmittal sheet, which captures relevant information about the batch, such as:

- A unique batch number.
- A batch date.
- A transaction code (indicating the type of transactions, such as a sales order or cash receipt).

- The number of records in the batch (record count).
- The total dollar value of a financial field (batch control total).
- The total of a unique nonfinancial field (hash total).

The information contained in the transmittal sheet is entered as a separate control record that the system uses to verify the integrity of the batch. The task of reconciling processing with the control record provides assurance that:

- All sales invoices and cash receipts records that were entered into the system were processed.
- No invoices or cash receipts were processed more than once.
- All invoices and cash receipts entered into the system are accounted for as either successfully processed or rejected because of errors.

TESTING BATCH CONTROLS.   The failure of batch controls to function properly can result in records being lost or processed multiple times. Tests of batch controls provide the auditor with evidence relating to the management assertions of *completeness* and *accuracy*.

Testing batch controls involves reviewing transmittal records of batches processed throughout the period and reconciling them to the batch control log. The auditor needs to investigate out-of-balance conditions to determine the cause. For example, assume that a batch's transmittal record shows 100 sales invoices with a total dollar value of $182,674.87 were entered into the system, but the completed batch log shows that only 96 records were processed with a batch total of $172,834.60. What caused this? Is the problem due to lost or changed invoices? Did the data entry clerk incorrectly calculate the batch control totals? Were error records rejected in processing and removed from the batch? Were rejected records corrected and resubmitted for processing?

The auditor should be able to obtain answers to these questions by reviewing and reconciling transaction listings, error logs, and logs of resubmitted records. Gathering such evidence, however, could involve scanning literally thousands of transactions. In modern systems, batch control logs are stored on-line in text files that can be read by word processing and spreadsheet programs. Modern audit software such as ACL is capable of searching log files for out-of-balance conditions.

PROCESS CONTROLS

Process controls include computerized procedures for file updating and restricting access to data. Depending on the level of computer technology in place, process controls may also include physical manual tasks. We begin by examining three control techniques related to file updating. Access and physical controls are then examined.

FILE UPDATE CONTROLS

Run-to-run controls use batch control data discussed in the previous section to monitor the batch as it moves from one programmed procedure (run) to another. These controls ensure that each run in the system processes the batch correctly and completely. After each major operation in the process, key fields such as invoice amount and record counts are accumulated and compared to the corresponding values stored in the control record. A discrepancy may indicate that a record was lost in processing, a record in the batch went unprocessed, or a record was processed more than once.

TRANSACTION CODE CONTROLS.   Revenue cycle systems are often designed to process multiple record types. For example, the order entry application may process both sales orders and returns and allowances transactions. The actual tasks performed by the application are determined by a transaction code assigned to each record. Errors in transaction codes, or in the program logic that interprets them, can cause incorrect processing of transactions and may result in materially misstated sales and accounts receivable balances.

SEQUENCE CHECK CONTROL.   In systems that use sequential master files, the order of the transaction records in the batch is critical to correct and complete processing. As the batch moves through the process, it must be re-sorted in the order of the master file used in each run. An out-of-sequence sales order record in a batch may prevent the remaining downstream records from being processed. A more serious problem can occur when the sequencing error is not detected and the downstream records are processed against the wrong customer accounts. A sequence check control should be in place to compare the sequence of each record in the batch with the previous record to ensure that proper sorting took place. Out-of-sequence records should be rejected and resubmitted for subsequent processing to allow the other records in the batch to be properly processed.

TESTING FILE UPDATE CONTROLS.   The failure of file update controls to function properly can result in records going unprocessed, being processed incorrectly (i.e., returns are treated as sales), or being posted to the wrong customer's account. Tests of file update controls provide the auditor with evidence relating to the assertions of *existence*, *completeness*, and *accuracy*.

We examined the audit procedures for reviewing batch controls previously as part of the discussion of input controls. Testing run-to-run controls is a logical extension of these procedures and needs no further explanation. Tests of transaction codes and sequence checks can be performed using ITF or the tests-data approach. The auditor should create test data that contain records with incorrect transaction codes and records that are out of sequence in the batch and verify that each was handled correctly. Implicit in this test is verifying the mathematical correctness of the computer operation. For example, consider a sales order for 5 units of product valued at $100. Assume that before processing the transaction current value of the customer's account is $1,000 and the inventory in question shows 250 units on hand. After processing, this transaction should increase the customer balance to $1,100 and reduce the inventory to 245 units.

The efficient use of logic-testing CAATTs like ITF requires careful planning. By determining in advance the input and process controls to be tested, a single audit procedure can be devised that performs all tests in one operation. For example, a single test designed to examine credit authorization controls, transaction code controls, and the mathematical accuracy of the update program can provide evidence that supports multiple audit objectives.

ACCESS CONTROLS

Access controls prevent and detect unauthorized and illegal access to the firm's assets. Inventories and cash are the physical assets of the revenue cycle. Traditional techniques used to limit access to these assets include:

* Warehouse security, such as fences, alarms, and guards.
* Depositing cash daily in the bank.

- Using a safe or night deposit box for cash.
- Locking cash drawers and safes in the cash receipts department.

Controlling access to accounting records is no less important. An individual with unrestricted access to data can manipulate the physical assets of the firm and cause financial statements to be materially misstated. Accounting files stored on magnetic media are particularly vulnerable to unauthorized access whether its cause is accidental, an act of malice by a disgruntled employee, or an attempt at fraud. The following are examples of risks specific to the revenue cycle:

1. An individual with access to the AR subsidiary ledger could remove his or her account (or someone else's) from the books. With no record of the account, the firm would not send the customer monthly statements.
2. Access to blank sales orders may enable an unauthorized individual to trigger the shipment of a product.
3. An individual with access to both cash and accounting records could remove cash from the firm and cover the act by adjusting the cash account.
4. An individual with access to physical inventory and inventory records could steal products and adjust the records to cover the theft.

TESTING ACCESS CONTROLS.   Access control is at the heart of accounting information integrity. In the absence of controls, invoices can be deleted, added, or falsified. Individual account balances can be erased, or the entire account receivable file can be destroyed. Evidence gathered about the effectiveness of access controls tests the management assertions of *existence, completeness, accuracy, valuation and allocation, right and obligations*, and *presentation and disclosure*.

Computer access controls are both system-wide and application-specific. Access control over revenue cycle applications depends upon effectively controlling access to the operating systems, the networks, and the databases with which they interact. The control techniques discussed in previous chapters—including passwords, data encryption, firewalls, and user views—apply also in preventing unauthorized access to revenue cycle processes. The auditors will typically test these controls as part of their review of general controls.

PHYSICAL CONTROLS

SEGREGATION OF DUTIES.   Proper segregation of duties ensures that no single individual or department processes a transaction in its entirety. The number of employees in the organization and the volume of transactions being processed will influence how tasks are divided. In general, the following three rules apply:

Rule 1. Transaction authorization should be separate from transaction processing. For example, within the revenue cycle, the credit department is segregated from the rest of the process, so that the formal authorization of material transactions is an independent event. The importance of this separation is clear when one considers the potential conflict in objectives between the individual salesperson and the organization. Often, sales staff compensation is based on their sales levels. To achieve their personal objective of maximizing sales volume, sales personnel may not always consider the creditworthiness of the prospective customer. The credit department, acting as an independent authorization group, detects risky customers and discourages poor and irresponsible sales decisions.

Rule 2. Asset custody should be separate from the record-keeping task. In the sales order processing system, the inventory warehouse clerk with custody of the physical assets should not also maintain the inventory records. Similarly, the cash receipts clerk (with custody of cash) should not record accounts receivable.

Rule 3. The organization should be so structured that the perpetration of a fraud requires collusion between two or more individuals. The record-keeping functions must be carefully divided. Specifically, the subsidiary ledgers (AR and inventory), the journals (sales and cash receipts), and the general ledger should be separately maintained. An individual with total record-keeping responsibility, in collusion with someone with asset custody, is in a position to perpetrate fraud. By separating these tasks, collusion must involve more people, which increases the risk of detection and is, therefore, less likely to occur.

SUPERVISION.   Some firms have too few employees to achieve an adequate separation of functions and must rely on supervision as a compensating control. By closely supervising employees who perform potentially incompatible functions, a firm can compensate for the exposure inherent in a system.

Supervision can also provide control in systems that are properly segregated. For example, the mail room is a point of exposure for any firm. The individual who opens the mail has access both to cash (the asset) and to the remittance advice (the record of the transaction). A dishonest employee may use this opportunity to steal the check, cash it, and destroy the remittance advice, thus leaving no evidence of the transaction. Ultimately, this sort of fraud will come to light when the customer receives another bill and, in response, produces the canceled check. However, by the time the firm gets to the bottom of this problem, the perpetrator may have committed the crime many times over and left the organization. Detecting crimes after the fact accomplishes little. Prevention is the best solution. The deterrent effect of supervision can provide an effective preventive control.

INDEPENDENT VERIFICATION.   The purpose of independent verification is to review the work performed by others at key junctures in the process to identify and correct errors. Two examples in the revenue cycle are:

1. The shipping department verifies that the goods sent from the warehouse are correct in type and quantity. Before the goods are sent to the customer, the stock release document and the packing slip are reconciled to identify discrepancies.
2. The billing department reconciles the shipping notice with the sales invoice to ensure that customers are billed only for the items and quantities that were actually shipped.

TESTING PHYSICAL CONTROLS.   Inadequate segregation of duties and the lack of effective supervision and independent verification can result in fraud and material errors. The exposure issues here are similar to the access control issues discussed earlier. Inappropriate access privileges are often associated with incompatible duties. Similarly, the purpose of collusion is to achieve unauthorized access to assets as well as the information needed to conceal the crime. In the absence of supervision and independent verification activities, errors and fraud may go undetected. Evidence gathered from reviewing job descriptions and organizational charts, and by observing physical processes, could be used to test *all* of the management assertions presented in Table 8–1.

The auditor's review of organizational structure should disclose the more egregious examples of incompatible tasks, such as one individual opening the mail, depositing the check, and recording receipts in the customer accounts. Covert relationships that lead to collusion may not be apparent from an organizational chart. For example, married employees (or other relations) who work in incompatible areas go unnoticed. The auditor should verify that the organization has rules for appropriately dealing with nepotism issues.

Many tasks that are normally segregated in manual systems are consolidated in the data processing function of computer-based systems. Computer programs in the revenue cycle perform inventory control, accounts receivable, billing, and general ledger tasks. In this situation, the auditor's concern should focus on the integrity of the computer programs that perform these tasks. The following questions need answers: Is the logic of the computer program correct? Has anyone tampered with the application since it was last tested? Have changes been made to the program that could have caused an undisclosed error?

Answers to these questions come from the auditor's review of systems development and maintenance controls and by reviewing organizational structure. Recall from earlier chapters that duties pertaining to the design, maintenance, and operation of computer programs need to be separated. Programmers who write the original computer programs should not be responsible for making program changes. Also, individuals who operate the computer system should not be involved in systems design, programming, or maintenance activities. Personal relationships (i.e., marriage) between individuals in these incompatible areas may require further investigation.

OUTPUT CONTROLS

Output controls are designed to ensure that information is not lost, misdirected, or corrupted and that system processes function as intended. For example, managers receive daily summaries of sales orders placed by customers, goods shipped, and cash received, and use such data to monitor the status of their operations. Output control can be designed to identify potential problems. For example, an exception report derived from the customer open order file listing end-of-day open sales orders can identify orders placed but not shipped. Such a report can help management assess the operational performance of the shipping process.

Reconciling the general ledger is an output control that can detect certain types of transaction processing errors. For example, the total of all credit sales recorded by billing should equal the total increases posted to the accounts receivable subsidiary accounts. A sales transaction that is entered in the journal but not posted to the customer's account would be detected by an imbalance in the general ledger. The specific cause of an out-of-balance condition could not be determined at this point, but the error would be noted. Finding the error may require examining all the transactions processed during the period. This could be time-consuming. For this reason, rather than summarizing an entire day's transactions in a single batch, entities often group transactions into small batches of 50 to 100 items. This facilitates reconciling balances by isolating a problem to a specific batch.

Another important element of output control is the maintenance of an **audit trail**. To resolve transaction processing errors, each detected error needs to be traced to its source. It is not sufficient to know that 100 transactions entered the system and only 99 came out. Details of transaction processing produced at intermediate points can provide an audit trail that reflects activity through every stage of operations. The following are examples of audit trail output controls.

ACCOUNTS RECEIVABLE CHANGE REPORT

This is a summary report that shows the overall change to accounts receivable from sales orders and cash receipts. These numbers should reconcile with total sales, total cash receipts (on account), and the general ledger.

TRANSACTION LOGS

Every transaction successfully processed by the system should be recorded on a transaction log, which serves as a journal. A transaction log serves two purposes. First, the transaction log is a permanent record of valid transactions. The original transaction file produced at the data input phase is usually only a temporary file. Once processed, the records on this file are erased (scratched) to make room for the next batch of transactions. Second, not all of the records in the temporary transaction file will always be successfully processed. Some of these records may fail validity tests and will be rejected. A transaction log should contain only successful transactions. Rejected transactions should be placed in an error file. The transaction log and error files combined should account for all the transactions in the batch. The validated transaction file may then be scratched with no loss of data.

TRANSACTION LISTINGS

The system should produce a (hard copy) transaction listing of all successful transactions. These listings should go to the appropriate users to facilitate reconciliation with input. For example, a listing of cash receipts processed will go to the controller to be used for a bank reconciliation.

LOG OF AUTOMATIC TRANSACTIONS

Some transactions are triggered internally by the system. For example, EDI sales orders are accepted and processed without human authorization. To maintain an audit trail of these activities, all internally generated transactions must be placed in a transaction log, and a listing of these transactions should be sent to the appropriate manager.

UNIQUE TRANSACTION IDENTIFIERS

Each transaction processed by the system must be uniquely identified with a transaction number. This is the only practical means of tracing a particular transaction through a database of thousands or even millions of records. In systems that use physical source documents, the unique number printed on the document can be transcribed during data input and used for this purpose. In real-time systems, which do not use source documents, each transaction should be assigned a unique number by the system.

ERROR LISTING

A listing of all error records should go to the appropriate user to support error correction and resubmission.

TESTING OUTPUT CONTROLS

The absence of adequate output controls has adverse implications for operational efficiency and financial reporting. Evidence gathered through tests of output controls relates to the *completeness* and *accuracy* assertions.

Testing output controls involves reviewing summary reports for accuracy, completeness, timeliness, and relevance to the decisions that they are intended to support. In addition, the auditor should trace sample transactions through audit trail reports, including transaction listings, error logs, and logs of resubmitted records. Gathering such evidence, however, may involve sorting through thousands of transactions.

In modern systems, audit trails are usually stored on-line in text files. Data extraction software such as ACL can be used to search log files for specific records to verify the completeness and accuracy of output reports. Alternatively, the auditor can test output controls directly using ITF. A well-designed ITF system will permit the auditor to produce a batch of sample transactions, including some error records, and trace them through all phases of processing, error detection, and output reporting.

SUBSTANTIVE TESTS OF REVENUE CYCLE ACCOUNTS

This section deals with the substantive tests that an auditor may perform to achieve audit objectives related to the revenue cycle. The strategy used in determining the nature, timing, and extent of substantive tests derives from the auditor's assessment of inherent risk, unmitigated control risk, materiality considerations, and the need to conduct the audit in an efficient manner.

REVENUE CYCLE RISKS AND AUDIT CONCERNS

In general, the auditor's concerns in the revenue cycle pertain to the potential for overstatement of revenues and accounts receivable rather than their understatement. Overstatement of accounts can result from material errors in the processing of normal transactions that occur throughout the year. In addition, the auditor should focus attention on large and unusual transactions at or near period-end. Examples of specific issues that give rise to these concerns include:

- Recognizing revenues from sales transactions that did not occur.
- Recognizing sales revenues before they are realized (i.e., billing customers for items still being manufactured at period-end).
- Failing to recognize period-end cutoff points, thus allowing reported sales revenues for the current period to be inflated by post-period transactions.
- Underestimating the allowance for doubtful accounts, thus overstating the realizable value of accounts receivable.
- Shipping unsolicited products to customers in one period that are returned in a subsequent period.
- Billing sales to the customer that are held by the seller. Special terms associated with such transactions may require no payment for a lengthy period of time.

In resolving these concerns, the auditor will seek evidence by performing a combination of tests of internal controls and substantive tests. Tests of controls include testing both general controls (discussed in Chapters 2 through 6) and application controls specifically related to revenue cycle procedures. Various application control techniques were examined in Chapter 6. For example, the auditor may use an integrated test facility (ITF) to test the accuracy of sales transaction postings to the accounts receivable file. While positive results from such a test may enable the auditor to reduce the degree of substantive testing needed to gain assurance about the mathematical accuracy of account processing, they offer no assurance about the collectibility of those accounts receivable. Similarly, ITF can be used to test the credit-limit logic of the edit program to provide assurance that the organization's credit policy is being properly implemented. This test, however, provides no evidence that proper cutoff procedures were followed in calculating the total value of accounts receivable.

From these examples, we see that in addition to tests of controls, the auditor must perform substantive tests to achieve audit objectives. The remainder of this chapter deals with audit objectives related to the revenue cycle and the substantive tests most commonly performed. Keep in mind that the quality of internal controls bears on the nature and extent of substantive tests determined by the auditor to be necessary. Normally, not all of the tests described below will be performed.

UNDERSTANDING DATA

The tests described below involve accessing and extracting data from accounting files for analysis. To do this, the auditor needs to understand the systems and controls that produced the data, as well as the physical characteristics of the files that contain them. Much of this chapter has been devoted to explaining alternative revenue cycle configurations and their control implications. The previous chapter described several common file structures and their audit implications. The discussion that follows presumes that the auditor is using ACL for performing the audit tests. Before we proceed, however, we need to review a few salient points regarding file preparation.

First, the auditor must verify that he or she is working with the correct version of the file to be analyzed. To do so the auditor must understand the file backup procedures and, whenever possible, work with the original files. Secondly, ACL can read most sequential files and relational database tables directly, but esoteric and/or complex file structures may require "flattening" before they can be analyzed. This may involve additional procedures and special programs to produce a copy of the original file in a format that ACL can accept. If the client organization's systems personnel perform the flattening process, the auditor must verify that the correct version of the original file was used and that all relevant records from the original were transferred to the copy for analysis.

The discussion that follows presumes that any joining of tables or file copying necessary to produce test data was done so under adequate controls to preserve data integrity. These files may reside on either a mainframe or a PC. The audit tests described below are applicable to both environments. The focus is on explaining the logic underlying various substantive tests and on illustrating the functionality of ACL in achieving audit objectives. The audit procedures described are based on the file structure in Figure 8–8. These structures indicate the key data and logical linkages between files. A description of each file follows.

CUSTOMER FILE

The Customer master file contains address and credit information about customers. The Credit Limit value is used to validate sales transactions. If the sum of the customer's outstanding account balance and the amount of current sales transaction exceeds the preestablished credit limit, then the transaction is rejected.

SALES INVOICE FILE

This file, along with the Line Item File, captures sales transaction data for the period. The **Sales Invoice file** contains summary data for each invoice. When an order is

FIGURE 8-8   File Structures for the Revenue Cycle

shipped to a customer, a record is added to the file. Summing Invoice Amount for all records in the file yields total sales (sale journal) for the period. When cash receipts are received, they are matched to the open invoice record, which is then closed by placing the current date in the Closed Date field. Also, the Remittance Number, which is the primary key of the of the cash receipt record, is added to the invoice record as a cross-reference. The accounts receivable balance for a particular customer is calculated by summing the Invoice Amount fields for all of the customer's open invoices. Total accounts receivable for financial reporting purposes is the sum of all the open invoice records in the file.

LINE ITEM FILE

The Line Item file contains a record of every product sold. Since a single transaction can involve one or more products, each record in the Sales Invoice file is associated with (linked to) one or more records in this file. Notice that the file contains two primary keys—Invoice Number and Item Number. Both keys are needed to uniquely define each record in the file. They also provide links to related records in the Sales Invoice and Inventory files. While financial reporting of sales and accounts receivable information requires only the data contained in the Sales Invoice file, the Line Item file is needed for operational tasks such as billing, customer service, marketing, and auditing. For example, sales details in the file allow marketing to evaluate the demand for its products. These data also provide audit evidence needed to corroborate the accuracy of price times quantity calculations that are summarized in the **sales invoices**.

INVENTORY FILE

The Inventory file contains quantity, price, supplier, and warehouse location data for each item of inventory. When products are sold, the Quantity On Hand field in the associated records is reduced by the value of the Quantity field in the Line Item record. The Quantity On Hand field is increased by inventory receipts from suppliers. This activity is discussed in the next chapter.

SHIPPING LOG FILE

The shipping log is a record of all sales orders shipped to customers. The primary key of the file is the bill of lading (BOL) number. The data in this file are useful for verifying that all sales reflected in the Sales Invoice file were shipped in the period under review. As an efficiency tool, these data can also be used to determine if customer orders are being shipped in a timely manner.

FILE PREPARATION PROCEDURES

The data contained in the files shown in Figure 8–8 provide evidence that may either corroborate or refute audit objectives. Most of the tests described in the following section involve using ACL to access and extract data from these files. For a detailed explanation of ACL commands review the instruction manual contained on the CD that accompanies this text and consult ACL's on-line Help feature.

As a preliminary step in using ACL, each file needs to be defined in terms of its physical location and its structure. Through a series of easy-to-use pop-up menus, the auditor specifies the name of the file and where it resides on the mainframe or PC. ACL then prompts the auditor to define the file's structure in terms of the length of each field and the data type contained in each field (i.e., numeric, character, or date). When the file definition is completed, it is saved under a unique name assigned by the auditor. All future file access is accomplished by simply selecting the file definition from an ACL menu. ACL automatically locates the file and presents it on screen, where the auditor can review and manipulate its contents.

Sometimes the contents of a data field are different from what they are supposed to be. For example, a numeric field in one or more records may contain alphabetic data because of a program error or a clerical mistake. Also, a field may contain corrupted data because of an error in the file-flattening process. Whatever the cause, prior to performing any substantive tests on a new file, it is important to validate its contents. Invalid data will distort the test results and may cause a system failure. ACL's *verify* command analyzes the data fields in the selected file to ensure that their contents are consistent with the field type in the file definition. Any validity errors detected by ACL need to be traced to their source and resolved. For purposes of discussion, we will assume that the files used in all tests described hereafter have been properly defined and verified.

TESTING THE ACCURACY AND COMPLETENESS ASSERTIONS

The audit procedures described in this section provide evidence relating to management assertions of *accuracy* and *completeness*. Auditors often precede substantive tests of details with an **analytical review** of account balances. In the case of the revenue cycle, an analytical review will provide the auditor with an overall perspective for trends in sales, cash receipts, sales returns, and accounts receivable. Analytical procedures do not necessarily require computer technology. For example, the auditor may compare reported sales for the quarter with those for the same period in previous years. Ratio analysis may be used to compare total sales to cost of goods sold, sales to accounts receivable, and allowance for doubtful accounts to accounts receivable. Significant variations in account balances over time, or unusual ratios, may signify financial statement misrepresentations. On the other hand, analytical procedures can provide assurance that transactions and accounts are reasonably stated and complete and may thus permit the auditor to reduce substantive tests of details on these accounts.

A medium-to-large sized organization's sales and accounts receivable data may constitute thousands or perhaps millions of records. Substantive tests of details of such volumes of data cannot be effectively accomplished using manual techniques. The following examples of substantive tests that can be performed using ACL are based on the file structures depicted in Figure 8–8.

REVIEW SALES INVOICES FOR UNUSUAL TRENDS AND EXCEPTIONS

A useful audit procedure for identifying potential audit risks involves scanning data files for unusual transactions and account balances. For example, scanning accounts receivable for excessively large balances may indicate that the organization's credit policy is being improperly applied. Credit balances in accounts receivable may suggest unusual sales return activity or errors in the application of cash receipts to customer accounts.

The auditor can use ACL's *stratify* feature to identify such anomalies. This function groups data into predetermined intervals and counts the number of records that fall into each interval. Using data similar to the sample data illustrated on the next page for the Sales Invoice file, the stratify function will produce the report presented in Figure 8–9.

Invoice Number	Customer Number	Invoice Amount	Sales Date	Due Date	Closed Date	Remittance Number
214088	065003	13.08	12/04/01	12/14/01	12/11/01	611243
214114	065003	9.76	12/04/01	12/14/01		
214129	065003	116.72	12/04/01	12/14/01		
214121	165006	29.40	12/04/01	12/14/01	12/12/01	613457
214185	165009	9.17	12/04/01	12/14/01	12/23/01	614476
213309	376005	–931.55	12/04/01	12/14/01		
213355	376005	–374.71	12/04/01	12/14/01		

The report groups the Invoice Amount field into ten intervals based upon the upper and lower limits of the data in the field. Analysis of the results allows the auditor to identify unusual trends and exceptions. For example:

- The minimum invoice amount was $ –931.55 and the maximum was $5,549.19.
- Twenty-nine items constitute $17,355.17 of negative sales.
- Fifty-eight percent of the sales are between $310 and $1,620.
- Only two items were sales over $4,894.

The auditor can use other ACL features to seek answers to questions raised by the preceding analysis. For example, since this is a Sales Invoice file, it should normally contain only positive numbers. Negative numbers may have been inserted into the records in a number of ways. For example, they could be the result of a defective computer program, unintentional clerical errors, an effort to reverse the effects of erroneous sales

FIGURE 8–9

Stratification of
Sales Invoice File

@ STRATIFY ON **Invoice Amount** INTERVAL 10 TO SCREEN

Page . . . 1   09/23/01 14:34:39

Produced with ACL by: Workbook

<<< STRATIFY over –1,000.00–> 5,549.19 >>>

>>> Minimum encountered was –931.55

>>> Maximum encountered was 5,549.19

Interval			COUNT	<— %	% —>	Invoice Amount
–1,000.00	–>	–345.09	29	3.86%	–3.47%	–17,355.17
–345.08	–>	309.83	216	28.72%	0.45%	2250.97
309.84	–>	964.75	308	40.96%	37.66%	188,622.25
964.76	–>	1,619.67	129	17.15%	31.82%	159,371.25
1,619.68	–>	2,274.59	42	5.59%	15.74%	78,824.30
2,274.60	–>	2,929.51	12	1.60%	6.16%	30,835.20
2,929.52	–>	3,584.43	11	1.46%	7.16%	35,840.18
3,584.44	–>	4,239.35	2	0.27%	1.50%	7,490.28
4,239.36	–>	4,894.27	1	0.13%	0.88%	4,426.14
4,894.28	–>	5,549.19	2	0.27%	2.10%	10,503.83
			752	100.00%	100.00%	50,0809.23

transactions, or a fraudulent attempt to reduce a customer's accounts receivable balance. Although the auditor cannot specifically identify from the stratification which records are causing the anomalies, the potential problem has been flagged. The auditor will probably want to pursue this matter further, but to do so will require more detailed information.

ACL provides a *filter capability* that can be used to select or ignore specific records from an entire file. Using this feature, the auditor can select from the Sales Invoice file only those records with negative invoice amounts. The resulting view of the file is much smaller and provides the auditor with the details needed to investigate the anomalies. Sample records from the filtered file are listed below. With knowledge of specific customer account numbers, invoice numbers, and sales dates, the questionable items can be traced to their sources for resolution.

Invoice Number	Customer Number	Invoice Amount	Sales Date	Due Date	Closed Date	Remittance Number
213309	376005	−931.55	12/04/01	12/14/01		
213355	376005	−374.71	12/04/01	12/14/01		
212297	784647	−537.36	12/04/01	12/14/01		
214389	262001	−300.39	12/10/01	12/20/01		
214390	641464	−46.77	12/10/01	12/20/01		
214391	222006	−62.15	12/10/01	12/20/01		
213699	878035	−378.45	12/07/01	12/20/01		
213700	878035	−742.75	12/07/01	12/20/01		

REVIEW SALES INVOICE AND SHIPPING LOG FILES FOR MISSING AND DUPLICATE ITEMS

Searching for missing and/or duplicate transactions is another important test that helps the auditor corroborate or refute the completeness and accuracy assertions. Duplicate and missing transactions in the revenue cycle may be evidence of over- or understated sales and accounts receivable. Duplicate sales invoice records may indicate a computer program error that materially overstates sales and accounts receivable. A missing sales invoice may point to an unrecorded sale that was shipped but not billed, thus understating these accounts. On the other hand, it may indicate nothing more than an invoice that was issued and voided because of a clerical error.

ACL is capable of testing a designated field for out-of-sequence records, gaps in sequence numbers, and duplicates for the entire file. Using this feature, the auditor can scan the Invoice Number field of all records in the Sales Invoice file. The ACL system would return an on-screen report similar to the one below.

@ GAPS ON INVOICE DUPLICATES ERRORLIMIT 10 TO SCREEN

Page . . . 1   09/24/01 14:56:24

Produced with ACL by: Workbook

*** Duplicate key fields at record   7, Key:12857
*** Gap detected between 12867 and 12869
*** Duplicate key fields at record   22, Key:12872
*** Gap detected between 12877 and 12889

> •
>
> •
>
> •

*** Keys out of sequence at record	330, Key:13193
*** Duplicate key fields at record	331, Key:13193
*** Duplicate key fields at record	332, Key:13193

5 data sequence errors detected

22 gaps and/or duplicates detected

The above report shows that 22 records in the Sales Invoice file are either duplicated or missing. In resolving this issue, the auditor will need to interview management and employees involved in the process and seek answers to the following types of questions:

- Are procedures in place to document and approve voided invoices?
- How are gaps in sales invoices communicated to management?
- What physical controls exist over access to sales invoice source documents?
- Are batch totals used to control total transactions during data processing?
- Are transaction listings reconciled and reviewed by management?

Tests for missing and duplicate documents can also be performed on the Shipping Log file. Consider the following sample data, which is based on the file structure in Figure 8–8.

BOL Number	Invoice Number	Shipping Date	Carrier Code
50449	214088	11/29/99	538
50450	214090	11/29/99	530
50451	214089	11/30/99	531
50452	214087	11/30/99	532
50453	214092	12/14/99	533
50455	214093	12/10/99	523

In this example, the auditor would test the Invoice Number field for gaps and duplicate records. A duplicate record may indicate that the same product was shipped to the customer twice. If we presume that the customer was billed only once, then the organization has forfeited the revenue from the second shipment. Missing invoices may denote that some customer orders are not shipped at all. Depending upon the circumstances, sales and accounts receivable may be overstated.

Here is an example of how a single test procedure can support more than one audit objective. Invoices missing from the shipping log provide evidence that tests the *valuation/allocation* assertion. The auditor seeks assurance that sales revenue is recognized only when appropriate criteria are met. In most organizations, this means that sales are recognized only when the products are shipped. The auditor should review the shipping log for the following period to determine if the missing invoice numbers are recorded there. If so, this would indicate that the merchandise was shipped after the cut-off period. It may be necessary to adjust the sales and accounts receivable balances accordingly.

REVIEW LINE ITEM AND INVENTORY FILES FOR SALES PRICE ACCURACY

Evidence from testing the product prices charged to customers supports the audit objective of *accuracy*. Sometimes sales personnel are given limited authority to negotiate prices with customers. Significant discrepancies between the suggested retail price and the price actually charged, however, may indicate incompetence, clerical errors, or sales personnel exceeding their authority. A retail outlet such as a department store will usually establish a non-negotiable pricing policy. Sales prices are calculated automatically by the point-of-sale system to eliminate salesperson intervention and clerical errors. Pricing inconsistency in such a setting may indicate a computer program error or the use of obsolete pricing data.

Traditionally, auditors would verify pricing accuracy by comparing sales prices on the invoices with the published price list. But because of the physical effort involved with this approach, it could be done only on a sample basis. Therefore, out of thousands of sales records, perhaps only one or two hundred would be tested. ACL allows the auditor to compare the prices charged on every invoice in the file for the period under review. Based on the file structures for the Line Item and Inventory files presented in Figure 8–8, we can illustrate this procedure using the sample data on the following page.

This procedure involves a few simple steps. First, notice that the actual sales price charged is stored in the Sales Price field in the Line Item file. The suggested retail price for each product is the Retail Price field in the Inventory file. In addition, the two files have Item Number as a common field. This is the key field on which the two files are related. Using this common field, the objective of the test is to match each record in the Line Item file with the corresponding record in the Inventory file. We can compare the Sales Price and Retail Price fields for constancy. Significant discrepancies can then be identified and investigated. The actual steps in this test are described next.

First, both files need to be ordered according to their common key. Item number is the primary key of the inventory master file, and we will assume that this file is already in the proper sequence. Since the Line Item file contains the details of the Invoice file, it is probably organized by Invoice Number at this time. It is therefore necessary to sort this file on the Item Number field to place it in the same order as the Inventory file. This involves simply opening the file and invoking ACL's *Sort* feature.

The next step is to combine the two files to create a third. ACL accomplishes this with its *Join* feature. The auditor has several options when joining files. The one most relevant to this test is to create a third file that consists only of matched records. In other words, the new file will contain only the Line Item and Inventory records whose value for the Item Number field match. Any Inventory records that are not matched with a Line Item record will not be part of the new file.

ACL's join feature permits the auditor to specify the fields from the two input files that are to be passed to the new output file. Usually, it is neither necessary nor desirable to include all fields from both of the original files. In this example, the fields needed from the Line Item file to verify pricing accuracy are Invoice Number, Item Number, and Sales Price; from the Inventory file, the fields are Description and Retail Price. The file structure of the new file and some sample records are presented below.

Invoice Number	Item Number	Description	Sales Price	Retail Price
214297	030303413	8 OZ BALL PEIN HAMMER	4.69	4.69
214297	030303403	12 OZ BALL PEIN HAMMER	5.29	5.29
214297	030303343	STRAIGHT CLAW HAMMER	12.98	12.98
214298	130305603	#4 SMOOTH PLANE	16.00	22.98
214298	030302303	MITRE BOX 21"	44.95	54.95

Line Item File

Invoice Number	Item Number	Sales Price	Quantity	Extended Price
214297	030303413	4.69	20	93.88
214297	030303403	5.29	10	52.90
214297	030303343	12.98	2	25.96
214298	130305603	16.00	5	80.00
214298	030302303	44.95	12	539.40

Inventory File

Item Number	Description	Warehouse Location	Quantity On Hand	Reorder Point	Order Quantity	PO Number	Unit Cost	Retail Price	Vendor Number
030303413	8 OZ BALL PEIN HAMMER	03	1,248	510	1,500		3.90	4.69	10879
030303403	12 OZ BALL PEIN HAMMER	03	536	550	1,200	111104	4.12	5.29	12248
030303343	STRAIGHT CLAW HAMMER	03	735	550	1,600		8.83	12.98	10951
130305603	#4 SMOOTH PLANE	03	804	800	2,000	107427	14.12	22.98	10879
030309373	HEAVY DUTY BRACE	03	842	900	1,200	108123	10.12	16.98	10951
030302903	4 PC CHISEL SET	03	795	620	1,200		10.12	16.98	13411
030302303	MITRE BOX 21"	03	600	650	1,200	129124	41.23	54.95	11182

At this point, the resulting file may still be vary large. Scanning the file visually for price differences could be time-consuming and ineffective. Here again is an application for a *filter*. Through a series of pop-up menus, the auditor can easily create a filter that will ignore all records in which Sales Price and Retail Price are equal. The resulting file will thus contain only price discrepancies. Using other ACL features, the auditor can calculate the total price variance and make a determination as to its materiality. If material, this issue would need to be pursued with management.

TESTING FOR UNMATCHED RECORDS.   A variation on the preceding test can be used to address some related issues. By selecting a different join option, the auditor can produce a new file of only unmatched records. There are two possible causes for unmatched records. The first is because the value of Item Number field in the Line Item record is incorrect and does not match an Inventory record. Since the operational assumption is that the inventory master file is correct, then any Line Item records in the unmatched file are errors. The presence (or absence) of such errors is evidence that refutes or corroborates the accuracy assertion.

The second source of unmatched records is the Inventory file. The presence of Inventory records in the unmatched file means that there were no corresponding records in the Line Item file. This is not an error; it means that these products did not sell during the period. After adjusting for any seasonal influences on sales, such evidence may refute the valuation assertion. The auditor may require that the inventory be written down to reflect its market value.

TESTING THE EXISTENCE ASSERTION

One of the most widely performed tests of existence is the **confirmation of accounts receivable**. This test involves direct written contact between the auditors and the client's customers to confirm account balances and transactions. *Statement on Auditing Standards No. 67* (SAS 67), *The Confirmation Process*, states that auditors should request confirmations of accounts receivable except in the following three situations: (1) accounts receivable are immaterial; (2) based on a review of internal controls, the auditor has assessed control risk to be low; or (3) the confirmation process will be ineffective.

This last point is worthy of further explanation. Because of the way some organizations account for their liabilities, they may be unable to respond to requests for confirmation. For example, government agencies and large industrial organizations often use an **open-invoice system** for liabilities. Under this approach, invoices are recorded individually rather than being summarized or grouped by creditor. In this environment, no accounts payable subsidiary ledger exists. Each invoice is paid (closed) as it comes due. For financial reporting purposes, total accounts payable is calculated simply by summing the open (unpaid) invoices. Determining the liability due to a particular creditor, which may consist of multiple open invoices, is not such a simple task. The auditor should not assume that an organization using this approach would invest the time needed to respond to the confirmation request. Under such circumstances, the confirmation process would be ineffective.

In the discussion that follows, we assume that accounts receivable are material and that the auditor has decided to request confirmations from the client's customers. The confirmation process involves three stages: selecting the accounts to confirmation, preparing confirmation requests, and evaluating the responses.

SELECTING ACCOUNTS TO CONFIRM

Given the file structures used in our example, selecting accounts receivable for confirmation involves processing data that are contained in both the Customer and the Sales

Invoice files. Each customer record is associated with one or more sales invoice records. Recall from a previous discussion that the accounts receivable balance for a particular customer is calculated by summing the open sales invoices (those with no values in the Closed Date and Remittance Number fields) for the customer. Once cash is received in payment of an invoice, it is closed by placing the payment date and the cash receipt number in the respective fields. Thus, the Sales Invoice file provides the financial information needed for the confirmation requests, and the customer mailing information is contained in the Customer file. Obtaining a set of accounts for confirmation requires three steps: consolidate the invoices by customer, join the data from the two files, and select a sample of accounts from the joined file.

CONSOLIDATE INVOICES.   The first step in the process is to consolidate all the open invoices for each customer. Using the sample data presented in Figure 8–10, ACL's *classify* command allows the auditor to set a filter to select only the open sales invoices (those with blanks in the Remittance Number field) and to summarize the Invoice Amount field for each record based on the Customer Number. The summarized records are then passed to a new file called Classified Invoices, presented in Figure 8–11.

JOIN THE FILES.   The next step in the confirmation process is to join the Classified Invoices file and the Customer file (illustrated in Figure 8–12 with sample data) to produce another new file called Accounts Receivable, which is presented in Figure 8–13. Recall that when using ACL's join feature both files must be ordered on the same key. This requires first sorting the Classified Invoices file by Customer Number to place it in the same sequence as the Customer master file. As noted previously, the join feature allows the auditor to select only relevant fields from each of the input files when creating the new file. In this example, Credit Limit, which is not needed for preparing the confirmations, has been dropped from the new Accounts Receivable file structure.

FIGURE 8–10	Invoice Number	Customer Number	Invoice Amount	Sales Date	Due Date	Closed Date	Remittance Number
Sales Invoice File	212209	376005	931.55	12/04/01	12/14/01		
	212255	376005	377.71	12/04/01	12/14/01		
	212297	784647	537.36	12/04/01	12/14/01		
	214088	065003	13.08	12/04/01	12/14/01	12/11/01	611243
	214389	262001	300.39	12/10/01	12/20/01		
	214100	641464	46.77	12/10/01	12/20/01		
	214114	065003	9.76	12/04/01	12/14/01		
	214129	262001	116.72	12/04/01	12/14/01		
	214121	165006	29.40	12/04/01	12/14/01	12/12/01	613457
	214185	165009	9.17	12/04/01	12/14/01	12/23/01	614476

FIGURE 8–11	Customer Number	Invoice Amount
Classified Invoices File	376005	1,279.26
	784647	537.36
	262001	417.11
	641464	46.77
	065003	9.76

FIGURE 8–12

Customer File Structure with Sample Data

Customer Number	Customer Name	Street Address	City	State	Zip Code	Credit Limit
065003	ACCEL ENTERPRISES	1000 STRAYER RD	BROOKLINE	MA	02167	72,000
262001	CONNECTICUT CORP.	600 PARAGON DR	BROOKLYN	NY	11201	80,000
376005	BULLY INDUSTRIES	8 WEST STREET	LAS VEGAS	NV	89109	53,000
641464	FIRST HEALTHCARE	88 STATE ST	AUSTIN	TX	78752	28,000
784647	SALT BANK OF AMER.	401 N BROADWAY	BENTONVILLE	AR	72712	27,000

FIGURE 8–13

Accounts Receivable File Structure

Customer Number	Customer Name	Street Address	City	State	Zip Code	Invoice Amount
065003	ACCEL ENTERPRISES	1000 STRAYER RD	BROOKLINE	MA	02167	9.76
262001	CONNECTICUT CORP.	600 PARAGON DR	BROOKLYN	NY	11201	417.11
376005	BULLY INDUSTRIES	8 WEST STREET	LAS VEGAS	NV	89109	1,279.26
641464	FIRST HEALTHCARE	88 STATE ST	AUSTIN	TX	78752	46.77
784647	SALT BANK OF AMER.	401 N BROADWAY	BENTONVILLE	AR	72712	537.36

SELECT A SAMPLE OF ACCOUNTS.   In a moderate-to-large sized organization, the Accounts Receivable file may contain thousands of records. Rather than confirming all of these accounts, the auditor will probably choose to select a sample of records. To assist the auditor in this task, ACL's *sample* feature offers two basic sampling methods: *random (record) sampling* and *monetary unit sampling (MUS)*. The choice of methods will depend on the auditor's strategy and the composition of the Accounts Receivable file. If the account balances are fairly evenly distributed, the auditor may want an unbiased sample and will thus choose the random sample approach. Under this method, each record, regardless of the size of the accounts receivable balance, has an equal chance of being included in the sample. If, on the other hand, the file is heavily skewed with large customer account balances, the auditor may select MUS, which will produce a sample biased toward the larger dollar amounts.

ACL's *size* command helps the auditor calculate sample size and sampling intervals based on the auditor's desired confidence level, the size of the population being sampled, and the assessed materiality threshold. These parameters are entered into ACL to draw a physical sample from the Accounts Receivable file that is sent to a new output file called AR-Sample. The structure of this file is the same as the Accounts Receivable file, but it contains far fewer records. For example, from the several thousand records in the accounts receivable population, perhaps only 150 records are selected for the sample.

PREPARING CONFIRMATION REQUESTS

The next stage in the confirmation process involves preparing confirmation requests that contain the information captured in the AR-Sample file. The requests, which usually take the form of a letter, are drafted and administered by the auditor, but are written in the client entity's name. A sample confirmation letter is presented in Figure 8–14.

POSITIVE AND NEGATIVE CONFIRMATIONS.   The letter shown in Figure 8–14 is an example of a **positive confirmation**. Recipients are asked to respond whether their records agree or disagree with the amount stated. Positive confirmations are particularly useful when the auditor suspects that a large number of accounts may be in

FIGURE 8–14

Confirmation
Letter

> ***Client Letterhead***
>
> ***(Client Name and Address)***
>
> ***(Name and Address of Client's Customer)***
>
> To whom it may concern:
>
> In accordance with the request from our external auditors, we ask that you confirm your outstanding account balance with our organization. Our records indicate that your account balance as of ***(end-of-period date)*** amounted to ***($ amount).***
>
> If your records agree with this balance, please indicate by signing in the space provided below and return this letter directly to our auditors using the enclosed envelope. Your prompt compliance with this request is greatly appreciated.
>
> If the amount indicated is not in agreement with your records, inform the auditors directly using the enclosed envelope. In your response, please show the amount owed according to your records and include full details of the discrepancy.
>
> Sincerely,
> ***(Name of Entity)***
>
> The amount stated above is correct: ***(Customer Name)***

dispute. They are also used when confirming unusual or large balances or when a large proportion of total accounts receivable arises from a small number of significant customers.

A problem with positive confirmations is poor response rate. Customers that do not dispute the amount shown in the confirmation letter may not respond. The auditor cannot assume, however, that lack of response means agreement. To obtain the highest response rate possible, second and even third requests may need to be sent to non-respondents.

Negative confirmations request the recipient to respond only if they disagree with the amount shown in the letter. This technique is used primarily when accounts receivable consist of a large number of low-value balances and the control risk of misstatement is considered to be low. The sample size for this type of test is typically large and may include the entire population. Evidence from non-returned negative confirmations selected from a large population provides indirect evidence to support the auditor's expectation that accounts receivable are not materially misstated.

On the other hand, responses to negative confirmations, particularly if they are widespread in a large population, may indicate a potential problem. Since the negative confirmations approach does not prove that the intended recipients actually received and reviewed the confirmation letters, evidence of individual misstatements provided by returned responses cannot be projected to the entire population. In other words, responses to negative confirmations cannot be used as a basis for determining the total dollar amount of the misstatement in the account. Such evidence can be used, however, to reinforce the auditor's prior expectation that the account balance may be materially misstated and that additional testing of details is needed to determine the nature and amount of the misstatement.

Once the auditor decides upon the nature and the wording of the confirmation letter, it can be created using a word processor. ACL's *export* feature can greatly facilitate the physical task of inserting the relevant financial data for each customer into the individual letters. Using this option, the auditor can produce a text version of the

AR-Sample file that can be integrated with the confirmation letter text using the mail/merge feature of a word processing package such as Microsoft Word or Word-Perfect. This facility greatly reduces the clerical effort traditionally associated with confirmation activities.

EVALUATING AND CONTROLLING RESPONSES

Maintaining control over the confirmation process is critical to its integrity. Evidence provided through confirmations is less reliable when contact between the auditor and the debtor is disrupted by client intervention. The auditor should take all reasonable steps to ensure the following procedures are observed:

- The auditor should retain custody of the confirmation letters until they are mailed.
- The confirmation letters together with self-addressed stamped envelopes should be addressed to the auditor, rather than the client organization.
- The confirmation request should be mailed by the auditor. If client mail room personnel participate in the process, they should be adequately supervised.

When responses are returned to the auditor, discrepancies in the amount owed should be investigated. The auditor should evaluate exceptions to determine if they represent isolated instances or signify a larger potential problem. For example, frequent complaints by debtors that the client is slow to record cash payments may indicate misappropriations of cash and the lapping of accounts receivable. Lapping is discussed in Chapter 10.

Non-responses to positive confirmations also need to be investigated. SAS 67 requires auditors to use alternative procedures to resolve this issue. A commonly used procedure is to review the following period's closed invoices to determine if the accounts were actually paid. Since it is unlikely that a customer will pay an account that is not owed, subsequent cash payments is good evidence of the *existence, accuracy,* and *valuation* objectives.

TESTING THE VALUATION/ALLOCATION ASSERTION

The auditor's objective regarding proper valuation and allocation is to corroborate or refute that accounts receivable are stated at net realizable value. This objective rests on the reasonableness of the allowance for doubtful accounts, which is derived from aged accounts receivable balances. To achieve this objective, the auditor needs to review the accounts receivable aging process to determine that the allowance for doubtful accounts is adequate.

AGING ACCOUNTS RECEIVABLE

As accounts age, the probability that they will ultimately be collected is decreased. Hence, as a general rule, the larger the number of older accounts that are included in an organization's accounts receivable file, the larger the allowance for doubtful accounts needs to be to reflect the risk. Historical trends in collection success also play an important part in estimating the bad debt losses for the period. A key issue for auditors to resolve, therefore, is whether the allowance calculated by the client is consistent with the composition of their organization's accounts receivable portfolio and with prior years. In addition, the auditor needs to determine that the allowance is consistent with current economic conditions. For example, an organization entering into a period of economic decline may experience an increased percentage of bad debts relative to prior, more prosperous, years. Under such circumstances, a larger portion of past-due accounts may need to be included in the allowance calculation than had previously been the case. As a starting point in an attempt to gain assurance on these issues, the auditor may decide to recalculate the aging schedule.

The following describes ACL's accounts receivable aging feature using the Sales Invoice file presented in Figure 8–10. The key data fields used in calculation are Invoice Amount and Due Date. The system compares the Due Date in the record with a specified cutoff date to produce aged summaries of the Invoice Amount data. The default intervals used are 30, 60, 90, and 120 days past due. These, however, can be changed to any values that better suit the auditor's needs.

Keep in mind that the Sales Invoice file contains all sales invoices for the period. Only the open sales invoices (those with blanks in the Remittance Number field) as of the cutoff date should be considered in the calculation. By filtering on the Remittance Number field, ACL will ignore all closed invoices. Upon executing the *Age* command, a report similar to the one below will be produced.

Aging of Accounts Receivable Produced with ACL

<<< AGE over 0-> 10,000 >>>

>>> Minimum encountered was 124

>>> Maximum encountered was 834

Due		Count	<— %	% —>	Invoice Amount
< 0		255	33.03%	46.30%	217,113.27
0 ->	29	259	33.55%	38.66%	181,252.50
30 ->	59	170	22.02%	11.66%	54,676.94
60 ->	89	58	7.51%	1.81%	8,496.10
90 ->	119	17	2.20%	1.52%	7,137.88
120 ->	10,000	13	1.68%	0.04%	204.00
		772	100.00%	100.00%	468,880.69

The aging report provides a clear picture of the accounts receivable composition. The total balance of accounts receivable outstanding at the end of the audit period is $468,880.69. As of the cutoff date, $217,113.27 of the outstanding balance is not past due. However, 17 invoices are between 90 and 120 days past due, and 13 invoices are over 120 days past due. The auditor should review past-due balances with the credit manager to obtain information for basing an opinion on their collectibility. The auditor's objective is not to assess the collectibility of each account, but to determine that the methods used by the credit manager to estimate the allowance for doubtful accounts is adequate and that the overall allowance is reasonable.

SUMMARY

This chapter examined audit procedures associated with the revenue cycle. The chapter began with a review of alternative technologies used in both legacy and modern systems. The emphasis was on key operational tasks under alternative technologies. The second main section of the chapter presented revenue cycle audit objectives and controls. In this section, we examined the tests of controls that an auditor may perform. Evidence gathered from tests of controls contributes to audit objectives and may permit the auditor to limit the scope, timing, and extent of substantive tests. The last section described the use of ACL in performing the more common substantive tests. The tests were presented in relation to the management assertions that they were designed to corroborate or refute.

KEY TERMS

analytical review	negative confirmation
audit trail	open-invoice system
batch control totals	packing slip
bill of lading	positive confirmation
confirmation of accounts receivable	reengineering
credit authorization	sales invoice
customer open order file	sales invoice file
customer order	sales order
cycle billing	shipping notice
events database	stock release (picking ticket)

REVIEW QUESTIONS

1. What document initiates the sales process?
2. Distinguish between a packing slip, shipping notice, and a bill of lading.
3. What are three input controls?
4. What are the three rules that ensure that no single employee or department processes a transaction in its entirety?
5. What is automation and why is it used?
6. What is the objective of reengineering?
7. Distinguish between an edit run, sort run, and update run.
8. How is the record's primary key critical in preserving the audit trail?
9. What are the advantages of real-time processing?
10. Why does billing receive a copy of the sales order when the order is approved but does not bill until the goods are shipped?
11. How do tests of controls relate to substantive tests?
12. List the audit objectives [derived from management assertions] that pertain to the revenue cycle.

DISCUSSION QUESTIONS

1. Distinguish between the sales, billing, and accounts receivable departments. Why can't the sales or accounts receivable departments prepare the bills?
2. Explain the risks associated with mail room procedures.
3. How could an employee embezzle funds by issuing an unauthorized sales credit memo if the appropriate segregation of duties and authorization controls were not in place?
4. What task can the accounts receivable department engage in to verify that all checks sent

by the customers have been appropriately deposited and recorded?

5. Why is access control over revenue cycle documents just as important as the physical control devices over cash and inventory?

6. For a batch processing system using sequential files, describe the intermediate and permanent files that are created after the edit run has successfully been completed when processing the sales order file and updating the accounts receivable and inventory master files.

7. Why has the use of magnetic tapes as a storage medium declined in recent years? What are their primary uses currently?

8. Discuss both the tangible and intangible benefits of real-time processing.

9. Distinguish between positive and negative confirmations.

10. What is the purpose of analytical reviews in the audit of revenue cycle accounts?

11. Explain the open-invoice system. What effect might it have on confirmation responses?

MULTIPLE-CHOICE QUESTIONS

1. Which document is NOT prepared by the sales department?
   a. packing slip
   b. shipping notice
   c. bill of lading
   d. stock release

2. Which document triggers the update of the inventory subsidiary ledger?
   a. bill of lading
   b. stock release
   c. sales order
   d. shipping notice

3. Which function should NOT be performed by the billing department?
   a. Record the sales in the sales journal.
   b. Send the ledger copy of the sales order to accounts receivable.
   c. Send the stock release document and the shipping notice to the billing department as proof of shipment.
   d. Send the stock release document to inventory control.

4. When will a credit check approval most likely require specific authorization by the credit department?
   a. When verifying that the current transaction does not exceed the customer's credit limit
   b. When verifying that the current transaction is with a valid customer

   c. When a valid customer places a materially large order
   d. When a valid customer returns goods

5. Which type of control is considered to be a compensating control?
   a. segregation of duties
   b. access control
   c. supervision
   d. accounting records

6. Which of the following is NOT an output control?
   a. The shipping department verifies that the goods sent from the warehouse are correct in type and quantity.
   b. General ledger clerks reconcile journal vouchers that were independently prepared in various departments.
   c. The use of prenumbered sales orders.
   d. The billing department reconciles the shipping notice with the sales invoice to ensure that customers are billed only for the quantities shipped.

7. CMA Adapted 684 3-29
   Which one of the following poses the biggest threat with respect to potential losses?
   a. The petty cash custodian has the ability to steal petty cash. Documentation for all disbursements from the fund must be submitted with the request for replenishment of the fund.

b. An inventory control clerk at a manufacturing plant has the ability to steal one completed television set from inventory a year. The theft probably will never be detected.

c. An accounts receivable clerk, who approves sales returns and allowances, receives customer remittances and deposits them in the bank. Limited supervision is maintained over the employee.

d. A clerk in the invoice processing department fails to match a vendor's invoice with its related receiving report. Checks are not signed unless all appropriate documents are attached to a voucher.

e. An accounting clerk has the ability to record unauthorized journal entries. All journal entries are reviewed by an accounting department supervisor each month.

8. CMA 1288 3-26
In a well-designed internal control structure in which the cashier receives remittances from the mail room, the cashier should not

a. endorse the checks.
b. prepare the bank deposit slip.
c. deposit remittances daily at a local bank.
d. prepare a list of mail receipts.
e. post the receipts to the accounts receivable subsidiary ledger cards.

9. CMA 689 3-15
Which one of the following situations represents an internal control weakness in accounts receivable?

a. Internal auditors confirm customer accounts periodically.
b. Only the sales manager reviews delinquent accounts.
c. The cashier is denied access to customers' records and monthly statements.
d. Customers' statements are mailed monthly by the accounts receivable department.
e. Customers' subsidiary records are maintained by someone who has no access to cash.

PROBLEMS

1. Describe the procedures, documents, and departments involved when insufficient inventory is available to fill a customer's approved order.

2. Refer to Figure 8–1 in the chapter and explain where the batch totals come from and which accounts in the general ledger are affected by the end-of-day batch process.

3. Document Flowchart Analysis
CMA Adapted 1287 5-7 through 5-12
Use the flowchart on the following page to answer the following questions:
a. The customer checks accompanied by the control tape (refer to Symbol A) would be forwarded to whom?
b. The appropriate description that should be placed in Symbol B would be what?
c. The next action to take with the customer remittance advices (refer to Symbol C) would be to do what?
d. The appropriate description that should be placed in Symbol D would be what?

e. The appropriate description that should be placed in Symbol E would be what?
f. The flowchart can be best described as representing what type of processing system?

4. Document Authorization and Transfer
CMA Adapted 690 5-1 through 5-5
Marport Company is a manufacturing company that uses forms and documents in its accounting information systems for record-keeping and internal control. The departments in Marport's organizational structure and their primary responsibilities are shown in the table on the following page. Using this information, answer the following questions:
a. The initiation of the purchase of materials and supplies would be the responsibility of what department?
b. The document generated by the department identified in (a) above to initiate the purchasing process would be what?
c. Multiple copies of the purchase order are prepared for record-keeping and distribu-

Problem 3: Document Flowchart Analysis

Problem 4: Document Authorization and Transfer

Accounts payable—authorize payments and prepare vouchers	Payroll—compute and prepare the company payroll
Accounts receivable—maintain customer accounts	Personnel—hire employees, as well as maintain records on job positions and employees
Billing—prepare invoices to customers for goods sold	Purchasing—place orders for materials and supplies
Cashier—maintain a record of cash receipts and disbursements	Production—manufacture finished goods
Credit department—verify the credit rating of customers	Production planning—decide the types and quantities of products to be produced
Cost accounting—accumulate manufacturing costs for all goods produced	Receiving—receive all materials and supplies
Finished goods storeroom—maintain the physical inventory and related stock records of finished goods	Sales—accept orders from customers
General accounting—maintain all records for the company's general ledger	Shipping—ship goods to customers
Internal audit—appraise and monitor internal controls, as well as conduct operational and management audits	Stores control—safeguard all materials and supplies until needed for production
Inventory control—maintain perpetual inventory records for all manufacturing materials and supplies	Timekeeping—prepare and control time worked by hourly employees
Mail room—process incoming, outgoing, and interdepartmental mail	

tion with one copy sent to the vendor and one retained by the purchasing department. In addition, for proper information flow and internal control purposes, a version of the purchase order would be distributed to what other departments?

d. What documents must the accounts payable department review before it can properly authorize payment for the purchase of materials and supplies?

e. Which document is used to transfer responsibility for goods between the seller of goods and a common carrier?

5. Segregation of Functions
   CMA Adapted
   Refer to the Marport Company in Question 4 and determine whether the following situations represent a proper segregation of functions in the processing of orders from customers.
   a. Invoice preparation by the billing department and posting to the customers'

accounts by the accounts receivable department

b. Approval of a sales credit memo because of a product return by the sales department with subsequent posting to the customer's account by the accounts receivable department

c. Shipping of goods by the shipping department that have been retrieved from stock by the finished goods storeroom department

d. Posting to the appropriate general ledger accounts by general accounting on the basis of batch totals prepared and verified by the billing department

6. **Internal Controls**
CMA 688 5-2
Jem Clothes, Inc., is a 25-store chain, concentrated in the Northeast, that sells ready-to-wear clothes for young men and women. Each store has a full-time manager and an assistant manager, both of whom are paid a salary. The cashiers and sales personnel are typically young people working part-time who are paid an hourly wage plus a commission based on sales volume. The accompanying flowchart depicts the flow of a sales transaction through the organization of a typical store. The company uses unsophisticated cash registers with four-part sales invoices to record each transaction. These sales invoices are used regardless of the payment type (cash, check, or bank card).

On the sales floor, the salesperson manually records his or her employee number and the transaction (clothes, class, description, quantity, and unit price), totals the sales invoice, calculates the discount when appropriate, calculates the sales tax, and prepares the grand total. The salesperson then gives the sales invoice to the cashier, retaining one copy in the sales book.

The cashier reviews the invoice and inputs the sale. The cash register mechanically validates the invoice by automatically assigning a consecutive number to the transaction. The cashier is also responsible for getting credit approval on charge sales and approving sales paid by check. The cashier gives one copy of the invoice to the customer and retains the second copy as a store copy and the third for a bank card, if deposit is needed. Returns are handled in exactly the reverse manner, with the cashier issuing a return slip.

At the end of each day, the cashier sequentially orders the sales invoices and takes cash register totals for cash, bank card, and check sales, and cash and bank card returns. These totals are reconciled by the assistant manager to the cash register tapes, the total of the consecutively numbered sales invoices, and the return slips. The assistant manager prepares a daily reconciliation report for the store manager's review.

Cash, check, and bank card sales are reviewed by the manager, who then prepares the daily bank deposit (bank card sales invoices are included in the deposit). The manager makes the deposit at the bank and files the validated deposit slip.

The cash register tapes, sales invoices, and return slips are then forwarded daily to the central data processing department at corporate headquarters for processing. The data processing department returns a weekly sales and commission activity report to the manager for review.

Required:
a. Identify six strengths in the Jem Clothes system for controlling sales transactions.
b. For each strength identified, explain what problem(s) Jem Clothes has avoided by incorporating the strength in the system for controlling sales transactions.

Use the following format in preparing your answer.

1. *Strength*   2. *Problem(s) Avoided*

7. **Stewardship**
Identify which department has stewardship over the following journals, ledgers, and files:
a. Customer open order file
b. Sales journal
c. Journal voucher file
d. Cash receipts journal
e. Inventory subsidiary ledger
f. Accounts receivable subsidiary ledger
g. Sales history file
h. Shipping report file
i. Credit memo file
j. Sales order file
k. Closed sales order file

8. **Control Weaknesses**
For the past 11 years, Elaine Wright has been an employee of the Star-Bright Electrical Supply store. Elaine is a very diligent employee who rarely calls in sick and takes her vacation days staggered throughout the year so that no one else gets bogged down with her tasks for more than one day. Star-Bright is a small store

Problem 6: Internal Controls

that employs only four people other than the owner. The owner and one of the employees help customers with their electrical needs. One of the employees handles all receiving, stocking, and shipping of merchandise. Another employee handles the purchasing, payroll, general ledger, inventory, and accounts payable functions. Elaine handles all of the point-of-sale cash receipts and prepares the daily deposits for the business. Furthermore, Elaine opens the mail and deposits all cash receipts (about 30 percent of the total daily cash receipts). Elaine also keeps the accounts receivable records and bills the customers who purchase on credit.

Required:

a. Point out any control weaknesses you see in the above scenario.

b. List some recommendations to remedy any weaknesses you have found working under the constraint that no additional employees can be hired.

`9. Internal Control
Iris Plant owns and operates three floral shops in Magnolia, Texas. The accounting functions have been performed manually. Each of the shops has a manager who oversees the cash receipts and purchasing functions for the shop. All bills are sent to the central shop and are paid by a clerk who also prepares payroll checks and maintains the general journal. Iris is seriously considering switching to a computerized system. With so many information systems packages on the market, Iris is overwhelmed. Advise Iris as to which business modules you think her organization could find beneficial. Discuss advantages, disadvantages, and internal control issues.

10. Internal Control
You are investing your money and opening a fast-food Mexican restaurant that accepts only cash for payments. You plan on periodically issuing coupons through the mail and in local newspapers. You are particularly interested in access controls over inventory and cash. Design a carefully controlled system and draw a document flowchart to represent it. Identify and discuss the key control issues.

11. Data Processing
The computer processing portion of a sales order system is represented by the flowchart on the following page. Answer the following questions:

a. What type of data processing system is this? Explain, and be specific.

b. The auditor suggests that this system can be greatly simplified by changing to direct access files. Explain the major operational changes that would occur in the system if this were done.

c. The auditor warns of control implications from this change that must be considered. Explain the nature of the control implications.

d. Sketch a flowchart (the computerized portion only) of the proposed new system. Use correct symbols and label the diagram.

12. Microcomputer AIS packages
Visit a microcomputer store that carries accounting information system packages. Examine and compare four packages on cost, capabilities (number of business modules), file constraints, flexibility, built-in controls, and support. Rank these systems and write a report supporting your recommendation.

INTERNAL CONTROL CASES

1. F&Y Computer Sales, Inc. (Prepared by Todd Feinman, Coopers & Lybrand LLP)

F&Y is in the business of selling computers. Its main competition is other major mail-order computer companies. It has a small market share compared to the industry leaders, but it hopes to increase its share by being more responsive to its customers' orders by reengineering its sales order processing system. F&Y has 147 employees, and the main office is located in St. Paul, Minnesota.

F&Y sells desktop computer systems that it primarily manufactures itself, with a few parts purchased from third-party companies.

Problem 11: Data Processing

It offers many different packages to accommodate its end-user customers, about 15 different bundles in all. Customers pay on credit

terms and get a satisfaction guarantee for up to 30 days after receipt of their computers. F&Y's suppliers include a few different microcomputer chip and software manufacturers whose products F&Y packages with its computers. F&Y's warehouse is located at the main office in St. Paul and is very large.

Last year, F&Y's market share dropped in comparison to its competition. A survey revealed that one reason was because customers were not getting their computers on time. The lead times were too long and were always a day or two late. Customer orders need to be sent out the day they are received, and inventory records need to be updated as orders are placed to be able to accurately tell customers how long a lead time is or whether a back-order is necessary. The board of directors also suspects that internal control weaknesses exist that might lead to internal fraud.

When customers need to order new computers for their homes or offices, they call F&Y to place an order. All sales are made either via the actual order document that F&Y gives its usual customers to complete and mail or fax back, or through a telephone call where sales representatives transcribe the order to a formal sales order document. Existing customers pay via credit, usually through existing accounts, while new customers must have a new account established. A customer's account record includes his or her name, address, phone number, background history with the company, and of course F&Y's formally assigned unique customer number. Usually Sam, from the sales department, will create the formal sales order and send it to Alice in the credit department.

Alice's job is to check the customer's credit and make sure he or she has the funds available to pay for the order. If so, the customer receives a credit approval, and Alice creates a stock release so that the order can continue to be processed. Credit that is not approved gets filed, and Alice calls the customer to notify him or her that the order has been canceled. For approved credit, Alice staples the approved sales order to the stock release and sends it to the warehouse (shipping) department.

Willie, a warehouse employee, receives the stock release, picks the goods, and calls either Federal Express, UPS, or a service requested by the customer. Willie also then proceeds to update the inventory subsidiary ledger to account for the computers he is going to load on the trucks. When Willie is too busy to ship the computers, he can ask most any other employee to do it because once inside the warehouse, any employee can transport any item out of the warehouse onto a delivery truck. Due to this easy transportation of goods, F&Y wants to ensure that it is not easy for unauthorized people to get into the warehouse. F&Y has implemented codes, to be punched in on the door's keypad, to open the warehouse doors, instead of a key since keys can be stolen or lost. Willie now prepares the bills of lading and shipping notices. The shipping companies arrive every day at 4:30 P.M., and Willie gives them the bill of lading, shipping notice, and computers to be shipped. After he knows the goods are on their way to the customer, the stock release, copy of shipping notice, and sales order are stapled together and sent to Bob in the billing department.

Bob receives and files the stock release, prepares the invoice, makes a copy of it, and mails it to the customer. Every Friday afternoon, Bob updates the sales journal and then sends the original invoice, sales order, stock release, and shipping notice to the accounts receivable department.

Adam, in the accounting (accounts receivable) department, files those documents that Bob sent him and updates the accounts receivable and general ledger for the customer's account. The accounts receivable is sorted according to customer number for Adam's ease since each customer number is unique. Every week he goes through the accounts and calls customers who are overdue on the payments. If a customer defaults on payment, Adam reclassifies the account as "doubtful."

When a customer receives his or her goods and invoice, the company is usually mailed a check for payment. Mickey, in the mail room, receives the checks and sends them to cash receipts. Mickey's boss, Muhammad, also works in the mail room, but is too busy with administrative work in his office behind closed doors to supervise the opening of the mail. This structure allows mail room clerks like Mickey to listen to music while they work and not disturb Muhammad. Mickey also happens to be Adam's (accounts receivable) son. Adam thought it would be wise to get his son's foot in the company's door by getting him a low-level job in the mail room.

Karen, the cash receipts clerk, receives the checks and stores them in her top drawer until the end of the week, at which point she prepares a deposit slip and deposits the checks at the Bank of New York. Karen returns from the bank with a bank receipt, files it, and updates the cash receipts journal.

At the end of each month, Adam makes sure all transactions are reconciled in the general ledger. If they are not, he asks the corresponding department to verify the books and report back to him. Usually the department in question can identify and correct the problem and tell Adam what adjusting entries to make.

Upon receipts of the goods, the customer sends F&Y the payment check as described above. Within 30 days of this date, the customer has the option to return the computer for any reason, including dissatisfaction with performance or malfunctioning parts. Customers call Willie in the warehouse and get a return authorization number to ship their computer back. Willie enters what item(s) the customer is going to ship back under the return authorization number and waits for arrival of goods. When goods arrive, he updates the inventory subsidiary ledger and prepares a return slip and sends it to Sam in sales.

Sam prepares the credit memo and forwards it, along with the return slip, to Bob in billing. The credit memo authorizes that the customer get reimbursed for his or her expense. Bob updates the sales journal and forwards both documents to Adam in accounting. Adam files the two documents and updates the accounts receivable file and general ledger. The customer should no longer be charged for the purchase.

Required:

a. Prepare a data flow diagram for the system described in the case.

b. Prepare a document flowchart for the system described in the case.

c. Identify the internal control weaknesses in the system. Structure your discussion around the six classes of internal control activities described in SAS 78.

d. Redesign the system to take advantage of computer technology, such as batch with sequential files or batch with direct access files, etc. Explain your choice of computer technology. Prepare a flowchart of the new system.

2. EXPOSE (Prepared by Jennifer Fernicola, Deloitte & Touche LLP)

EXPOSE is one of the United States' leading direct sellers of beauty and related products. All cosmetics are available in a wide range of gorgeous fashion-forward colors, incorporating state-of-the-art skin technology to help the customer best achieve a beautiful, smooth complexion.

The products are marketed and sold nationwide. Annual sales reach more than $4.5 billion. EXPOSE has over 40 retail stores and over 50,000 representatives nationwide.

EXPOSE cosmetics are sold either through the retail stores, from a local representative (usually a beauty technician at a beauty salon), or through a monthly catalog. The products are marketed as a high-quality, expensive line of cosmetics unavailable in department stores. They are, in essence, "department store makeup without having to go to the department store."

New customers are attracted to EXPOSE by the seasonal shows the company has at select locations in shopping malls, beauty salons, and its retail stores. At the shows, EXPOSE representatives demonstrate beauty techniques on models. Free makeovers and color consultations are given. Once a customer knows her color "code," she may order through a catalog with the confidence that the color of the product she is buying will match her skin tone and hair color. EXPOSE carries over 45 codes, and it is very specific for accuracy. Regular customers are sent the catalog. They can order through phone sales or an order form. They may also purchase the product from a retail store or beauty salon that carries the product line. (The beauty salons may not have all items in stock, however, and the items may have to be ordered.) The goods are typically shipped within 24 hours of receipt of the order. All representatives must go through a four-week intensive program to qualify as an EXPOSE Expert.

All raw materials are sent to the manufacturing headquarters in Whippany, New Jersey, where most of the products are produced. Other smaller plants are located in southern New Jersey and eastern Pennsylvania. The raw materials include some natural extracts such as sage and comfrey. Other raw materials are synthetic pellets produced by EXPOSE's main supplier, Crystallan. Other suppliers are fairly small and located outside of the continental United States. EXPOSE has a strong supplier relationship with Crystallan and has had no serious problems with quality or late deliveries in the past. For the past two years, Gateway Plastics has supplied the plastic pellets that EXPOSE uses to melt down and mold its packaging.

Production is based on projections of customer orders. Raw materials are shipped in batches, but are based on projected demand. For example, when EXPOSE projects a demand for 400,000 Pink Ice Lipsticks, it orders the raw materials necessary to produce that many lipsticks in that color. Four distribution centers are located across the United States.

Recently, EXPOSE's internal auditors have discovered serious flaws in the revenue cycle. Specifically, both the cash sales in the retail stores and the sales order processing of phone sales and cash receipts of credit sales appear to be in violation of SAS 78 Controls. Further, the retail stores seem to have a problem with overstocking certain inventory items and having shortages of other items. The procedures used by the 40,000 EXPOSE retail stores and the catalog sales are discussed below. (The controls for sales by the 100,000 agents operating in beauty salons are not considered to be problematic, and thus are not discussed.)

The catalog sales process of EXPOSE begins with a customer contacting the sales department by calling a toll-free number (1-800-GORGEOUS). Telephone operators assist the customers, gather the appropriate information, and prepare four-copy sales orders. Included on each sales order is the customer account number; the name, number, and description of the items sold; and the quantity and unit prices of each item sold. The sales order is sent to the credit department. Once credit is approved, the sales department is notified and sent the approved sales order and the sales order clerk, Christina, updates the sales journal. The approved sales order is filed in the sales department. Then Christina delivers three copies of the sales order to the warehouse.

When the warehouse receives the sales order copies from the credit department, the warehouse clerk, Brandon, locates and releases the inventory and also adjusts the inventory subsidiary ledger. One copy is kept in the warehouse and two copies are sent along with the goods to the shipping department. Once the shipping department receives the goods and the sales order copies from the warehouse, the shipping clerk, Jenny, draws up a shipping notice, which will inform the billing department that the customer's order has been filled and shipped. She then packages the goods and prepares a bill of lading, which is a formal contract between the seller and the shipping company that transports the goods to the customer. Jenny then transfers the custody of the goods and the bill of lading to the carrier, who then ships the goods to the customer. After recording the shipment in the shipping log, she sends the two copies of the sales orders and the shipping notice to the billing department.

Once Donna, in the billing department, receives these documents, she sends one copy of the sales order and the shipping notice to the sales department in order for them to send the billing department a sales invoice, which will serve as the customer's bill. The sales department then files a copy of the invoice, the shipping notice, and the sales order. The billing department files the other sales order in an open file. When the billing department receives the invoice from the sales department, Donna then reconciles the invoice with the sales order in the file and then sends the invoice to the customer. The sales order is then sent to accounts receivable. At the end of each day, Christina in the sales department summarizes all of the entries in the sales journal and prepares a journal voucher, which is then sent to the general ledger. Accounts receivable also updates the accounts receivable subsidiary ledger at the end of the day from the sales orders copies and sends it to the general ledger. Alex then updates the general ledger from the journal voucher and keeps the forms in a journal voucher file.

Once the mail room receives the checks and the source documents (remittance advice), the mail room clerk, Brian, records each check onto a list. The list is then filed in the mail room. Brian sends the checks and remittance advices to the accounts receivable department. The cashier in accounts receivable, Kristen, then records the cash receipts in the cash receipts journal. At the end of the week she sends the checks and a deposit slip to the bank and posts from the remittance advice and updates the subsidiary ledger. The remittance advice is then filed in accounts receivable. At the end of each week, Kristen prepares a journal voucher and a summary of the AR subsidiary accounts and sends them to the general ledger. Once the general ledger department receives these documents, Donald puts them in a file until the end of each month. When Donald receives all documents for the month, he updates the accounts receivable control and cash control accounts by using the documents received from accounts receivable. The account summary and journal voucher are then filed in Donald's desk.

The retail sales process begins when a customer brings the items she wishes to purchase up to the register. Due to the small size of the retail stores, 350 square feet, only one register is located in each store. Any one of the sales associates working at the time enters the product code number and sales price from a sticker on the item into the register. A sales associate places the stickers on the items when they are unpacked. Next, the register calculates the amount due by the customer, and either cash or credit cards are accepted. When cash is tendered, the sales associate accepts the cash and gives the customer her receipt and change. For credit sales, the credit cards are swiped through a machine and the transaction is either rejected or approved via a telecommunications link with a bank network. If approved, an approval code is recorded. A tape of all transactions entered into for the day is kept inside the cash register. At the end of the day, the manager counts the cash and credit card receipts and reconciles them with the daily sales. Any cash shortages are divided by the number of people working that day and deducted from their next paycheck. This policy is believed to be one of the reasons for the high turnover of sales associates.

The cash and credit slips are kept overnight in a safe in the back of the store. The following morning, the manager prepares a deposit slip, takes the cash and credit slips to the bank, and receives a deposit receipt, which she files. The tape totals the sales by cash and credit. Further, the register produces totals of all items sold, and these tapes are sent to corporate headquarters for inventory tracking purposes and order replenishment decisions.

Required:

a. Prepare a data flow diagram for the system described in the case.

b. Prepare a document flowchart for the system described in the case.

c. Identify the internal control weaknesses in the system. Structure your discussion around the six classes of internal control activities described in SAS 78.

d. Redesign the system to take advantage of computer technology, such as batch with sequential files or batch with direct access files, etc. Explain your choice of computer technology. Prepare a flowchart of the new system.

3. Horox, Inc. (Prepared by Megan Gillette, Lehigh University)

Horox, Inc., is a manufacturer of portable compact disc (CD) players located outside of Philadelphia, Pennsylvania. It employs 1,500 workers at a centrally located, 15-acre production facility. It distributes its products worldwide through three nearby distribution centers. Sales are currently $20 million per year and growing. Horox was formed ten years ago; its management was relatively inexperienced and their technical knowledge was lacking. Since 1995, Horox has been expanding into new research areas and in the past three years has reported enormous profits in its financial statements.

Its major competitors for the little market share they have are electronic giants. Horox has managed to edge its way into retail chains and privately owned stores through the aggressiveness and wit of its sales staff. Horox supplies the major electronic chains and department stores, requiring payment for all orders within 30 days of the order or upon receipt.

The salespersons work partly on salary. They also take home large commissions as an incentive to work hard. Since the salespersons are traveling to retailers most of the time, the purchase orders come in throughout the day over the fax machine or by telephone to Eddie in the sales department. Eddie has been with the company for a long time; he knows the sales process well and performs credit checks simultaneously with sales order processing. Once Eddie prepares copies of the sales order, he sends a copy to billing and two copies to the inventory warehouse. He files one copy.

Once the sales orders reach Rosemary in the inventory warehouse, she prepares the packing slip and collects the CD players from inventory. Rosemary then updates the inventory records and sends the merchandise, a copy of the sales order, and the packing slip to Kelly in the shipping department. She files one copy of the sales order. Once received by the shipping department, Kelly prepares two shipping notices and bills of lading.

Once the order is ready to be distributed to the customer, it is sent out with the bills of lading, shipping notice, and packing slip. Kelly files one copy of the sales order and shipping notice.

In the billing department, the sales order is processed into an invoice with prices. The remittance advice is also created. Both are sent out to the customer as a bill. The sales journal is updated by Wendy, the billing clerk. The sales department reconciles with the billing department periodically.

Once the customer receives the bill requesting payment, he or she sends a check along with the remittance advice back to the company. Here the mail room sorts the checks by company and gives the checks and remittance advices accompanying the checks to Katie, the billing department secretary. Katie updates the cash receipts journal and credits the customer's account. Katie deposits the checks in the company account at the bank. She then files the remittance advices in a file for two months, and afterwards she discards them.

Required:
a. Prepare a data flow diagram for the system described in the case.
b. Prepare a document flowchart for the system described in the case.
c. Identify the internal control weaknesses in the system. Structure your discussion around the six classes of internal control activities described in SAS 78.
d. Redesign the system to take advantage of computer technology, such as batch with sequential files or batch with direct access files, etc. Explain your choice of computer technology. Prepare a flowchart of the new system.

ACL ASSIGNMENTS

The **AR** and **Customer** files used for the following assignments are located in the **workbook.acl** document on the CD that accompanies this text. The AR file is actually an invoice file that contains several related records as designated by the Trans Type field:

IN = Sales invoice
PM = Payment from customer
CN = Credit Note (Credit Memo)
TR = Transfer (write off)

Sales invoices should be represented by positive Trans Amount values, while the other transaction types are negative.

Some of the assignments below employ the ACL's *relation* and *join* features. For detailed information on the use of these and other commands, consult ACL's on-line Help.

1. Open the **AR** file, *profile* the data, and *stratify* on the Trans Amount field. Print the Last Results window and write an analysis providing possible explanations for the results obtained.

2. Open the **AR** file, stratify the file on the Trans Amount field, and use the expression builder to create filters that limit the strata to:
   a. sales invoice transactions only
   b. credit note (memo) transactions only
   c. payment transactions only
   d. transfer (write off) transactions

3. Open the **AR** file and use the expression builder to create a filter that screens for invalid transaction types. Print the results and comment.

4. Using the *relation* feature create a view from data in both the **AR** and **Customer** files that shows customer details (**name** and **street address**) for payment transactions with abnormal (positive) amount values. Print the view and comment on the results.

5. Using the *join* feature create a view from data in both the **AR** and **Customer** files that show customer details (**name** and **address**) for payment transactions with abnormal (positive) amount values. Print the view and comment on the results.

chapter 9

AUDITING THE EXPENDITURE CYCLE

This chapter examines audit procedures associated with the expenditure cycle. The chapter is divided into three main sections. It begins with a review of computer technologies used in both legacy and modern systems. The focus is on the way that key operational tasks are performed under different technological environments. The second section discusses the expenditure cycle audit objectives, controls, and tests of controls that an auditor would normally perform to gather the evidence needed to limit the scope, timing, and extent of substantive tests. The last section describes substantive tests in relation to expenditure cycle audit objectives that can be performed using ACL software.

LEARNING OBJECTIVES

After studying this chapter, you should:

- Understand the primary tasks associated with the expenditure cycle under different levels of technology.
- Understand audit objectives related to the expenditure cycle.
- Be familiar with expenditure cycle control issues related to alternative technologies.
- Recognize the relationship between expenditure cycle audit objectives, controls, and tests of controls.
- Understand the nature of substantive tests in achieving expenditure cycle audit objectives.
- Be familiar with common features and functions of ACL that are used to perform substantive tests.

OVERVIEW OF EXPENDITURE CYCLE TECHNOLOGIES

This section examines alternative information technologies used in the expenditure cycle. The first of these is a purchases and cash system that employs batch processing and uses sequential files for storing accounting records. This is an example of an early legacy system. This approach characterizes the era of data ownership in which files were designed exclusively for the use of a single user. Data sharing is virtually impossible in this setting and results in a great deal of data redundancy and data obsolescence. Secondly, we review the operational features of a modern system that employs real-time processing and uses direct access files or databases. The final example depicts a modern payroll system that uses real-time processing and database technology.

You should recognize that space limitations prohibit a review of all possible configurations of processing technologies, techniques, and file structures. The objective, instead, is to present examples of fundamentally different approaches that are typically found in practice and examine their control and audit implications.

PURCHASES AND CASH DISBURSEMENT PROCEDURES USING BATCH PROCESSING TECHNOLOGY

Many of the manual functions in the batch system presented in Figure 9–1 are the same as those found in manual purchase systems. The principal difference is that the routine accounting tasks are automated. The following section describes the sequence of events as they occur in this system.

DATA PROCESSING DEPARTMENT: STEP 1

The purchasing process begins in the data processing department, where the inventory control function is performed. The revenue cycle (in retailing firms) or the conversion cycle (in manufacturing firms) actually initiates this activity. When inventories are reduced by sales to customers or usage in production, the system determines if the affected items in the **inventory subsidiary file** have fallen to their reorder points.[1] If so, a record is created in the open requisition file. Each record in the open requisition file defines a separate inventory item to be replenished. The record contains the inventory item number, a description of the item, the quantity to be ordered, the standard unit price, and the vendor number of the primary supplier. The information needed to create the requisition record is selected from the inventory subsidiary record. The inventory subsidiary record is then flagged "On Order" to prevent the item from being ordered again before it arrives.

At the end of the day, the system sorts the open requisition file by vendor number and consolidates multiple items from the same vendor onto a single requisition. Next, vendor mailing information is retrieved from the valid vendor file to produce purchase requisition documents. Copies of these documents go to manual procedures in the purchasing and accounts payable departments.

PURCHASING DEPARTMENT

Upon receipt of the purchase requisition, the purchasing department prepares a five-part purchase order. Copies go to the vendors, accounts payable, receiving, data processing, and the purchasing department's own file.

The system in Figure 9–1 employs manual procedures to control the ordering process. A computer program identifies inventory requirements and prepares

---

1.   This may be batch or real time, depending on the revenue and conversion cycle systems that interface with the expenditure cycle. The raw materials and finished goods inventory files link these three transaction cycles together. The design of one system influences the others. For example, if sales processing (revenue cycle) reduces inventories in real time, the system will naturally identify inventory requirements in real time also. This is true even if the purchases system is batch-oriented.

FIGURE 9–1   Batch Purchases System

FIGURE 9-1 (continued)

Data Processing Cash Disbursements System

traditional purchase requisitions, thus allowing the purchasing agent to verify the purchase transaction before placing the order. Some firms use this technique to reduce the risk of placing unnecessary orders with vendors due to a computer error. However, such manual intervention creates delays in the ordering process. If sufficient computer controls are in place to prevent or detect purchasing errors, then more efficient ordering procedures can be implemented.

Before continuing with our example, we need to discuss alternative approaches for authorizing and ordering inventories. Figure 9–2 illustrates three different methods. In *alternative one*, the system advances the procedures shown in Figure 9–1 one-step further. This system prepares the purchase order documents and sends them to the purchasing department for review and signing. The purchasing agent then mails the approved purchase orders to the vendors and distributes copies to other internal users.

The system shown in *alternative two* expedites the ordering process by distributing the purchase orders directly to the vendors and internal users, thus bypassing the purchasing department completely. This system produces a transaction list of items ordered for the purchasing agent's review.

Alternative three represents a reengineering system that uses *electronic data interchange (EDI)*. This method produces no physical documents (purchase orders or sales orders). Instead, the computer systems of both the buying and selling companies are connected via a special telecommunications link. The buyer and seller are parties in a trading partner arrangement in which the entire ordering process is automated and unimpeded by human intervention.

In each of the three alternatives, the authorization and the ordering steps in the process are consolidated and performed by the computer system. Purchase requisition documents serve no purpose in such systems and are not produced. However, requisition records may still exist on magnetic disk or tape to provide an audit trail.

DATA PROCESSING DEPARTMENT: STEP 2

Returning to Figure 9–1, the purchase order is used to create an open purchase order record and to transfer the corresponding record(s) in the open purchase requisition file to the closed purchase requisition file.

RECEIVING DEPARTMENT

When the goods arrive from vendors, the receiving clerk prepares a receiving report. Copies go to purchasing, accounts payable, and data processing.

DATA PROCESSING DEPARTMENT: STEP 3

The data processing department runs a batch job (Step 3) that updates the inventory subsidiary file from the receiving reports and removes the "On Order" flag from the inventory records. The system calculates batch totals of inventory receipts for the general ledger update procedure and then closes the corresponding records in the open purchase order file to the closed purchase order file.

ACCOUNTS PAYABLE

When the accounts payable clerk receives the supplier's invoice, he or she reconciles it with the supporting documents that were previously placed in the accounts payable pending file. The clerk then prepares a voucher, files it in the open voucher file, and sends a copy of the voucher to data processing.

FIGURE 9–2   Alternative Inventory Ordering Procedures

ALTERNATIVE ONE

ALTERNATIVE TWO

ALTERNATIVE THREE

DATA PROCESSING DEPARTMENT: STEP 4

A batch program validates the voucher records against the valid vendor file, adds them to the voucher register (or open accounts payable subsidiary file), and prepares batch totals for posting to the accounts payable control account in the general ledger.

CASH DISBURSEMENT: DATA PROCESSING DEPARTMENT

Each day, the system scans the Due Date field of the voucher register for items due. Checks are printed for these items, and each check is recorded in the check register (cash disbursements journal). The check number is recorded in the voucher register to close the voucher and transfer the items to the **closed accounts payable file**. The checks, along with a transaction listing, are sent to the cash disbursements department. Finally, batch totals of closed accounts payable and cash disbursements are prepared for the general ledger update procedure.

At the end of the day, batch totals of open (unpaid) and closed (paid) accounts payable, inventory increases, and cash disbursements are posted to the accounts payable control, inventory control, and cash accounts in the general ledger. The totals of closed accounts payable and cash disbursements should balance.

CASH DISBURSEMENT: CASH DISBURSEMENTS DEPARTMENT

The cash disbursements clerk reconciles the checks with the transaction listing and submits the negotiable portion of the checks to management for signing. The checks are then mailed to the suppliers. One copy of each check goes to accounts payable, and the other copy is filed in cash disbursements along with the transaction listing.

CASH DISBURSEMENT: ACCOUNTS PAYABLE

Upon receipt of the check copies, the accounts payable clerk matches them with open vouchers and transfers these closed items to the closed voucher file. The expenditure cycle process concludes with this step.

REENGINEERING THE PURCHASES/CASH DISBURSEMENT SYSTEM

The automated system just described simply replicates many of the procedures in a manual system. In particular, the accounts payable task of reconciling supporting documents with supplier invoices is labor intensive and costly. The following example shows how reengineering this process can produce considerable savings.

The Ford Motor Company employed over 500 clerks in its North American accounts payable department. Analysis of the function showed that a large part of their accounts payable clerks' time was devoted to reconciling discrepancies between supplier invoices, receiving reports, and purchase orders. The first step in solving the problem was to bring about fundamental changes in the business environment. Ford initiated trading partner agreements with suppliers in which they agreed in advance to terms of trade such as price, quantities to be shipped, discounts, and lead times. With these sources of discrepancy eliminated, Ford reengineered the workflow to take advantage of the new environment. The flowchart in Figure 9–3 depicts key features of a reengineered system.

FIGURE 9–3   Reengineered Purchases/Cash Disbursement System

DATA PROCESSING

The following tasks are performed automatically:

1. The inventory file is searched for items that have fallen to their reorder point.
2. A record is entered in the purchase requisition file for each item to be replenished.
3. Requisitions are then consolidated according to vendor number.
4. Vendor mailing information is retrieved from the valid vendor file.
5. Purchase orders are prepared and sent to the vendor. Alternatively, these may be transmitted using EDI technology.
6. A record of each transaction is added to the open purchase order file.
7. A transaction listing of purchase orders is sent to the purchasing department for review.

RECEIVING DEPARTMENT

When the goods arrive, the receiving clerk accesses the open purchase order file in real time by entering the purchase order number taken from the packing slip. The receiving screen, illustrated in Figure 9–4, then prompts the clerk to enter the quantities received for each item on the purchase order.

FIGURE 9–4

Receiving
Screen

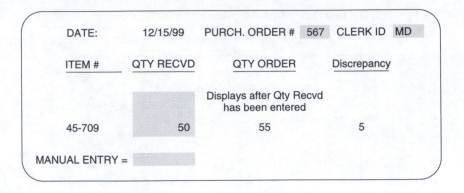

DATA PROCESSING

The following tasks are performed automatically by the system:

1. Quantities of items received are matched against the open purchase order record, and a "Y" value is placed in a logical field to indicate the receipt of inventories.
2. A record is added to the receiving report file.
3. The inventory subsidiary records are updated to reflect the receipt of the inventory items.
4. The general ledger inventory control account is updated.
5. The record is removed from the open purchase order file and added to the open accounts payable file, and a due date for payment is established.

Each day, the Due Date fields of the accounts payable records are checked for items due to be paid. The following procedures are performed for the selected items:

1. Checks are printed, signed, and distributed to the mail room for mailing to vendors. EDI vendors receive payment electronically.
2. The payments are recorded in the check register file.
3. Items paid are transferred from the open accounts payable file to the closed accounts payable file.
4. The general ledger accounts payable and cash accounts are updated.
5. Reports detailing these transactions are transmitted via terminal to the accounts payable and cash disbursements departments for management review and filing.

Since the financial information about purchases is known in advance from the trading partner agreement, the **vendor's invoice** provides no critical information that cannot be derived from the receiving report. By eliminating this source of potential discrepancy, Ford was able to eliminate the task of reconciling vendor invoices with the supporting documents for the majority of purchase transactions. As a result of its reengineering effort, the company was able to reduce its accounts payable staff from 500 to 125.

CONTROL IMPLICATIONS

The technology control issues (i.e., those pertaining to the use of sequential files versus direct access files) are general in nature. The points made in the last chapter apply to the expenditure cycle also. Therefore, let's examine only the issues specific to this cycle by focusing on the differences between an automated versus a reengineered system.

THE AUTOMATED SYSTEM

Improved Inventory Control.   The greatest advantage of the automated (batch) system over its manual counterpart is its improved ability to manage inventory needs. Inventory requirements are detected as they arise and are processed automatically. As a result, the risks of accumulating excessive inventory or of running out of stock are reduced. However, with this advantage comes a control concern. Authorization rules governing purchase transactions are consolidated within a computer program. Program errors or flawed inventory models can cause firms to be suddenly inundated with inventories or desperately short of stock. Therefore, it is extremely important to monitor automated decisions. A well-controlled system will provide management with adequate summary reports on inventory purchases, inventory turnover, spoilage, and slow-moving items.

Better Cash Management.   This type of system promotes effective cash management by scanning the voucher file daily for items due, thus avoiding early payments and missed due dates. In addition, by writing checks automatically, the firm reduces labor cost, saves processing time, and promotes accuracy.

As a control against unauthorized payments, comparing the vendor number on the voucher with a valid vendor file validates all entries in the voucher file. If the vendor number is not on file, the record is presumed to be invalid and is diverted to an error file for management review.

In this system, a manager in the cash disbursements department physically signs the checks, thus providing control over the disbursement of cash. However, many computer systems automate check signing with special printing equipment, which is more efficient when check volume is high but relinquishes some control. To offset this exposure, firms often set a materiality threshold for check writing. Checks for amounts below the threshold are signed automatically, and an authorized manager or the treasurer signs those above the threshold.

Time Lag.   A lag exists between the arrival of goods in the receiving department and recording inventory receipts in the inventory file. Depending on the type of sales order system in place, this lag may affect sales negatively. Because of this time lag, sales clerks will not know the current status of inventory, and sales may be lost.

Purchasing Bottleneck.   In this hypothetical batch system, the purchasing department is directly involved with all purchase decisions. For many firms, this creates additional work that extends the time lag in the ordering process. A vast number of routine purchases could be automated. By freeing purchasing agents from routine work, such as preparing purchase orders and mailing them to the vendors, attention can be focused on problem orders (such as special items or those in short supply), and the purchasing staff can be reduced.

Excessive Paper Documents.   The basic batch system is laden with paper documents. All operations departments create documents, which are sent to data processing and which data processing must then convert to magnetic media. A number of costs are associated with paper documents, since the paper must be purchased and the documents filed, stored, handled by internal mail carriers, and converted by data processing personnel. Organizations with high volumes of transactions benefit considerably from reducing or eliminating paper documents in their systems.

THE REENGINEERED SYSTEM.   This system addresses many of the operational weaknesses found in the basic batch system. Specifically, the improvements in this system are that (1) it uses real-time procedures and direct-access files to shorten the lag time in record-keeping; (2) it eliminates routine manual procedures through automating; and (3) it achieves a significant reduction in paper documents by using electronic communications between departments and by storing records on direct-access media. These operational improvements, however, carry control implications.

Segregation of Duties. This system removes the fundamental separation between authorization and transaction processing. Here, computer programs authorize and process purchase orders and authorize and issue checks to vendors. To compensate for this exposure, the system needs to provide management with detailed transaction listings and summary reports. These documents describe the automated actions taken by the system and allow management to spot errors and any unusual events that warrant investigation.

Accounting Records and Access Controls. This system maintains accounting records exclusively on magnetic disks. To preserve the integrity of these records, the organization must implement controls that limit access to the disks. Unauthorized access to magnetic records carries the same consequences as access to source documents, journals, and ledgers in a manual environment. Organizations can employ a number of physical and software techniques to provide adequate access control. However, keep in mind that some techniques are costly, and management must justify these costs against their expected benefits.

OVERVIEW OF PAYROLL PROCEDURES

Payroll processing is actually a special expenditure system. In theory, payroll checks could be processed through the regular accounts payable and cash disbursements system. However, as a practical matter, this approach would have a number of drawbacks, including:

1. A firm can design general expenditure procedures that apply to all vendors. However, payroll procedures differ greatly between classes of employees. For example, different procedures are used for hourly employees, salaried employees, piece workers, and commissioned employees. Also, payroll processing requires special accounting procedures for employee deductions and withholdings for taxes. Cash disbursements for trade accounts do not require special processing. Therefore, general expenditure systems are not designed to deal with these complications.
2. Writing checks to employees requires special controls. It is easier to conceal payroll fraud when payroll checks are combined with trade account checks.
3. General expenditure procedures are designed to accommodate a relatively smooth flow of transactions. Business enterprises are constantly purchasing inventories and disbursing funds to vendors. Naturally, they design systems to deal adequately with their normal level of transaction activity. Payroll activities are discrete rather than continuous. Disbursements to employees occur weekly, biweekly, or monthly. To periodically impose this processing burden on the general system may have an overwhelming peak-load effect.

Because payroll systems run infrequently (weekly or monthly), they are often well suited to batch processing and sequential files. Figure 9–5 shows a flowchart for such a system. The data processing department receives the personnel action forms and time cards, which it converts to sequential files. Batch computer programs perform the detailed record-keeping, check-writing, and general ledger functions.

FIGURE 9-5 Batch Payroll System with Sequential Files

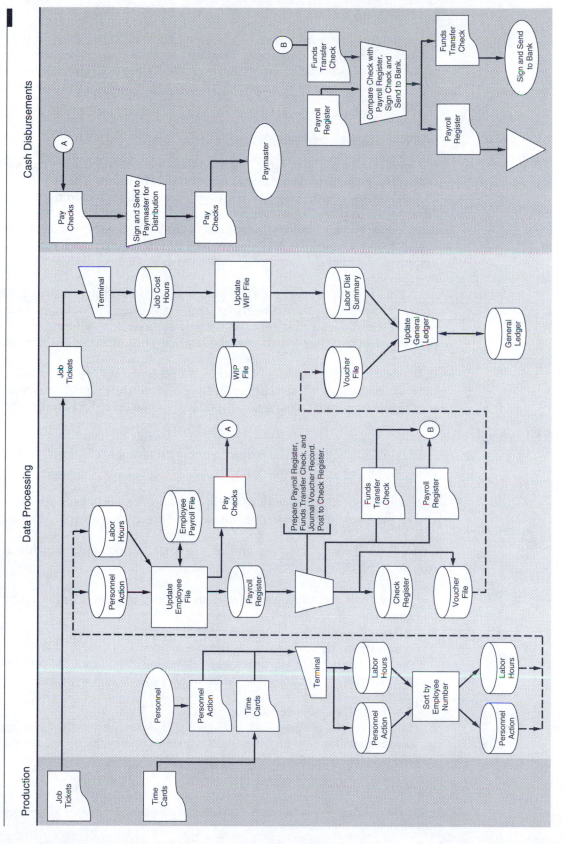

CONTROL IMPLICATIONS

The strengths and weaknesses of this system are similar to those in the batch system for general expenditures discussed earlier. This system promotes accounting accuracy and reduces check-writing errors. Beyond this, it does not significantly enhance operational efficiency; however, for many types of organizations, this level of technology is adequate.

REENGINEERING THE PAYROLL SYSTEM

For moderate-sized and large organizations, payroll processing is often integrated within the **human resource management (HRM) system**. The HRM system captures and processes a wide range of personnel-related data, including employee benefits, labor resource planning, employee relations, employee skills, personnel actions (pay rates, deductions, and so on), as well as payroll. HRM systems must support real-time access to personnel files for purposes of direct inquires and recording changes in employee status as they occur. Figure 9–6 illustrates a payroll system as part of an HRM system.

This system differs from the simple automated system above in the following ways: (1) operations departments transmit transactions to data processing via terminals, (2) direct access files are used for data storage, and (3) many processes are now performed in real time. We discuss the key operating features of this system below.

PERSONNEL.   The personnel department makes changes to the employee file in real time via terminals. These changes include additions of new employees, deletions of terminated employees, changes in dependents, changes in withholding, and changes in job status (pay rate).

COST ACCOUNTING.   The cost accounting department enters job cost data (real time or daily) to create the **labor usage file**.

TIMEKEEPING.   Upon receipt of the approved time cards from the supervisor at the end of the week, the timekeeping department creates the current **attendance file**.

DATA PROCESSING.   At the end of the work period, the following tasks are performed in a batch process:

1.   Labor costs are distributed to various work-in-process, overhead, and expense accounts.
2.   An on-line labor distribution summary file is created. Copies of the file go to the cost accounting and general ledger departments.
3.   An on-line payroll register is created from the attendance file and the **employee file**. Copies of the files go to the accounts payable and cash disbursements departments.
4.   The employee records file is updated.
5.   Payroll checks are prepared and signed. They are sent to the treasurer for review and reconciliation with the payroll register. The paychecks are then distributed to the employees.[2]

---

2.   For added internal control, many companies encourage their employees to have their checks directly deposited in their bank accounts.

FIGURE 9-6 Payroll System with Real-Time Elements

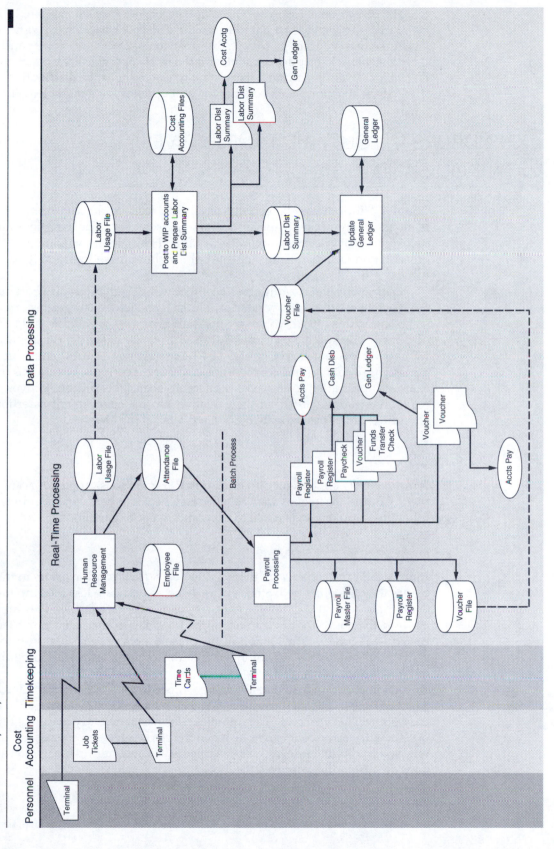

6. The disbursement voucher file is updated and a check is prepared for the funds transfer to the imprest payroll account. The check and a hard copy of the disbursement voucher go to cash disbursements. One copy of the voucher goes to the general ledger department, and the final copy goes to accounts payable.

7. At the end of processing, the system retrieves the labor distribution summary file and the disbursements voucher file and updates the general ledger file.

EXPENDITURE CYCLE AUDIT OBJECTIVES, CONTROLS, AND TESTS OF CONTROLS

Chapter 1 introduced the concept of audit objectives derived from general management assertions about financial statement presentation. The assertions are existence or occurrence, completeness, accuracy, rights and obligations, valuation or allocation, and presentation and disclosure. Table 9-1 shows how these translate to specific expenditure cycle audit objectives.[3]

Achieving these audit objectives requires designing audit procedures to gather evidence that either corroborates or refutes management assertions. As we saw in the last chapter, this often involves a combination of tests of controls and substantive tests of details. The specific controls addressed here are based on the application controls framework presented in Chapter 6, which classifies controls into three broad categories: input controls, process controls, and output controls. Within this framework, we examine application controls, tests of controls, and the audit objectives to which they relate. Substantive tests and their relationship to management assertions and corresponding audit objectives are considered later in the chapter.

INPUT CONTROLS

Input controls are designed to ensure that transactions are valid, accurate, and complete. Control techniques vary considerably between batch and real-time systems. The following input controls relate to expenditure cycle operations.

DATA VALIDATION CONTROLS

Input validation controls are intended to detect transcription errors in transaction data before they are processed. Since errors detected early are less likely to infiltrate the accounting records, validation procedures are most effective when they are performed as close to the source of the transaction as possible. In the batch purchases system depicted in Figure 9–1, validation of purchase orders occurs only after they have been sent to the vendor. Because of inevitable transcription errors that occur in preparation of source documents, such systems are characterized by the need for extensive error correction and transaction resubmission procedures. On the other hand, the real-time input of time-card data illustrated in Figure 9–6 can identify and resolve most errors as they occur. This approach also minimizes human data entry and thus reduces the risk of data entry errors. For example, when the clerk enters the employee number, the system automatically retrieves his or her name, mailing address, pay rate, and other relevant data from the employee file.

---

3.   Adapted from *Montgomery's Auditing*, 12th ed. (New York: Cooper's & Lybrand, L.L.P., 1998), p. 18-4.

TABLE 9-1

Relationship between Management Assertions and Expenditure Cycle Audit Objectives

Management Assertions	Expenditure Cycle Audit Objectives
Existence or Occurrence	Verify that the accounts payable balance represents amounts actually owed by the organization at the balance sheet date.
	Establish that purchases transactions represent goods and services actually received during the period covered by the financial statements.
	Determine that payroll transactions represent wages for services actually performed during the period covered by the financial statements.
Completeness	Determine that accounts payable represent all amounts owed by the organization for purchases of goods and services as of the balance sheet date.
	Ensure that the financial statements reflect all goods and services received by the organization, less returns, for the period covered.
	Verify that the financial statements reflect all wages for services performed during the period covered.
Accuracy	Establish that purchases transactions are accurately computed and based on correct prices and correct quantities.
	Ensure that the accounts payable subsidiary ledger is mathematically correct and agrees with the general ledger accounts.
	Verify that payroll amounts are based on correct pay rates and hours worked and are accurately computed.
Rights and Obligations	Establish that the accounts payable and accrued payroll recorded at the balance sheet date are legal obligations of the organization.
Valuation or Allocation	Verify that accounts payable are stated at correct amounts owed.
Presentation and Disclosure	Ensure that accounts payable, accrued payroll, and expenses reported for the period are properly described and classified in the financial statements.

Chapter 6 presented a number of general types of validation tests. Examples that are relevant to the expenditure cycle are reviewed below.

Missing data checks are used to examine the contents of a field for the presence of blank spaces. An employee number missing from an attendance record, the quantity-received value missing from a receiving report, or an incomplete mailing address in a purchase order record will cause the transaction to be rejected. When the validation program detects a blank where it expects to see a data value, this will be interpreted as an error.

Numeric-alphabetic data checks determine whether the correct form of data is in a field. For example, the quantity field in a purchase order should not contain alphabetic data. As with blanks, alphabetic data in a numeric field may cause serious processing errors.

Limit checks determine if the value in the field exceeds an authorized limit. For example, if the firm has a policy that no employee works more than 44 hours per week, the payroll system validation program can interrogate the hours-worked field in the weekly payroll records for values greater than 44.

Range checks assign upper and lower limits to acceptable data values. This technique can be used to control orders placed with vendors. For example, a range of 500

to 1,000 units can be set as the normal order quantity for a particular class of product. A range check is also useful for controlling payroll transactions. If the range of pay rates for hourly employees in a firm is between 8 and 20 dollars, all payroll records can be checked to see that this range is not exceeded. The purpose of this control is to detect keystroke errors that shift the decimal point one or more places. It would not detect an error where a correct pay rate of, say, 9 dollars is incorrectly entered as 15 dollars.

Validity checks compare actual values in a field against known acceptable values. This control is used to verify such things as state abbreviations or employee job skill codes. If the value in the field does not match one of the acceptable values, the record is determined to be in error.

Check digit controls identify keystroke errors in key fields by testing their internal validity. A check digit could be used to verify a vendor number on a purchase order record.

TESTING VALIDATION CONTROLS.   Data entry errors that slip through edit programs undetected can cause recorded accounts payable and expense amounts to be materially misstated. The audit procedures described below provide evidence about the *accuracy* assertion.

The central audit issue is whether the validation programs in the data editing system are functioning correctly and have functioned as intended throughout the period. Testing the logic of a validation program, however, represents a significant undertaking. The auditor may decide to rely on the quality of other controls to provide the assurance needed to reduce substantive testing. For example, after reviewing systems development and maintenance controls, the auditor may determine that controls over original program design and testing and subsequent changes to programs are effective. This evidence permits the auditor to assess the risk of material program errors at a low level and thus reduce the substantive tests related to the audit objective of accuracy.

If controls over systems development and maintenance are weak, however, the auditor may decide that testing data editing controls will be more efficient that performing extensive substantive tests of details. In such a case, ITF or the test data approach can enable the auditor to perform explicit tests of the validation logic. This would require the auditor to gain a familiarity with all of the validation procedures in place. The auditor would need to create a comprehensive set of test transactions that include both valid and erroneous data values that fall within and outside of the test parameters. An analysis of the test results will show the auditor which types of errors, if any, can pass undetected by the validation program. This evidence will help the auditor determine the nature, timing, and extent of subsequent substantive tests.

In addition to direct testing of program logic, the auditor can achieve some degree of assurance by reviewing error listings and error logs. These documents provide evidence of the effectiveness of the data entry process, the types and volume of errors encountered, and the manner in which the errors are corrected and reentered into the system. Recall from the last chapter that error listings and logs do not provide evidence of undetected errors. An analysis of error conditions not present in the listing can, however, guide the auditor in designing substantive tests to perform. For example, assume that the error listing of the purchase order file contains no order-quantity range errors. This may simply mean that data entry personnel are skilled and no transcription errors of that sort occurred. On the other hand, it may mean that the validation program does not test for this type of error. To determine whether material order-quantity discrepancies existed, the auditor can perform substantive tests that compare the actual quantity ordered on purchase orders with the order-quantity data stored in the inventory records.

BATCH CONTROLS

Batch controls are used to manage high volumes of transaction data through a system. The objective of batch control is to reconcile output produced by the system with the input originally entered into the system. Batch control is initiated at the data input stage and continues through all phases of data processing. For example, a batch of supplier invoices enters the system at the data entry stage; after each subsequent processing stage, the batch is reviewed for completeness.

The information contained in the transmittal sheet is entered as a separate control record that the system uses to verify the integrity of the batch. Periodic reconciliation between the data in the transmittal record and actual processing results provides assurance that:

- All invoices that were entered into the system were processed.
- No invoices were processed and paid more than once.
- All invoices entered into the system are accounted for as either successfully processed or rejected because of errors.

TESTING BATCH CONTROLS.   The failure of batch controls to function properly can result in records being lost or processed multiple times. Tests of batch controls provide the auditor with evidence relating to the assertions of *completeness* and *accuracy*.

Testing batch controls involves reviewing transmittal records of batches processed throughout the period and reconciling them to the batch control log. The auditor needs to investigate out-of-balance conditions to determine their cause. For example, assume that the transmittal record for a batch of supplier invoices shows that 100 records with an invoice total of $285,458.86 entered the system. The completed batch log, however, shows that 101 records were processed with a batch total of $288,312.50. What caused this? Did the system process one record twice, due to a programming error? Was an extra record entered into the system during processing? Did the data entry clerk incorrectly calculate the batch control totals? By reviewing and reconciling transaction listings and error logs, the auditor should be able to obtain answers to these questions.

PURCHASES AUTHORIZATION CONTROLS

Purchases authorization actually occurs in the revenue cycle when goods are sold to customers. At that time, the system compares the quantity on hand with the reorder point to determine if the inventory needs to be reordered. If so, a purchases requisition for the standard order quantity is created and the item is flagged "On Order" to prevent subsequent orders from being placed. In the expenditure cycle, the purchase requisition file is sorted by vendor number and purchases orders are then prepared.

TESTING PURCHASES AUTHORIZATION CONTROLS.   Incorrectly functioning purchase authorization controls can cause unnecessary and incorrect orders to be placed with vendors. The following tests of controls provide evidence pertaining to the *accuracy* and *valuation* assertions.

Since purchase requisitions are internally generated, they should be free from clerical errors and do not need validating. However, computer logic errors in this procedure can cause negative operational and financial consequences that may go undetected. Two concerns are of particular importance. First, the auditor needs to verify that the correct order quantity is used when a requisition is created. Errors in programming logic (or data entry) may cause an intended order quantity of 1,000 to be recorded as

100 or 10,000. This sort of error can result in unanticipated stock-outs, excessive ordering costs, or overinvestment in inventory. Second, the auditor should verify that the inventory record is flagged "On Order" when a requisition is first prepared. Failure to do so will result in overinvestment in inventory due to multiple orders being placed for the same item. Testing these controls using CAATTs involves creating test inventory records and sales transactions that reduce the inventory items below their reorder point. The resulting purchase requisitions and inventory records can then be examined for evidence of properly functioning controls.

EMPLOYEE AUTHORIZATION

The personnel department prepares and submits personnel action forms to the payroll department. These documents are used to affect changes in hourly pay rates, payroll deductions, and job classification. They also identify employees who are authorized to receive a paycheck. This information plays an important role in preventing errors and payroll fraud. A common form of fraud is to submit time cards on behalf of employees who are not employed by the firm. To prevent this, someone in the payroll department should be designated to compare time cards with the list of unauthorized employees sent from personnel.

When employee authorization procedures are computerized, the payroll program matches each attendance record with a corresponding record in the current personnel action file. Any attendance records that do not match should be rejected and investigated by management.

TESTING EMPLOYEE AUTHORIZATION PROCEDURES. Failure to implement employee authorization procedures can result in payroll distributions to unauthorized individuals. The tests of controls described below provide evidence pertaining to the *existence, accuracy, valuation*, and *rights and obligation* assertions.

The auditor needs to determine that effective procedures exist in the personnel department to identify current employees, communicate their status completely and correctly to the payroll function, and monitor adherence to employee authorization procedures. Using either the test data or integrated test facility (ITF) approaches, the auditor can assess the correctness of programmed procedures that validate employee authenticity. This involves creating a dummy authorized employee file and a corresponding attendance file containing both records that match and some that do not. The auditor can analyze the processing results to determine if the payroll application correctly identified and rejected the invalid transactions.

The integrity of standing data is an important consideration in the preceding test. A correctly functioning payroll application cannot successfully validate payroll transactions if the authorized employee file is itself invalid. The auditor can obtain assurance that the file has integrity when following controls exist: access to the authorized employee file is password controlled; additions to and deletions from the file are restricted to authorized individuals in the personnel department; and the employee records stored on the file are encrypted.

PROCESS CONTROLS

Process controls include computerized procedures for file updating and restricting access to data. Depending on the level of computer technology in place, process controls may also include physical controls associated with manual activities. We begin by examining three control techniques related to file updating. Access and physical controls are examined later.

FILE UPDATE CONTROLS

Run-to-run controls use batch control data discussed in the previous section to monitor the batch as it moves from one programmed procedure (run) to another. These controls ensure that each run in the system processes the batch correctly and completely. After each major operation, key fields such as invoice amount and record counts are accumulated and compared to the corresponding values stored in the transmittal record. A discrepancy may indicate that a record was lost in processing, a record in the batch went unprocessed, or a record was processed more than once.

SEQUENCE CHECK CONTROL.   In systems that use sequential master files, the order of the transaction records in the batch is critical to correct and complete processing. As the batch moves through the process, it must be re-sorted in the order of the master file used in each run. An out-of-sequence supplier's invoice record in a batch will prevent other downstream records from being processed. In more serious cases, the downstream records may be processed against the wrong suppliers' accounts. A sequence check control needs to be in place to compare the sequence of each record in the batch with the previous record to ensure that proper sorting took place. Out-of-sequence records should be rejected and resubmitted, thus allowing the other records in the batch to be processed.

LIABILITY VALIDATION CONTROL.   An important control in purchases/accounts payable systems is the validation of the liability prior to making payment. The process involves reconciling supporting documents including the purchase order, receiving report, and supplier's invoice. When these documents agree as to the items and quantities ordered and received, and the prices charged match the expected prices, then a liability (account payable) should be recognized and recorded. At a future date, cash will be disbursed to pay the liability.

In business environments where discrepancies in prices charged and quantities received are commonplace, the validation process is difficult to automate. Programmed decision rules must be implemented to accept less-than-perfect matches between supporting documents. For example, the system may be designed to accept invoice prices that are within 5 percent of expected prices. Discrepancies in the items and quantities ordered and received, however, are more difficult to resolve. Dealing with these problems often requires reordering inventory and/or making adjustments to accounts payable records. In this type of business setting, many organizations employ manual procedures for reconciling supporting documents and validating the liability.

Trading partner relationships (such as the Ford example described earlier) stabilize the business environment and permit organizations to depart from traditional accounting procedures. Since prices, quantities, and product quality are guaranteed by the trading partner agreement, the liability validation process can be greatly simplified and automated. For example, matching the receiving report to the original purchase order is all that is necessary to establish the liability.

VALID VENDOR FILE.   The **valid vendor file** is similar to the authorized employee file discussed earlier. This file consists of a list of vendors with whom the organization normally does business. Fraudulent transactions in the expenditure cycle often culminate in a payment to someone posing as a legitimate vendor. Before payment, the recipient of the cash disbursement should be validated against the valid vendor file. Any record that does not match should be rejected and investigated by management.

TESTING FILE UPDATE CONTROLS.   Failure of file update controls to function properly can result in transactions (1) not being processed (liabilities are not recognized and recorded), (2) being processed incorrectly (i.e., payments are approved for unauthorized recipients), or (3) being posted to the wrong supplier's account. Tests of file update controls provide the auditor with evidence relating to the management assertions of *existence, completeness, rights and obligations*, and *accuracy*.

Tests of sequence checks can be performed using either ITF or the test data approach. The auditor should create test data that contain records that are out of sequence in the batch and verify that each was handled correctly. In addition, the auditor needs to verify the mathematical correctness of the procedure. For example, a receiving report record of 1,000 units of product costing $10,000 should increase the quantity-on-hand of that inventory item by 1,000 units and increase its total carrying value by $10,000. Similarly, a payroll record of $1,000 updating an employee's year-to-date earnings record of $10,000 should produce a new balance of $11,000.

Testing the liability validation logic requires understanding the decision rule for matching supporting documents. By creating test purchase orders, receiving reports, and supplier invoices, the auditor can verify whether decision rules are being correctly applied. Similarly, the ITF and test data methods can be used to test the effectiveness of valid vendor control. This involves creating a reference file of valid vendors and a file of supplier invoices (accounts payable) to be paid. Invoice records with vendor numbers that do not match to a valid vendor record should be rejected by the program and passed to an error file for management review.

The efficient use of logic-testing CAATTs such as ITF requires determining in advance the input and process controls to be tested. A single audit procedure can be devised that performs many or all of the needed tests. For example, when testing payroll, a single transaction that tests employee authorization controls, sequence checks, and mathematical accuracy can provide evidence that supports multiple audit objectives.

ACCESS CONTROLS

Access controls prevent and detect unauthorized and illegal access to the firm's assets. Inventories and cash are the physical assets of the expenditure cycle. Traditional techniques used to limit access to these assets include:

- Warehouse security, such as fences, alarms, and guards.
- Moving assets promptly from the receiving dock to the warehouse.
- Paying employees by check rather than cash.

Controlling access to accounting records is no less important. An individual with unrestricted access to data can manipulate the physical assets of the firm and cause financial statements to be materially misstated. Accounting files stored on magnetic media are particularly vulnerable to unauthorized access, whether its cause is accidental, an act of malice by a disgruntled employee, or an attempt at fraud. The following are examples of risks specific to the expenditure cycle:

1. An individual with access to the AP subsidiary ledger (and supporting documents) could add his or her account (or someone else's) to the file. Once recognized by the system as a legitimate liability, the account will be paid even though no purchase transaction transpired.
2. Access to employee attendance cards may enable an unauthorized individual to trigger an unauthorized paycheck.
3. An individual with access to both cash and accounts payable records could remove cash from the firm and record the act as a legitimate disbursement.

4. An individual with access to physical inventory and inventory records can steal products and adjust the records to cover the theft.

TESTING ACCESS CONTROLS.   Access control lies at the heart of accounting information integrity. In the absence of adequate controls, supplier invoices can be deleted, added, or falsified. Individual payroll account balances can be erased or the entire accounts payable file can be destroyed. Evidence gathered about the effectiveness of access controls tests the management assertions of *existence, completeness, accuracy, valuation and allocation, rights and obligations*, and *presentation and disclosure*.

Since payments to false vendors carries such potential for material loss, the auditor is concerned about the integrity of the valid vendor file. By gaining access to the file, a computer criminal can place his or her name on it and masquerade as an authorized vendor. The auditor should therefore assess the adequacy of access controls protecting the file. These include password controls, restricting access to authorized managers, and using data encryption to prevent the file contents from being read or changed.

As discussed in previous chapters, computer access controls are both system-wide and application-specific. Access control includes controlling access to the operating systems, the networks, and the databases with which all applications interact. The auditors will typically test these controls as part of their review of general controls.

PHYSICAL CONTROLS

Physical controls include manual activities and human actions to initiate computer procedures to safeguard the assets of the organization. The relevant physical controls for the *purchases* and *payroll* systems follow.

PURCHASES SYSTEM CONTROLS

Segregation of Inventory Control from the Warehouse.   The primary assets at risk in the expenditure cycle are inventory and cash. Warehouse clerks responsible for asset custody should not be given responsibility for maintaining inventory records. Otherwise, inventory could be removed from the warehouse and the accounting records adjusted to conceal the event.

Segregation of the General Ledger and Accounts Payable from Cash Disbursements. An individual with the combined responsibilities of writing checks, posting to the cash account, and maintaining accounts payable could perpetrate fraud against the firm. An individual with such access could withdraw cash and then adjust the cash account accordingly to hide the transaction. Also, he or she could establish fraudulent accounts payable (to an associate in a nonexistent vendor company) and then write checks to discharge the phony obligations. By segregating these functions, the organization's management can greatly reduce this exposure.

Supervision of Receiving Department.   Large quantities of valuable assets flow through the receiving department on their way to the warehouse. Close supervision here reduces the chances of two types of exposure: (1) failure to properly inspect the assets and (2) the theft of assets.

Inspection of Assets.   When goods arrive from the supplier, receiving clerks must inspect items for proper quantities and condition (damage, spoilage, and so on). For this reason, the receiving clerk receives a blind copy of the original purchase order from purchasing. A blind purchase order has all the relevant information about the goods being received except for the quantities and prices. To obtain the information on quantities, which is needed for the receiving report, the receiving personnel are forced to physically count and inspect the goods. If receiving clerks were provided with quantity information through formal documentation (that is, the purchase order), they may be tempted to transfer this information to the receiving report without performing a physical count. Inspecting and counting the items received protects the firm from incomplete orders and damaged goods. Supervision is critical at this point to ensure that the clerks properly carry out these important duties. Incoming goods are accompanied by a packing slip containing quantity information that could be used to circumvent the inspection process. A supervisor should take custody of the packing slip while receiving clerks count and inspect the goods.

Theft of Assets.   Receiving departments are sometimes hectic and cluttered during busy periods. In this environment, incoming inventories are exposed to theft until they are securely placed in the warehouse. Improper inspection procedures coupled with inadequate supervision can create a situation that is conducive to the theft of inventories in transit.

Reconciliation of Supporting Documents.   The accounts payable department plays a vital role in controlling the disbursement of cash to vendors. Copies of supporting documents flow into this department for review and comparison. Each document contains unique facts about the purchase transaction, which the accounts payable clerk needs to verify before the obligation is recognized. These include:

1. The purchase order, which shows that the purchasing agent ordered only the needed inventories from a valid vendor.[4]
2. The receiving report, which is evidence of the physical receipt of the goods, their condition, and the quantities received. The reconciliation of this document with the purchase order signifies the point of realization of the obligation.
3. The supplier's invoice, which provides the financial information needed to record this obligation as an account payable. The accounts payable clerk verifies that the prices on the invoice are reasonable (in compliance with organizational policy) compared with the expected prices stated on the purchase order.

PAYROLL SYSTEM CONTROLS

Verification of Time Cards.   The **time card** is the formal record of daily attendance. Each day at the beginning of the shift, employees place their time cards in a special clock that records arrival. They "clock out" for their lunch period and at the end of the shift. Before sending time cards to payroll, the supervisor must verify their accuracy and sign them.

Supervision.   Sometimes an employee will "clock in" for another worker who is late or absent. Supervisors should observe the clocking process and reconcile the time cards with actual attendance.

---

4.   Firms often establish a list of valid vendors with whom they do regular business. Purchasing agents must acquire inventories only from valid vendors. This technique deters certain types of fraud such as an agent buying from suppliers with whom he or she has a relationship (a relative or friend) or buying at excessive prices from vendors in exchange for a kickback or bribe.

Paymaster.   The use of an independent **paymaster** to distribute checks (rather than the normal supervisor) helps verify the existence of the employees. This is useful in uncovering a fraud whereby the supervisor is pretending to distribute paychecks to nonexistent employees.

Payroll Imprest Account.   Employee paychecks are drawn on a special **payroll imprest** bank account, which is used only for payroll. Funds must be transferred from the general cash account to this imprest account before the paychecks can be cashed. The amount of the funds transfer is determined from the payroll register, which is reviewed for correctness and approved by accounts payable. The imprest account technique physically limits the organization's exposure. Individual checks that exceed the imprest amount will not clear. This will expose the existence of checks written in error (duplicates) or created through fraudulent activities.

TESTING PHYSICAL CONTROLS.   Inadequate segregation of duties and lack of supervision can result in fraud and errors that can cause financial statements to be materially misstated. The exposure issues here are similar to the access control issues discussed earlier. Granting inappropriate access privileges is often due to assigning incompatible duties to an individual. Similarly, the purpose of collusion is to achieve unauthorized access to assets as well as the information needed to conceal the crime. Evidence gathered by reviewing the segregation of duties can be used to test *all* of the management assertions outlined in Table 9–1.

The auditor's review of organizational structure should disclose the more egregious examples of incompatible tasks, such as one individual opening and approving time cards, authorizing employee payments, and receiving and distributing the paychecks. Covert relationships that may lead to collusion may not be apparent from an organizational chart. For example, married employees (or other relations) who work in incompatible areas may go unnoticed. The auditor should determine whether the organization has an effective policy for dealing with nepotism.

Many tasks that are normally segregated in manual systems are consolidated in the data processing function of computer-based systems. Computer programs in the expenditure cycle authorize purchases, place orders, update inventory records, approve payments to vendors, and write the checks. In automated environments, the auditor's concern should focus on the integrity of the computer programs that perform these tasks. The following questions need to be answered: Is the logic of the computer program correct? Has anyone tampered with the application since it was last tested? Have changes been made to the program that could have caused an undisclosed error?

Answers to these questions come from the auditor's review of systems development and maintenance controls and by reviewing organizational structure. Recall from earlier chapters that duties pertaining to the design, maintenance, and operation of computer programs need to be separated. Programmers who write the original computer programs should not be responsible for making program changes. Also, individuals who operate the computer system should not perform systems design, programming, or maintenance activities. Personal relationships (i.e., marriage) between individuals in these incompatible areas may require further investigation.

OUTPUT CONTROLS

Output controls are designed to ensure that information is not lost, misdirected, or corrupted and that system processes function as intended. For example, daily summaries of cash disbursements to vendors and inventory receipts should go to managers to report the status of their operations. Output control can be designed to identify operational and internal control problems. For example, an exception report derived from the Suppliers Invoice (accounts payable) file listing past-due liabilities can identify discounts lost and help management assess the operational performance of the accounts payable process. Output, however, is not limited to end-of-day reporting. System output is also needed at intermediate junctures where processing accuracy can be reviewed and verified and errors can be detected quickly and corrected.

Reconciling the general ledger can detect certain types of transaction processing errors. For example, the total of all reductions to accounts payable should equal the total cash disbursements to vendors. A cash disbursement that is entered in the journal but not posted to the vendor's account would be detected by an imbalance in the general ledger. The specific cause of an out-of-balance condition may not be apparent at this point, but the error would be noted. Finding the error may require examining all the transactions processed during the period and could be time-consuming. For this reason, rather than summarizing an entire day's transactions in a single batch, entities often group transactions into small batches of 50 to 100 items. This facilitates reconciling balances by isolating a problem to a specific batch.

Another important element of output control is the maintenance of an audit trail. Details of transaction processing produced at intermediate points can provide an audit trail that reflects activity through every stage of operations. The following are examples of audit trail output controls.

ACCOUNTS PAYABLE CHANGE REPORT

This is a summary report that shows the overall change to accounts payable. These figures should reconcile with total vendor invoices received, total cash disbursements, and the general ledger.

TRANSACTION LOGS

Every transaction successfully processed by the system should be recorded on a **transaction log**, which serves as a journal. Transactions rejected because of input errors should be placed in an error file, corrected, and resubmitted. The transaction log and error files together thus account for all economic activity.

TRANSACTION LISTINGS

The system should produce a (hard copy) **transaction listing** of all successful transactions. Listings should go to the appropriate users to facilitate reconciliation with input. For example, a listing of cash disbursements processed will go to the controller to be used for the bank reconciliation.

LOG OF AUTOMATIC TRANSACTIONS

Some transactions are triggered internally by the system. For example, EDI purchase orders are initiated and processed without human authorization. To maintain an audit trail of these activities, all internally generated transactions must be placed in a transaction log, and a listing of these transactions should be sent to the appropriate manager.

UNIQUE TRANSACTION IDENTIFIERS

Each transaction processed by the system must be uniquely identified with a transaction number. This is the only practical means of tracing a particular transaction through a database of thousands or even millions of records. In systems that use physical purchase orders, the unique number printed on the document can be transcribed during data input and used for this purpose. In real-time systems, which do not use source documents, each purchase order should be assigned a unique number by the system.

ERROR LISTING

A listing of all error records should go to the appropriate user to support error correction and resubmission.

TESTING OUTPUT CONTROLS

The absence of adequate output controls has adverse implications for operational efficiency and financial reporting. Evidence gathered through tests of output controls relates to the *completeness* and *accuracy* assertions.

Testing output controls involves reviewing summary reports for accuracy, completeness, timeliness, and relevance to the decision that they are intended to support. In addition, the auditor should trace sample transactions through audit trail reports, including transaction listings, error logs, and logs of resubmitted records. Gathering such evidence, however, may involve sorting through thousands of transactions.

In modern systems, audit trails are usually stored on-line as text files that can be read by word processing and spreadsheet programs. Data extraction CAATTs such as ACL are capable of searching log files for specific records to verify completeness and accuracy of the output reports. Alternatively, the auditor can test output controls directly using ITF. A well-designed ITF system will permit the auditor to produce a batch of sample transactions, including some error records, and trace them through all phases of processing, error detection, and output reporting.

SUBSTANTIVE TESTS OF EXPENDITURE CYCLE ACCOUNTS

This section deals with the substantive tests that an auditor may perform to achieve audit objectives related to the expenditure cycle. The strategy used in determining the nature, timing, and extent of substantive tests derives from the auditor's assessment of inherent risk, unmitigated control risk, materiality considerations, and the need to conduct the audit in an efficient manner.

EXPENDITURE CYCLE RISKS AND AUDIT CONCERNS

Taking the most narrow attest-function view, external auditors are concerned primarily with the potential for understatement of liabilities and related expenses. Reported balances usually consist of items that have been reviewed, validated, and acknowledged by management. Attempts to improve financial statement presentation may involve actions to suppress the recognition and reporting of valid liabilities related to the period under review. Substantive tests of expenditure cycle accounts are therefore directed toward gathering evidence of understatement and omission of material items rather than their overstatement. Broader operational audit concerns, however, include process efficiency, fraud, and losses due to errors. Within this context, overstatement of liabilities and related expenses are also important.

In resolving these concerns, the auditor will seek evidence by performing a combination of tests of internal controls and substantive tests. Tests of controls include testing both general controls (discussed in Chapters 2 through 6) and application controls specifically related to the expenditure cycle. Various application control-testing techniques were examined in Chapter 7 and specific tests related to the expenditure cycle were described in this chapter. In addition to tests of controls, the auditor must perform substantive tests to achieve audit objectives. The remainder of this chapter deals with audit objectives related to expenditure cycle accounts and the substantive tests most commonly performed. Keep in mind that the quality of internal controls bears on the nature and extent of substantive tests determined by the auditor to be necessary. Normally, not all of the following tests will be performed.

UNDERSTANDING DATA

The substantive tests described below involve extracting data from accounting files for analysis. To do this, the auditor needs to understand the systems and controls that produced the data as well as the physical characteristics of the files that contain them. Much of this chapter was devoted to explaining various expenditure cycle configurations and their control implications. Chapter 8 described several common file structures and their audit implications. The discussion that follows presumes that the auditor is using ACL for performing the audit tests. Before we proceed, however, we need to review a few salient points regarding file preparation.

First, the auditor must verify that he or she is working with the correct version of the file to be analyzed. To do so, the auditor must understand the file backup procedures and, whenever possible, work with the original files. Second, ACL can read most sequential files and relational database tables directly, but esoteric and/or complex file structures may require "flattening" before they can be analyzed. This may involve additional procedures and special programs to produce a copy of the original file in a format that ACL can accept. If the organization's systems personnel perform the flattening process, the auditor must verify that the correct version of the original file was used and that all relevant records from the original were transferred to the copy for analysis.

The discussion that follows presumes that any file copying necessary to produce test data was performed under adequate controls to preserve data integrity. Furthermore, the tests described are applicable to both mainframe and PC environments. The focus of this material is on explaining the logic underlying various substantive tests and on illustrating the functionality of ACL in achieving audit objectives. The audit procedures described are based on the file structure in Figure 9–7. These structures indicate the key data and logical linkages between files. A description of each file follows.

INVENTORY FILE

The Inventory file contains quantity, price, supplier, and warehouse location data for each item of product inventory. The purchasing process begins with a review of the inventory records to identify inventory items that need to be ordered. In a retail organization, this step is performed when sales of finished goods to customers are recorded in the inventory records. In this case, the purchasing process involves replenishing the finished goods inventory. Purchasing systems of manufacturing firms replenish raw materials inventory as these items are used in the production process. In either case, when inventory items are sold or used in production, the Quantity-On-Hand field is reduced accordingly by a computer application. With each inventory reduction, the system tests for a "reorder" condition, which occurs when the quantity-on-hand falls below the reorder point. At that time, the system prepares a purchase order, which is sent to the vendor, and adds a record to the Purchase Order file. The quantity-on-hand

FIGURE 9-7   File Structures for the Expenditure Cycle

value will remain below the reorder-point until the inventory is received from the supplier. This may take days or even weeks. To signify that the item is on order and prevent it from being reordered each time the computer application detects the same reorder condition, a computer-generated purchase order number is placed in the PO-Number field of the inventory record. Normally, this field is blank.

PURCHASE ORDER FILE

This file contains records of purchases placed with suppliers. The record remains open until the inventory arrives. Placing the receiving report number in the dedicated field closes the record.

PO LINE ITEM FILE

The Line Item file contains a record of every item ordered. Since a single transaction can involve one or more products, each record in the Purchase Order file is associated with (linked to) one or more records in this file. Notice that the file contains two primary keys—Purchase Order Number and Item Number. Both keys are needed to uniquely define each record in the file. They also provide links to related records in the Purchase Order and Inventory files.

RECEIVING REPORT FILE

When the ordered items arrive from the supplier, they are counted and inspected and receiving documents are prepared. Via terminal, the receiving clerk enters information about the items received. The system automatically performs the following tasks: (1) increases the Quantity-On-Hand field in the inventory record(s); (2) removes the reorder condition by resetting the PO-Number field to its normal blank state; (3) creates a receiving report record of the event; and (4) closes the purchase order record by placing the receiving report number in the designated field.

DISBURSEMENT VOUCHER FILE

For most companies, discrepancies between amounts ordered, received, and billed are legitimate concerns that must be resolved before payment to the vendor is approved. Because of its complexity, this reconciliation is often a manual process that is triggered by receipt of the supplier's invoice. The accounts payable clerk reviews the supporting records in the Purchase Order and Receiving Report files and compares them to the invoice. If the items, quantities, and prices match, then a cash disbursement voucher is created. Based on the supplier's terms of trade and the company's payment policy, the payment due date is determined and placed in the voucher record.

Each payment day, the Cash Disbursement application selects the items due, flags them "paid' by entering the current date in the Check-Date field, and cuts the check, which is then mailed to the supplier. The **Disbursement Voucher file** provides three important pieces of information for the auditor: (1) it is a record of the timing and amount of vendor invoices received; (2) it is a journal of checks written in payment of trade accounts for the period; and (3) at any point in time, the open items (unpaid vouchers) in the file constitute the company's outstanding accounts payable balance.

FILE PREPARATION PROCEDURES

The data contained in the preceding files provide evidence that may either corroborate or refute audit objectives. Most of the tests described in the following section involve using ACL to access and extract data from these files. Recall from the previous chapter that each file needs to be defined in terms of its physical location and its structure. Through a series of easy-to-use pop-up menus, the auditor specifies the name of the file and where it resides on the mainframe or PC. ACL then prompts the auditor to define the file's structure in terms of the length of each field and the data type contained in each field (i.e., numeric, character, or date). When the **file definition** is completed, it is saved under a unique name assigned by the auditor. All future file access is accomplished by simply selecting the file definition from an ACL menu. ACL automatically locates the file and presents it on screen, where the auditor can review and manipulate its contents.

Sometimes the contents of a data field are different from what they are supposed to be. For example, a numeric field in one or more records may contain alphabetic data because of a program error or a clerical mistake. Also, a field may contain corrupted data because of an error in the file-flattening process. Whatever the cause, prior to performing any substantive tests on a new file, it is important to validate its contents. Invalid data will distort the test results and may cause a system failure. ACL's *verify* command analyzes the data fields in the selected file to ensure that their contents are consistent with the field type in the file definition. Any validity errors detected by ACL need to be traced to their source and resolved. For purposes of discussion, we will assume that the files used in all tests described hereafter have been properly defined and verified.

TESTING THE ACCURACY AND COMPLETENESS ASSERTIONS

The audit procedures described in this section provide evidence relating to management assertions of *accuracy* and *completeness*. We saw in the last chapter that auditors often precede substantive tests of details with an *analytical review* of account balances. Analytical procedures can identify relationships between accounts and risks that are not otherwise apparent. In the case of the expenditure cycle, an analytical review can provide the auditor with an overall perspective for trends in accounts payable and related expenses. Current expenses may be compared to historical expenses and management budgets. For example, the auditor may compare current payroll expenses for the quarter with those for the same period in previous years. Unusual trends or variances should be noted and examined for cause. Analytical procedures may indicate trends, even in adequately controlled organizations, that lead the auditor to extend substantive tests. On the other hand, they can provide assurance that transactions and accounts are reasonably stated and complete and may thus permit the auditor to reduce substantive testing.

A medium-to-large sized organization's expenses and accounts payable data may constitute thousands or perhaps millions of records. Unlike analytical procedures, which can be performed without CAATTs, substantive tests of details of such volumes of data cannot be effectively accomplished without using CAATTs. The following substantive tests that can be performed using ACL are based on the file structures depicted in Figure 9–7.

REVIEW DISBURSEMENT VOUCHERS FOR UNUSUAL TRENDS AND EXCEPTIONS

A useful audit procedure for identifying potential audit risks involves scanning data files for unusual transactions and account balances. For example, scanning accounts payable for excessively large balances may indicate abnormal dependency on a particular supplier. On the other hand, a high number of vendors with small balances may indicate the need to consolidate business activity. Various corporate surveys have estimated the cost of processing a purchase order at between $50 and $125. Restricting the number of vendors with whom the organization does business can reduce this expense.

The auditor can use ACL's *stratify* and *classify* features to identify various characteristics and anomalies associated with accounts payable procedures. Both of these functions are used to group data into predetermined intervals, count the number of records that fall into each interval, and accumulate a financial value for each interval. The stratify function groups financial data into specific strata. Using data similar to those in Figure 9–8, we demonstrate its use for stratifying disbursement vouchers by accumulating the Amount field for each strata. The classify function forms strata based on nonfinancial (and non-numeric) data. In our example, this feature is used to group the vouchers by vendor number. In this case also, the Amount field is accumulated. The results of the two procedures are presented in Figures 9–9 and 9–10, respectively.

The first report gives the auditor an overall perspective for the nature of the purchasing process. Notice that 78 percent of the total number of disbursement vouchers constitutes only 15 percent of the business volume for the period. The second report shows the business activity associated with individual vendors. Over 53 percent of the organization's purchases are from a single vendor, while most of the other vendors receive only a small percentage of the total business. These findings may reflect a natural business phenomenon, or they may signify potential risks.

Excessive purchases from a single supplier may reflect an unusual business dependency that may prove harmful to the firm if the supplier raises prices or cannot deliver on schedule. This may also signify a fraudulent relationship involving kickbacks to purchasing agents or other management.

The large number of small volume suppliers is evidence of a highly inefficient purchasing process. Management may consider reducing the number of suppliers and increasing the size of their order quantities to reduce the number of orders placed. This situation may also be a signal to the auditor that a valid vendor approach to purchasing is *not* in use. It is unlikely that an organization would add vendors to the file for control purposes unless they expect significant levels of business.

REVIEWING FOR ACCURATE INVOICE PRICES

Comparing prices on supplier invoices to original purchase order prices provides evidence for testing the management assertion of *accuracy*. Significant discrepancies between expected prices and the prices actually charged may be due to clerical errors, failure to review supporting documents before authorizing payment, or accounts payable personnel exceeding their authority in dealing with price discrepancies.

Traditionally, auditors verify pricing accuracy by comparing invoice prices with the purchase orders on a sample basis only. Of the thousands of invoices processed

FIGURE 9–8

Disbursement Voucher Sample Data

Voucher Number	PO Number	Amount	Due Date	Check Number	Check Date	Supplier Invoice Number	Vendor Number
12655	12923	158.32	12/21/95	6484	01/02/96	1223467	28788
512973	12958	1,802.63	01/15/96	6537	01/09/96	67783pl	15545
511810	12960	10,815.75	01/12/96	6567	01/09/96	88746pl	15545
1064	12998	4,427.99	01/15/96	6571	01/09/96	667223	28847
1060	13002	117,667.60	01/03/96	6611	01/09/96	844001	28847
77696	13006	150.95	12/04/95	6641	01/09/96	po2298	1564485

FIGURE 9–9

Stratified
Disbursement
Voucher Data

@ STRATIFY ON Amount ACCUMULATE Amount MINIMUM –7000 MAXIMUM 120000

INTERVAL 10 TO SCREEN

<<< Graphable Data >>>

Page . . . 1   10/25/98 13:50:52

Produced with ACL by: ACL for Windows Workbook

<<< STRATIFY over -7,000.00-> 120,000.00 >>>

>>> Minimum encountered was –3,333.09

>>> Maximum encountered was 117,667.60

Interval			COUNT	<— %	% —>	Invoice Amount
–7,000.00	–>	5,699.99	248	78.23%	15.12%	252,718.04
5,700.00	–>	18,399.99	52	16.40%	36.42%	608,507.30
18,400.00	–>	31,099.99	7	2.21%	9.12%	152,406.07
31,100.00	–>	43,799.99	2	0.63%	4.16%	69,552.83
43,800.00	–>	56,499.99	3	0.95%	8.88%	148,321.19
56,500.00	–>	69,199.99	2	0.63%	7.75%	129,488.07
69,200.00	–>	81,899.99	0	0.00%	0.00%	0.00
81,900.00	–>	94,599.99	1	0.32%	5.27%	88,043.63
94,600.00	–>	107,299.99	1	0.32%	6.24%	104,267.30
107,300.00	–>	120,000.00	1	0.32%	7.04%	117,667.60
			317	100.00%	100.00%	1,670,972.03

during the period, perhaps only one or two hundred can be tested manually. ACL allows the auditor to compare the prices charged on every invoice in the file for the period under review. The test will involve the Disbursement Voucher file and the Purchase Order file, which is illustrated with some sample data in Figure 9–11.

Testing pricing accuracy involves matching records from the two files using ACL's *join* feature. This can be accomplished in a few simple steps. First, recall from Chapter 8 that both files being joined need to be ordered on a common key. In this example, PO Number is a common secondary key. Reorganizing both files on this field requires opening each file separately, invoking ACL's *sort* function, specifying the sort field, and designating the file name to receive the sorted output. The results of this process will be two new files ordered in the same sequence.

The next step is to combine the two files to create a third output file. The auditor achieves this with the *join* command. Several options are available when joining files. The relevant option in this case is to create an output file that consists only of matched records from the two files. ACL's *join* feature permits the auditor to specify the fields from the two input files that are to be passed to the new output file. Usually, it is neither necessary nor desirable to include all fields from both of the original files. In this example, the fields needed from the Purchase Order file to verify pricing accuracy are PO Number and PO Amount; from the Disbursement Voucher file the fields are Voucher Number, Amount, Check Number, and Vendor Number. The file structure of the new combined PO/Disbursement file with some sample records is presented in Figure 9–12.

FIGURE 9-10

Disbursement
Voucher Data
Classified on
Vendor Number

@ CLASSIFY ON Vendor_Number ACCUMULATE Amount TO SCREEN

<<< Graphable Data >>>

Page . . . 1   10/25/98 13:52:39

Produced with ACL by: ACL for Windows Workbook

Vendor_Number	COUNT	<— %	% —>	Amount
11494	5	1.58%	4.91%	82,011.60
15545	33	10.41%	2.33%	38,891.82
1564189	17	5.36%	1.76%	29,487.27
1564218	2	0.63%	0.01%	225.16
1564396	6	1.89%	2.82%	47,154.24
1564485	2	0.63%	0.00%	0.00
1581597	15	4.73%	1.16%	19,443.83
1581600	11	3.47%	1.71%	28,500.00
1581605	4	1.26%	0.06%	980.29
1598209	3	0.95%	0.75%	12,578.57
1599477	3	0.95%	0.23%	3,809.04
1599690	2	0.63%	0.00%	0.00
1615020	1	0.32%	1.36%	22,778.06
1615041	17	5.36%	15.51%	259,112.93
170507	12	3.79%	3.26%	54,399.57
21255	1	0.32%	0.05%	775.37
23542	1	0.32%	–0.20%	(3,333.09)
25152	70	22.08%	3.98%	66,583.42
28529	8	2.52%	0.08%	1,313.61
28788	24	7.57%	0.38%	6,339.02
28847	66	20.82%	53.46%	893,379.11
41191	4	1.26%	6.22%	104,003.84
56853	6	1.89%	0.20%	3,396.09
57780	1	0.32%	–0.08%	(1,270.64)
99598	3	0.95%	0.02%	412.92
	317	100.00%	100.00%	1,670,972.03

At this point, the resulting file may be quite large. Scanning the file visually for price differences can be time-consuming and ineffective. Here again is an application for a *filter*. Through a series of pop-up menus, the auditor can easily write an expression to create a filter that will ignore all records in which PO Amount and Amount are equal. The resulting file will thus contain only price discrepancies. Using other ACL features, the auditor can calculate the total price variance and make a determination as to its materiality. If material, the matter should be pursued with management.

TESTING THE COMPLETENESS, EXISTENCE, AND RIGHTS AND OBLIGATIONS ASSERTIONS

Inventories received from valid suppliers in response to authorized purchase orders constitute liabilities. In most systems, however, the trigger that causes the liability to

FIGURE 9-11

Purchase Order File

PO Number	PO Amount	PO Date	PO Approver	Vendor Number	Rec. Rpt Number
12821	493.05	12/16/95	Controller	25152	10134
12838	138.95	01/24/96	PurchMgr	25152	10101
12848	14,463.75	01/10/96	Controller	28847	10787
12891	2,845.57	01/30/96	Controller	28847	11663
12894	252.54	12/06/95	PurchMgr	28529	11922
12946	238.65	12/13/95	PurchMgr	28529	11475
12958	1,802.63	12/16/95	Controller	15545	11668

FIGURE 9-12

Combined PO/Disbursement File

PO Number	PO Amount	Voucher Number	Amount	Check Number	Vendor Number
12821	493.05	121655	493.05	6484	25152
12838	138.95	512973	138.95	6537	25152
12848	14,463.75	511810	14,875.95	6537	28847
12891	2,845.57	105436	2,905.67	6541	28847
12894	252.54	102360	252.54	6544	28529
12946	238.65	776756	238.65	6555	28529
12958	1,802.63	514760	1,802.63	6652	15545

be recognized and recorded as an account payable (in our example, a disbursement voucher) is the receipt of the supplier's invoice, which often lags the receipt of the merchandise. Normally, the time lag between liability realization and recognition does not impact financial reporting. At period-end closing, however, it becomes an issue requiring special attention. Items of inventory received at the end of the audit period, whose related invoice is not received until early into the following period, may not be included as an accounts payable. Management should have procedures for identifying invoices received in a subsequent period that relate to the audit period and adjusting the liabilities accordingly. The search for unrecorded liabilities described below provides evidence that tests the *completeness, existence,* and *rights and obligations* assertions.

SEARCHING FOR UNRECORDED LIABILITIES

The search for unrecorded liabilities involves the Disbursement Voucher and Receiving Report files, illustrated without data in Figure 9–13. Each record of an inventory receipt contained in this file for the period should match a corresponding record in the Disbursement Voucher file. Again, using the *join* feature, the two files can be compared for the existence of mismatched records.

FIGURE 9-13

Disbursement Voucher and Receiving Report Files

Disbursement Voucher File

Voucher Number	PO Number	Amount	Due Date	Check Number	Check Date	Supplier Invoice Number	Vendor Number

Receiving Report File

Rec. Rpt. Number	PO Number	Carrier Code	Date Received	Vendor Number

As in the previous example, the two files being joined need to be ordered on a common key, which, again, is PO Number. Since the Disbursement Voucher file was previously sorted on this key, that sorted output file can be used for this test also. Therefore, only the Receiving Report file needs to be reorganized. The next step is to joint the two files to create a combined output file. This time, however, the output option is different from the previous example. The relevant option in this case is to create an output file that consists only of *unmatched* records from the *primary* file. Remember, the auditor is attempting through this test to identify receiving report records that have not been recorded as liabilities. The primary file in this instance is the Receiving Report file, and the Disbursement Voucher file is the secondary file. In choosing this option, all the inventory receipts that were correctly recorded as liabilities will be ignored by the *join* process. Only the unmatched receiving report records will be contained in the new output file. The structure of the file is the same as the Receiving Report file in Figure 9–13. If the output file contains any records, the auditor needs to review this information with management to determine if the appropriate adjustments were made to the accounts payable balance.

SEARCHING FOR UNAUTHORIZED DISBURSEMENT VOUCHERS

A variation on the preceding test can be used to address questions pertaining to over-stated accounts payable. By selecting the Disbursement Vouchers file as the primary file and the Receiving Report file as the secondary file, the preceding test will produce a file of vouchers for which the organization has no record of inventory receipts. This might indicate that payments are approved solely on the basis of receiving a supplier's invoice rather than also verifying that inventories were ordered and actually received. Unsupported disbursement vouchers may signify an attempt at fraud or a poor control environment in which multiple payments are made for the same purchase. The latter situation is examined further below.

REVIEW FOR MULTIPLE CHECKS TO VENDORS

Corporate losses from multiple payments to vendors for the same merchandise have been estimated to be in the hundreds of millions of dollars per year. Malfunctioning computer programs, data entry errors, and the failure of authorization controls usually cause duplicate payments. Occasionally, however, they are the result of dishonest vendors who attempt to circumvent internal controls by sending two supplier invoices with different invoice numbers for the same purchase. Sometimes they send multiple copies of the same invoice or simply add a letter behind one of the invoice numbers to differentiate them. The auditor can test for duplicate records in a large file by employing ACL's *duplicate* feature. This technique is demonstrated below using the Disbursement Voucher file in Figure 9–13.

Any field or combination of fields can be used to test for duplicate records. The auditor, however, needs to understand the relationship between the files to draw meaningful conclusions from the test results. For instance, in our example each disbursement voucher is issued in payment of a single supplier's invoice, and each supplier invoice relates to a single purchase order. Recognizing this relationship, the auditor can conclude that the same PO Number value should not normally exist in two or more records in the Disbursement Voucher file. A search for duplicate records in the file produces the report on the following page.

DUPLICATES ON PO_Number ERRORLIMIT 10 TO SCREEN

Page . . . 1   10/27/98 08:42:37

Produced with ACL by: Workbook

*** Keys out of sequence at record	4, Key:12084
*** Keys out of sequence at record	5, Key:12068
*** Keys out of sequence at record	7, Key:15036
*** Keys out of sequence at record	9, Key:15165
*** Keys out of sequence at record	11, Key:11181
*** Keys out of sequence at record	12, Key:15506
*** Keys out of sequence at record	13, Key:14906
*** **Duplicate key fields at record**	15, Key:17769
*** Keys out of sequence at record	16, Key:15124
*** **Duplicate key fields at record**	18, Key:15139
*** Keys out of sequence at record	20, Key:12734

10 data sequence errors detected

2 gaps and/or duplicates detected

The report indicates that in addition to several out-of-sequence records, two records (boldfaced) have duplicate purchase order numbers. The cause of this situation will require further examination in consultation with the appropriate management. The explanation may simply be that vouchers were created in error, voided, and resubmitted. On the other hand, the results may signify that, on two occasions, duplicate checks were issued for the same merchandise. This may be due to a computer error or an internal control problem in the voucher approval process.

AUDITING PAYROLL AND RELATED ACCOUNTS

Testing accrued payroll and related accounts for completeness and accuracy consist primarily of analytical procedures and reviews of cash disbursements made in the following period. The auditor should test the mathematical accuracy of payroll summaries and trace totals to the payroll records and to the general ledger accounts. The average salary per employee in the current period can be compared to the previous year's averages. ACL's *stratify* feature can help the auditor detect unusual trends and abnormal balances in the payroll file. Substantive test of details, however, are normally not performed on payroll expense accounts unless analytical procedures or severe weaknesses in internal controls indicate the need for additional testing.

SUMMARY

This chapter examined audit procedures associated with the expenditure cycle. It began with a review of alternative technologies used in both legacy and modern systems. The focus was on the key operational tasks that constitute the purchases, cash disbursement, and payroll procedures. The second section explained expenditure cycle audit objectives, controls, and tests of controls that an auditor normally performs. Evidence from such procedures is used to determine the nature, timing, and extent of substantive tests. The last section described substantive tests in relation to expenditure cycle assertions based upon ACL software applications.

KEY TERMS

attendance file
closed accounts payable file
closed voucher file
disbursement voucher file
employee file
file definition
human resource management (HRM) system
inventory subsidiary file
labor usage file

log of automatic transactions
paymaster
payroll imprest account
supplier's (vendor's) invoice
time card
transaction listing
transaction log
valid vendor file
vendor's invoice

REVIEW QUESTIONS

1. Differentiate between a purchase requisition and a purchase order.
2. What purpose does a purchasing department serve?
3. Distinguish between an accounts payable file and a vouchers payable file.
4. What are the three logical steps of the cash disbursements system?
5. What general ledger journal entries are triggered by the purchases system?
6. What two types of exposure can close supervision of the receiving department reduce?
7. What steps of independent verification does the general ledger department perform?
8. What is (are) the purpose(s) of maintaining a valid vendor file?
9. How do computerized purchasing systems help to reduce the risk of purchasing bottlenecks?
10. What is a personnel action form?
11. What tasks does a payroll clerk perform upon receipt of hours-worked data from the production department?
12. What documents constitute the audit trail for payroll?

DISCUSSION QUESTIONS

1. What is the importance of the job ticket? Illustrate the flow of this document and its information from inception to impact on the financial statements.

2. What documents support the payment of an invoice? Discuss where these documents originate and the resulting control implications.

3. Discuss the time lags between realizing and recognizing economic events in the purchase and payroll systems. What is the accounting profession's view on this matter as it pertains to these two systems?

4. Discuss the importance of supervision controls in the receiving department and the reasons behind blind fields on the receiving report, such as quantity and price.

5. How does the procedure for determining inventory requirements differ between a basic batch processing system and batch processing with real-time data input of sales and receipts of inventory?

6. What advantages are achieved in choosing:
   a. a basic batch computer system over a manual system?
   b. a batch system with real-time data input over a basic batch system?

7. Discuss the major control implications of batch systems with real-time data input. What compensating procedures are available?

8. Discuss some specific examples of how information systems can reduce time lags that positively affect an organization.

9. Discuss some service industries that may require their workers to use job tickets.

10. Payroll is often used as a good example of batch processing using sequential files. Explain why.

MULTIPLE-CHOICE QUESTIONS

1. Which document helps to ensure that the receiving clerks actually count the number of goods received?
    a. packing list
    b. blind copy of purchase order
    c. shipping notice
    d. invoice

2. When the goods are received and the receiving report has been prepared, which ledger may be updated?
    a. standard cost inventory ledger
    b. inventory subsidiary ledger
    c. general ledger
    d. accounts payable subsidiary ledger

3. Which statement is NOT correct for an expenditure system with proper internal controls?
    a. Cash disbursements maintains the check register.
    b. Accounts payable maintains the accounts payable subsidiary ledger.
    c. Accounts payable is responsible for paying invoices.
    d. Accounts payable is responsible for authorizing invoices.

4. Which duties should be segregated?
    a. matching purchase requisitions, receiving reports, and invoices and authorizing payment
    b. authorizing payment and maintaining the check register
    c. writing checks and maintaining the check register
    d. authorizing payment and maintaining the accounts payable subsidiary ledger

5. Which documents would an auditor most likely choose to examine closely in order to ascertain that all expenditures incurred during the accounting period have been recorded as a liability?
    a. invoices
    b. purchase orders

    c. purchase requisitions
    d. receiving reports

6. Which task must still require human intervention in an automated purchases/cash disbursements system?
    a. determination of inventory requirements
    b. preparation of a purchase order
    c. preparation of a receiving report
    d. preparation of a check register

7. CMA 686 3-12
    In a well-designed internal control structure, two tasks that should be performed by different persons are
    a. preparation of purchase orders and authorization of monthly payroll.
    b. preparation of bank reconciliations and recording of cash disbursements.
    c. distribution of payroll checks and approval of credit sales.
    d. posting of amounts from both the cash receipts journal and cash disbursements journal to the general ledger.
    e. posting of amounts from the cash receipts journal to the general ledger and distribution of payroll checks.

8. CMA 689 3-17
    Which one of the following situations represents a strength in the internal control for purchasing and accounts payable?
    a. Prenumbered receiving reports are issued randomly.
    b. Invoices are approved for payment by the purchasing department.
    c. Unmatched receiving reports are reviewed on an annual basis.
    d. Vendors' invoices are matched against purchase orders and receiving reports before a liability is recorded.
    e. The purchasing department reconciles the accounts payable subsidiary vendor ledger with the general ledger control account.

PROBLEMS

1. **Document Preparation**
    Create the appropriate documents (purchase requisition, purchase order, receiving report, inventory record, and disbursement voucher) and prepare any journal entries needed to process the following business events for Jethro's Boot & Western Wear Manufacturing Company (this is a manual system):
    a. On October 28, 19x4, the inventory subsidiary ledger for Item 2278, metal pins, indicates that the quantity on hand is 4,000 units (valued at $76.00), the reorder point is 4,750, and units are on order. The economic order quantity is 6,000 units. The supplier is Jed's Metal Supply Company (vendor number 83682). Our customer number is 584446. The current price per unit is $0.02. Inventory records are kept at cost. The goods should be delivered to Inventory Storage Room 2.
    b. On November 8, the goods were received (the scales indicated that 4,737 units were received).
    c. On November 12, an invoice (number 9886) was received for the above units, which included freight of $6.00. The terms were 1/10, net 30. Jethro's likes to keep funds available for use as long as possible without missing any discounts.

2. **Flowchart Analysis**
    Examine the diagram on page 383 and indicate any incorrect initiation and/or transfer of documentation. What problems could this cause?

3. **Accounting Records and Files**
    Indicate which department—accounts payable, cash disbursements, data processing, purchasing, inventory, or receiving—has ownership over the following files and registers:
    a. open purchase order file
    b. purchase requisition file
    c. open purchase requisition file
    d. closed purchase requisition file
    e. inventory
    f. closed purchase order file
    g. valid vendor file
    h. voucher register
    i. open vouchers payable file
    j. receiving report file
    k. closed voucher file
    l. check register (cash disbursements journal)

4. **Source Documents Identification**
    Explain, in detail, the process by which the information is obtained and the source of information for each of the fields in the expenditure cycle files. (See the accompanying Figure on page 384 for a complete listing of files and fields.)

5. **Data Processing**
    Explain how the processing procedures would differ, if at all, for the transactions listed in Problem 1 if a computer-based system with
    a. a basic batch processing system were implemented.
    b. a batch processing system with real-time data input were used.

6. **Internal Control**
    Using the flowchart on page 385 of a purchases system, identify six major control weaknesses in the system. Discuss and classify each weakness in accordance with SAS 78.

7. **Purchase Discounts Lost**
    Estimate the amount of money that could be saved by the accounts payable and cash disbursements departments if a basic batch processing system were implemented. Assume that the clerical workers cost the firm $12 per hour, that 13,000 vouchers are prepared, and that 5,000 checks are written per year. Assume that total cash disbursements to vendors amount to $5 million per year. Due to sloppy bookkeeping, the current system takes advantage of only about 25 percent of the discounts offered by vendors for timely payments. The average discount is 2 percent if payment is made within ten days. Payments are currently made on about the 15th day after the invoice is received. Make your own assumptions (and state them) regarding how long specific tasks

Problem 2: Flowchart Analysis

Problem 4: Source Documents Identification

Inven Num	Description	Qnty on Hand	Reorder Point	Qnty On Order*	EOQ	Vendor Number	Standard Cost	Total Inven. Cost	Inventory Master File

Pur Req Number	Inven Num	Qnty on Order	Vendor Number	Unit Standard Cost	Purchase Requisition File

Vendor Number	Address	Terms of Trade	Date of Last Order	Lead Time	Vendor File

PO Num	Pur Req Number	Inven Num	Qnty On Order	Vendor Number	Address	Standard Cost	Expected Invoice Amount	Rec Flag	Inven Flag	Open (and Closed) Purchase Order File

Voucher Number	Check Num	Invoice Num	Invoice Amount	Acct Cr	Acct DR	Vendor Number	Open Date	Due Date	Close Date

Voucher Register (Open AP File)

* A value in this field is a "flag" to the system not to order item a second time.
When inventories are received, the flag is removed by changing this value to zero.

will take. Also discuss any intangible benefits of the system. (Don't worry about excessive paper documentation costs.)

8. **Data Processing Output**
Using the information provided in Problem 7, discuss all transaction listings and summary reports that would be necessary for a batch system with real-time input of data.

9. **Internal Control**
Discuss any control weaknesses found in the flowchart on page 386. Recommend any necessary changes.

10. **Internal Control**
CMA 1288 5-3
Lexsteel is a leading manufacturer of steel furniture. While the company has manufacturing plants and distribution facilities throughout the United States, the purchasing, accounting, and treasury functions are centralized at corporate headquarters.

While discussing the management letter with the external auditors, Ray Lansdown, controller of Lexsteel, became aware of potential problems with the accounts payable system. The auditors had to perform additional audit procedures to attest to the validity of accounts payable and cutoff procedures. The auditors have recommended that a detailed systems study be made of the current procedures. Such a study would not only assess the exposure of the company to potential embezzlement and fraud, but would also identify ways to improve management controls.

Landsdown has assigned the study task to Dolores Smith, a relatively new accountant

Problem 6: Internal Control

Vendor	Purchases	Inventory Control	Receiving	Accounts Payable	Cash Disbursments	General Ledger

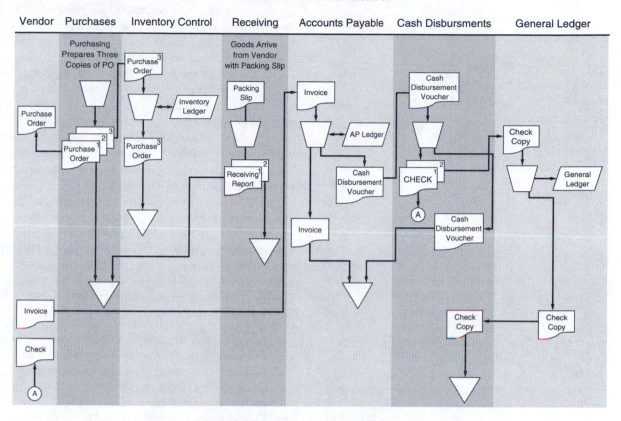

in the department. Because Smith could not find adequate documentation of the accounts payable procedures, she interviewed those employees involved and constructed a flowchart of the current system. This flowchart is presented on page 387. A description of the current procedures follows.

Computer Resources Available
The host computer mainframe is located at corporate headquarters with interactive, remote job-entry terminals at each branch location. In general, data entry occurs at the source and is transmitted to an integrated database maintained on the host computer. Data transmission is made between the branch offices and the host computer over leased telephone lines. The software allows flexibility for managing user access and editing data input.

Procedures for Purchasing Raw Materials
Production orders and appropriate bills of materials are generated by the host computer at corporate headquarters. Based on these bills of materials, purchase orders for raw materials are

generated by the centralized purchasing function and mailed directly to the vendors. Each purchase order instructs the vendor to ship the materials directly to the appropriate manufacturing plant. Assuming that the necessary purchase orders have been issued, the manufacturing plants proceed with the production orders received from corporate headquarters.

When goods are received, the manufacturing plant examines and verifies the count to the packing slip and transmits the receiving data to accounts payable at corporate headquarters. In the event that raw material deliveries fall behind production, each branch manager is given the authority to order materials and issue emergency purchase orders directly to the vendors. Data about the emergency orders and verification of materials receipt are transmitted via computer to accounts payable at corporate headquarters. Since the company employs a computerized perpetual inventory system, physical counts of raw materials are deemed not to be cost-effective and are not performed.

Problem 9: Internal Control

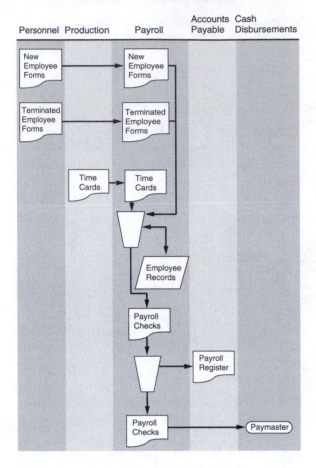

Personnel Production | Payroll | Accounts Payable | Cash Disbursements

Accounts Payable Procedures

Vendor invoices are mailed directly to corporate headquarters and entered by accounts payable personnel when received; this often occurs before the receiving data are transmitted from the branch offices. The final day of the invoice term for payment is entered as the payment due date. This due date must often be calculated by the data entry person using information listed on the invoice.

Once a week, invoices due the following week are printed in chronological entry order on a payment listing, and the corresponding checks are drawn. The checks and the payment listing are sent to the treasurer's office for signature and mailing to the payee. The check number is printed by the computer and displayed on the check, and the payment listing is validated as the checks are signed. After the checks are mailed, the payment listing is returned to accounts payable for filing. When there is insufficient cash to pay all the invoices, certain checks and the payment listing are retained by the treasurer until all checks can be paid. When the remaining checks are mailed, the listing is then returned to accounts payable. Often, weekly check mailings include a few checks from the previous week, but rarely are there more than two weekly listings involved.

When accounts payable receives the payment listing back from the treasurer's office, the expenses are distributed, coded, and posted to the appropriate plant or cost center accounts. Weekly summary performance reports are processed by accounts payable for each cost center and branch location reflecting all data entry to that point.

Required:

a. Identify and discuss three areas where Lexsteel Corporation may be exposed to fraud or embezzlement due to weaknesses in the procedures described, and recommend improvements to correct these weaknesses.

b. Describe three areas where management information could be distorted due to weaknesses in the procedures, and recommend improvements to correct these weaknesses.

c. Identify three strengths in the procedures described and explain why they are strengths.

11. Human Resource Data Management

In a payroll system with real-time processing of human resource management data, control issues become very important. List some items in this system that could be very sensitive or controversial. Also describe what types of data must be carefully guarded to ensure that they are not altered. Discuss some control procedures that might be put into place to guard against unwanted changes to employee's records.

INTERNAL CONTROL CASES

1. F&Y Computer Sales, Inc. (Prepared by Jon Young, Lehigh University)

F&Y is in the business of selling computers. Its main competition is other major

Problem 10: Internal Control

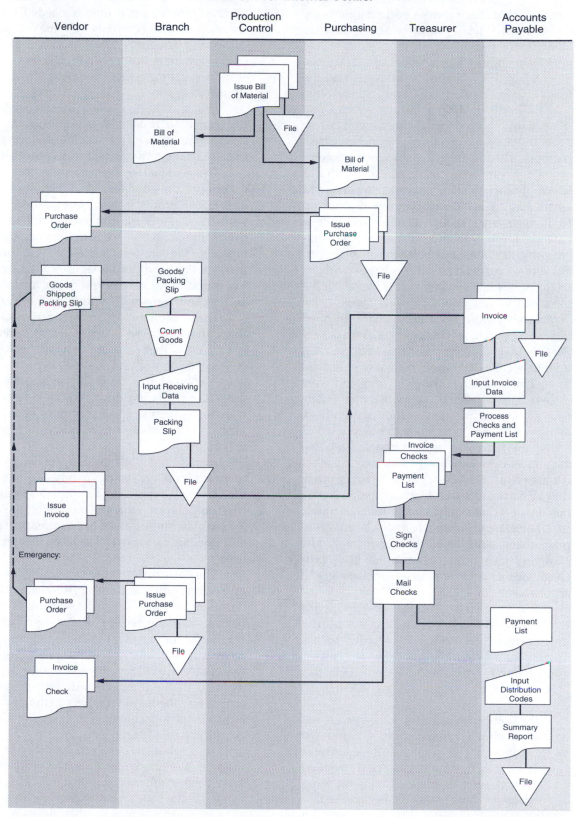

mail-order computer companies. It has a small market share compared to the industry leaders, but it hopes to increase its share by being more responsive to its customers' orders by reengineering its sales order processing system. F&Y has 147 employees, and the main office is located in St. Paul, Minnesota.

F&Y sells desktop computer systems that it primarily manufactures itself, with a few parts purchased from third-party companies. It offers many different packages to accommodate its end-user customers, about 15 different bundles in all. Customers pay on credit terms and get a satisfaction guarantee for up to 30 days after receipt of their computers. F&Y's suppliers include a few different microcomputer chip and software manufacturers whose products F&Y packages with its computers. F&Y's warehouse is located at the main office in St. Paul and is very large.

Last year, F&Y's market share dropped in comparison to its competition. A survey revealed that one reason was because customers were not getting their computers on time. The lead times were too long and were always a day or two late. Customer orders need to be sent out the day they are received, and inventory records need to be updated as orders are placed to be able to accurately tell customers how long a lead time is or whether a back-order is necessary. The board of directors also suspects that internal control weaknesses exist that might lead to internal fraud.

The expenditure cycle for F&Y consists of purchasing and cash disbursements. The company uses three departments in its purchasing function: warehouse, purchasing, and accounting.

The purchasing function begins in the warehouse department when inventories drop below predetermined reorder points. The inventory clerk observes this and collects information for the purchase requisitions that will be sent to the purchasing department each Friday.

The computer industry is fast paced and new products are constantly being introduced to the market. The purchasing department spends most of its time finding new suppliers and products, as well as negotiating the terms of purchase of these products. Because of this, it prefers to deal with all straight reorders on Fridays. Not as much time is needed for reorders, and the company can make use of large order discounts. The company generally keeps high inventories with high safety stocks of its best-selling items to combat weekly adjustments.

The purchasing department prepares five purchase orders. Two copies go to the vendor, one goes to the warehouse, one goes to accounting, and one is filed in purchasing.

The warehouse then files the purchase order until the goods arrive. When the goods arrive, Willie, in the warehouse, sends some workers to check the purchase order against the packing slip and the actual goods. Unfortunately, the workers have been reporting many of the goods as damaged. The company has found that many of the goods are fragile and become inoperable with little damage.

Three receiving reports are then made by the warehouse. One is sent back to purchasing to notify them the product was received, one goes to accounting, and one is filed in the warehouse. At this time, the warehouse updates its records and the inventory ledger. The warehouse then sends a summary of this information to accounting to update the general ledger.

Accounting waits until it gets the invoice to match it up against the purchase order and the receiving report. It then updates the purchasing journal and the accounts payable ledger. Accounting uses the summary report and purchasing journal to update the general ledger.

The cash disbursements system consists of the accounting and cash disbursements departments. The cash disbursements system begins with the receipt of the invoice. The purchasing department often negotiates early payment discounts with its suppliers. For this reason and simplicity, the accounting department sends the purchase order, the receiving report, and the invoice directly to the cash disbursements department after updating the accounts payable ledger.

The cash disbursements department then prepares the checks for Gus, the head of the cash disbursements department. He then compares the records and signs the check. The check is sent to the supplier, and one copy is kept and filed along with the other remaining records. The check register is then updated and a voucher is sent to accounting to update the general ledger.

The payroll system consists of the accounting and cash disbursements departments. Department heads collect and check time cards for accuracy and send them to the accounting department. The time cards are then compared to the personnel action forms that accounting maintains to make sure that proper wage-per-hour figures are used in determining employee paychecks. The accounting department then prepares the paychecks and develops the payroll register. They then send these items to the cash disbursements department.

The cash disbursements department then signs the paychecks and distributes them to the various department heads to distribute to the employees. They also update the check register and send any checks needed to the bank to the payroll imprest account. They then send the payroll register back to accounting, where it is filed.

Required:

a. Prepare a data flow diagram for the system described in the case.

b. Prepare a document flowchart for the system described in the case.

c. Identify the internal control weaknesses in the system. Structure your discussion around the six classes of internal control activities described in the chapter.

d. Redesign the system to take advantage of computer technology, such as batch with sequential files or batch with direct access files, etc. Explain your choice of computer technology. Prepare a flowchart of the new system.

2. EXPOSE (Prepared by Dawn Lotito, Lehigh University)
EXPOSE is one of the United States' leading direct sellers of beauty and related products. All cosmetics are available in a wide range of gorgeous fashion-forward colors, incorporating state-of-the-art skin technology to help the customer best achieve a beautiful, smooth complexion.

The products are marketed and sold nationwide. Annual sales reach more than $4.5 billion. EXPOSE has over 40 retail stores and over 50,000 representatives nationwide. EXPOSE cosmetics are sold either through the retail stores, from a local representative (usually a beauty technician at a beauty salon), or through a monthly catalog. The products are marketed as a high-quality, expensive line of cosmetics unavailable in department stores. They are, in essence, "department store makeup without having to go to the department store."

New customers are attracted to EXPOSE by the seasonal shows the company has at select locations in shopping malls, beauty salons, and its retail stores. At the shows, EXPOSE representatives demonstrate beauty techniques on models. Free makeovers and color consultations are given. Once a customer knows her color "code," she may order through a catalog with the confidence that the color of the product she is buying will match her skin tone and hair color. EXPOSE carries over 45 codes, and it is very specific for accuracy. Regular customers are sent the catalog. They can order through phone sales or an order form. They may also purchase the product from a retail store or beauty salon that carries the product line. (The beauty salons may not have all items in stock, however, and the items may have to be ordered.) The goods are typically shipped within 24 hours of receipt of the order. All representatives must go through a four-week intensive program to qualify as an EXPOSE Expert.

All raw materials are sent to the manufacturing headquarters in Whippany, New Jersey, where most of the products are produced. Other smaller plants are located in southern New Jersey and eastern Pennsylvania. The raw materials include some natural extracts such as sage and comfrey. Other raw materials are synthetic pellets produced by EXPOSE's main supplier, Crystallan. Other suppliers are fairly small and located outside of the continental United States. EXPOSE has a strong supplier relationship with Crystallan and has had no serious problems with quality or late deliveries in the past. For the past two years, Gateway Plastics has supplied the plastic pellets that EXPOSE uses to melt down and mold its packaging.

Production is based on projections of customer orders. Raw materials are shipped in batches, but are based on projected demand. For example, when EXPOSE projects a demand for 400,000 Pink Ice Lipsticks, it orders the raw materials necessary to produce that many lipsticks in that color. Four distribution centers are located across the United States.

In the manufacturing facility in Whippany, New Jersey, the purchases subsystem begins with Jane in inventory control recognizing a need for raw materials after reviewing the records in the inventory ledger. She prepares three purchase orders and sends one to the supplier and one to the receiving department (also called the warehouse). Jane updates the inventory records, sends a summary to general ledger, and then files the purchase order.

When the raw materials are received, the workers in the receiving department are instructed to compare the packing slip from the supplier to the purchase order. After this is done, the purchase order is sent to accounts payable, and the packing slip is filed.

Marcia in accounts payable uses the purchase order and the invoice from the supplier to post to the purchases journal. She files the purchase order and the invoice. She then prepares a journal voucher from the purchases journal and sends it to general ledger.

Bob in the general ledger department uses the journal voucher and the summary from inventory control to post to the control accounts and reconcile. He then files the journal voucher and summary information.

The cash disbursements subsystem begins with Mary in accounts payable. She reviews the accounts payable file for items due and prepares the checks, as well as signs them and distributes them to the suppliers. She updates the check register and the accounts payable subsidiary ledger. She sends the journal voucher from the check register and the summary information from the accounts payable ledger to the general ledger.

Bob in general ledger reconciles the journal voucher and summary from Mary and posts to the control accounts. He then files the journal voucher and summary information.

Required:

a. Prepare a data flow diagram for the system described in the case.

b. Prepare a document flowchart for the system described in the case.

c. Identify the internal control weaknesses in the system. Structure your discussion around the six classes of internal control activities described in the chapter.

d. Redesign the system to take advantage of computer technology, such as batch with sequential files or batch with direct access files, etc. Explain your choice of computer technology. Prepare a flowchart of the new system.

3. Horox, Inc. (Prepared by Kate Cannon, Lehigh University)

Horox, Inc., is a manufacturer of portable compact disc (CD) players located outside of Philadelphia, Pennsylvania. It employs 1,500 workers at a centrally located, 15-acre production facility. It distributes its products worldwide through three nearby distribution centers. Sales are currently $20 million per year and growing. Horox was formed ten years ago; its management was relatively inexperienced and their technical knowledge was lacking. Since 1995, Horox has been expanding into new research areas and in the past three years has reported enormous profits in its financial statements.

Its major competitors for the little market share they have are electronic giants. Horox has managed to edge its way into retail chains and privately owned stores through the aggressiveness and wit of its sales staff. Horox supplies the major electronic chains and department stores, requiring payment for all orders within 30 days of the order or upon receipt.

Within the expenditure cycle, the company needs to purchase raw materials such as plastics and special computer chips and send these materials to the conversion cycle. The expenditure cycle also maintains the payroll department. John, a purchasing department clerk, monitors the inventory levels and determines whether purchases are necessary. He then prepares a purchase requisition. If purchases are needed, he prepares six copy purchase order forms. Two purchase orders are sent directly to the vendor. One is placed in an open purchase order file in the purchasing department, and another is used to update the records of the purchasing department. Both accounts payable and the receiving department get a purchase order. Upon receiving the goods with a packing slip, the receiving department creates five receiving reports. A receiving report is sent to the stores and the accounts payable department. Two receiving reports are sent to the purchasing department, where one is filed and one is used to update records. The final report is filed in the receiving department with the purchase order and packing slip. Vendors send the accounts payable department invoices, which are updated to the accounts payable subledger and the purchases journal and filed. A voucher is created from the purchases journal, and it is sent to the general ledger.

In the cash disbursements department, Larry prepares and signs the checks for the suppliers. He receives the information from the accounts payable department such as the purchase requisition, purchase order, receiving report, invoice, and the cash disbursements voucher. After preparation of the checks, these documents are sent back to the accounts payable department, and a journal voucher is sent to general ledger. A copy of the check is filed after the original is sent to the supplier. Within the general ledger, the journal voucher is reconciled with the summary sent by the accounts payable department. After reconciliation, the voucher and the summary are filed.

Required:
a. Prepare a data flow diagram for the system described in the case.
b. Prepare a document flowchart for the system described in the case.
c. Identify the internal control weaknesses in the system. Structure your discussion around the six classes of internal control activities described in the chapter.
d. Redesign the system to take advantage of computer technology, such as batch with sequential files or batch with direct access files, etc. Explain your choice of computer technology. Prepare a flowchart of the new system.

ACL ASSIGNMENTS

The files used for the following assignments are located in the **workbook.acl** document on the CD that accompanies this text. Some of the assignments employ the ACL's *relation* and *join* features. For detailed information on the use of these and other commands, consult ACL's on-line Help.

1. Open the **AP_Trans** (purchases) file and stratify it on the Quantity field. Print the last results window and comment on the action to be taken by the auditor.

2. Using the *relation* feature create a view from data in both the **AP_Trans** (purchases) and **Inventory** files that shows product details (**product description** and **quantity on-hand**). Print the view and comment on the results.

3. Open the **EMPMAST** (employee master file) and test for duplicate employee records. Prepare a last-results report that identifies anomalies or potential errors. Print the report and comment on the results.

4. Using the *relation* feature create a view of data from both the **Empmast** and **Payroll** files that test for paychecks to non-existent employees.

5. Using the *join* feature create a view of data from both the **Empmast** and **Payroll** files that tests for paychecks to non-existent employees.

10

FRAUD AND FRAUD DETECTION

Over the centuries, the practice of auditing developed concurrently with accounting because it was considered useless to keep accounts unless it was possible to ensure that they were kept accurately. Although auditing is a comparatively modern profession, the necessity for some independent check (attestation) of the accounts was consistently felt in ancient Egypt, the Roman Empire, and the great mercantile establishments of the Middle Ages.[1]

This chapter examines the two closely related subjects of ethics and fraud and their implications for auditing. We begin with a survey of ethical issues that highlight an organization's conflicting responsibilities to its employees, shareholders, customers, and the general public. Organization managers have an ethical responsibility to seek a balance between the risks and benefits to these constituents that result from their decisions. Similarly, employees have an ethical responsibility to their employers. Management, employees, and auditors need to recognize the implications of new information technologies for such historic issues as working conditions, the right to privacy, and the potential for fraud.

The second section is devoted to the subject of fraud. No major aspect of the independent auditor's role has caused more concern for the public accounting profession than the auditor's responsibility for detecting fraud during an audit. Although the term *fraud* is very familiar in today's financial press, it is not always clear what constitutes fraud. In this section, we examine the nature and meaning of fraud, differentiate between employee fraud and management fraud, explain fraud-motivating forces, and review common fraud techniques. The chapter concludes with a review of ACL tests that can be performed to detect fraud.

LEARNING OBJECTIVES

After studying this chapter, you should:

- Understand the broad issues pertaining to business ethics.
- Know why the subject of ethics is important to the study of accounting information systems.

---

1.   R. Lindberg and T. Cohn, *Operation Auditing* (New York: American Management Association, 1972).

- Have a basic understanding of ethical issues related to the use of information technology.
- Be able to distinguish between management fraud and employee fraud.
- Be familiar with the common fraud techniques used in both manual systems and computer-based systems.
- Be aware of the gap that exists between the expectations of financial statements users and the ability of auditors to detect fraud.

ETHICS

With scandals in the banking industry, stories of computer crimes and viruses, and almost daily charges of impropriety and illegalities by public officials in Washington, one cannot help but wonder about the current state of ethics in America. Such business activities as kickbacks, fraud, consumer deception, conflicts of interest, and the selling of products that are banned in the United States to Third World countries are all too common. Countless journal and newspaper articles, books, television programs, and movies are concerned with ethics or, more precisely, the lack of ethics in business, politics, education, and everyday life.

Ethical standards are derived from societal mores and deep-rooted personal beliefs about issues of right and wrong that are not universally agreed upon. It is quite possible for two individuals, both of whom consider themselves to be acting ethically, to be on opposite sides of an issue. Often, we confuse ethical issues with legal issues. When the Honorable Gentleman from the state of ———, who is charged with ethical misconduct, stands before Congress and proclaims that he is "guilty of no wrongdoing," is he really saying that he did not break the *law*?

WHAT IS BUSINESS ETHICS?

Ethics pertains to the principles of conduct that individuals use in making choices and guiding their behavior in situations that involve the concepts of right and wrong. More specifically, **business ethics** involves finding the answers to two questions:

1. How do managers decide on what is right in conducting their business?
2. Once managers have recognized what is right, how do they achieve it?

Ethical issues in business can be divided into four areas: equity, rights, honesty, and the exercise of corporate power. Figure 10–1 identifies some of the business practices in each of these areas that have ethical implications.

While interest in business ethics has increased significantly over the last decade, the subject has concerned both scholars and the public since the beginnings of the Western economy. Concerns about the moral shortcomings of financiers, bankers, and investors are found in many historical writings. In fact, many contemporary debates about the nature of business ethics are centuries old.[2]

John F. Akers, the former chairman of the board and CEO of IBM Corporation, states: "Our ethical standards come out of the past—out of our inheritance as a people:

---

2.   D. Vogel, "Business Ethics Past and Present," *Public Interest* (Winter 1991): 49–64.

FIGURE 10–1

Ethical Issues
in Business

ETHICAL ISSUES IN BUSINESS	
Equity	Executive Salaries Comparable Worth Product Pricing
Rights	Corporate Due Process Employee Health Screening Employee Privacy Sexual Harassment Affirmative Action Equal Employment Opportunity Whistleblowing
Honesty	Employee and Management Conflicts of Interest Security of Organization Data and Records Misleading Advertising Questionable Business Practices in Foreign Countries Accurate Reporting of Shareholder Interests
Exercise of Corporate Power	Political Action Committees Workplace Safety Product Safety Environmental Issues Divestment of Interests Corporate Political Contributions Downsizing and Plant Closures

religious, philosophical, historical. And the more we know of that past, the more sure-footedly we can inculcate ethical conduct in the future."[3]

Ethical behavior and personal gain are closely related issues. Medieval Catholicism deemed capitalism and money making to be morally wrong: "a Catholic could no more have been an ethical moneylender six centuries ago than he could be a socially responsible drug dealer today."[4] Many medieval merchants did act unscrupulously by any standards. But if their business was thought to be fundamentally immoral, why should they try to perform it ethically? How could they?

The Protestant Reformation made it possible for the successful business person to be an ethical individual as well. Profit and heaven were thus no longer mutually exclusive pursuits. A diligent worker could be rewarded financially as a sign of God's favor. Further, the acquisition of personal wealth could be socially beneficial. Hence, business people were rewarded with profits for fulfilling the needs and expectations of their customers, employees, and investors.

Protestant business ethics has had a significant impact on Western culture. Nineteenth-century Americans were very concerned with the relationship between the moral character of individuals and success in business. Contemporary business ethics shifts the focus away from the individual's character to the organization's actions. In addition, current discussions about business ethics have taken on a secular tone. Nonetheless, we remain preoccupied with the relationship of ethics and profit.

---

3.   J.F. Akers, "Ethics and Competitiveness—Putting First Things First," *Sloan Management Review* (Winter 1989): 69–71.

4.   Vogel, "Business Ethics Past and Present."

In today's world, many people believe that the term *business ethics* is an oxy-moron. However, good ethical behavior should also be good for business. This does not mean that firms that act ethically will prosper. Ethical behavior is a necessary but not a sufficient condition for business success. An equally important corollary is that firms that act unethically should be punished.

HOW SOME FIRMS ADDRESS ETHICAL ISSUES

In 1990, the Business Roundtable, composed of the chief executive officers of 200 major corporations, set up a task force that included several ethicists as consultants. The group studied ethics programs at ten companies and made recommendations that would help to ensure ethical practices within organizations. These included greater commitment of top management to improving ethical standards, written codes that clearly communicate management expectations, programs to implement ethical guide-lines, and techniques to monitor compliance.[5]

Some very successful companies have long emphasized ethics. For example, Boe-ing uses line managers to lead ethics training sessions and maintains a toll-free num-ber to enable employees to report violations. General Mills has published guidelines for dealing with vendors, competitors, and customers, and emphasizes open decision making. Johnson & Johnson's "credo" of corporate values is integral to its culture. It holds companywide meetings that challenge the credo tenets and uses surveys to as-certain compliance.[6]

THE ROLE OF MANAGEMENT IN MAINTAINING THE ETHICAL CLIMATE

Organization managers must create and maintain an appropriate ethical atmosphere; they must limit the opportunity and temptation for unethical behavior within the firm. It is not enough for managers to appeal to each individual's conscience. The individual must be made aware of the firm's commitment to ethics above short-term increases in profit and efficiency.[7]

Although top management's attitude toward ethics sets the tone for business practice, in many situations it is up to lower-level managers to uphold a firm's ethical standards. Poor ethical standards among employees are a root cause of employee fraud and other abuses. Reported abuses in Wall Street scandals have typically been perpe-trated by relatively junior employees. According to one study, half of American work-ers believe that the way to get ahead is through politics and cheating.[8] A survey of 9,175 employees in three different industries revealed that one-third of them had stolen property and supplies from their employers.[9] The Ethics Resource Center's 1994 study of employee transgressions found that the two most common types of abuse were fal-sifying reports (41 percent) and theft (35 percent).[10]

Methods need to be developed for including lower-level managers and employ-ees in the ethics schema of the firm. Managers and employees alike should be made

---

5.   J.A. Byrne, "Businesses Are Signing up for Ethics 101," *Business Week*, 15 February 1988, pp. 56–57.

6.   *Ibid*.

7.   S.W. Gellerman, "Managing Ethics from the Top Down," *Sloan Management Review* (Winter 1989): 73–79.

8.   P. Kim and J. Patterson, *The Day America Told the Truth* (New York, 1992).

9.   R. Hollinger and J. Clark, *Theft by Employees* (Lexington, MA, 1983).

10.   Ethics Resource Center, Inc., *Ethics in American Business: Policies, Programs, and Perceptions* (Washing-ton D.C., 1994).

aware of the firm's code of ethics, be given decision models, and participate in training programs that explore ethical issues.

ETHICAL DEVELOPMENT

Most individuals develop a code of ethics as a result of their family environment, formal education, and personal experiences. Behavioral stage theory suggests that we all go through several stages of moral evolution before settling on one level of ethical reasoning.[11] The levels in the stage theory model are presented in Figure 10–2. Managers who achieve Stage 6 are guided by self-chosen ethical principles and are not influenced by social pressure, fear, or guilt in their decisions.

MAKING ETHICAL DECISIONS

Business schools can and should be involved in the ethical development of future managers. Business programs can teach students analytical techniques to use in trying to understand and put into perspective a firm's conflicting responsibilities to its employees, shareholders, customers, and the public.

Every ethical decision has both risks and benefits. For example, implementing a new computer-based information system in an organization may cause some

FIGURE 10–2   Behavioral Stage Theory

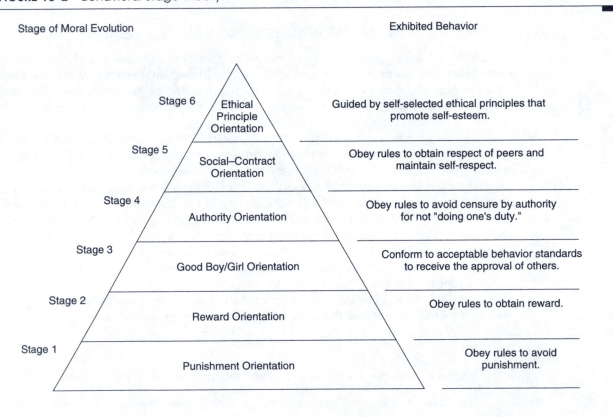

11.   G. Baxter and C. Rarick, "Education for the Moral Development of Managers: Kohlberg's Stages of Moral Development and Integrative Education," in James A. O'Brien, *Management Information Systems: A Managerial End User Perspective* (Boston: Irwin, 1993), p. 545.

employees to lose their jobs, while those who remain enjoy the benefit of improved working conditions. Seeking a balance between these consequences is the managers' **ethical responsibility**. The following ethical principles provide some guidance in the discharge of this responsibility.[12]

> *Proportionality.* The benefit from a decision must outweigh the risks. Furthermore, there must be no alternative decision that provides the same or greater benefit with less risk.

> *Justice.* The benefits of the decision should be distributed fairly to those who share the risks. Those who do not benefit should not carry the burden of risk.

> *Minimize Risk.* Even if judged acceptable by the above principles, the decision should be implemented so as to minimize all of the risks and avoid any unnecessary risks.

WHAT IS COMPUTER ETHICS?

The use of information technology in business has had a major impact on society and thus raises significant ethical issues regarding computer crime, working conditions, privacy, and more. **Computer ethics** is "the analysis of the nature and social impact of computer technology and the corresponding formulation and justification of policies for the ethical use of such technology . . . [This includes] conerns about software as well as hardware and concerns about networks connecting computers as well as computers themselves."[13]

Bynum has defined three levels of computer ethics: pop, para, and theoretical.[14] *Pop* computer ethics is simply the exposure to stories and reports found in the popular media regarding the good or bad ramifications of computer technology. The society at large needs to be aware of such things as computer viruses and computer systems designed to aid handicapped persons. *Para* computer ethics involves taking a real interest in computer ethics cases and acquiring some level of skill and knowledge in the field. All systems professionals need to reach this level of competency so they can do their jobs effectively. Students of accounting information systems should also achieve this level of ethical understanding. The third level, *theoretical* computer ethics, is of interest to multidisciplinary researchers who apply the theories of philosophy, sociology, and psychology to computer science with the goal of bringing some new understanding to the field.

A NEW PROBLEM OR JUST A NEW TWIST ON AN OLD PROBLEM?

There are many ethical issues to which students should be exposed. Some will argue that the pertinent issues have already been examined in some other domain. For example, the issue of property rights has been explored and has resulted in copyright, trade secret, and patent laws. Although computer programs are a new type of asset, many believe that they should not be considered as different from other forms of property. So a fundamental question is whether computers represent new ethical problems

---

12.   M. McFarland, "Ethics and the Safety of Computer System," *Computer*, February 1991.
13.   J.H. Moor, "What Is Computer Ethics?" *Metaphilosophy* 16 (1985): 266–75.
14.   T.W. Bynum, "Human Values and the Computer Science Curriculum" (Working paper for the National Conference on Computing and Values, August 1991).

or just create new twists on old problems. Where the latter is the case, we need only to understand the generic values that are at stake and the principles that should then apply.[15] However, a large contingent vociferously disagrees with the premise that computers are no different than other technology. For example, many reject the notion of intellectual property being the same as real property. There is, as yet, no consensus on this matter.

Below we have listed several issues of concern for the student of accounting information systems. This listing is not presumed to be exhaustive, and a full discussion of each of the issues is beyond the scope of this chapter. Instead, the issues are very briefly defined, and several trigger questions are provided. It is hoped that these questions will serve as discussion starters in the classroom. To give each of them a label and separate treatment, some overlap between issues is unavoidable.

PRIVACY

People desire to be in full control of what and how much information about themselves is available to others, and to whom it is available. This is the issue of **privacy**. "[P]rivacy is a matter of the restricted access to persons or information about persons."[16] The creation and maintenance of huge, shared databases makes it necessary to protect people from the potential misuse of data. This raises the issue of **ownership** in the personal information industry.[17] Should the privacy of individuals be protected through policies and systems? No laws currently govern this industry, yet the demand for personal information (for targeted mailing lists, for example) is ever-growing. What information about oneself does the individual "own"? Why can firms that are unrelated to individuals buy and sell information about these individuals without their permission?

SECURITY (ACCURACY AND CONFIDENTIALITY)

Computer **security** is an attempt to avoid such undesirable events as a loss of confidentiality or data integrity. Security systems attempt to prevent fraud and other misuse of computer systems; they act to protect and further the legitimate interests of the system's constituencies. The ethical issues involving security arise from the emergence of shared, computerized databases that have the potential to cause irreparable harm to individuals by disseminating inaccurate information to authorized users, such as through incorrect credit reporting.[18] There is a similar danger in disseminating accurate information to persons unauthorized to receive it. However, increasing security can actually cause other problems. For example, security can be used both to protect personal property and to undermine freedom of access to data, which may have a deleterious effect on some individuals. Which is the more important goal? Automated monitoring can be used to detect intruders or other misuse, yet it can also be used to spy on legitimate users, thus diminishing their privacy. Where is the line to be drawn? What is an appropriate use and level of security? Which is most important: security, accuracy, or confidentiality?

---

15.   G. Johnson, "A Framework for Thinking about Computer Ethics" in J. Robinette and R. Barquin (eds.), *Computers and Ethics: A Sourcebook for Discussions* (Brooklyn: Polytechnic Press, 1989), pp. 26–31.

16.   J.H. Moor, "The Ethics of Privacy Protection," *Library Trends* 39 (1990): 69–82.

17.   W. Ware, "Contemporary Privacy Issues" (Working paper for the National Conference on Computing and Human Values, August 1991).

18.   K.C. Laudon, "Data Quality and Due Process in Large Interorganizational Record Systems," *Communications of the ACM* (1986): 4–11.

OWNERSHIP OF PROPERTY

Laws designed to preserve real property rights have been extended to cover what is referred to as intellectual property, that is, software. The question here becomes, what can an individual (or organization) own? Ideas? Media? Source code? Object code? A related question is whether or not owners and users should be constrained in their use or access. Copyright laws have been invoked in an attempt to protect those who develop software from having it copied. Unquestionably, the hundreds and thousands of program development hours should be protected from piracy. However, many believe the copyright laws can cause more harm than good. For example, should the "look and feel" of a software package be granted copyright protection? The League for Programming Freedom argues that this flies in the face of the original intent of the law. Whereas the purpose of copyrights is to "promote the progress of science and the useful arts," allowing a user interface the protection of copyright may do just the opposite. The best interest of computer users is served when industry standards emerge; copyright laws work to disallow this. This same group also argues against the use of patents for software. Patents protect the holder against anyone using the same basic process, even if it is independently developed. Since patent searches are very expensive and quite unreliable, programmers may be sued for inadvertently using a process on which someone else holds the patent. Firms exist whose only mission is to obtain patents, then sue software developers for patent infringement. In trying to resolve these issues, social goals (such as preservation and dissemination of information, justice of distribution, and maximum potential of resources) are found to conflict with personal goals (recognition and credit, control, empowerment). Part of the problem lies in the uniqueness of software, its ease of dissemination, and the possibility of exact replication. Does software fit with the current categories and conventions regarding ownership?

RACE

While African-Americans and Hispanics constitute about 20 percent of the U.S. population, they make up only 7 percent of management information systems (MIS) professionals.[19] What causes this difference? Our society often tries to make restitution for past social wrongs. Should something special be done in this situation? If so, what, and how can reverse discrimination then be avoided? Or should it?

EQUITY IN ACCESS

Some barriers to access are intrinsic to the technology of information systems, but some are avoidable through careful system design. Several factors, some of which are not unique to information systems, can limit access to computing technology. The economic status of the individual or the affluence of an organization will determine the ability to obtain information technology. Culture also limits access, for example, where documentation is prepared only in one language or is poorly translated. Safety features, or the lack thereof, have limited access to pregnant women, for example. How can hardware and software be designed with consideration for differences in physical and cognitive skills? What is the cost of providing equity in access? For what groups of society should equity in access become a priority?

---

19.   J.S. Bozman, "MIS Dream Jobs Still Elude Blacks," *Computerworld*, 18 January 1988, p. 1.

ENVIRONMENTAL ISSUES

Computers with high-speed printers allow for the production of printed documents faster than ever before. It is probably easier just to print a document than to consider seriously whether it should be printed and how many copies really need to be made. It may be more efficient or more comforting to have a hard copy in addition to the electronic version. However, paper comes from trees, a precious natural resource, and ends up in landfills if not properly recycled. Should organizations limit nonessential hard copies? Can *nonessential* be defined? Who can and should define it? Should proper recycling be required? How can it be enforced?

ARTIFICIAL INTELLIGENCE

A new set of social and ethical issues has arisen out of the popularity of expert systems. Because of the way these systems have been marketed, that is, as decision-makers or replacements for experts, some people rely on them significantly. Therefore, both knowledge engineers (those who write the programs) and domain experts (those who provide the knowledge about the task being automated) must be concerned about their responsibility for faulty decisions, incomplete or inaccurate knowledge bases, and the role given to computers in the decision-making process.[20] Additionally, the proliferation of knowledge-based systems has the potential to cause a displacement of "experts" (most of whom are in middle management positions) similar to that which occurred to artisans during the Industrial Revolution. Further, since expert systems attempt to clone a manager's decision-making style, an individual's prejudices may implicitly or explicitly be included in the knowledge base. Some of the questions that need to be explored are: Who is responsible for the completeness and appropriateness of the knowledge base? Who is responsible for a decision made by an expert system that causes harm when implemented? Who owns the expertise once it is coded into a knowledge base?

UNEMPLOYMENT AND DISPLACEMENT

Many jobs have been and are being changed as a result of the availability of computer technology. People unable or unprepared to change are displaced and are finding it difficult to obtain new jobs. Should employers be responsible for retraining workers who are displaced as a result of the computerization of their functions? As mentioned above, even white-collar professionals are at risk for displacement. Should there be a concern over the exploitation of experts? How can the good provided by information systems be reconciled with their potential for harm?

MISUSE OF COMPUTERS

Computers can be misused in many ways. Copying proprietary software, using a company's computer for personal benefit, and snooping through other people's files are just a few obvious examples.[21] Although copying proprietary software (except to make a personal backup copy) is clearly illegal, it is commonly done. Why do people feel that

---

20.   R. Dejoie, G. Fowler, and D. Paradice (eds.), *Ethical Issues in Information Systems* (Boston: Boyd & Fraser, 1991).

21.   K.A. Forcht, "Assessing the Ethic Standards and Policies in Computer-Based Environments," in R. Dejoie, G. Fowler, and D. Paradice (eds.), *Ethical Issues in Information Systems* (Boston: Boyd & Fraser, 1991).

it is not necessary to obey this law? Are there any good arguments for trying to change this law? What harm is done to the software developer when people make unauthorized copies? A computer is not an item that deteriorates with use, so is there any harm to the employer if it is used for an employee's personal benefit? Does it matter if the computer is used during company time or outside of work hours? Is there a difference if some profit-making activity takes place rather than, for example, using the computer to write a personal letter? Does it make a difference if a profit-making activity takes place during or outside of working hours? Is it okay to look through paper files that clearly belong to someone else? Is there any difference between paper files and computer files?

INTERNAL CONTROL RESPONSIBILITY

A business cannot meet its financial obligations or achieve its objectives if its information is unreliable. Therefore, managers must establish and maintain a system of appropriate internal controls to ensure the integrity and reliability of their data.[22] Because much of the internal control system relates to the transaction processing system, information systems professionals and accountants are central to ensuring control adequacy.

Deadlines for putting new systems into place often become unachievable. For example, cutting corners by omitting audit trails and other controls might be suggested as a way to complete a project on time.[23] What are the ramifications of cutting certain corners? Is it ever appropriate? What is the purpose of an audit trail? What are the consequences for a system without one? How much control is adequate?

FRAUD

The lack of ethical standards is fundamental to business fraud. No major aspect of the independent auditor's role has caused more difficulty for the public accounting profession than the responsibility for the detection of fraud during an audit. Over the last 20 years, the structure of the U.S. financial reporting system has become the subject of congressional inquiries, and the issue of the auditor's role in detecting fraud has gathered momentum to the point where the public accounting profession today faces a crisis in public confidence in its ability to perform the independent attestation function.

The Securities and Exchange Commission, the courts, and the public, along with Congress, are focusing more and more on business failures and questionable practices by the management of corporations that engage alleged fraud. The question consistently being asked is, "Where were the auditors?"

Although fraud is a very familiar term in today's financial press, its meaning is not always clear. For example, in cases of bankruptcies and business failures, alleged fraud is more often poor management decisions or adverse business conditions. Under such circumstances, it becomes necessary to clearly define and understand the nature and meaning of fraud.

Fraud denotes a false representation of a material fact made by one party to another party with the intent to deceive and induce the other party to justifiably rely on

---

22.   All companies registered with the Securities and Exchange Commission are required by law (Foreign Corrupt Practices Act of 1977) to maintain such a system of internal control.
23.   E. Cohen and L. Cornwell, "A Question of Ethics: Developing Information Systems Ethics," *Journal of Business Ethics* 8 (1989): 431–37.

the fact to his or her detriment. According to common law, a fraudulent act must meet the following five conditions:

1. *False representation.* There must be a false statement or a nondisclosure.
2. *Material fact.* A fact must be a substantial factor in inducing someone to act.
3. *Intent.* There must be the intent to deceive or the knowledge that one's statement is false.
4. *Justifiable reliance.* The misrepresentation must have been a substantial factor on which the injured party relied.
5. *Injury or loss.* The deception must have caused injury or loss to the victim of the fraud.

Fraud in the business environment has a more specialized meaning. It is an intentional deception, misappropriation of a company's assets, or manipulation of its financial data to the advantage of the perpetrator. In the accounting literature, fraud is also commonly known as "white-collar crime," "defalcation," "embezzlement," and "irregularities." The auditor deals with fraud typically at two levels: management fraud and employee fraud. It is essential to distinguish between these two types of fraud since each has different responsibilities and implications for auditors.

Employee fraud or frauds by nonmanagement employees are generally designed to directly convert cash or other assets to the employee's personal benefit. Typically, the employee circumvents the company's internal control system for personal gain. If a company has an effective system of internal control, defalcations or embezzlements can usually be prevented or detected.

Employee fraud usually involves three steps: (1) stealing something of value (an asset), (2) converting the asset to a usable form (cash), and (3) concealing the crime to avoid detection. The third step is often the most difficult. It may be relatively easy for a storeroom clerk to steal inventories from his employer's warehouse, but altering the inventory records to hide the theft is more of a challenge.

Management fraud is more insidious than employee fraud and often escapes detection until irreparable damage or loss has been suffered by the organization. Usually management fraud does not involve the direct theft of assets. The Treadway Commission on Fraudulent Financial Reporting observes that on a macrolevel, management may engage in fraudulent activities to obtain a higher price from a stock or debt offering or just to meet the expectations of investors. The Commission on Auditors' Responsibilities calls it a "performance fraud" that often uses deceptive practices to inflate earnings or to forestall the recognition of either insolvency or a decline in earnings. Management fraud on a microlevel may typically involve materially misstating financial data and reports to gain additional compensation, to garner a promotion, or to escape the penalty for poor performance. Management fraud typically contains three special characteristics:[24]

1. The fraud is perpetrated at levels of management above the one to which internal control structures generally relate.
2. The fraud frequently involves using the financial statements to create an illusion that an entity is more healthy and prosperous than it actually is.

---

24.   R. Grinaker, "Discussant's Response to a Look at the Record on Auditor Detection of Management Fraud," *Proceedings of the 1980 Touche Ross University of Kansas Symposium on Auditing Problems* (Kansas City: University of Kansas, 1980).

3. If the fraud involves misappropriation of assets, it frequently is shrouded in a maze of complex business transactions, often involving related third parties.

The preceding characteristics of management fraud suggest that management can often perpetrate irregularities by overriding an otherwise effective internal control structure (that is, an internal control structure that would prevent similar irregularities by other employees). When management uses the financial statements to create an illusion, "the input data usually is manipulated to include false or questionable transactions or to include false or questionable judgment with respect to expense allocations or revenue recognition."[25]

FACTORS THAT CONTRIBUTE TO FRAUD

According to one study, people engage in fraudulent activity as a result of an interaction of forces both within an individual's personality and the external environment. These forces are classified into three major categories: (1) **situational pressures**, (2) **opportunity**, and (3) **personal characteristics (ethics)**. Figure 10–3 graphically displays the interplay of these three fraud-motivating forces.[26]

FIGURE 10–3   Fraud-Motivating Forces

25.   *Ibid.*
26.   M. Romney, W.S. Albrecht, and D.J. Cherrington, "Auditors and the Detection of Fraud," *Journal of Accountancy* (May 1980).

Figure 10–3 suggests that a person with a high level of personal ethics and limited pressure and opportunity to commit fraud is most likely to behave honestly. Similarly, an individual with less personal integrity, when placed in situations with increasing pressure and given the opportunity, is most likely to commit fraud.

While these factors, for the most part, fall outside of the auditors' sphere of influence, auditors can develop a *red-flag* checklist to detect possible fraudulent activity. To that end, a questionnaire approach could be used to help external auditors uncover motivations for committing fraud. Some of the larger public accounting firms have developed checklists to help uncover fraudulent activity during an audit. Questions for such a checklist might include:[27]

- Do key executives have unusually high personal debt?
- Do key executives appear to be living beyond their means?
- Do key executives engage in habitual gambling?
- Do key executives appear to abuse alcohol or drugs?
- Do any of the key executives appear to lack personal codes of ethics?
- Do any of the key executives appear to be unstable (e.g., have frequent job or residence changes or mental or emotional problems)?
- Are economic conditions unfavorable within the company's industry?
- Does the company use several different banks, none of which sees the company's entire financial picture?
- Do any key executives have close associations with suppliers?
- Is the company experiencing a rapid turnover of key employees, either through quitting or being fired?
- Do one or two individuals dominate the company?

A review of some of these questions suggests that the contemporary auditor may use special investigative agencies to run a complete but confidential background check on the key managers of existing and prospective client firms.

FINANCIAL LOSSES FROM FRAUD

A 1996 study by Certified Fraud Examiners (CFE) estimated losses from fraud and abuse to be six percent of annual revenues.[28] The actual cost of fraud is difficult to quantify for a number of reasons: (1) not all fraud is detected; (2) of that detected, not all is reported; (3) in many fraud cases, incomplete information is gathered; (4) information is not properly distributed to management or law enforcement authorities; and (5) too often, business organizations decide to take no civil or criminal action against the perpetrator(s) of fraud. In addition to the direct economic loss to the organization, indirect costs including reduced productivity, the cost of legal action, increased unemployment, and business disruption due to investigation of the fraud need to be considered.

The CFE study examined organizations in 12 different industries. The median dollar loss by industry is presented in Table 10–1. The study concluded that organizations with 100 or fewer employees were the most vulnerable to fraud. The education industry suffered the smallest losses, while the real estate financing industry suffered the largest losses. The large losses in the real estate segment reflect the savings and loan debacle of the late 1980s.

---

27.   *Ibid.*
28.   *Report to the Nation: Occupational Fraud and Abuse*, Association of Fraud Examiners, 1996, p. 15.

TABLE 10-1

Losses from
Fraud by Industry

Industry	Loss from Fraud
Real Estate and Finance	$475,000
Manufacturing	274,000
Banking	200,000
Oil & Gas	173,000
Construction	142,000
Health Care	105,000
Retail	100,000
Service	95, 000
Insurance	72,000
Government	50,000
Utility	50,000
Education	32,000

THE PERPETRATORS OF FRAUDS

The CFE study examined the personal characteristics of fraud perpetrators. The median financial loss was calculated for the following classifications: position in the organization, gender, age, and education. The results of the study are presented in the tables that follow.

MEDIAN LOSS BY POSITION WITHIN THE ORGANIZATION

The study indicated that 58 percent of the reported fraud cases were committed by non-managerial employees, 30 percent by managers, and 12 percent by owner/executives. However, the median fraud perpetrated by non-managerial employees was significantly lower than the management and executive frauds. Table 10–2 shows that non-managerial employees were responsible for a median loss of $60,000, compared to $250,000 for managers and $1 million for executives.

MEDIAN LOSS BY GENDER

Table 10–3 shows shows that the median loss per case caused by males ($185,000) was nearly four times that caused by females ($48,000).

TABLE 10-2

Losses from
Fraud by Position

Position	Percent of Frauds	Dollar Value
Owners	12	$1,000,000
Management	30	250,000
Employees	58	60,000

TABLE 10-3

Losses from
Fraud by Gender

Gender	Loss From Fraud
Male	$185,000
Female	48,000

MEDIAN LOSS BY AGE

Table 10–4 indicates that perpetrators 25 years of age or younger cause median losses of about $12,000, while employees 60 and older are perpetrated frauds that were on average 28 times larger—$346,000.

MEDIAN LOSS BY MARITAL STATUS

Table 10–5 shows that married employees commit the greatest number of frauds with the largest median losses.

MEDIAN LOSS BY EDUCATION

Table 10–6 shows a relationship between the perpetrator's educational level and the median loss caused by his or her fraud. The frauds of high school graduates averaged only $50,000, while those with advanced degrees averaged $275,000.

CONCLUSIONS TO BE DRAWN

What do these results tell us? On the surface they seem to suggest that an organization can reduce or eliminate fraud by hiring only unmarried, adolescent, female dropouts from high school. A little deeper analysis, however, takes us back to a point that was made earlier. Notwithstanding the importance of personal ethics, *situational pressures* and *opportunity* contribute greatly to fraud.

TABLE 10–4

Losses from
Fraud by Age

Age Range	Loss
< 25	$ 12,000
26 – 20	50,000
31 – 35	54,000
36 – 40	100,000
41 – 50	196,000
51 – 60	280,000
> 60	346,000

TABLE 10–5

Losses from
Fraud by
Marital Status

Marital Status	Loss
Married	$150,000
Divorced	80,000
Single	54,000
Separated	50,000

TABLE 10–6

Losses from
Fraud by
Education

Education Level	Loss
High School	$ 50,000
College	200,000
Post Graduate	275,000

SITUATIONAL PRESSURES.   As people age, they tend to marry and assume greater responsibilities. Life creates significant situational pressures that at one time or another
will test the ethics and honesty of most people. If we assume that heads of households
tend to feel situational pressures more severely other family members, and recognize
that more heads of households (in the economic sense) are men than women, then
some of the variance due to gender is explained.

OPPORTUNITY.   The real culprit responsible for explaining the loss variance presented
above is opportunity. Opportunity can be redefined as control over assets or access to
assets. Indeed, control and access are essential elements of opportunity. The financial
loss differences associated with most of the classifications above are explained by the
opportunity factor.

- *Gender.* While the demographic picture is changing, more men than women occupy positions of authority in business organizations, which provide them
  greater access to assets.
- *Position.* Those in the highest positions have the greatest access to company
  funds and assets.
- *Age.* Older employees tend to occupy higher-ranking positions and therefore
  generally have greater access to company assets
- *Education.* Generally, those with more education occupy higher positions in their
  organizations and therefore have greater access to company funds and other
  assets.

FRAUD SCHEMES

Fraud schemes can be classified in a number of different ways. For purposes of discussion, this section presents the classification format derived by the Association of
Certified Fraud Examiners. Three broad categories of fraud schemes are defined: fraudulent statements, corruption, and asset misappropriation.[29]

FRAUDULENT STATEMENTS

Fraudulent statements are associated with management fraud. While all fraud involves
some form of financial misstatement, to meet the definition under this class of fraud
scheme, the statement itself must bring direct or indirect financial benefit to the perpetrator. In other words, the statement is not simply a vehicle for obscuring or covering a
fraudulent act. For example, misstating the cash account balance to cover the theft of
cash does not fall under this class of fraud scheme. On the other hand, understating liabilities to present a more favorable financial picture of the organization does qualify.
Fraudulent statements account for about 5 percent of the fraud cases covered in the
CFE fraud study.

CORRUPTION

Corruption involves an executive, manager, or employee of the organization in collusion with an outsider. The CFE study identifies four principal types of corruption:
bribery, illegal gratuities, conflicts of interest, and economic extortion. Corruption accounts for about 10 percent of occupational fraud cases.

---

29.   *Ibid*, pp. 31–34.

BRIBERY.   **Bribery** involves giving, offering, soliciting, or receiving things of value to influence an official in the performance of his or her lawful duties. Officials may be employed by government (or regulatory) agencies or by private organizations. Bribery defrauds the entity (business organization or government agency) of the right to honest and loyal services from those employed by it. The following is an example of bribery.

> The manager of a meat-packing company offers a U.S. health inspector a cash payment. In return, the inspector suppresses his report of health violations discovered during a routine inspection of the meat-packing facilities. In this situation, the victims are those who rely upon the honest reporting of inspector. The loss is salary paid to the inspector for work not performed and any damages that result from failure to perform.

ILLEGAL GRATUITIES.   An **illegal gratuity** involves giving, receiving, offering, or soliciting something of value because of an official act that has been taken. This is similar to a bribe, but the transaction occurs after the fact. The following is an example of an illegal gratuity.

> The plant manager in a large corporation uses his influence to ensure that a request for proposals is written in such a way that only that one contractor will be able to submit a satisfactory bid. As a result, the favored contractor's proposal is accepted at a noncompetitive price. In return, the contractor secretly makes a financial payment to the plant manager. The victims in this case are those who expect a competitive procurement process. The loss is the excess costs incurred by the company because of the noncompetitive pricing of the construction.

CONFLICTS OF INTEREST.   Every employer should expect that his or her employees will conduct their duties in a way that serves the interests of the employer. A **conflict of interest** occurs when an employee acts on behalf of a third party during the discharge of his or her duties or has self-interest in the activity being performed. When the employee's conflict of interest is unknown to the employer and results in financial loss, then fraud has occurred. The preceding examples of bribery and illegal gratuities also constitute conflicts of interest. This type of fraud can exist, however, when bribery and illegal payments are not present, but the employee has an interest in the outcome of the economic event. The following is an example.

> A purchasing agent for a building contractor firm is also part owner in a plumbing supply company. The agent has sole discretion in selecting vendors for the plumbing supplies needed for buildings under contract. The agent directs a disproportionate number of purchase orders to his company, which charges above-market prices for its products. The agent's financial interest in the supplier is unknown to his employer.

ECONOMIC EXTORTION.   **Economic extortion** is the use (or threat) of force (including economic sanctions) by an individual or organization to obtain something of value. The item of value could be a financial or economic asset, information, or cooperation to obtain a favorable decision on some matter under review. The following is an example of economic extortion.

> A contract procurement agent for a state government threatens to blacklist a highway contractor if he does not make a financial payment to the agent. If the

contractor fails to cooperate, the blacklisting will effectively eliminate him from consideration for future work. Faced with a threat of economic loss, the contractor makes the payment.

ASSET MISAPPROPRIATION

The most common form of fraud scheme involves some type of asset misappropriation. Eighty-five percent of the frauds included in the CFE study fall into this category. Assets can be misappropriated either directly or indirectly for the perpetrator's benefit. Certain assets are more susceptible than others to misappropriation. Transactions involving cash, checking accounts, inventory, supplies, equipment, and information are the most vulnerable to abuse. Examples of fraud schemes involving asset misappropriation are described below.

CHARGES TO EXPENSE ACCOUNTS.   The theft of an asset creates an imbalance in the basic accounting equation (assets = equities), which the criminal must adjust if the theft is to go undetected. The most common way to conceal the imbalance is to charge the asset to an expense account and reduce equity by the same amount. For example, the theft of $20,000 cash could be charged to a miscellaneous operating expense account. The loss of the cash reduces the firm's assets by $20,000. To offset this, equity is reduced by $20,000 when the miscellaneous expense account is closed to retained earnings, thus keeping the accounting equation in balance. This technique has the advantage of limiting the criminal's exposure to one period. When the expense account is closed to retained earnings, its balance is reset to zero to begin the new period.

LAPPING.   **Lapping** involves the use of customer checks, received in payment of their accounts, to conceal cash previously stolen by an employee. For example, the employee first steals and cashes a check for $500 sent by Customer A. To conceal the accounting imbalance caused by the loss of the asset, Customer A's account is not credited. Later (the next billing period), the employee uses a $500 check received from Customer B and applies this to Customer A's account. Funds received in the next period from Customer C are then applied to the account of Customer B, and so on.

Employees involved in this sort of fraud often rationalize that they are simply borrowing the cash and plan to repay it at some future date. This kind of accounting cover-up must continue indefinitely or until the employee returns the funds. Lapping is usually detected when the employee leaves the organization or becomes sick and must take time off work. Unless the fraud is perpetuated, the last customer to have funds diverted from his or her account will be billed gain, and the lapping technique will be detected. Employers can deter lapping by periodically rotating employees into different jobs and forcing them to take scheduled vacations.

TRANSACTION FRAUD.   **Transaction fraud** involves deleting, altering, or adding false transactions to divert assets to the perpetrator. This technique may be used to ship inventories to the perpetrator in response to a fraudulent sales transaction or to disburse cash in payment of a false liability. A common type of transaction fraud involves the distribution of fraudulent paychecks to nonexistent employees. For example, an employee who has left the organization is kept on the payroll by her immediate supervisor. Each week, the supervisor continues to submit time cards to the payroll department just as if the employee was still working for the firm. The fraud works best in organizations that distribute employee paychecks to the supervisor, who then distributes them to the employees. The supervisor forges the ex-employee's signature and then cashes the check. Although the organization has lost cash, the fraud can go undetected because the credit to the cash account is offset by a debit to payroll expense.

COMPUTER FRAUD SCHEMES.   Since computers lie at the heart of most organizations' accounting information systems today, the topic of **computer fraud** is of special importance to auditors. While the objectives of the fraud are the same—misappropriation of assets—the techniques used to commit computer fraud vary greatly.

No one knows for sure how much businesses lose each year to computer fraud, but estimates ranging from $500 million to $10 billion per year give some indication of the problem's magnitude. One reason for the discrepancy between these estimates is that computer fraud is not well defined. For example, we saw in the ethics section of this chapter that some people do not view copying commercial computer software to be unethical. On the other side of this issue, software vendors consider this to be a criminal act. Regardless of how narrowly or broadly computer fraud is defined, most agree that it is a rapidly growing phenomenon.

For our purposes, computer fraud includes the following:

- The theft, misuse, or misappropriation of assets by altering computer-readable records and files
- The theft, misuse, or misappropriation of assets by altering the logic of computer software
- The theft or illegal use of computer-readable information
- The theft, corruption, illegal copying, or intentional destruction of computer software
- The theft, misuse, or misappropriation of computer hardware.

The General Model for Accounting Information System shown in Figure 10–4 portrays, conceptually, the key stages of an information system. Each stage in the model—data collection, data processing, database management, and information generation—is a potential area of risk for certain types of computer fraud.

Data Collection.   **Data collection** is the first operational stage in the information system. The objective is to ensure that event data entering the system are valid, complete, and free from material errors. In many respects, this is the most important stage in the system. Should transaction errors pass through data collection undetected, the organization runs the risk that the system will process the errors and generate erroneous and unreliable output. This, in turn, could lead to incorrect actions and poor decisions by the users.

Two rules govern the design of data collection procedures: relevance and efficiency. The information system should capture only relevant data. A fundamental task of the system designer is to determine what is and what is not relevant. He or she does so by analyzing the user's needs. Only data that ultimately contribute to information are relevant. The data collection stage should be designed to filter irrelevant facts from the system.

Efficient data collection procedures are designed to collect data only once. These data can then be made available to multiple users. Capturing the same data more than once leads to data redundancy and inconstancy. Information systems have limited collection, processing, and data storage capacity. Data redundancy overloads facilities and reduces the overall efficiency of the system. Inconsistency among data elements can result in inappropriate actions and bad decisions.

The simplest way to perpetrate a computer fraud is at the data collection or data entry stage. This is the computer equivalent of the transaction fraud discussed

FIGURE 10–4   The General Model for Accounting Information Systems

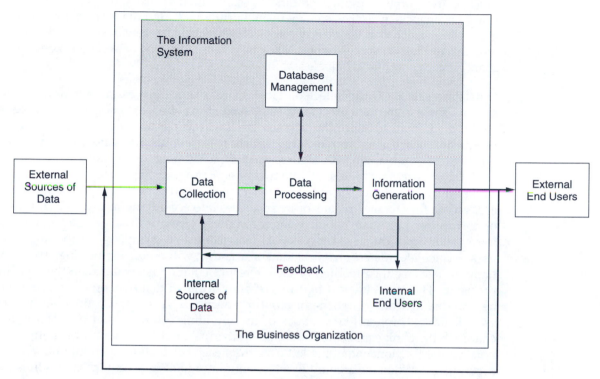

previously. Frauds of this type require little or no computer skills. The perpetrator need only understand how the system works to enter data that it will process. The fraudulent act involves falsifying data as it enters the system. This can be to delete, alter, or add a transaction. For example, to commit a payroll fraud, the perpetrator may insert a fraudulent payroll transaction along with other legitimate transactions. Unless the insertion is detected by internal controls, the system will generate an additional paycheck for the perpetrator. A variation on this type of fraud is to change the Hours Worked field in an otherwise legitimate payroll transaction to increase the amount of the paycheck.

Still another variant on this fraud is to disburse cash in payment of a false account payable. By entering fraudulent supporting documents (purchase order, receiving report, and supplier invoice) into the data collection stage of the accounts payable system, a perpetrator can fool the system into creating an accounts payable record for a nonexistent purchase. Once the record is created, the system will presume it is legitimate and, on the due date, will disperse funds to the perpetrator in payment of a bogus liability.

The trend toward distributed data processing and networking increasingly exposes organizations to transaction frauds from remote locations. "Masquerading," "piggybacking," and "hacking" are examples of such fraud techniques. Masquerading involves a perpetrator gaining access to the system from a remote site by pretending to be an authorized user. This usually requires first gaining authorized access to a password. Piggybacking is a technique in which the perpetrator at a remote site taps into the telecommunications lines and latches onto an authorized user who is logging into the system. Once in the system, the perpetrator can masquerade as the authorized user. Hacking may involve piggybacking or masquerading techniques. Hackers are distinguished from other computer criminals because their motives are not usually to defraud for financial gain. They are motivated primarily by the challenge of breaking into the system rather than the theft of assets. Nevertheless, hackers have caused extensive damage and loss to organizations. Many believe that the line between hackers and the more classic computer criminals is thin.

Data Processing.   Once collected, data usually require processing to produce information. Tasks in the data processing stage range from simple to complex. Examples include mathematical algorithms (such as linear programming models) used for production scheduling applications, statistical techniques for sales forecasting, and posting and summarizing procedures used for accounting applications.

Data processing frauds fall into two classes: program fraud and operations fraud. **Program fraud** includes the following techniques: (1) creating illegal programs that can access data files to alter, delete, or insert values into accounting records; (2) destroying or corrupting a program's logic using a computer virus; or (3) altering program logic to cause the application to process data incorrectly. For example, the program a bank uses to calculate interest on its customers' accounts will produce rounding errors. This happens because the precision of the interest calculation is greater than the reporting precision. Therefore, interest figures that are calculated to a fraction of one cent must be rounded to whole numbers for reporting purposes. A complex routine in the interest-calculation program keeps track of the rounding errors so that the total interest charge to the bank equals the sum of the individual credits. This involves temporarily holding the fractional amounts left over from each calculation in an internal memory accumulator. When the amount in the accumulator totals one cent (plus or minus), the penny is added to the customer's account that is being processed. In other words, one cent is added to (or deleted from) customer accounts randomly. A type of program fraud called the *salami fraud* involves modifying the rounding logic of the program so it no longer adds the one-cent randomly. Instead, the modified program always adds the plus-cent to the perpetrator's account but still adds the minus-cent randomly. This can divert a considerable amount of cash to the perpetrator, but the accounting records stay in balance to conceal the crime.

Operations fraud is the misuse or theft of the firm's computer resources. This often involves using the computer to conduct personal business. For example, a programmer may use the firm's computer time to write software that he sells commercially. A CPA in the controller's office may use the company's computer to prepare tax returns and financial statements for her private clients. Similarly, a corporate lawyer with a private practice on the side may use the firm's computer to search for court cases and decisions in commercial databases. The cost of accessing the database is charged to the organization and hidden among other legitimate charges.

Database Management.   The organization's database is its physical repository for financial and nonfinancial data. Database management involves three fundamental tasks: storage, retrieval, and deletion. The *storage* task assigns keys to new records and stores them in their proper location in the database. *Retrieval* is the task of locating and extracting an existing record from the database for processing. After processing is complete, the storage task restores the updated record to its place in the database. *Deletion* is the task of permanently removing obsolete or redundant records from the database.

Database management fraud includes altering, deleting, corrupting, destroying, or stealing an organization's data. Because access to database files is an essential element of this fraud, it is usually associated with transaction or program fraud. The most common technique is to access the database from a remote site and browse the files for useful information that can be copied and sold to competitors. Disgruntled employees have been known to destroy company data files simply to harm the organization. One method is to insert a destructive routine called a *logic bomb* into a program. At a specified time, or when certain conditions are met, the logic bomb erases the data files that the program accesses. For example, a disgruntled programmer who was contemplating leaving an organization inserted a logic bomb into the payroll system. Weeks later, when the system detected that the programmer's name had been removed from the payroll file, the logic bomb was activated and erased the payroll file.

Information Generation.   Information generation is the process of compiling, arranging, formatting, and presenting information to users. Information can be an operational document such as a sales order, a structured report, or a message on a computer screen. Regardless of physical form, useful information has the following characteristics: **relevance**, **timeliness**, **accuracy**, **completeness**, and **summarization**.

- *Relevance.* The contents of a report or document must serve a purpose. This could be to support a manager's decision or a clerk's task. We have established that only data relevant to a user's action have information content. Therefore, the information system should present only relevant data in its reports. Reports containing irrelevancies waste resources and may be counterproductive to the user. Irrelevancies detract attention from the true message of the report and may result in incorrect decisions or actions.
- *Timeliness.* The age of information is a critical factor in determining its usefulness. Information must be no older than the time period of the action it supports. For example, if a manager makes decisions daily to purchase inventory from a supplier based upon an inventory status report, then the information in the report should be no more than a day old.
- *Accuracy.* Information must be free from material errors. However, materiality is a difficult concept to quantify. It has no absolute value; it is a problem-specific concept. This means that in some cases, information must be perfectly accurate. In other instances, the level of accuracy may be lower. Material error exists when the amount of inaccuracy in information causes the user to make poor decisions or to fail to make necessary decisions. We sometimes must sacrifice absolute accuracy to obtain timely information. Often perfect information is not available within the decision time frame of the user. Therefore, in providing information, system designers seek a balance between information that is as accurate as possible, yet timely enough to be useful.
- *Completeness.* No piece of information essential to a decision or task should be missing. For example, a report should provide all necessary calculations and present its message clearly and unambiguously.
- *Summarization.* Information should be aggregated in accordance with user's needs. Lower-level managers tend to need information that is highly detailed. As information flows upward through the organization to top management, it becomes more summarized. Later in this chapter, we shall look more closely at the effects that organizational structure and managerial level have on information reporting.

A common form of fraud at the information generation stage is to steal, misdirect, or misuse computer output. One simple but effective technique called **scavenging** involves searching through the trash cans of the computer center for discarded output. A perpetrator can often obtain useful information from the carbon sheets removed from multipart reports or from paper reports that were rejected during processing. Sometimes output reports are misaligned on the paper or slightly garbled during printing. When this happens, the output must be reprinted and the original output is often thrown in the trash.

Another form of fraud called **eavesdropping** involves listening to output transmissions over telecommunications lines. Technologies are readily available that enable perpetrators to intercept messages being sent over unprotected telephone lines and microwave channels. Most experts agree that it is practically impossible to prevent a determined perpetrator from accessing data communication channels. Data encryption can, however, render useless any data captured through eavesdropping.

AUDITOR'S RESPONSIBILITY FOR DETECTING FRAUD

The auditor has a responsibility to plan and perform the audit to obtain reasonable assurance about whether the financial statements are free of material misstatement, whether caused by error or fraud. SAS 82, *Consideration of Fraud in a Financial Statement Audit*, is the current authoritative standard for describing the auditor's responsibility for detecting and reporting fraud. The following outlines the key elements of this document.[30]

SCOPE

The predecessor document, SAS 53, dealt with financial statement misstatements due to both errors and irregularities. SAS 82 provides an expanded description of fraud and deals only with the auditor's consideration of fraud.

RISK ASSESSMENT

The auditor is required to assess the risk of material misstatement of the financial statements due to fraud and should factor the **risk assessment** into the design of audit procedures. The assessment should include risk factors that relate to both fraudulent financial reporting and the misappropriation of assets.

FRAUDULENT FINANCIAL REPORTING

Risk factors that relate to fraudulent financial reporting are grouped according to classifications:

- *Management's Characteristics and Influence over the Control Environment.* These factors relate to the tone-at-the-top regarding internal control, management style, situational pressures, and the financial reporting process.
- *Industry Conditions.* This includes the economic and regulatory environment in which the entity operates. For example, a company in a declining industry or

---

30.   This section is based on *Comparison of SAS No. 82, Consideration of Fraud in a Financial Statement Audit, with SAS No. 53, The Auditor's Responsibility to Detect and Report Error and Irregularities* (New York AICPA, 1998).

with key customers experiencing business failures is at greater risk to fraud than one whose industry base is stable.

- *Operating Characteristics and Financial Stability.* This pertains to the nature of the entity and the complexity of its transactions. For example, an organization involved with related-party transactions with organizations that are not audited may be at risk to fraud.

MISAPPROPRIATION OF ASSETS

The risk factors related to misappropriation of assets are:

- *Susceptibility of Assets to Misappropriation.* The susceptibility of an asset pertains to its nature and the degree to which it is subject to theft. Liquid assets such as cash and bearer bonds are more susceptible to misappropriation than nonliquid assets such as steel girders and physical plant equipment.
- *Controls.* This class of risk factors involves the inadequacy or lack of controls designed to prevent or detect misappropriation of assets. For example, a database management system that does not adequately restrict access to accounting records increases the risk of asset misappropriation.

AUDITOR'S RESPONSE TO RISK ASSESSMENT

The auditor's judgments about the risk of material misstatements due to fraud may affect the audit in the following ways:

- *Engagement Staffing and Extent of Supervision.* The knowledge, skill, and ability of personnel assigned to the engagement should be commensurate with the assessment of the level of risk of the engagement.
- *Professional Skepticism.* Exercising professional skepticism involves maintaining an attitude that includes a questioning mind and critical assessment of audit evidence.
- *Nature, Timing, and Extent of Procedures Performed.* Fraud risk factors that have control implications may limit the auditor's ability to assess control risk below the maximum and thus reduce substantive testing.

RESPONSE TO DETECTED MISSTATEMENTS DUE TO FRAUD

To some degree, the risk of material misstatement due to fraud always exists. The auditor's response is thus influenced by the degree of assessed risk. In some cases, the auditor may determine that currently planned audit procedures are sufficient to respond to the risk factors. In other cases, the auditor may decide to extend the audit and modify planned procedures. In rare instances, the auditor may conclude that procedures cannot be sufficiently modified to address the risk, in which case the auditor should consider withdrawing from the engagement and communicating the reasons for withdrawal to the audit committee.

When the auditor has determined that fraud exists but has had no material effect on the financial statements, the auditor should:

- Refer the matter to an appropriate level of management at least one level above those involved.
- Be satisfied that implications for other aspects of the audit have been adequately considered.

When the fraud has had a material effect on the financial statements or the auditor is unable to evaluate its degree of materiality, the auditor should:

- Consider the implications for other aspects of the audit.
- Discuss the matter with an appropriate level of management that is at least one level above those involved and with senior management.
- Attempt to determine whether the fraud is material.
- Suggest that the client consult with legal counsel, if appropriate.

DOCUMENTATION REQUIREMENTS

The auditor should document in the working papers the criteria used for assessing the fraud risk factors. Where risk factors are identified, the documentation should include (1) those risk factors identified and (2) the auditor's response to them.

FRAUD DETECTION TECHNIQUES

Because of the need to falsify accounting records, many fraud schemes leave a trail in the underlying accounting data that the forensic auditor can follow if he or she knows what to look for. For businesses with a large volume of transactions, however, finding the telltale trail using manual procedures may be impossible. Computer-based data extraction and analysis tools such as ACL are thus essential.

To find the trail in the masses of data, the auditor first develops a "fraud profile" that identifies the data characteristics that one would expect to find in a specific type of fraud scheme.[31] This requires an understanding of the enterprise's processes and internal controls (and their weaknesses). Once the fraud profile is developed, ACL can be used to manipulate the organization's data to search for transactions that fit the profile. In this section, we examine the operational and data characteristics of three common fraud schemes. The ACL features used for fraud detection are outlined in Chapters 8 and 9 and explained in detail in the ACL workbook that accompanies this text. The following discussion presumes that the reader is familiar with that material.

PAYMENTS TO FICTITIOUS VENDORS

The purchasing function is particularly vulnerable to fraud, and for many organizations represents a significant area of risk. A common fraud scheme involves making a payment to a fictitious company. A preliminary step in this scheme requires the perpetrator to create a phony vendor organization and establish it in the victim organization's records as a legitimate supplier. The embezzler then submits invoices from the fake vendor, which are processed by the accounts payable system of the victim-company. Depending on the organizational structure and internal controls in place, this type of fraud may require collusion between two or more individuals. For example, the purchasing agent prepares a purchase order for items from the fake vendor and the receiving clerk prepares a fictitious receiving report for the items. Accounts payable receives these documents, which appear to be legitimate, and matches them to the phony

---

31.   D. Johnson, "Finding the Needle in the Haystack," *ACL Services Ltd. (internal publication)* (Vancouver BC, Canada, 1997).

invoice when it arrives. An accounts payable is recorded and payment is subsequently made. In smaller organizations, a single individual with the authority to authorize payments can hatch a simpler version of the scheme. The fraud profile describing the false-vendor scheme and the audit procedures are described below.

SEQUENTIAL INVOICE NUMBERS

Since the victim-organization is the only recipient of the invoices, the supporting invoices "issued" by the phony vendor may actually be in something close to an unbroken numerical sequence.

AUDIT PROCEDURE.   Use ACL to *sort* the records of the Invoice file by invoice number and vendor number. This will highlight records that possess series characteristics, which can then be retrieved for further review.

VENDORS WITH P.O. BOXES

Most legitimate suppliers have a complete business address. Since fake suppliers have no physical facilities, the perpetrator of the fraud will sometimes rent a P.O. box to receive payments by mail. While it is also possible for a legitimate vendor to use a P.O. box, they are candidates for further review.

AUDIT PROCEDURE.   Using ACL's expression builder, create a *filter* to select vendor records from the Invoice File that use P.O. box addresses. From this list, verify the legitimacy of the vendor.

VENDORS WITH EMPLOYEE ADDRESSES

Rather than rent a P.O. box, the perpetrator may use his or her home address on the invoice. While it is also possible that an employee's home-based business is a legitimate supplier, this is not likely and should be investigated.

AUDIT PROCEDURE.   Use ACL to *join* the Employee File and the Invoice File using the address fields as the common key for both files. Only records that match should be passed to the resulting combined file. These records can then be reviewed further.

MULTIPLE COMPANIES WITH THE SAME ADDRESS

To divert attention away from excessive purchases made from the same vendor, a perpetrator may create several phony suppliers that share the same mailing address.

AUDIT PROCEDURE.   Use ACL's *duplicates* command to generate a listing of mailing addresses that are common to two or more vendors.

INVOICE AMOUNTS SLIGHTLY BELOW THE REVIEW THRESHOLD

Many organizations control disbursements by establishing a materiality threshold. A management review and signature is required for all checks that exceed the threshold. Those that fall below the limit are not reviewed. Knowing this, the perpetrator may falsify payments that fall just under the threshold to maximize his or her benefit from the fraud.

AUDIT PROCEDURE.   Use ACL's expression builder to create a value range around the control threshold. To highlight suspicious activity that warrants further investigation, *sort* payments records that fall within this range by vendor.

PAYROLL FRAUD

The two common forms of **payroll fraud** are overpayment of employees and payments to nonexistent employees. The first scheme typically involves inflating the number of hours worked and/or issuing duplicate payroll checks. The second approach involves entering fictitious employees into the payroll system. A supervisor, who then receives the resulting payroll checks, usually perpetrates this type of fraud. A variation on this scheme is to keep a terminated employee on the payroll. Suggested audit procedures for detecting these frauds are described below.

TEST FOR EXCESSIVE HOURS WORKED

AUDIT PROCEDURE.   Use ACL's expression builder to select payroll records that reflect excessive hours worked. The determination of what is excessive will depend on the nature of organization and its policies. If moderate overtime is fairly common, then filtering records with hours worked of greater than 50 hours may uncover instances of fraud. Using this filter to review employee records over time may disclose a pattern of abuse.

TEST FOR DUPLICATE PAYMENTS

AUDIT PROCEDURE.   Use ACL's *duplicates* function to search payroll records for employees with:

- Same employee number, same name, same address, etc., (duplicate payments).
- Same name with different mailing addresses.
- Same name with different checking accounts.
- Same name with different social security numbers.
- Same mailing address with different employee names.

Some duplicate records detected in the search will be due to natural phenomena (i.e., unrelated individuals who happen to have the same name). The results, however, provide the auditor with a basis for further review.

TESTS FOR NONEXISTENT EMPLOYEES

AUDIT PROCEDURE.   Use ACL's *join* feature to link the payroll and employee files using Employee Number as the common attribute. The resulting joined file should contain only those records from the payroll file that do not match valid employee records. These records need to be reviewed with management.

LAPPING ACCOUNTS RECEIVABLE

Lapping was described earlier in the chapter as the theft of a customer's check received in payment on their account. The perpetrator then covers the theft in the following period by applying cash received from a second customer to the account of the first. The simplicity of this fraud technique is key to its success because it presents a very obscure fraud profile. The only evidence of fraud in the underlying data is in the timing difference between when payment is received and when it is recorded. Depending on how the organization structures its accounts receivable, this may be difficult to detect. The problem is illustrated by comparing two common methods of managing accounts receivable.

THE BALANCE FORWARD METHOD

The **balance forward method** is used extensively for consumer accounts. Total sales to customers for the period are itemized and billed at the period end. Customers are required to pay only a minimum amount off the balance. The rest of the balance, plus interest, is carried forward to the next period.

Lapping is difficult to detect in this type of system. For example, assume the perpetrator embezzles a customer payment of $500. This amount would not be posted to the customer's account in the current period and the balance carried forward to the next period would be overstated by $500. In the following period, cash taken from another customer would be used to cover this amount. Since balances carried forward are commonplace, an overstated amount does not draw attention internally. The customer, however, may complain that the payment was not recorded. If the embezzler himself deals with the complaint, he could explain that the payment was received too late to be reflected on the current statement but would show up in the next period.

THE OPEN INVOICE METHOD

The **open invoice method** is often used to manage trade accounts receivable (sales to other business organizations). Each invoice is recorded as a separate item in the invoice file. Checks received from customers are usually in payment of individual invoices. Since good credit relations between customer and supplier are critical, payments tend to be on time and in full. Partial payments resulting in balances carried forward are the exception rather than the norm.

To illustrate lapping in this situation, assume that Customer "A" remits a check for $1,523.61 in payment of an open invoice for the same amount. The perpetrator pockets the check, but does not close the invoice. Therefore, the invoice balance is carried forward. In the next period, Customer "B" remits a check for $2,636.88 in full payment of an open invoice. The embezzler applies $1,523.61 of this payment to Customer A's open invoice, thus closing it. The remainder ($1,113.27) is applied to Customer B's invoice, which remains open. The balance of $1,523.61 is carried forward into the next period. This carry-forward characteristic provides the forensic auditor with a basis for constructing a fraud profile. To illustrate, refer to invoice record structure in Figure 10–5.

The Invoice Amount field in Figure 10–5 is the accounts receivable amount due. The Due Date field is calculated at the time of the sale, and the Closed Date field is entered when the payment is received. The Remittance Amount field reflects the amount of payment received from the customer.

AUDIT PROCEDURE.   Lapping is a fraud that must to be actively continued by the perpetrator. The fraud profile is thus best observed over time. If the organization

FIGURE 10–5	Invoice Number	Customer Number	Invoice Amount	Sales Date	Due Date	Closed Date	Remittance Number
Sales Invoice File	77885	23671	2,636.88	02/12/99	02/25/99	03/28/98	1,113.27

follows proper backup procedures, the invoice file will be copied frequently throughout the period, thus producing several archived versions of the file. Collectively, these files reflect the invoice amounts carried forward from month to month for the period under review. If the auditor suspects lapping, he or she may employ the following ACL tests:

- Use ACL's expression builder to select items from each file version whose Remittance Amount is greater than zero and less than the Invoice Amount field. These sets of records may contain legitimate items that are being disputed by the customers. For example, damaged goods, overcharges, and refused deliveries may result in customers making only partial payments. The auditor will need to sift through these legitimate issues to identify lapping.
- *Merge* the resulting carry-forward files into a single file reflecting activity for the entire period.
- Create a *calculated field* of the amount carried forward (Invoice Amount— Remittance Amount)
- Use the *duplicates* command to search the file for calculated carry-forward amounts that are the same. Following the example illustrated above, a carry-forward pattern of $1,523.61 will emerge.

SUMMARY

This chapter began by examining ethical issues that societies have pondered for centuries. It is increasingly apparent that good ethics is a necessary condition for the long-term profitability of a business. This requires that ethical issues be understood at all levels of the firm, from top management to line workers. In this section, we identified several ethical issues for auditors to consider in their fraud risk assessment.

In the second section, we examined fraud and its relationship to auditing. Fraud falls into two general categories: management fraud and employee fraud. Management fraud typically involves the material misstatement of financial data and reports to attain additional compensation or promotion or to escape the penalty for poor performance. Managers that perpetrate fraud often do so by overriding the internal control structure. Employee frauds are generally designed to convert cash or other assets directly to the employee's personal benefit. Typically, the employee circumvents the company's internal control structure for personal gain. However, if a company has an effective system of internal control, defalcations or embezzlements can usually be prevented or detected. The section examined several well-documented fraud techniques used in both manual and computer-based systems.

The chapter concluded with a review of fraud detection techniques. Three common forms of fraud were examined: false payments to vendors, payroll fraud, and lapping. Audit procedures employing ACL technology were presented.

KEY TERMS

accuracy
balance forward method
bribery
business ethics
completeness

computer ethics
computer fraud
conflict of interest
database management fraud
data collection

eavesdropping
economic extortion
employee fraud
ethical responsibility
ethics
fraud
illegal gratuity
lapping
management fraud
open invoice method
operations fraud
opportunity
ownership

payroll fraud
personal characteristics (ethics)
privacy
program fraud
relevance
risk assessment
scavenging
security
situational pressures
summarization
timeliness
transaction fraud

REVIEW QUESTIONS

1. What is ethics?
2. What is business ethics?
3. What are the four areas of ethical business issues?
4. What is a business code of ethics?
5. What are three ethical principles that may provide some guidance for ethical responsibility?
6. What is computer ethics?
7. How do the three levels of computer ethics—pop, para, and theoretical—differ?
8. Are computer ethical issues new problems or just a new twist on old problems?
9. What are the computer ethical issues regarding privacy?
10. What are the computer ethical issues regarding security?
11. What are the computer ethical issues regarding ownership of property?
12. What are the computer ethical issues regarding race?
13. What are the computer ethical issues regarding equity in access?
14. What are the computer ethical issues regarding the environment?
15. What are the computer ethical issues regarding artificial intelligence?
16. What are the computer ethical issues regarding unemployment and displacement?
17. What are the computer ethical issues regarding misuse of computers?
18. What are the computer ethical issues regarding internal control responsibility?
19. What are the five conditions that constitute fraud under common law?
20. What is fraud in the business environment?
21. What is management fraud?
22. What is employee fraud?
23. What are the three forces within an individual's personality and the external environment that interact to promote fraudulent activity?
24. How can external auditors attempt to uncover motivations for committing fraud?
25. What is lapping?
26. What is kiting?
27. What is transaction fraud?
28. What is computer fraud and what types of activities does it include?
29. At which stage of the general accounting model is it easiest to commit computer fraud?

DISCUSSION QUESTIONS

1. Distinguish between ethical issues and legal issues.

2. Some argue against corporate involvement in socially responsible behavior because the costs incurred by such behavior place the organization at a disadvantage in a competitive market. Discuss the merits and flaws of this argument.

3. Although top management's attitude toward ethics sets the tone for business practice,

sometimes it is up to lower-level managers to uphold a firm's ethical standards. John, an operations-level manager, discovers that the company is illegally dumping toxic materials and is in violation of environmental regulations. John's immediate supervisor is involved in the dumping. What action should John take?

4. When a company has a strong internal control structure, stockholders can expect the elimination of fraud. Comment on the soundness of this statement.

5. Distinguish between employee fraud and management fraud.

6. The estimates of losses annually due to computer fraud vary widely. Why do you think obtaining a good estimate of this figure is difficult?

7. What are the five conditions necessary for an act to be considered fraudulent?

8. Distinguish between exposure and risk.

9. Explain the characteristics of management fraud.

10. The text discusses many questions about personal traits of employees that might help uncover fraudulent activity. Name three.

11. Give two examples of employee fraud and explain how the theft might occur.

12. Discuss the fraud schemes of bribery, illegal gratuities, and economic extortion.

13. Explain at least three forms of computer fraud.

14. Why are the computer ethics issues of privacy, security, and property ownership of interest to accountants?

MULTIPLE-CHOICE QUESTIONS

1. To conceal the theft of cash receipts from customers in payment of their accounts, which journal entry below should the bookkeeper make?

	DR	CR
a.	Miscellaneous Expense	Cash
b.	Petty Cash	Cash
c.	Cash	Accounts Receivable
d.	Sales Returns	Accounts Receivable
e.	None of the above	

2. Which of the following controls would best prevent the lapping of accounts receivable?
   a. Segregate duties so that the clerk responsible for recording in the accounts receivable subsidiary ledger has no access to the general ledger.
   b. Request that customers review their monthly statements and report any unrecorded cash payments.
   c. Require customers to send payments directly to the company's bank.
   d. Request that customers make the check payable to the company.

3. Which of the following is NOT a necessary condition under common law to constitute a fraudulent act?
   a. injury or loss
   b. material fact
   c. written documentation
   d. justifiable reliance

4. The fraud scheme that is similar to the "borrowing from Peter to pay Paul" scheme is
   a. expense account fraud.
   b. kiting.
   c. lapping.
   d. transaction fraud.

5. Which ethical principle states that the benefit from a decision must outweigh the risks, and that there is no alternative decision that provides the same or greater benefit with less risk?
   a. minimize risk
   b. justice
   c. informed consent
   d. proportionality

6. Individuals who acquire some level of skill and knowledge in the field of computer ethics

are involved in which level of computer ethics?

a. para computer ethics
b. pop computer ethics
c. theoretical computer ethics
d. practical computer ethics

7. All of the following are issues of computer security except
a. releasing incorrect data to authorized individuals.
b. permitting computer operators unlimited access to the computer room.
c. permitting access to data by unauthorized individuals.
d. providing correct data to unauthorized individuals.

8. Which characteristic is NOT associated with software as intellectual property?
a. uniqueness of the product
b. possibility of exact replication
c. automated monitoring to detect intruders
d. ease of dissemination

9. For an action to be called fraudulent, all of the following conditions are required except
a. poor judgment.
b. false representation.
c. intent to deceive.
d. injury or loss.

10. One characteristic of employee fraud is that the fraud
a. is perpetrated at a level to which internal controls do not apply.

b. involves misstating financial statements.
c. involves the direct conversion of cash or other assets to the employee's personal benefit.
d. involves misappropriating assets in a series of complex transactions involving third parties.

11. Forces that may permit fraud to occur do not include
a. a gambling addiction.
b. lack of segregation of duties.
c. centralized decision-making environment.
d. questionable integrity of employees.

12. Which of the following best describes lapping?
a. applying cash receipts to a different customer's account in an attempt to conceal previous thefts of funds
b. inflating bank balances by transferring money among different bank accounts
c. expensing an asset that has been stolen
d. creating a false transaction

13. Operations fraud includes
a. altering program logic to cause the application to process data incorrectly.
b. misusing the firm's computer resources.
c. destroying or corrupting a program's logic using a computer virus.
d. creating illegal programs that can access data files to alter, delete, or insert values.

PROBLEMS

1. Expense Account Fraud
While auditing the financial statements of the Petty Corporation, the certified public accounting firm of Trueblue and Smith discovered that its client's legal expense account was abnormally high. Further investigation of the records indicated the following:
- Since the beginning of the year, several disbursements totaling $15,000 had been made to the law firm of Swindle, Fox, and Kreip.

- Swindle, Fox, and Kreip were not the Petty Corporation's attorneys.
- A review of the canceled checks showed that they had been written and approved by Mary Boghas, the cash disbursements clerk.
- Boghas's other duties included performing the end-of-month bank reconciliation.
- Subsequent investigation revealed that Swindle, Fox, and Kreip are representing Mary Boghas in an unrelated embezzle-

ment case in which she is the defendant. The checks had been written in payment of her personal legal fees.

Required:

a. What control procedures could the Petty Corporation have employed to prevent this unauthorized use of cash? Classify each control procedure in accordance with the SAS 78 framework (authorization, segregation of functions, supervision, and so on).

b. Comment on the ethical issues in this case.

2. Tollbooth Fraud

Collectors at Tollbooths A and B (see following figure) have colluded to perpetrate a fraud. Each day, Tollbooth Collector B provides A with a number of toll tickets prestamped from Tollbooth B. The price of the toll from Point B to Point A is 35 cents. The fraud works as follows:

Drivers entering the turnpike at distant points south of B will pay tolls up to $5. When these drivers leave the turnpike at Point A, they pay the full amount of the toll printed on their tickets. However, the tollbooth collector replaces the tickets collected from the drivers with the 35-cent tickets provided by B, thus making it appear that the drivers entered the turnpike at Point B. The difference between the 35-cent tickets submitted as a record of the cash receipts and the actual amounts paid by the drivers is pocketed by Tollbooth Collector A and shared with B at the end of the day. Using this technique, Collectors A and B have stolen over $20,000 in unrecorded tolls this year.

Required:

What control procedures could be implemented to prevent or detect this fraud? Classify the control procedures in accordance with SAS 78.

3. CMA 1289 3-Y6

Causes of Fraud

The studies conducted by the National Commission on Fraudulent Financial Reporting (the Treadway Commission) revealed that fraudulent financial reporting usually occurs as the result of certain environmental, institutional, or individual influences and opportune situations. These influences and opportunities, present to some degree in all companies, add pressures and motivate individuals and companies to engage in fraudulent financial reporting. The effective prevention and detection of fraudulent financial reporting requires an understanding of these influences and opportunities, while evaluating the risk of fraudulent financial reporting that these factors can create in a company. The risk factors to be assessed include not only internal ethical and control factors but also external environmental conditions.

Required:

a. Identify two situational pressures in a public company that would increase the likelihood of fraud.

b. Identify three corporate circumstances (opportune situations) where fraud is easier to commit and detection is less likely.

c. For the purpose of assessing the risk of fraudulent financial reporting, identify the external environmental factors that should be considered in the company's
   i. industry.
   ii. business environment.
   iii. legal and regulatory environment.

d. List several recommendations that top management should incorporate to reduce the possibility of fraudulent financial reporting.

4. Financial Aid Fraud

Harold Jones, the financial aid officer at a small university, manages all aspects of the financial aid program for needy students. Jones receives requests for aid from students, determines whether the students meet the aid criteria, authorizes aid payments, notifies the applicants that their request has been either approved or denied, writes the financial aid checks on the account he controls, and requires that the students come to his office to receive the checks in person. For years, Jones has used his position of authority to perpetrate the following fraud:

Jones encourages students who clearly will not qualify to apply for financial aid. Although the students do not expect aid, they apply on the "off chance" that it will be awarded. Jones modifies the financial information in the students' applications so that it falls within the established guidelines for aid. He then approves aid and writes aid checks payable to the students. The students, however, are informed that aid was denied. Since the students expect no aid, the checks in Jones's office are never collected. Jones forges the students' signatures and cashes the checks.

Required:
Identify the internal control procedures (classified per SAS 78) that could prevent or detect this fraud.

5. Kickback Fraud
    The kickback is a form of fraud often associated with purchasing. Most organizations expect their purchasing agents to select the vendor that provides the best products at the lowest price. To influence the purchasing agent in his or her decision, vendors may grant the agent financial favors (cash, presents, football tickets, and so on). This activity can result in orders being placed with vendors that supply inferior products or charge excessive prices.

Required:
Describe the controls that an organization can employ to deal with kickbacks. Classify each control as either preventive, detective, or corrective.

ACL ASSIGNMENT

1. False Vendor Fraud
    You are the auditor of a large company. You suspect that employees may have established themselves as false vendors. A copy of the Vendor and Empmast (employee master) files are located in the ACL Workbook document on the CD that accompanies this textbook. Perform the necessary audit tests to produce a list of employees that may be guilty of this fraud scheme.

GLOSSARY

The chapter in which the term is first defined is set in parentheses following the definition.

Access controls: Controls that ensure that only authorized personnel have access to the firm's assets. (1)

Access method: The technique used to locate records and to navigate through the database. (3)

Access tests: Tests that ensure that the application prevents authorized users from unauthorized access to data. (6)

Accounting records: The documents, journals, and ledgers used in transaction cycles. (1)

Accuracy tests: Tests that ensure that the system processes only data values that conform to specified tolerances. (6)

American National Standards Institute (ANSI): The most popular EDI standard in the United States. (5)

Amplitude: Strength of transmission signal. (5)

Assurance services: Professional services that are designed to improve the quality of information, both financial and nonfinancial, used by decision-makers. (1)

Asynchronous: Transmission method in which there is no continuous synchronization between the sending and receiving devices. (5)

Attendance file: File created by the time-keeping department upon receipt of approved time cards. (9)

Attributes: Equivalents to adjectives in the English language that serve to describe the objects. (3)

Audit objectives: Audit goals derived from management assertions that lead to the development of audit procedures. (1)

Audit opinion: Opinion of auditor regarding the presentation of financial statements. (1)

Audit planning: Stage at which the auditor identifies the financially significant applications and attempts to understand the controls over the primary transactions that are processed by these applications. (1)

Audit procedures: Tasks performed by auditors to gather evidence that supports or refutes management assertions. (1)

Audit risk: Probability that the auditor will render unqualified opinions on financial statements that are, in fact, materially misstated. (1)

Audit trail: Accounting records that trace transactions from their source document to the financial statements. (2)

Auditing: Form of independent attestation performed by an expert who expresses an opinion about the fairness of a company's financial statements. (1)

Authenticity tests: Tests verifying that an individual, a programmed procedure, or a message attempting to access a system is authentic. (6)

Backbone systems: Basic system structure on which to build. (4)

Base case system evaluation (BCSE): Variant of the test data technique, in which comprehensive test data are used. (6)

Batch controls: Effective method of managing high volumes of transaction data through a system. (6)

Batch control totals: Record that accompanies the sales order file through all of the data processing runs. (8)

Bill of lading: Formal contract between the seller and the shipping company that transports the goods to the customer. (8)

Biometric devices: Devices that measure various personal characteristics, such as fingerprints, voice prints, retina prints, or signature characteristics. (3)

Bus topology: Nodes in the topology that are connected to a common cable. (5)

Call-back device: Hardware component that asks the caller to enter a password and then breaks the connection to perform a security check. (5)

Carrier sensing: Random access technique that detects collisions when they occur. (5)

Check digit: Method for detecting data coding errors. A control digit is added to the code when it is originally designed to allow the integrity of the code to be established during subsequent processing. (6)

Client-server topology: Topology involving the distribution of data processing between the user's application—the client—and the server. (5)

Compilers: Language translation modules of the operation system. (2)

Completeness tests: Tests identifying missing data within a single record and entire records missing from a batch. (6)

Conceptual design: The production of several alternative designs for the new system. (4)

Control activities: Policies and procedures used to ensure that appropriate actions are taken to deal with the organization's risks. (1)

Control environment: The foundation of internal control. (1)

Control risk: Likelihood that the control structure is flawed because controls are either absent or inadequate to prevent or detect errors in the account. (1)

Corrective controls: Actions taken to reverse the effects of errors detected in the previous step. (1)

Customer open order file: File containing a copy of the sales order. (8)

Customer order: Document that indicates the type and quantity of merchandise being requested. (8)

Cycle billing: Method of spreading the billing process out over the month. (8)

Data definition language (DDL): Programming language used to define the database to the database management system. (3)

Data dictionary: Description of every data element in the database. (3)

Data encryption: Technique that uses an algorithm to scramble selected data, making it unreadable to an intruder browsing the database. (3)

Data encryption standard (DES): Approach that uses a single key known to both the sender and the receiver of the message. (5)

Data manipulation language (DML): Language used to insert special database commands into application programs written in conventional languages. (3)

Data normalization: Process that promotes effective database design. (7)

Data structures: Techniques for physically arranging records in the database. (3)

Database administrator: The individual responsible for managing the database resource. (2)

Database authorization table: Table containing rules that limit the actions a user can take. (3)

Database lockout: Software control that prevents multiple simultaneous access to data. (3)

Database management system (DBMS): Software system that controls access to the data resource. (3)

Deletion anomaly: The unintentional deletion of data from a table. (7)

Detailed design: Design of screen outputs, reports, and operational documents; entity relationship diagrams; normal form designs for database tables; updated data dictionary; designs for all screen inputs and source documents; context diagrams for overall system; low-level data flow diagrams; and structure diagrams for program modules. (4)

Detection risk: Risk that auditors are willing to take that errors not detected or prevented by the control structure will also not be detected by the auditor. (1)

Detective controls: Devices, techniques, and procedures designed to identify and expose undesirable events that elude preventive controls. (1)

Disaster recovery plan (DRP): Comprehensive statement of all actions to be taken before, during, and after a disaster, along with documented, tested procedures that will ensure the continuity of operations. (2)

Disk locks: Devices that prevent unauthorized individuals from accessing the floppy disk drive of a computer. (2)

Documentation: Written description of how the system works. (4)

Echo check: Technique that involves the receiver of the message returning the message to the sender. (5)

Electronic data interchange (EDI): The intercompany exchange of computer-processible business information in standard format. (5)

Embedded audit module (EAM): Technique in which one or more specially programmed modules embedded in a host application select and record predetermined types of transactions for subsequent analysis. (7)

Employee file: A file used with the attendance file to create an on-line payroll register. (9)

Employee fraud: Performance fraud by non-management employees generally designed to directly convert cash or other assets to the employee's personal benefit. (10)

Empty shell: Arrangement that involves two or more user organizations that buy or lease a building and remodel it into a computer site, but without the computer and peripheral equipment. (2)

Encryption: Technique that uses a computer program to transform a standard message being transmitted into a coded (ciphertext) form. (5)

End users: Users for whom the system is built. (4)

Entity: A resource, event, or agent. (3)

Error file: Transaction file that lists any detected errors. (6)

Ethics: Principles of conduct that individuals use in making choices in guiding their behavior in situations that involve the concepts of right and wrong. (10)

Exposure: Absence or weakness of a control. (1)

Firewall: Software and hardware that provide a focal point for security by channeling all network connections through a control gateway. (5)

Frequency: Number of cycles or oscillations occurring per second. (5)

Front end processors (FEP): A special purpose computer that manages the flow of data between the host computer and the communication's network. (5)

Full duplex: Transmission method that allows signals to be sent and received simultaneously. (5)

Generalized audit software (GAS): Software that allows auditors to access electronically coded data files and perform various operations on their contents. (6)

Grandparent-parent-child (GPC): Backup technique used in sequential batch systems. (3)

Hash total: Control technique that uses non-financial data to keep track of the records in a batch. (6)

Hashing structure: Structure employing an algorithm that converts the primary key of a record directly into a storage address. (7)

Hierarchical data model: A database model that represents data in a hierarchical structure and permits only a single parent record for each child. (3)

Hierarchical topology: Topology where a host computer is connected to several levels of subordinate smaller computers in a master-slave relationship. (5)

Indexed random file: Randomly organized file that is accessed via an index. (7)

Indexed sequential access method (ISAM): Sequential structure used for large table files that can be accessed by an index. (7)

Indexed sequential file: Sequential file structure that is accessed via an index. (7)

Indexed structure: A class of file structure that use indexes for its primary access method. (7)

Inference controls: Controls that prevent users from inferring specific data values through normal query features. (3)

Inherent risk: Risk that is associated with the unique characteristics of the business or industry of the client. (1)

Insertion anomaly: The unintentional insertion of data into a table. (7)

Integrated test facility (ITF): Automated technique that enables the auditor to test an application's logic and controls during its normal operation. (6)

Internal control system: Policies a firm employs to safeguard the firm's assets, ensure accurate and reliable accounting records and information, promote efficiency, and measure compliance with established policies. (1)

Internal view: The physical arrangement of records in the database. (3)

Interpreters: Language translation modules of the operating system that convert one line of logic at a time. (2)

Invented list: A cross reference created from multiple indexes. (7)

Lapping: Use of customer checks, received in payment of their accounts, to conceal cash previously stolen by an employee. (10)

Local area networks: Network generally confined to a close geographical area. (5)

Logic bomb: Destructive program, such as a virus, that is triggered by some predetermined event. (2)

Logical key pointer: A pointer containing the primary key of the related record. (7)

Management assertions: Explicit or implicit statements made by management within the financial statements pertaining to the financial health of the organization. (1)

Management fraud: Performance fraud that often uses deceptive practices to inflate earnings or to forestall the recognition of either insolvency or a decline in earnings. (10)

Modem: Hardware device that performs the modular-demodulator task. (5)

Modulation: Process of converting from digital to wave form. (5)

Monitoring: The process by which the quality of internal control design and operation can be assessed. (1)

Multiplexer: Device that permits the simultaneous transmission of multiple signals while maintaining a separation between each of them. (5)

Mutual aid pact: Agreement between two or more organizations (with comparable computer facilities) to aid each other with their data processing needs in the event of a disaster. (2)

Navigational models: Model that possesses explicit links or paths among data elements. (3)

Network model: Variation of the hierarchical model. (3)

Network protocols: Rules and standards governing the degree of hardware and software that permit users of networks manufactured by different vendors to communicate and share data. (5)

Network topology: Physical arrangement of the components. (5)

New systems development: Process that involves five steps: identifying the problem, understanding what needs to be done, considering alternative solutions, selecting the best solution, and implementing the solution. (4)

Object-oriented design: Building information systems from reusable standard components or modules. (4)

Objects: Equivalent to nouns in the English language. (4)

Packing slip: Document that travels with the goods to the customer to describe the contents of the order. (8)

Parallel simulation: Technique that requires the auditor to write a program that simulates key features of processes of the application under review. (6)

Parity check: Technique that incorporates an extra bit into the structure of a bit string when it is created or transmitted. (5)

Partitioned database approach: Database approach that splits the central database into segments or partitions that are distributed to their primary users. (3)

Password: Secret code entered by the user to gain access to the data files. (2)

Payroll imprest account: A account into which a single check for the entire amount of the payroll is deposited. (9)

Pointer structure: A structure in which the address (pointer) of one record is stored in the field on a related record. (7)

Polling: Popular technique for establishing communication session in WANs. (5)

Preventive controls: Passive techniques designed to reduce the frequency of occurrence of undesirable events. (1)

Private branch exchange (PBX): Method used for switching data and voice communications locally with a firm. (5)

Project planning: Allocation of resources to individual applications within the framework of the strategic plan. (4)

Project schedule: Document that formally presents management's commitment to the project. (4)

Protocols: Rules and standards governing the design of hardware and software that permit network users to communicate and share data. (5)

Public key encryption: Technique that uses two keys: one for encoding the message, the other for decoding it. (5)

Recovery operations center (ROC): Arrangement involving two or more user organizations that buy or lease a building and remodel it into a completely equipped computer site. (2)

Redundancy tests: Tests that determine that an application processes each record only once. (6)

Reengineering: The identification and elimination of non-value-added tasks by replacing traditional procedures with those that are innovative and different. (8)

Replicated databases: Database approach in which the central database is replicated at each IPU site. (3)

Request-response technique: Technique in which a control message from the sender and a response from the sender are sent at periodic synchronized intervals. (5)

Reusable password: A network password that can be used more than one time. (2)

Ring topology: Topology that eliminates the central site. All nodes in this configuration are of equal status. (5)

Risk assessment: The identification, analysis, and management of risks relevant to financial reporting. (1)

Rounding error tests: Tests that verify the correctness of rounding procedures. (6)

Run-to-run controls: Controls that use batch figures to monitor the batch as it moves from one programmed procedure to another. (6)

Salami frauds: Fraud in which each victim is unaware of being defrauded. (6)

Sales order: Source document that captures such vital information as the name and address of the customer making the purchase; the customer's account number; the name, number, and description of product; quantities and unit price of items sold; and other financial information. (8)

Schema (conceptual view): Description of the entire database. (3)

Segregation of duties: Separation of employee duties to minimize incompatible functions. (1)

Sequential structure: A data structure in which all records in the file lie in contiguous storage spaces in a specified sequence arranged by their primary key. (7)

Servers: Special-purpose computers that manage common resource, such as programs, data, and printers of the LAN. (5)

Shipping notice: Document that informs the billing department that the customer's order has been filled and shipped. (8)

Simplex: Transmission method allowing transmission in one direction only. (5)

Stakeholders: Entities either inside or outside an organization that have direct or indirect interest in the firm. (4)

Steering committee: An organizational committee consisting of senior-level management responsible for systems planning. (4)

Stock release (picking ticket): Document that identifies which items of inventory must be located and picked from the warehouse shelves. (8)

Structured design: Disciplined way of designing systems from the top down. (4)

Subschema (user view): User view of the database. (3)

Substantive tests: Tests that determine whether database contents fairly reflect the organization's transactions. (1)

Supervision: A control activity involving the critical oversight of employees. (1)

Supplier's (vendor's) invoice: The bill sent from the seller to the buyer showing unit costs, taxes, freight, and other charges. (9)

Synchronous: Transmission method that uses a separate timing signal to keep the receiving end's device in constant synchronization. (5)

System survey: Determination of what elements, if any, of the current system should be preserved as part of the new system. (4)

Systems analysis: Two-step process that involves a survey of the current system and then an analysis of the user's needs. (4)

Systems development life cycle (SDLC): Formal process consisting of two major phases: new systems development and maintenance. (4)

Systems planning: Linking of individual system projects or applications to the strategic objectives of the firm. (4)

Test data method: Technique used to establish application integrity by processing specially prepared sets of input data through production applications that are under review. (6)

Tests of controls: Tests that establish whether internal controls are functioning properly. (1)

Token passing: Transmission of a special signal (token) around the network from node to node in a specific sequence. (5)

Tracing: Test data technique that performs an electronic walkthrough of the application's internal logic. (6)

Transaction authorization: Procedure to ensure that employees process only valid transactions within the scope of their authority. (1)

Transcription errors: Type of error that can corrupt a data code and cause processing errors. (6)

Transfer Control Protocol/Internet Protocol (TCP/IP): The basic protocol that permits communication between Internet nodes. (5)

Transposition errors: Error that occurs when digits are transposed. (6)

Trojan horse: Program that attaches to another legitimate program but does not replicate itself like a virus. (2)

Turnkey systems: Completely finished and tested systems that are ready for implementation. (4)

Update anomaly: The unintentional updating of data in a table, resulting from data redundancy. (7)

User views: The set of data that a particular user needs to achieve his or her assigned tasks. (3)

Valid vendor file: A file containing vendor mailing information. (9)

Validation controls: Controls intended to detect errors in transaction data before the data are processed. (6)

Value-added banks (VAB): Banks that can accept electronic disbursements and remittance advices from its clients in any format. (5)

Value-added network (VAN): Network that provides service by managing the distribution of the messages between trading partners. (5)

Vendor-supported systems: Custom systems that organizations purchase from commercial vendors. (4)

Virtual table: A table derived from the base tables that is a partial representation of the actual physical base tables. (7)

Virus: Program that attaches itself to a legitimate program to penetrate the operating system. (2)

Walkthrough: Analysis of system design to ensure the design is free from conceptual errors that could become programmed into the final system. (4)

Wide area network: Network that exceeds the geographic limitations of a local area network. (5)

Worm: Software program that "burrows" into the computer's memory and replicates itself into areas of idle memory. (2)

INDEX

A

Access control list, defined, 54

Access controls: audit objectives and procedures for, 106-107; and biometric devices, 104; and data encryption, 104; and database authorization tables, 103-104; and disasters, 19-20; and electronic commerce, 196-200; and electronic data interchange, 204, 206; and the expenditure cycle, 364-365; and fraud, 19; and inference controls, 104-106; purpose of, 19, 102; and the revenue cycle, 309-310; and user views, 103; and user-defined procedures, 104

Access method, defined, 87, 252

Access privileges, controlling, 55-57, 64

Access tests, defined, 236

Access token, defined, 54

Accountants: and distributed databases 102; and the SDLC, 118-119

Accounting records: and data consolidation, 19-20; and internal control, 18-19; in the IT environment, 19

Accounts payable change report, described, 368

Accounts receivable change report, described, 313

Accuracy assertion: and the expenditure cycle, 359, 360, 361, 362, 364, 365, 369, 373-376;

and the revenue cycle, 305, 307, 308, 309, 310, 313, 318-324

Accuracy of information, and computer fraud, 413

Accuracy tests, defined, 236

ACL software: customizing a view, 278-279; for data extraction, 276-281; described, 276-277; and expenditure cycle testing, 369-379; filtering data, 279; and fraud detection, 416-420; input file definition, 277-278; and revenue cycle testing, 314-329; for statistical analysis, 281; stratifying data, 279-281

Aging accounts receivable, described, 328-329

American Institute of Certified Public Accountants: and auditing standards, 3

American National Standards Institute (ANSI), defined, 191

Amplitude, defined, 176

Analytical review: in the expenditure cycle, 373; in the revenue cycle, 318

Anomalies: deletion, 265-266; insertion, 265; update, 264-265

Application controls: CAATT tests of, 239-245; and data extraction and analysis, 271-281; defined, 15, 24, 214; and the expenditure cycle, 358-369; input controls, 215-228, 304-308, 358-362; output

controls, 231-235, 312-314, 367-369; processing controls, 228-230, 308-312, 362-367; and the revenue cycle, 304-314; testing, 235-245

Application-level firewalls, defined, 196

Application software: and the DBMS, 82; defined, 63

AR update and billing run, described, 296-297

Artificial intelligence, and computer ethics, 400

Assertions of management: and auditing, 5-6; and the expenditure cycle, 359, 373-379; and obtaining evidence, 6-7; and the revenue cycle, 305, 318-329

Assets: access to, 19-20; misappropriation of, 409-414, 415

Associations: and data normalization, 267-268; defined, 88; illustrated, 89; types of, 88-89

Assurance services: defined, 2; versus attest services, 1-5

Asynchronous transmission, 175

Attendance file, defined, 356

Attest services: defined, 1-2; requirements applying to, 2; versus assurance services, 1-5

Attributes, in a relational data model, 94

Audit logs, use of, 60, 61

Audit objectives: and audit trails, 61; and backup controls, 110, 111; categories of, 6;

INSTALLING ACL FOR WINDOWS VERSION 5.0

To install ACL for Windows on your Windows 3.x or Windows 95:

1. Insert the CD-ROM into the CD-ROM drive.
2. From the menu bar, select File in Windows 3.x or Start in Windows 95, and choose Run to display the Run dialog box.
3. In the Command Line text box, type the location of the CD-ROM (for example, e:) and the location of the ACL setup application, e:\Introacl\Setup.exe
4. Click OK to continue the installation process and then follow the instructions on your screen.

When the installation is complete, ACL displays the ACL for Windows Version 5 icon in a program group with the same name.

OPENING THE "INTRODUCING ACL FOR WINDOWS" ELECTRONIC BOOKLET (INTROACL.PDF)

On the CD-ROM is an electronic booklet entitled "Introducing ACL for Windows." This booklet will help you get started with ACL and get acquainted with its basic features. Copy Introacl.pdf to your hard drive using File Manager in Windows 3.x or Windows Explorer in Windows 95. To open this booklet you will need Adobe Acrobat Reader installed on your computer. Open the file by double-clicking on it, or by selecting Open from the File menu in Adobe Acrobat Reader and locating the file.

If you do not have Adobe Acrobat Reader installed on your computer, download the latest version from the Adobe Web site:

http://www.adobe.com/prodindex/acrobat/readstep.html

and install it following Adobe's instructions.